REGIONS A

This book is to be returned on
or before the date stamped below

1 4 DEC 2001

- 9 DEC 2003

EADI BOOK SERIES 23

REGIONS AND DEVELOPMENT: POLITICS, SECURITY AND ECONOMICS

edited by

SHEILA PAGE

FRANK CASS

LONDON • PORTLAND, OR

in association with

EADI   European Association of Development Research
and Training Institutes, Geneva

First published in 2000 in Great Britain by
FRANK CASS PUBLISHERS
Newbury House, 900 Eastern Avenue
London IG2 7HH, England

and in the United States of America by
FRANK CASS PUBLISHERS
c/o ISBS
5804 N.E. Hassalo Street
Portland, Oregon 97213–3644

Website: www.frankcass.com

Copyright © 2000 Frank Cass & Co. Ltd.

British Library Cataloguing in Publication Data

Regions and development : politics, security and economics.
  – (EADI book series ; no. 23)
  1. Regional economics. 2. Regionalism – Developing countries
  I. Page, Sheila, 1946–
  338.9
  ISBN 0-7146-5023-4 (cloth)
  ISBN 0-7146-4465-X (paper)

Library of Congress Cataloging-in-Publication Data

Regions and development : politics, security, and economics/ edited
  by Sheila Page.
    p. cm. – (EADI book series, ISSN 1462-2181 ; 23)
  "In association with the European Association of Development
Research and Training Institutes (EADI), Geneva."
  Includes bibliographical references and index.
    ISBN 0-7146-5023-4 (cloth) ISBN 0-7146-4465-X (pbk.)
  1. Developing countries – Economic integration. 2 Regionalism –
Developing countries. 3. International economic integration.
  4. International economic relations. I. Page, Sheila.
  II. European Association of Development Research and Training
Institutes. III. Series.
  HC59.7.R372   1999
  337–dc21

99–41946
CIP

Printed in Great Britain by
Antony Rowe Ltd, Chippenham, Wilts

Contents

List of Tables and Figures

List of Contributors

Claude Auroi, Institute of Development Studies, Geneva.

Lino Briguglio, Foundation for International Studies, Islands and Small States Institute, Malta.

Stephen F. Burgess, Hofstra University, Hemstead, New York.

Heribert Dieter, German Foundation for International Development, Berlin.

James J. Hentz, Virginia Military Institute, Lexington, VA.

Björn Hettne, Department of Peace and Development Research (PADRIGU), Göteborg University, Sweden.

Philippe Hugon, CERED FORUM, Université Paris X-Nanterre, Nanterre.

Sheila Page, Overseas Development Institute, London.

Siegfried Schultz, German Institute of Economic Research, Berlin.

Sandro Sideri, Institute of Social Studies, The Hague.

Meine Pieter van Dijk, Erasmus University, Rotterdam.

Katarzyna Żukrowska, IRISS, Institute of Development and Strategic Studies, Warsaw.

Introduction

SHEILA PAGE

- Why do countries come together in regions?

- Why do some regions succeed?

- Are regions economic or political tools, intended for development or for negotiation?

At the 1996 EADI Conference, the papers presented in the World Trade and Trade Policy workshop looked at the new trends in regionalism from a variety of points of view for different institutions. They were searching for the effects of regions and for their implications for policy and performance in the developing countries and for international economic institutions, and trying to interpret them in terms of economic and political theory.

It is too early to reach structured conclusions. The regions are too new, and evidence on their success and their effects is still limited. Nevertheless, three conclusions start to emerge:

- There is some evidence for a more widespread interest in formal regional organisations, although these are taking too wide a range of forms to be treated as a single phenomenon.

- The general analyses and comparisons of regions suggest that studying trade motives and effects is not enough; regionalism is a political decision, although some of the individual studies find significant economic effects.

- Other forces and influences in international relations remain important, and cut across regional interests.

These chapters are based on papers written in 1996, and therefore take no account of changes in the region or in the world economy since then.

Nevertheless, the regions which were identified then as likely to endure have all survived, and continued to develop, and the tentative conclusions stated here still seem valid.

The first four chapters look at the general nature of regionalism. Sandro Sideri gives a broad survey of the nature of change in the world economy. Sideri, Hettne and Hugon are all interested in putting regionalism into the context of what they see as probably the more important trend, that towards globalisation. For Sideri, globalisation is driven by technology and by company networks. He argues that the primary aim of regions is to re-establish control where globalisation has removed companies or other actors from national control. It is an attempt to resist full globalisation. This suggests that regions are a move to more 'managed' trade. He introduces what became a common theme: the complex nature of regionalism; it is not just removal of trade barriers, but establishment of institutions, networks, infrastructure, etc. Björn Hettne, like Sideri, interprets regionalisation as a counter-movement to globalisation, a form of popular resistance to globalisation. His approach is to place regionalism in the context of the shift from a 'Westphalian', state-based, international order to one with new actors. The new regionalism has emerged from the new multipolar global system.

The chapters by Page and Hugon start to move from the general to individual cases, by taking a comparative as well as analytic approach. Sheila Page takes up Sideri's emphasis on non-trade integration, and attempts to combine quantitative analysis of economic linkages with a framework for analysing and 'counting' political and institutional links. This is used to compare thirteen existing regions. For all of them, political characteristics and motives are important; in contrast, there is no common economic link. The most integrated appear to be the European Union and MERCOSUR, with both economic and policy integration, followed by SACU and ANZCERTA. Philippe Hugon sees regions as a response to the asymmetric power in global relationships, and explores how different theoretical approaches to analysing international economics can shed light on globalisation and regionalisation. He includes growth, industrial, and institutional approaches. He then applies this analysis to examine regionalism in East Asia and sub-Saharan Africa. In the first, economic success and concentration led to regions without institutions, while in the second, institutions were unable to compensate for economic failure.

The next seven chapters give more detail on the importance of regionalism in individual areas. Stephen Burgess uses a comparison of the EU and SADC to analyse how countries face the institutional problems of regions: managing inequality among countries, achieving policy convergence, and creating institutions in the face of still-strong national interests. He emphasises the importance of institutions (in the region, but also in the individual countries) and, like Page, attempts to apply a quantitative analysis to them. James Hentz complements this by looking specifically at South Africa's policy on regions, and also emphasises the importance of ideas and political ideology as a motive for interest in regional integration. He notes the break in economic policy from 1994, and the new emphasis on economic liberalism, and explores its implications for the future of SADC.

Heribert Dieter looks at the biggest, although also the least integrated, region: APEC. He is interested in the effects of regions on the multilateral system. He argues that it is the big regions which could threaten the multilateral system; the small developing country regions are more numerous, but not significant at world level. He follows Sideri's view, that regions are attempts to get some of the advantages of global openness, but without giving up the ability to control economic actors and ensure national standards and interests. He believes that the interest of APEC is not in completely free trade and not only in trade. He stresses international policy-making, security dialogue, and political integration as more important. Siegfried Schultz looks at the investment linkages between APEC and the EU, and specifically flows of investment into Europe. He uses the eclectic approach to analysing foreign investment, looking at ownership, location advantages, and internalisation. In a detailed analysis of Asian investment in the EU by country and sector, he does not find that regional influences add to these traditional explanations.

Claude Auroi looks at Latin America, the developing continent with the longest and most extensive history of regions, and finds that they have stemmed from forces within each sub-region, not a single, general explanation. While regionalism can contribute to development by stimulating regional trade, economies of scale, and technological integration, it is not possible to apply the success of, for example, MERCOSUR, to the Andean Group where political conflicts mean that the conditions for convergence found in MERCOSUR are not met. Katarzyna Żukrowska looks at CEFTA, formed within Eastern Europe, which is unusual in being seen as a step towards full integration with the EU. She examines the shift of interests, from concentration on EU links to agreeing to separate regional integration, and argues that this arose out of internal reasons, rejecting (like Auroi and other contributors) the view that regions form as reactions to others. Although the CEFTA countries maintain their ultimate objective of joining the EU, she also notes how, once formed, CEFTA has widened to include new countries and deepened in coverage, following the history of other regions.

The final two chapters look at the interests of developing countries in the global system as a whole, and are a reminder that they do not and cannot act only within regions. Lino Briguglio looks at the special problems of small island countries. He analyses their special vulnerability, to natural as well as economic and political influences from outside. He therefore shows that they have a common interest which cuts across regions. But while their interests are common, one of the reasons he gives for their importance is precisely their diversity. Some of the problems which he finds in small countries are similar to those analysed by Hugon for the African economies, with factors like poor transport and dependence on developed countries acting for both as an obstacle to close regional integration. Meine Pieter van Dijk looks at the trade prospects for developing countries more broadly. These have changed after the trade policy reforms of the Uruguay Round and are continuing to change with the new multilateral negotiations, the special arrangements for least developed countries, and the negotiations on the 'new' areas of the environment, competition policy, and labour standards. Like Dieter, he emphasises the potential conflict between global and regional rule systems, and argues that future progress on world-level trade agreements may pre-empt progress in regions.

The authors show different preferences between regions and globalisation, but all see advantages and disadvantages from both. They emphasise the importance of the existing conditions in countries, and their natural and institutional linkages, in setting the conditions for whether regions or globalisation can be beneficial. These constraints make simple judgements on regions unattainable.

PART I

REGIONALISATION AND GLOBABLISATION

1

Globalisation and Regional Integration

SANDRO SIDERI

I. INTRODUCTION

While the fascination with globalisation, and its effects, is growing fast, the shift towards regionalism is also becoming quite clear. It is the intention here to analyse these two apparently contrasting phenomena in order to assess their relevance and the eventual connection between the two processes. In terms of the chapter's structure, the first section deals with globalisation and its impact, particularly on the nation-state. The second section considers the emergence of regionalism, its causes, and the complications created by the rising demand for devolution, including the analysis of regional integration efforts in Europe and Asia. Some reflections and tentative conclusions are presented in the third section.

II. GLOBALISATION AND ITS IMPACT

Globalisation is essentially a process driven by economic forces, the immediate causes of which are the spatial reorganisation of production and of international trade, and, finally, the integration of financial markets. It affects most capitalist economic and social relations and represents by far the most significant aspect of current international relations.[1] Being largely responsible for the end of the cold war and therefore for the universalisation of the operations of capitalism, although its regional spread is still uneven, globalisation is reorganising power at world level as well as at national or sub-national levels. The apparent universalisation of capitalism justifies the contention that there is also a single path of economic, political, and social development for the entire world – that of free markets and political liberalism. Hence Fukuyama's contention of 'the end of history'.

By allowing nations to specialise in different branches of manufacturing and even in different stages of production within a specific industry, international

The author wishes to thank Professor J. Hillorst and two anonymous referees for their helpful comments on an earlier draft of this contribution. A more extensive version of this study appears in *The European Journal of Development Research* (Vol.9, No.1, June 1997, pp.38–79).

trade has contributed to the creation of the present global manufacturing system. This dispersion of production capacity to a wide number of developed countries (DCs) as well as developing countries (LDCs), each performing tasks in which it has a cost advantage, has been made possible both by new forms of investment and financing, promoted by specific government policies, and by technological advance. The latter has prompted the 'knowledge era' in which the creation, storage and use of knowledge are becoming the basic economic activity. The result is distinctive patterns of spatial and social organisation.

Globalisation implies both multilateralism, that is, mainly multilateral trade liberalisation and trade policy, and microeconomic phenomena, particularly firms' competitiveness at the global level and the profound transformation of work organisation.[2] In fact, the creation of a world market for labour and production has been made possible by the segmentation of the manufacturing process into multiple partial operations which, combined with the development of cheap transportation and communications networks, has brought the increasing division of production into separate stages carried out in different locations. This massive industrial de-location or redeployment of productive activities ('global localisation' is the expression created by Sony's boss Akio Morita), supported by direct foreign investment, has then made it possible 'to explode the value-added chain' and to create the multinational corporation (MNC), causing, in turn, large-scale migratory flows and the feminisation of labour. As domestic industries transfer a growing amount of their production abroad, land becomes less valuable than technology, knowledge, and direct investment, and 'the function of the state is being further redefined' [*Rosecrance, 1996: 46*].

Clearly, globalisation is affecting the class structure, the labour process, the application of technology, the structure and organisation of capital, family life, the organisation of cities and the use of space. The spatial reorganisation of production has also been enhanced by the need to cope with the exchange-rate fluctuations brought about by the financial deregulation. The world economy is therefore characterised by a growing share of its GDP depending directly on international trade (the share of trade in world output has increased from 7 per cent to 20 per cent between 1950 and 1995 [*Boltho, 1996: Table 2, 256*] and foreign capital and globalisation indicate the integration of free markets, financial flows, trade and information.[3]

The speeding up of international competition and the transformation of production systems (industry is now based on a 'flexible production' system) are fast creating a truly international labour market 'and workers are more likely to be in the service sector, working part-time or engaged in informal sector activities' [*UNRISD, 1995: 9*]. Hence the risk that globalisation and technological change will penalise and marginalise the less educated and less skilled labour – those left-behinds who are the poor in the US and the unemployed in Europe – while economic growth and expansion of firms no longer imply increased employment. Having established a powerful set of rules and standards for how countries have to behave if they are to attract investment capital, globalisation causes higher remuneration of capital because of its greater global mobility compared to labour.

Labour reductions, made possible by technological and organisational changes, also contribute to the higher remuneration of capital. Clearly increases in productivity no longer translate necessarily into more jobs and higher wages. Whilst in the past 'higher profits meant more job security and better wages', global competition 'tends to delink the fate of the corporation from the fate of its employees' [*Schwab and Smadja, 1996*]. Nor is it any longer possible to assume that the jobs that are eliminated within the advanced economies will end up in LDCs, since their opening up to world commerce – synonymous with integration – attracts investment but also world-competitive imports which destroy local manufactures. Contrary to what is happening in the traditional industrial countries, the linkage between growth of real output and employment and labour income remains an important aspect of the pattern of development and industrialisation in Asia, and particularly in Asia Pacific.

The emergence of a global economy entails the diffusion to distant countries of identical consumer goods, as well as consumerism, patterns of demand and the homogenisation of markets' rules and structures. It also entails the spread of values, such as the dominance of market forces, and of the preference for liberal democracy, even though this is a more contentious point than the pre-eminence of the market. The growing exchange of goods across frontiers also involves that of 'bads' such as narcotic drugs, pollution, etc. [*Griffin and Khan, 1992: 63*]. The phenomenon of globalisation is necessarily a 'totalising or homogenising force' whose scope extends beyond the realm of economics to embrace science, politics, culture and life-styles. Whilst it 'articulates with local structures in diverse ways' and allows 'distinct regional divisions of labour', globalisation enables 'the economy, politics, culture and ideology of one country to penetrate another', and distinct regional divisions of labour are 'ultimately subordinate to the globalisation process' [*Mittelman, 1994: 428 and 430*].

The analysis of the effects of globalisation is greatly helped by the discussion of whether increasing globalisation leads to an international economy or to a really global one. According to Hirst and Thompson [*1992: 358–60*] a world-wide international economy is one centred on nation-states, their growing strategic interdependence built first around the importance of international trade but progressively replaced by foreign investment. In this system the 'international and domestic policy fields either remain separated as distinct levels of governance or, allegedly, they work "automatically"', that is, under the impact of unorganised or spontaneous market forces, as with the

Gold Standard with its overt domestic policy interventions. The development of the current system is largely the result of the absence of a global hegemony and of political resistance to delegating authority to a supranational authority capable of generating a more disciplined order.

Within this world-wide international economic system, the MNC has risen and matured. Most companies trading from their bases in distinct national economies have not necessarily lost their national identity, a fact which explains why it seems inappropriate to call them transnational companies (TNCs).[4] Since 'national policies remain viable, indeed essential in order to preserve the distinct styles and strengths of the national economy base and the companies that trade from it', so the nation-state's regulation of business and negotiation of trade agreements provide some governance to the international economy [*Hirst and Thompson, 1995: 424, 408; 1992: 393*]. An important characteristic of the current international economic system, which is not entirely new,[5] is the bias towards disinflationary macroeconomic policies which the international capital market entails [*Hutton, 1995: 306*].

The following arguments can be made against the thesis of a truly globalised economy: (i) the number of genuine TNCs is small, most of what appears as supranational is due to the rapid growth in inter-firm partnerships and joint ventures; (ii) both foreign trade flows and patterns of foreign direct investment are highly concentrated in DCs and a few Newly Industrialised Countries (NICs); (iii) financial markets are not necessarily beyond regulation, as demonstrated by the success of the Plaza and Louvre accords; and (iv) even the rapid development of some areas of the Third World is not unprecedented and often depends on an authoritarian government's ability to repress political protest.

Even if the globalisation observable today is considered still quite limited, the scope of the nation-state's autonomy is certainly reduced, since its control over economic and social processes within its territory has become less exclusive, and its ability to maintain national distinctiveness and cultural homogeneity has been curtailed. Once considered the basic units of geopolitics, the dominant role and independence of nation-states are being undermined by diverse challenges, all connected to the process of globalisation. According to *The Economist* [*23 Dec. 1995–5 Jan. 1996: 17*], these challenges come from: (i) the transportation revolution which has 'demolished any lingering belief in national self-sufficiency'; (ii) the materialisation of the third dimension – the air – in the use of force, which has changed the nature of war and left countries naked to air attacks; and (iii) the information revolution and the globalisation of knowledge which are 'blurring the sense of national separateness'. By loosening the state's exclusiveness of control of its territory, communications and information technologies are 'reducing its capacity for cultural control and homogenisation', thus making exclusion more difficult [*Hirst and Thompson,*

1995: 419].[6] Furthermore, as Griffin and Khan [*1992: 63*] rightly observe, the arms technology and the militarisation of the oceans and outer space have made political boundaries largely irrelevant in most of the world. In the absence of an immediate enemy – as occurred at the end of the cold war when western countries lost the common purpose under which they had co-operated for so many years – the nation-state becomes less significant to the citizen.

It seems, then, that the diminished role of the state is accompanied by, and results from, the emergence of a multi-layered and overlapping system of governance by often competing institutions, agencies and centres of power. This complex system entails different levels and functions which vary from the global level, to the regional, national, sub-national, industrial district, and 'entity' levels. There is also another possible level, the trans-regional one made up by agreement between different regional groupings, for example, APEC (see later), the US and European Union (EU) agreement reconciling different approaches to competition policy, and, even more appropriately, the proposed Transatlantic Free Trade Area between NAFTA (North American Free Trade Area) and the EU.

Once it becomes apparent that the state has been internationalised [*Cox, 1981*] because it 'no longer serves primarily as a buffer or shield against the world economy' but, instead, has become an agent in the process of globalisation [*Mittelman, 1994: 431*], counter reactions develop: the emergence, or re-emergence, of local movements seeking autonomy or even independence from present nation-states, and a rush towards regionalism,[7] within which national sovereignty is also going to be curtailed. One manifestation of the conflict between the fragmentation and the unification generated by globalisation is the rapid homogenisation of markets and the rise of ethnic, cultural and regional identities, so that the conflict is then between economic integration and political separatism. Among these fragmenting tensions must be included the emergence of 'entities' such as the Palestinian Authority or the Bosnian accord. These are newly formed polities – not-quite nations, often the remnants of old nations – created by nationalist forces liberated at the end of the cold war. A phenomenon often identified with 'overlapping sovereignty', further fragmentation and/or killing on a large scale must be avoided and this is the most immediate task [*Dickey, 1995: 22 , 25*]. It is also argued that as the world becomes more democratic, so it splits into smaller political jurisdictions which, from an economic point of view, tend to be too small. If 'democratisation leads to secessions' – that is, 'too many nations may emerge as democracy spreads' and separation 'is to produce government policies that are "closer to the people"' [*Bolton et al., 1996: 701*] – economic integration also tends to encourage smaller entities to go it alone. Thus 'political separatism should go hand in hand with economic integration' [*Alesina and Spolaore, 1995: 2–3, 22*]. Since national self-determination derives its legitimacy from the notions of democracy and cultural homogeneity, when the state pushes its rights to the limits, devolution is no longer considered sufficient and it is secession that becomes associated with freedom and democracy.

The various governing powers 'need to be tied together'. 'Gaps' between different agencies and dimensions of governance must be closed by what Hirst and Thompson [*1995: 423*] aptly call a process of 'suturing' – a process to which regionalisation may contribute. The more extreme globalisation theorists, like Ohmae [*1993*], consider any attempt to build an institutional architecture to govern this complex system unnecessary, either because they believe it to be ungovernable, or because they see the market as a satisfactory mode of governance.[8] Yet, markets and companies cannot exist without the protection of the public power (even deregulation requires the active intervention of the state), just as 'the open international economy depends ultimately on western (particularly US) force and upon active public regulation backed by legal enforcement', that is by nation-states [*Hirst and Thompson, 1995: 427*]. Like the national market, the international one must be 'embedded' in a context of non-market social institutions and regulatory mechanisms, lest instability and inefficiency prevail [*Polanyi, 1957: Chs. 5, 6*]. Only the most extreme advocates of economic liberalism, or 'global neoclassicism', argue that a free market is a state of nature; it must be produced and regulated, just as property rights, without which there is no market, are not endowed by nature. Market and civil society cannot develop spontaneously, as the liberal myth assumes; instead both are moulded by the state, their effectiveness not necessarily proportional to their utilisation of democratic practices. Yet the global economy appears 'increasingly disembedded from the domestic social compact between state and society on which the political viability of the post-war international order has hinged' [*Ruggie, 1995: 525*]. Also for Gilpin [*1987: 389*] the growth in global interdependence has undermined 'the postwar "compromise of embedded liberalism" and the clash between domestic autonomy and international norms reasserted itself in the major economies of the international system'.

The erosion of national borders is being accelerated by the emergence of global collaborative R&D programmes, including Europe's supranational research schemes. The globalisation of R&D facilities is expected to continue at a fast pace for three main reasons [*Sigurdson, 1996: 25*]: (i) the ongoing process of mergers and acquisitions naturally leads to more and more R&D facilities being controlled by companies with their manufacturing and/or headquarters in another country; (ii) the need to adapt more and more sophisticated products and systems to local conditions requires the localisation of R&D; and (iii) more and more companies are sourcing their knowledge generation in countries and regions where such resources can more easily be

12

obtained and where the costs may be considerably lower.

If there has been a strengthening of the government's influence on the location of economic activity by international companies, the emphasis in the government's actions has shifted from removing structural distortions in domestic markets to facilitating the supply capabilities of their own firms 'by lowering transaction-related barriers, and by fostering the upgrading and structural redeployment of the assets within their jurisdiction' [*Dunning, 1993: 10–11, 345*].

Leaving aside its survival, the legitimacy, relevance and effectiveness of the nation-state are seriously challenged by the growing need to establish some form of governance of the globalised economy.[9] This governance, however, cannot be assured by the existing set of international institutions. Being mostly intergovernmental rather than supranational agencies, these are being rendered ineffective and obsolete by the weakening of the state caused by the process of globalisation. The task of global governance is complicated, however, by the recognition of the difficulties inherent in any attempt to regulate global markets and that growing interdependence might even cause disintegration.[10] In addition, there is the problem posed by the diseconomies of scale, which would certainly affect the management structure required by such a task, and at the same time the growing demand for more citizen participation which requires some decentralisation of the decision-making process [*Arndt, 1993: 280–81*]. Furthermore,

> there is now no doctrinally grounded and technically effective regime of macro-economic management that can produce sustained expansionary effects, [since] neither the financial markets nor the Brussels bureaucracy ... can impose or secure the forms of social cohesion and the policies that follow from them that national governments can [*Hirst and Thompson, 1992: 371–2*].

Meanwhile the growing degree of internationalisation of business forces governments as well as firms, particularly in industries dominated by MNCs, to adopt globally oriented macro-organisational strategies and microeconomic policies respectively, which, in turn, requires a reappraisal of the available policies [*Dunning, 1993: 9*].

Globalisation has also made financial markets much more volatile and local capital vulnerable to the strategies of corporate raiders. Hence the need for new norms for this market, or even an institutional framework. This need derives from an imbalance between the global dimension of the problems and the national dimension of the government structure of each economy. It still remains unsatisfied, because it requires co-operation among the principal governments.

Although many governments insist on only addressing national political agendas, it is 'the present urge to deregulate the state out of existence' which threatens international co-operation in many areas of macroeconomic policy [*Boltho, 1996: 259*]. This significant change in the regulatory climate, with the emphasis on competition and internationalisation, reflects a distinctly anti-Keynesian view (taking Keynesianism as implying that governments have the duty and the power to enhance national welfare through discretionary policy action) which Schor [*1992*] aptly refers to as 'global neoclassicism'. The same change in the regulatory climate militates against the institutionalisation of international co-operation, making it more difficult and less effective.[11]

A similar process of deregulation and globalisation has occurred within related professional activities. Greater competition in these services has led to the creation of new categories of specialists, such as 'design professionals' and to the emergence of 'mega' firms and factories. In the field of law, globalisation is stimulating a process of homogenisation and interconnection between national legal systems. Alongside the necessary technical communications infrastructure, particularly the global mass media, these developments raise 'the spectre of cultural homogenisation often in the form of "cultural imperialism" or "Americanisation"' [*Featherstone, 1990: 10*].

Since even the largest MNCs find it increasingly difficult to remain sufficiently competitive in all parts of the value-added chain, strategic alliances offer the option of concentrating on core competences and accessing remaining inputs from partners. The expansion of strategic alliances into a transborder corporate superstructure which mixes and matches nationalities, erodes the possibility of controlling the national system of innovation.

As 'economic globalisation both changes the spatial dimension of MNCs and creates a need for more flexible production and marketing systems, and new forms of organisation' [*Dunning, 1993: 202*], the global MNC is becoming a down-sized, out-sourced and largely stateless web of cross-border corporate alliances, spanning different industries and countries. The companies entering these strategic alliances, held together by common goals, act almost as a single firm, the so-called 'relationship-enterprise'. Such an arrangement is also useful for firms to side-step controls, like anti-trust laws, which governments place on companies, controls which even MNCs have not yet been able to escape since the home base most of them maintain makes them less global than they appear [*The Economist, 6 Feb. 1993: 65*]. By the same token, however, the globalisation of markets mainly takes place within a market structure which presents clear oligopolistic features such as high concentration, instability and asymmetry, and by the convergence of consumer needs and preferences at similar income levels [*Dunning, 1993: 202*].

If the process of globalisation has quickened the pace of change, economic as well as political, the speed and complexity with which capital, goods, services and people are moving around makes it difficult to predict even the immediate future. Hence the prevailing sense of a 'great global uncertainty' [*Robertson, 1990: 16*]. This uncertainty is further fuelled by the fact that

> political maps are being drawn and redrawn as myriad ethnic or political groups emerge to make new claims and stake out new territory. These changes have generated enormous social tensions that development policies have failed to tackle head-on [while] power has been transferred to institutions that have consistently ignored the social implications of their actions [*UNRISD, 1995: 8*].

One of the most dangerous temptations of globalisation correctly identified by Griffin and Khan [*1992: 66*] is the tendency 'to skimp on higher education in order not to lose resources through brain drain and to run a low wage, low human development economy in order to keep costs low and international competition at bay'.

In support of the recurrent suggestion that globalisation fosters inequality among countries and affects some countries' ability to obtain higher incomes, Krugman and Venables [*1994*] have developed a formal model which explains how the differentiation of countries into a rich core and a poor periphery takes place only after the world economy has reached a certain critical level of integration. Afterwards the rise of the core's income is partly at the expense of the periphery – the 'unequal development' of the 1960s and 1970s. Only when the process of integration has proceeded far enough to erode the advantages of the core, does the periphery's income start to rise 'partly at the core's expense'.

In addition, two issues contribute towards increasing hostility to globalisation: (i) cultural diversity outside the western world; and (ii) fears of a loss of social cohesion and economic well-being in the western countries. Differences in cultural preferences are brought to the fore by the acceleration of globalisation and the inclusion in the process of former Socialist countries and larger Asian economies. The danger of 'cultural pollution' has been attributed to audio-visuals and foreign companies' access to the print and film media, including conditions for television transmissions, and also to advertising, retailing and banking. Even the harmonisation of standards, which facilitates international exchange and renders products and services cheaper, becomes objectionable when one considers that it also erodes many of the distinctions between societies. The cry of a clash of values or ethics becomes unavoidable when attempting to build mechanisms to secure compliance with labour practices, human rights or environmental protection, by means of measures such as sanctions.

The accommodation of different business practices between countries whose approach to environmental protection and restrictions on child labour are sharply at odds is intrinsically hard and conflict-provoking. It may generate a backlash against the process of trade liberalisation. Even defining minimum international standards relating to the terms and conditions of employment, and the environment,[12] generates resistance and requires interventionist measures that contradict the process of globalisation. The West's fears relate to the depressing effect that international trade may have on the real wages of unskilled workers. Hence the demand for restrictions on 'unfair trade'.[13] Populist hostility has begun to materialise to globalisation and to regional agreements with less developed economies, for example US opposition to NAFTA and West European dissatisfaction with the EU's proposed inclusion of East European countries. Hence the preference for regional arrangements between rather similar economies which, being able to compete constructively, could avoid the destructive social consequences caused by a global system of unrestrained competition, largely influenced by the MNCs' increasingly warlike fashion of behaviour, which 'leads to winner take-all situations': those who come out on top win big while the losers risk becoming the left-behinds [*Schwab and Smadja, 1996*]. If competition between firms in different countries can never be 'fair', it may be so when it takes place in the same country or within a regional bloc. In the last resort, the integration of different economies into a single market transforms international trade into a domestic exchange.

Notwithstanding the fact that 'the politics of managing globalisation will not be easy' [*Cable, 1996: 246*], globalisation is clearly here to stay and will exercise an increasing influence on the pace and pattern of growth of the world economy and hence on the distribution of income and wealth. The large-scale disruptions arising from the process of globalisation are generating, in turn, sustained pressure for self-protection, a contradiction that clearly characterises a process as complex as globalisation, and which leads simultaneously to opportunities and challenges.

An important phenomenon which accompanies, or perhaps is caused by, the process of globalisation, is the rise of regional trading blocs.[14] These pose a special challenge to the multilateral system, hence to the global economy. This does not imply, however, that trade blocs will necessarily reverse globalisation; but they may, ultimately, contribute to its development. In both DCs and LDCs regionalism appears as the response to the declining effectiveness of the state and the need to shield some sectors and some areas from the less desirable effects of growing competitiveness among nations. Hence, states try to control at the regional level what they find increasingly difficult to manage at the national level (for example, by industrial policy) and impossible at the global level (notwithstanding the efforts to promote international co-operation based on home-country control of MNCs).

Despite the claims of the globalisation enthusiasts, nation-states and, increasingly, trade blocs remain the dominant players in a fragmented and unstable world characterised by free trade within each of these blocs and managed trade between them and other countries [*Sideri, 1993*]. And while the end of bipolarism, following the dismissal of the cold war, heightens the danger of continuous frictions and tensions, 'paradoxically, globalisation engenders the regionalisation of conflict' [*Mittelman. 1994: 440*], even though it seems very unlikely that regional arrangements could spark a global trade war [*Perroni and Whalley, 1996*]. Undoubtedly, integration of nations has ambiguous economic benefits and certainly carries political costs, both of them largely related to the level of development of the countries considered.

III. THE RESPONSE OF REGIONALISM

The need to adapt to the evolution of the world economic and political system explains the renewed interest in the potential of intra-regional co-operation through formal regional integration agreements (RIA), both multilateral and bilateral, or different kinds of informal arrangements. For most DCs the aim of regionalism is 'to recapture collective autonomy in relation to the United States, and to begin to organise a competitive response to the Japanese challenge' [*Streeck and Schmitter, 1991: 149*]. In the case of many LDCs the need to adapt to globalisation is complemented by the fact that the previous industrialisation strategy, namely import substitution, has come to be considered inadequate and to be replaced by one centred on exporting finished products and international competitiveness.[15]

Naturally, the constraints imposed by the process of globalisation matter much more for the medium and smaller countries than for the major powers.[16] In the global, multilateral, economy, market size strongly defines a country's negotiating power, hence the potential contribution of regional groupings [*Oman, 1994: 29*] in order to overcome the limitations faced by each country separately. Furthermore, as it is now widely recognised that economies of scale and the need to limit international labour mobility imply large nations (although large size also brings costs due to the growing heterogeneity of the population), regional integration enables both objectives to be met whilst allowing greater autonomy to sub-national entities (and so reducing the costs of heterogeneity).

The proliferation of RIAs which started in the early 1980s represents the third wave of regionalism in this century, following those of the 1930s and of the 1950–60s. Whereas the RIAs of the 1930s largely aimed to help countries withdraw from the world economy, and those of the second wave among LDCs were closely related to import-substitution strategies, the present wave is driven by the desire to facilitate participation in the world economy. Hence the declared aim of these arrangements is to pursue liberalisation and export- and foreign investment-led strategies. Whilst the second wave represented an attempt by LDCs to find an alternative to closer links with the industrial world,

17

the present wave is seen as an attempt to strengthen vertical as well as horizontal links. Furthermore, the present RIAs are characterised by a broader scope and tend to involve North and South economies. At any rate, more than 60 per cent of world trade now takes place within regional integration schemes.

Since the overall objective of all these RIAs is to enhance good and factor mobility while at the same time limiting the threat to territorially defined markets, most of them embody principles of managed as opposed to totally free trade. Hence the problem is how they can represent a route to multilateral free trade and the WTO's ultimate objective, in other words, whether regionalism ultimately complements the process of trade liberalisation or leads to the fragmentation of the world economy into feuding trading blocs.[17] A real paradox is the fact that, while LDCs have finally come to accept the case for free trade, DCs have been gradually turning away from it through various forms of creeping administrative protection. The current movement towards regional trading blocs is a culmination of this trend towards so-called managed trade [*Lal, 1993: 352*].[18]

Yet, such fragmentation may reduce but not necessarily stop the process of globalisation, because important progress in liberalising world trade has been made through unilateral actions and bilateral and regional agreements, particularly in the EU and the NAFTA [*Boltho, 1996: 250*]. Although bilateral and regional agreements are potentially useful means of reducing trade barriers, competition between regional blocs may increase the danger of global conflict, whose origin may lie in instability in the marginalised Third World (hence Mittelman's [*1994: 441*] 'truncated globalisation'), instability caused by poverty and undemocratic rule, but also by deeper cultural and political prejudices in antagonistic blocs.

By eroding national sovereignty, growing globalisation and interdependence help to unleash the demands emerging, or re-emerging, from below.[19] The forces of cultural pluralism and of the so-called 'sub-nationalism' [*Mittelman: 1994: 432*] grow stronger with the weakening of the state, but also in reaction to the homogenisation accompanying globalisation. Although it takes many forms, at the most general level sub-nationalism 'can be seen as manifestation of a search for community or identity different from the community or identity offered by shared citizenship of an existing state'. Yet, the search is sometimes accompanied by intolerance, since these movements, when carried to excess, become 'narrow and exclusive, socially divisive and sources of communal strife' [*Griffin and Khan, 1992: 75, 77*]. This means that, while globalisation is accompanied by widespread acceptance of the forms of democracy, the resistance to it on the part of the growing number of left-behinds, who experience the broadening of the distance between them and the force they are ruled by, may turn rather undemocratic. In fact, as widening globalisation causes growing internal marginalisation, widening democratisation offers

18

undemocratic and/or religious parties the means to exploit this coincidence to take power. This allows governments to justify their authoritarian rule in order to maintain their countries' competitiveness within a global system.

Devolution of power – that is, the assignment of the responsibility for governing – to emerging sub-national entities may be easier within the context of a regional scheme than within a single nation-state. Furthermore, the negative impact of the various types of diseconomies of scale that accompany the creation of smaller organisational units may be limited or eliminated by liberalisation and the availability of a wider regional market, and by transferring some administrative tasks and responsibilities to the regional power. Channelled in a constructive direction, the forces driving sub-nationalism can achieve the community and identity they seek, while enriching the region as well.

In Europe the possibility that geographical areas which form part of the territory of EU member states could become politically independent regions within the EU framework, with their citizens becoming citizens of Europe, is currently being discussed. The main advantages of what Drèze has called a 'Europe of regions' are that (i) more autonomy may lead to efficiency gains, and (ii) this arrangement may provide a more efficient framework for the exercise of regional autonomy than the alternatives of political independence or greater autonomy within the existing nation-state [*Drèze, 1993: 266*]. The standardisation process implicit in regional integration brings differences between regions or sub-national units to the fore, creating new opportunities for the latter's independence under the umbrella of the supranational unit. Regional integration facilitates sub-national movements because it tends to reduce the cost of secession. The transformation of these movements into autonomous entities functioning within the regional scheme could be partially or totally financed by the supranational government, depending on whether the countries of which they were formerly a part are willing to contribute to such an arrangement.

The loss of sovereignty involved in the creation of supra-regional institutions seems more acceptable than that implied by remote international agencies in which the weight of most countries is practically nil. Considering the difficulties of creating institutionalised governance mechanisms for the world economy and the limitations of national policies, sidelined by world market forces, many countries may turn to regionalism. The latter appears in fact useful for managing both the loss of control generated by the process of globalisation and the pressures for the devolution of power and diversification emanating from below [*Sideri, 1995*]. The sharing of common rules and institutions with other nation-states allows the concession of more autonomy to sub-national entities, while regional governance may also compensate for the ineffectiveness of national policies.

19

Also important for resorting to regionalism is a felt, if rarely openly stated, need by countries in Europe and elsewhere to avoid the establishment of a liberalised global economy in which the US, being the single hegemonic power, maintains the right to make exceptions in the pursuit of its own interests [*Bienefeld, 1994: 45*]. Such a focus may serve to strengthen the regional group's unity but is less useful for promoting international governance, including the re-regulation of the international economy.

Yet even Ohmae [*1993: 78, 81*], who considers the nation-state as 'an unnatural, even dysfunctional, unit for organising human activity and managing economic endeavour in a borderless world', theorises about the relevance of 'region states' as natural economic zones of between 5 and 20 million people, defined less by their economies of scale in production and more by their having reached efficient economies of scale in their consumption, infrastructure and professional services. Being shaped by modern marketing techniques and technologies, these 'region states' are a far cry from the present conception of the nation-state as an embodiment of common history, values and culture. What is more interesting about these 'region states' is the possibility that they represent a stepping stone not so much to globalisation but rather to trade bloc formation or, alternatively, the outcome of the breaking of a trade bloc or something in between the latter and a return to nation-states.

If national protection, especially in small countries, entails high costs in terms of economies of scale forgone, a generally inefficient cost structure, absence of competition, and a lower and more unequally distributed income, these negative effects are lessened in regional trading blocs which become even more useful when the expansion of the world economy proceeds only slowly. This means that 'the macro-economic policies in the OECD countries are likely to determine the relative strength of the forces of globalisation and regionalisation' [*Griffin and Khan, 1992: 68–9*].

Given that regionalism seems to occur alongside the spread of globalisation, it is plausible to link these two phenomena and to view regionalism as an attempt either to reduce the pace of globalisation and/or to minimise its cost and pain. This does not imply that steps towards greater regional integration are always defensive in nature; they can also be stepping stones to a more open world economy. Regionalism is not a process with uniform characteristics, but one occurring in many shapes and sizes and responding to a variety of forces. Yet, whether globalisation continues and, if it does, how it will develop, will depend largely on what happens to regionalism. There are those who already fear that 'the world trading system is currently in danger of entering the zone of excessive regionalisation' [*Frankel et al., 1995: 92*].

As to the effects of preferential trading arrangements (PTA) on the level of welfare and on the drive towards multilateral liberalisation, the traditional theory, based on the second-best approach, provides no definite answers. The net effect of the reduction or removal of trade barriers by means of PTAs on member countries' welfare is an empirical problem whose solution depends on the relative size of 'trade creation' and 'trade diversion'.

Only with the addition of dynamic effects [*Baldwin, 1989*] can it be argued that the increase of member countries' income may more than offset trade diversion, hence raising outside welfare. Therefore, the impact of PTAs on multilateral liberalisation largely depends on the rules governing their formation. It has been shown [*Kemp and Wan, 1976*] that in order to improve external welfare it is sufficient to offset any potential trade diversion created by a PTA by reducing external tariffs. This can be considered as an incentive to expand membership until multilateral free trade is reached – the first-best that maximises global welfare. Yet the rules of the General Agreement on Tariffs and Trade (GATT) 'ignore the issue of trade diversion and make no attempt to implement rules based on the Kemp/Wan insights' [*Lawrence, 1994: 369*]. Article XXIV of the GATT allows the formation of PTAs provided that external tariffs are not raised and barriers are removed on substantially all trade between member countries, that is, there is no selective liberalisation. The chance of trade diversion being larger than trade creation is considered to be nil when the prospective members of a free trade area (FTA) are close geographically [*Wonnacott and Lutz, 1989: 69*]. In this case – the EU being the perfect example at least as far as manufactured goods are concerned [*Jacquemin and Sapir, 1991: 169*] – integration is 'natural'. As members already trade a lot among themselves, integration neither causes much diversion nor penalises third parties [*Krugman, 1991*], unless trade creation is curbed by over-strict rules of origin.

Yet the effects of lowering border barriers to trade clearly fails to capture the full implications of current regional initiatives aiming to reconcile or harmonise different national policies, in other words, the deepening of the process of regional integration,[20] which impinges also on the role of the state *vis-à-vis* that of regional institutions. As 'not all states are effective at meeting and mediating international competitive pressures through national policy resources' [*Hirst and Thompson, 1992: 393–4*], the governance of large economic areas by trade blocs allows member countries to withstand global pressures on specific policy issues and to pursue objectives, particularly social and environmental ones, that they could not attempt independently [*Hirst and Thompson, 1995: 430*]. Furthermore, the creation of regional schemes may help to lessen the effect of the marginalisation – by neglect or exclusion – that globalisation apparently implies for the less developed parts of the world economy [*Sideri, 1993*]. In fact, since the benefits of global growth do not spread automatically to the poorest countries or the poorest people, the expansion of the global economy does not translate automatically into human development for the world's poor [*Griffin and Khan, 1992: 7*]. This is well illustrated by the case of Africa (where the percentage of poor in Sub-Saharan Africa is expected to increase from 16 to 32 per cent by 2000 [*WB, 1990: 139*]), and by many enclaves in other regions of the Third World.

If regionalism seems a more potent force among DCs, this is because of their greater diversity of trade, payments and investment regimes, plus a more pronounced tendency to use protectionist measures and closer control over trade transactions which, with few exceptions, are unilaterally decided and implemented. This trend has only been reversed from the mid-1980s when, alongside its further integration into the world economy, regionalism started to occur also in the developing world. Consequently, new and enlarged regional agreements are emerging from the process of continuing liberalisation, not necessarily to halt but to mute it, and to make its negative impact more tolerable and reduce the risks implicit in the process of globalisation.

In order to clarify the evolution of these linkages, the following sub-sections summarise the integration processes taking place in Europe and Asia, including their impact on the rest of the developing world.

The European Union

The European Community (EC) (founded in 1957) is deepening relationships between its members by completing the construction of the internal market (following its 'Europe 1992' initiative) and by moving to the European Union – including the introduction of a single currency – according to the Maastricht Treaty of 1992. At the same time, the EU has been widening its relations by first creating the European Economic Area and then admitting most of the nations of EFTA (formed in 1959 by the UK, the Scandinavian countries, Switzerland, Austria and Portugal, in part reflecting 'Britain's attempt to weaken the process of EC integration' [*Boltho, 1996: 250*]). The EU has also concluded association agreements with Eastern European countries, potentially expanding the bloc size from 370 million to more than 500 million people. These agreements are bound, however, to have a significant negative impact on exports of manufactured goods from some LDCs since both groups of countries produce and export low- and medium-technology products [*Sideri, 1992*].

The search for European unity seems driven by two competing visions 'both of which are based on the notion that competitiveness requires continent-wide approaches', but which lead to quite opposite results. The first holds that market forces should operate on a continental basis, hence the process of European integration should probably provide greater access to third parties. The second vision insists that 'intervention and rules, the social dimension, should be likewise', leading to a Europe which is more protectionist and closed to outsiders [*Lawrence, 1994: 377, 385*].[21]

Europe has not only become an 'outpost in changing globalisation trends to which other regions of the world will have to react', but also presents 'actual examples of economic integration beyond what we are used to consider an ideal' [*Bressand, 1990: 47, 63*]. The presence of the EC has forced the rest of the world to conform increasingly to its standards, to reduce their barriers to EC exports, and to seek lower barriers for their products in the EC market by concluding special association agreements with it, or, where possible, to join it. European integration shows that trade represents only one dimension of a much more complex and dynamic economic system centred on services, technology, advanced and integrated public infrastructures and corporate cross-border networking strategies.

In other words, European-based companies 'rather than simply seeking exports and economies of scale, are developing Euro-wide delivery systems, corporate alliances, production networks and electronic marketplaces'. The profound restructuring they are carrying out involves 'seeking customised, in-depth interactions with clients, suppliers and partners, through an expanding gamut of networking strategies, many of which have a strong information and advanced communication content'. In this they are strongly supported by Community programmes like RACE, ESPRIT, EUREKA, and also Erasmus and Comet, and institutions like ETSI (European Telecommunications Standardisation Institute) [*Bressand, 1990: 58–9*]. Furthermore, the EC has not hesitated to use sectoral protectionism, particularly towards Japan which seems to resent this measure less than the US 'attempt to force open' its economy [*Gilpin, 1987: 405*].

The ambitious social programme involving regional harmonisation and social homogeneity implies a serious redistribution of revenue within the EU. Although this can only be done at the Community level, the member states, at least the larger ones, remain crucial for constructing the political basis of consent needed for Community redistribution and macroeconomic policies, including fiscal, regulatory and industrial policies. Nation-states will also play a substantial role in the effective establishment of sub-national governments and rules.

Since 'the concept of the nation-state shakes hands with the concept of government by consent' and 'only the nation-state possesses the necessary sense of identity' [*The Economist, 23 Dec. 1995–5 Jan. 1996: 20*],[22] the subsidiarity principle has been introduced to defend the identity of member nations officially. Drawing on this principle at the European Council in Lisbon in 1992, the member states have even started reappropriating a substantial part of those common policies where their interests conflict most. The same principle can also be used by sub-national movements. In fact, the principle of subsidiarity has inspired most Constitutions of the federal type drawn up during this century, starting with Germany's *Grundgesetz*.

The system of governance that is emerging in Europe is 'unique and uniquely complex'. Although the constituent nation-states are becoming 'semi-sovereign', they will not disappear; consequently the Community's supranational institutions will have to share power with national as well as with international and transnational institutions, and eventually with sub-national ones. The main problem with this system is 'a profound *absence of hierarchy and monopoly* among a *wide variety of players of different but uncertain status'*. The inclusion of sub-national units among the already recognised players in European politics (nations, classes, sectors, and firms – the 'regionalisation of Europe') would heighten the complexity of the system while further eroding the domestic sovereignty of nation-states [*Streeck and Schmitter, 1991: 151, 154, 156, 159*] or forcing them to bargain with the MNCs.

Coming very close to the line which separates the pooling of their economic life from the merging of their politics, the EU member countries will soon have to decide whether or not they want to cross it.

Asia's Informal Regionalism-cum-Corporatism

The evolution of South and South-East Asia emphasises two quite different, but not necessarily opposing, trends: the intensification of both globalisation and regional integration. In fact, developing Asia's average share of world trade increased from 7.3 per cent between 1971 and 1980 to 16.2 per cent between 1991 and 1994 [*ADB, 1996: 183*], while Asia-Pacific's share of world production increased from 5 per cent in 1960 to 25 per cent. In addition, developing Asia's intra-trade rose from 22.3 per cent in 1980 to 41 per cent of their total exports in 1994 [*ibid.: 186–7, Table 3.1 and 3.2; WTO, 1995: 11, Chart 1.5*]. (Official figures probably underestimate the real size of the flow.)

It also appears that the vertical division of labour, in which Japan imported primary products from and exported semi-manufactured products to developing Asia which then re-exported many of the finished products outside the region, is being replaced by a horizontal one. This means an upswing in manufactured exports from Asia of slightly differentiated finished products, together with the incorporation of China into the region's manufacturing trade. Meanwhile markets outside the region continue to absorb a large share of Asia's growing export of manufactured goods. Since three-quarters of the Asian NICs' exports of finished goods are directed to the US and the EU, the region's penetration of, and dependence on, these two markets is quite evident (see also Yoshida et al. [*1994: 61–6, 104*]). Compared with their extra-regional trade, exchanges between the Asian NICs, between the largest ASEAN economies and between these two groups remain modest. Hence, the economic growth of the region, excluding Japan, continues to be dependent on outside markets [*Oman: 1994: 79–80*]. The trade barriers of the East Asian LDCs remain high, so further liberalisation of intra-regional trade and investment is needed. Asia's restructuring is helped by intra-regional foreign direct investment. In 1993 over

50 per cent of the total value of the stock of foreign direct capital in East and South-East Asia originated from within the Asian region, the largest source being the Asian NICs, followed by Japan, representing an important shift of these flows over time [*ADB, 1996: 196, 198–9, Figure 3.5*] (see also Yoshida *et al.* [*1994: 71–5 and 81–9*]).

Together with the expansion of trade, services have been growing rapidly, 90 per cent of the total exports of commercial services from the region being provided by Asian NICs [*ADB, 1996: 184*]. Intra-Asian movement of labour has also increased, the pattern having changed with Asian migration becoming chiefly intra-regional and some countries moving from a position of net emigration to one of net immigration.

The regionalism emerging in East Asia has been presented as a 'market-led' integration, in comparison with the 'policy-driven' and discriminatory type represented by the EU. Yet the fact that Asian regionalism is market-driven does not deny the crucial role played by national governments, as exemplified by the creation of Special Economic Zones and open areas in China and of 'growth triangles' all over Asia's Pacific Rim [*Arndt, 1993: 277*]. The inception of the intergovernmental arrangement known as APEC (Asia-Pacific Economic Co-operation established in 1989) represents another example of how Asian national governments intervene in, and attempt to guide, the economic process. Equally misleading is the label 'open regionalism'[22] attached by Drysdale and Garnaut [*1993*] to this phenomenon, as is that of a 'negotiating framework consistent with and complementary to GATT' [*Yoshida et al., 1994: 105*], based on the assumption that, without a formal trade agreement, the integration process is promoted if, and only if, it is consistent with the GATT and is not detrimental to other economies.

Given that the successful conclusion of the Uruguay Round protects the extra-regional interests of the region, and particularly those of the NICs, Asian regionalism should not be suspected of aiming to build an 'Asian Fortress' which would damage the world trade system as well as Asia's own interests [*Tang, 1995:18*]. More importantly, it has been argued that Japan is not interested in forming a trade bloc in Asia because: (i) it would not be able 'to cope with the subtle ways of sheltering the Japanese market (e.g. the distribution system'); (ii) the protectionist lobby 'is still stronger than that of consumer protection in basic agricultural items'; and (iii) 'there are more efficient ways for Japanese exports to enter the market of neighbouring countries' [*Langhammer, 1992: 225–6*]. Furthermore, until recently Japanese economic and security interests largely coincided with those of the US. More recently, however, the interests of the two countries may be leading them in different, not to say conflicting, directions and the 'region is emerging as a battleground for supremacy between the yen and the dollar' [*Stokes, 1996: 285*]. Hence Japan may reconsider the project of building an Asian bloc, even if it means tackling the difficult problem of China's role in it.

The East Asian experiment is also presented as a clear example of 'natural' regionalism, in the sense that the expansion of intra-regional trade and investment is 'a natural result of geographical and cultural proximity, not the outcome of political negotiations' [*Thomsen, 1994: 109*]. Likewise, Kreinin and Plummer (quoted in Lorenz [*1993: 238–9*]) regard an economic grouping comprising ASEAN and the Asian NICs, and certainly one consisting of them plus Japan, as a 'natural' bloc since it does not greatly distort its comparative advantage. In fact, East Asia's share of intra-regional trade rose from 19.0 per cent in 1965 to 29.3 per cent in 1990, an increase of over 50 per cent, even higher than EC's 32 per cent [*Frankel et al., 1995: Table 1, 63*].

Although it is considered by far the most successful Asian integration and co-operation scheme, ASEAN (Association of South-East Asian Nations, established in 1967; it now includes Brunei, Indonesia, Malaysia, the Philippines, Singapore, Thailand, and Vietnam) remains basically a PTA with such limited co-operation in industry that the level of its intra-regional trade has remained quite stable at around 17 per cent of total trade between 1970 and 1992. More relevant appear to be the following ASEAN features: (i) the formulation and representation of members' common interests in foreign affairs; (ii) a common 'perception of market forces as the driving element of development'; (iii) the creation of a strong internal network of consultation and software co-operation; and (iv) a permanent dialogue with the major OECD countries [*Langhammer and Hiemenz, 1990: 54–7*].

APEC, the other major regional initiative, is potentially the most sweeping trade agreement ever, since it involves economies that produce half the world's output. At the Bogor summit of 1994, the then 18 Asian and Pacific members (ten applications for membership have been submitted since) agreed to 'achieve free and open trade and investment in the region' by 2010 for industrial members and 2020 for the others. Even without a formal institutional framework, trade within the area covered by APEC has grown from 57 per cent of its total trade to 69 per cent between 1980 and 1992.

Although one of the main advantages of APEC is the inclusion of the US, which is seen as a counterweight to Japanese pre-eminence, APEC is unlikely to advance towards a FTA since simply eliminating tariffs does not guarantee that the US can penetrate some Asian economies, particularly Japan. Moreover, APEC's investment code is 'flimsy and not binding' [*The Economist, 16 Sept. 1996: 33*]. Bergsten's [*1996: 107*] contention that 'APEC has eliminated any possibility of the three-bloc world that was so widely feared a few years ago' does not seem very convincing.

By contrast, South-East and North-East Asia are involved in a strong and informal process of regionalism through the various 'growth triangles'[23] identified along the Pacific coasts. It is argued that the peculiar characteristics of this process distinguish it from other attempts and make it 'a distinctly Asian form of regional co-operation which has evolved from the area's experience with export processing zones, industrial and technological parks and other subnational zones' [*ADB, 1996: 179*]. These 'growth triangles', of which 'Greater China' is the most prominent example [*Sideri, 1994*], are localised economic co-operation zones that 'exploit complementarities between geographically contiguous areas of different countries to gain a competitive edge in export promotion'. They are more export-oriented than trade blocs, can be established at relatively low cost and within a short period of time, and can be expanded incrementally.

Aside from enabling an increase in exports despite rising labour costs, 'growth triangles' may also serve as protection from trade blocs and from increasing protectionism in other parts of the world [*Tang and Thant, 1994: 1, 23–4*]. Rather than trading in goods and services, they are mainly focused on the transnational movement of capital, labour, technology, and information and on the inter-country provision of infrastructure. 'Growth triangles' 'emphasise the complementarities of actual or potential resource bases of the constituent areas which arise from major differences in the supply and prices of factors' [*ADB, 1996: 179*]. The informality of these *de facto* arrangements enhances their flexibility, although the existence of an international treaty or agreement which all can read and which is more difficult to modify, would also enhance their credibility and stability and thereby attract more foreign investment [*Oman, 1994: 16*].

This rapid intensification of regional trade and investment is more the result of a need to compete globally and to take advantage of the various economies' complementarities and different factor availabilities than a need to pursue self-sufficiency. For most South-East Asian countries, opening up to the world economy by means of export-oriented policies is still accompanied by a definite policy of nurturing domestic infant industries. It is difficult, therefore, to reconcile this approach with 'open regionalism' which implies a willingness to extend to all trading partners, on a most-favoured-nation (MFN) basis, regionally negotiated tariff reductions. Such an arrangement differs from both the discriminatory GATT-notified regional integration scheme and the non-discriminatory exchange of tariff reductions in the multilateral negotiations under the GATT [*ADB, 1996, 181*].

Furthermore, South-East Asia's *de facto* regional integration also represents a response to the EU and to the creation of NAFTA: the more these two regional groupings become, or are perceived to become trading blocs, the stronger the pressure on the South-East Asian economies to follow suit and formalise their regional arrangements. Since their regionalism is a strategy to improve participation in the ongoing globalisation, they may resist preferential arrangements for as long as is feasible. 'Growth triangles' are quite dynamic institutions since both the intensity of the co-operation and the areas included in the triangle can be adjusted and changed. This makes them a new and potentially powerful tool of economic development. Yet, the continuous inflow of foreign direct investment, including intra-Asian investment, is crucial for the future of Asian 'growth triangles', and this inflow, in turn, requires the maintenance of a reasonably open global trading system and political stability. The majority of strategic alliances entered into by western, mostly American companies, have, until recently, been with Japanese, Korean and Taiwanese firms. In order to cope with the yen's overvaluation, the Japanese firms have started to relocate their manufacturing activities, a deployment which is estimated to involve one quarter of Japan's industrial production since the end of the 1980s [*Sigurdson, 1996: 3*]. It remains to be seen, however, whether the industrialisation and the regional division of labour emerging in Asia-Pacific, under Japan's guidance, are shaped by the pattern of co-operation and economic growth evoked by the poetic image of the 'flying geese'.

The emergence of 'Greater China', and the growing economic and financial integration of China's Southern provinces, Guandong and Fujian, with Hong Kong and Taiwan, have been largely driven by the private sector (particularly foreign investment, seeking to exploit factor price differentials), although there has also been some government support. The result is such that the economic integration within the triangle is mainly a vertical one, as the exchange of intra-industrial products and commodities is larger than that of final goods produced by the member economies themselves. As the demand and supply of 'Greater China' are both generated externally, its considerable vulnerability to market conditions in the outside world justifies the label of an 'outward-dependent growth triangle' [*Chen and Ho, 1994: 67*], although this arrangement has brought major net benefits to all participants. Finally, to obtain a more complete picture the triangle should be seen within the context of a larger global relationship which includes the technology of Japan and the markets of the US and other industrial countries [*Pochih Chen, 1994: 91*].

Asia's preference for this informal type of regional integration may be due to the following characteristics prevailing in the region: (i) still relatively low volume of intra-regional trade; (ii) little homogeneity of laws and regulations governing trade and investment; (iii) large differences in per capita income; (iv) wide geographical dispersion and often poor transportation and communication networks; and (v) very diverse political, social and economic systems [*Tang and Thant, 1994: 7–8*]. It is even argued [*Mittelman, 1994: 434*] that Asian regionalism 'paradoxically both shields the domestic society from and integrates it into the global division of labour'. Although the process of regional economic integration seems firmly established, and the phenomenon could be even more consistent than is indicated by aggregate trade trends, the most significant obstacles to the creation of an East Asian bloc are (i) the difficulty of harmonising the interventionist policies that all these countries, except Hong Kong, have used in order to promote export-led development; (ii) the general desire of avoiding Japanese pre-eminence; but also (iii) the impossibility of reconciling the presence of two hegemonic powers like China and Japan.

Even though transnational production networks tend to weaken the role of individual governments in formulating national development policies, and in determining how these economies are going to be linked to the global economic system [*Gereffi, 1993: 53*], an important aspect of Asia's evolution, and one which strongly impinges on both national economic development and regional co-operation, relates to so-called 'Asian corporatism'. Also referred to in the literature as 'neo-authoritarianism', this reflects an attempt to 'reconcile two apparently contradictory demands in the process of internationalisation: internal political control and external economic integration' [*Ling, 1996: 10*]. In other words, it involves the unpacking of the liberal project in order to re-fuse some of its components such as civil society and democracy and a minimal role for the state.

Asian corporatism, based on Confucian tradition and reflecting the developmental experiences of Meiji Japan and later Singapore, South Korea and Taiwan, offers the following alternative sets of developmental rationalisations for economic growth: (i) collective individualism – the neo-classical individual is placed within some social collective; (ii) utilitarian personalism – economic individuals apply a neo-classical utilitarian logic to hierarchically structured, historically conditioned, family- or clan-based personal connections; (iii) *patria economica* – Confucian family-state; and (iv) state-mobilised learning – economic development as a form of patriotism. The existence of this Asian corporatism (see particularly the case of China which currently represents the best example) 'signals the rise of an alternative, regional hegemonic order to liberal capitalism', out of which, however, Asian corporatism partly stems, so that it has also been considered 'another kind of capitalism' [*Ling, 1996: 14–15, 19*].

Although this may indicate that the spread of liberalism is not merely a one-way process and globalisation involves different communities adapting ideas and institutions to their respective needs, a sounder interpretation is that it reveals the authoritarian underpinning of the whole process and the crucial role of the state, contrary to the liberal myth propagated by international institutions [*Rodrik, 1994*]. The insistence on 'Asian values', allegedly to avoid succumbing to western individualism and other western excesses, in reality serves to qualify the acceptance of democracy and reflects the intention of the elites to run their countries like a family business. Consequently, the applicability of the Asian model to other parts of the world is seriously curtailed.

Finally, there remains the question of whether differences in the capitalist structures between East Asia, Europe and North America are so profound as to hinder the consolidation of the global economy and harden it into regional blocs – what Gilpin refers to as 'the Japan problem', but which also involves the Asian NICs. At issue is the resistance to their insertion into the world economy. In fact, compared with those of other DCs the Japanese economy shows 'extraordinary low inward-direct-investment ratios and import penetration' which explains why 'it has hardly shared in the internationalisation of the world economy over the last decade' [*Hutton, 1995, 306*]. A highly competitive export sector assured Japan's trade surplus. The export of capital, buying US debt during the 1980s, offset the trade surpluses and checked the upward movement of the yen. Yet, the net Japanese capital inflow into the US contributes to the US trade deficit since it pushes up the exchange rate of the dollar and thereby reduces American competitiveness in the world market.

Similar asymmetric trade relations characterise most of East Asia. Higher investment allows the region to obtain 'a rate of productivity and innovation with which European and American producers cannot compete, but access to the region's markets remains structurally difficult even while their own economies remain open' [*Hutton, 1995: 307*], owing to the fact that these economies tend to be highly regulated, compartmentalised, and segmented. Rather than trade barriers the real obstacle is their firms' anti-competitive behaviour, with their exclusive supplier or distributor arrangements (vertical *keiretsu* in Japan) and domination of particular markets. Hence the problem crystallises around the meaning given to liberalisation. Given the nature of the Japanese economy, and that of other East Asian countries, liberalisation cannot mean 'simply the removal of formal, external trade restrictions and, under certain circumstances, giving foreign firms "National Treatment"' but must go deeper, thus challenging 'inherent and crucial features of Japanese culture, social relations, and political structure'. In effect, unless Japan – and the other eastern Asian countries – 'becomes a liberal society in the Western sense', Europe and North America will find it increasingly difficult to maintain economic relations with them.

Hence the crucial question: 'can a liberal international economy long survive if it is not composed primarily of liberal societies as defined in the West … ?' [*Gilpin, 1987: 390–93*]. Reactions to the homogenisation implied by the international liberal order are the rise of economic nationalism and the refuge of regionalism. Following Gilpin [*1987: 395*], autonomy tends to gain over interdependence in order to minimise the latter's costs. If Japan decides not to open its market to the region's growing manufacturing production and not to export its capital surplus to the same, the chances of further integration in East and South-east Asia will be sharply reduced and confrontation with China may become unavoidable.

The Risk of Marginalisation for Other Parts of the Developing World

The difficulties encountered by many LDCs in creating their own regional schemes are an indication that the process of globalisation does not really involve them, or does so only marginally, as large parts of the Third World remain outside the global economy.

Latin America and Africa both have a rich experience with integration schemes and of failure, probably more so in Africa. Comparing earlier LDC regional initiatives with more recent ones, Langhammer and Hiemenz [*1990: 57–73*] identify the main differences as (i) the shift in emphasis from more formal types of internal integration to less binding project-oriented co-operation schemes; (ii) a greater scope allowed for pursuing trade liberation at different speeds; and (iii) the lower priority assigned to the planning and programming of regional industrialisation compared with co-operation in providing public goods, that is, building physical infrastructure, communications, transport, and the creation of software, namely training, research and technology. One important implication of these developments is that the role of supranational authorities in the decision-making process has been curtailed as national authorities have regained or maintained their rights to decide.

Langhammer and Hiemenz [*1990: 57–73*] explain the failure of many regional initiatives by LDCs in terms of internal rather than external factors, even though the negative impact of a deteriorating external economic environment is not excluded. Amongst the internal reasons cited are (i) the resistance to reducing barriers to trade and factor mobility; (ii) the macro-economic policies pursued; (iii) the fear of economic domination by a large or more advanced partner country; (iv) the problems inherent in any international co-ordination, particularly when no common threat exists; and (v) the influence of vested interests. Yet the negative outcome 'did not so much result from a misperception of the potential embodied in regional integration, but from the lack of incentives to implement integration policies in the given situation'.

Furthermore, since low wages are not a sufficient attraction for MNCs to locate labour-intensive production in countries with inadequate infrastructure and lacking in the human capital required by 'flexible production', these countries have also failed to attract direct foreign investment, except in some primary products. For the MNCs, the trend is in fact to neglect the production of low-wage goods for the world market and concentrate on production and sourcing networks at the regional level [*Oman, 1994: 93*]. The lack of progress in regional integration compounds the problems of poor infrastructure and human capital, thus increasing the risk of marginalisation for several LDCs and for large sections of some continents.[24]

What emerges is that, although globalisation tends to marginalise the less developed parts of the Third World, their capacity to react by forming regional groupings of their own is limited, mainly because the central institutions of government are crumbling, hence the expression 'failed states'. Their prospects are no better if the world economy comes to be dominated by trade blocs [*Gilpin, 1987: 400; Sideri, 1993*]. Although their chances of obtaining some economic support may be better in the latter case, their dependence on one of the trade blocs would also increase. Whereas globalisation implies their marginalisation with neglect, a system of trade blocs means total dependence: an unenviable predicament.

IV. CONCLUDING REMARKS

The globalisation process is creating a world economic system which is dominated by the private sector, fast-paced and largely averse to government action, particularly when perceived as an interference.

The existence of the world market renders the nation-state unable to deliver such valued benefits as job security and rising living standards to its citizens. Neither can regional integration necessarily accomplish this, but it may be better at reconciling global competitiveness with a heightened sense of social solidarity, and possibly, democratic legitimacy. National sovereignty is no longer the valuable commodity it once was; capital markets increasingly exercise their power of veto over the economic decisions of all states. If political independence does actually offer people less control over decisions that crucially affect them, the search for protection from globalisation becomes less attractive. This explains why in many countries deregulation often stimulates increased protection of domestic markets [*Gilpin, 1987: 407*].

Economic globalisation is entering a critical phase as the backlash against its effects is growing, primarily in the DCs. This, and the new brand of populism generated by globalisation, is propelling the search for alternative solutions which retain most of the achievements of globalisation, but minimise its disruptive impact on economic activity and social stability.

For DCs, regionalism appears as the instrument for protecting them from the risk of de-industrialisation. More importantly, regional integration is seen as reducing the impact of political or cultural globalisation, both of which are still less advanced than economic globalisation but no less threatening. However, the forces opposing the process of globalisation, namely nationalism and powerful sectional interests, are the same forces which regionalism must overcome, while the end of the Cold War has further contributed to the fragmentation of people's horizons [*Bliss, 1994: 134*].

LDCs also regard regional integration as a useful instrument for achieving those economies of scale required to increase their participation in international trade [*Krugman, 1988: 42*]. With respect to the least developed countries, regional integration may not be a viable option, mainly because their state machinery is unable to provide the necessary backing for the establishment and functioning of a regional scheme. Nevertheless, many LDCs are currently reconsidering regional integration which, coupled with a significant degree of trade liberalisation as required by structural adjustment programmes, they see as helping to test their firms' competitiveness regionally, before being fully exposed to the more taxing global environment.

Since it remains doubtful whether LDCs' segmented and unstable markets will become homogeneous and stable as is assumed by structural adjustment policies, trade liberalisation, privatisation and deregulation should focus on productivity and production in the enterprises, large and small, which serve the domestic and regional markets, rather than on exporting to the global market. Outward-oriented development strategies in particular require measures which encourage the emergence of entrepreneurial capabilities. These developments involve education and training, social approval, favourable legislation, and close co-operation with the enterprises of neighbouring countries through regional integration, as well as with more advanced countries in order to gain access to their larger markets. Both types of co-operation should be facilitated by globalisation. By contributing firm and committed finance, which is available neither locally nor centrally, foreign aid would provide incentives for rational economic behaviour not determined by market prices.

LDCs' rather negative experience of regional integration contrasts with that of DCs, notably the EU, and even with that of some groupings in the developing world, namely ASEAN, 'Greater China', and the Asian 'growth triangles' [*Sideri, 1994*]. Many LDCs, and particularly the least developed ones, lack the ingredients needed for the successful formation of a trade bloc or even a trade interest group, such as the Cairns group. They lack the impetus of shared political objectives and their interests start to diverge as soon as one gets down to details. More generally, large variations in their economic circumstances militate against the formation of a united front, and they often lack the cultural, political and historical closeness essential to any common endeavour. For large sections of the developing world the road to liberalisation necessarily passes through that of regionalism; in other words, if they could 'regionalise regionalism' this would help to strengthen the effectiveness and credibility of their governments and enable them to 'globalise globalisation', to adopt Oman's expression.

In the face of strong external pressures, the need to redefine one's identity is more pressing, so economic globalisation has gone hand in hand with political nationalism – the ideology which is probably the easiest to transplant globally. To check the growing forces of disintegration, a structure must be built between national and sub-national levels and the world system. Without denying that a regional framework tends to foster movements towards autonomy and even secession, it appears as the only instrument able to address the destabilising and destructive forces emanating from both globalisation and nationalism. In addition, regional integration agreements, even the most open and liberal with respect to trade and investment, may enable groups of countries with close political and cultural ties to establish the free movements of, and equal opportunities for, people within the region, whilst restricting rights of entry, residence, and citizenship for outsiders. Particularly in post-Maastricht Europe, regionalism is re-centralising state power at the regional level, eroding economic nationalism and increasing awareness of economic interdependence. It has become a useful laboratory for new approaches to deeper integration which can be applied multilaterally; it eases negotiations by reducing the number of players; and it encourages the codification and formalisation of rules and regulations affecting trade, making them more transparent and less discretionary [*Cable, 1994: 12*].

It follows that regionalism has two different meanings. On the one hand, it protects against the worse effects of globalisation and unites individual countries. On the other hand, it favours the prospering of sub-national movements, thereby heightening the dangers of national divisiveness. However, as the contradictions of globalisation become clearer – depletion of resources and the environment, reduced capacity of the state to provide public goods while 'many of the neoliberal forms of state have been authoritarian' [*Gill, 1995: 419–20*] – regionalism emerges as the stronger and more pervasive influence on the course of international policies.

The traditional analysis of RIAs, which focuses on the effect of lowering border barriers to trade, fails to capture fully the implications of current regional initiatives which aim to achieve deeper integration by means of the harmonisation and reconciliation of domestic policies among the member countries. The pressure of growing globalisation is forcing countries into regionalisation, but it is the latter which makes it necessary to address problems arising from different regulatory policies and to reduce differences by means of mutual recognition and a supranational mechanism for implementing common policies. The level of policy decision and implementation can vary, however. It can be transferred to the regional level but also to the sub-national level. Hence the problem of assigning authority for the different levels of the policy-making spectrum, that is, subsidiarity in general and fiscal federalism in this specific sector, with which to hold centrifugal forces together and retain an overall identity against the enveloping globalisation. Devolution of power involves extending consumer choice, or wild consumerism, but it also entails market volatility, concentrating power in private hands and the deflationary bias – monetarist preferences – generated by the current international financial and trading system. In sum, it means the prevalence of the values of finance over those of production and employment, as underlined by too many observers.

In addition, MNCs, particularly those most competitive globally, are much more interested in intra-regional than in inter-regional trade liberalisation. When MNCs invest in other regions, they organise their activities on a regional and fairly autonomous basis, regardless of the existence of a regional integration scheme. Since 'in those sectors in which MNCs are important, intra-firm trade[25] already appears to be a regional affair' [*Thomsen, 1994: 123–5*], MNCs would only object to any increase in the barriers to inter-regional investment, an eventuality considered unlikely even if the world economy becomes fragmented into a series of trading blocs. In any case, large MNCs from the OECD area are relatively sheltered from such a fragmentation since the redeployment of labour-intensive production to low-wage countries has become less relevant (see note 3). Furthermore, by multiplying international joint ventures, encouraging linkages among MNCs of different nationalities, and strengthening cross-cutting interests, sectoral protectionism may reduce the risk of destabilising conflict inherent in a system of regional blocs [*Gilpin, 1987: 404*].

As regionalism mitigates the negative effects of unfettered globalisation, the system of small and medium enterprises (SME) can likewise help to reassert the value of co-operation, without reducing efficiency. The success of SMEs and the growth of sub-regional economies are connected to the overall process of globalisation, as they can cope better with shifting and volatile patterns of international demand through their diversified and flexible production. By clustering together, by sharing work, expertise, collective services, and risk, inter-firm SMEs have demonstrated their ability to resist market shocks and adapt to rapid changes better than large firms organised hierarchically.

Clearly, SME inter-firm relationships are typified by a mixture of competition and co-operation, in which the co-operative aspects help to minimise the disadvantages of small size and the competitive aspects, along with the specialisation, convey the dynamism and flexibility that are often lacking in large integrated firms. SMEs' flexibility and strength are greatly enhanced by the development of a low-cost financial sector closely connected to the local economy and the sub-national governance. Being thus sheltered from some of the negative effects of globalisation, SMEs would support international openness whilst helping to retain some manufacturing activities. By allowing sub-national areas enough autonomy, the system of SMEs may develop and prosper, reducing both separatist pressures and tensions between the national level and the global one. Grafted on to the economic, political and social systems likely through decentralisation, federalism or even the recognition of sub-national entities' role and place, the system is 'embedded' in rules, norms and conventions established by trade unions, the state, political parties, religious affiliations and more informal community-based institutions. The result is a 'social market' which rests as much on economic forces as on solidarity.

The alternatives to a globalisation mitigated by regionalism and devolution are 'global neoclassicism' or feuding regional blocs. Neither of these will be able to provide a stable, secure and environment-friendly world order. Both will involve more marginalisation for the developing world and also for some economic sectors and social groups in DCs.

NOTES

1. This globalist view satisfies the Right's anti-political liberalism, since trade, multinational corporations (MNCs) and capital markets are freed from the constraints of politics and labour organisations and their operations are also made more secure by the emergence of a demilitarised world, thus denying 'both the need for strong international governance and the possibility of national level action'. The globalist view also satisfies the Left, since 'globalisation proves the reality of the world capitalist system and the illusory nature of national reformist strategies, even if this intellectual certainty is bought at the price of political impotence'. Both 'can thus mutually celebrate the end of the Keynesian era' [*Hirst and Thompson, 1995: 424, 414*]. A rather different distinction involving globalism sees it either as 'a Kantian-Grotian-Hegelian reasoning that promotes the rule of international law, universal human rights, a global ecological order, and other concerns of a liberal world order' or as a 'Gramscian international political economy where a capitalist "world-hegemony" turns states inside-out ... to service the needs of international production', what Cox [*1981: 44–6*] calls 'the internationalising of the state'. 'Both strands of globalism share a common conviction: international relations is homogenising ... and internationalisation ultimately leads to globalisation: that is, one world order' which basically is western-led [*Ling, 1996: 1–2*].

2. Oman [*1994: 57-8*] argues that the diffusion of the 'flexible production' system and the crisis of 'fordism' are shaping the dynamics of the present wave of regionalism. The 'flexible production' system implies a complete overhaul of the value-added chain based on simultaneous engineering, continuous innovation, extensive use of general or multipurpose machinery and skilled workers, and team work which closely integrates manual and mental tasks. This allows companies to produce differentiated products and small batches for niche markets. Competition is combined with co-operative links among firms: the horizontal integration of production is based on thick networks among firms and sub-contracting relations – the 'just-in-time' organisation. Also very flexible and variegated is the response to falling markets: namely, diversification of production, innovation, sub-contracting and lay-offs, while the 'forms of social regulation are mainly established at a local level, with an important role of specific local institutions' [*Garofoli, 1992: 3*]. The other system, namely Fordism, concerns mainly mass production of standard goods in big plants in which economies are obtained through fixed capital and labour productivity increases within the production process. 'The prevailing form of the market is the oligopolistic one and the management of the economy is organised at the national level, especially with the goal to offset the immanent tendency to over-production.' The resulting pattern of production is therefore determined by the combination of Taylorism and the Keynesian state [*ibid*].

    The main problem with this new system is that it is less 'robust', or more 'fragile', than Fordism owing to its dependence on the reliability of communication and transportation structures and on the quality of labour. This makes the flexible specialisation system less feasible for LDCs and explains the growing structural unemployment of DCs. Furthermore, since the 'flexible production' system tends to reduce the importance of the cost of labour –

its share of variable production cost declining – the need to move production into LDCs in order to exploit their comparative advantage becomes less pressing (see also note 2). Much more relevant is proximity, due to the synergic character of the relationship between firms, suppliers and clients. Hence the creation of production networks in each regional market, that 'global localisation' which contributes to current regionalism. This also explains why MNCs are often more interested in regional integration and less worried about commercial obstacles to inter-regional exchanges [*Oman, 1994: 86–91*]. Flexible production is also identified with global capitalism, that is, a capitalism that is no longer nationally based but has been deterritorialised and located in MNCs.

3. Over the past decade international trade has grown twice as fast as output (currently more than $4 trillion per year), while foreign direct investment has risen three times as fast. The turnover of international capital markets is now close to $100 trillion and foreign-exchange transactions approximate $1.3 trillion per day.

4. 'Beneath the surface, many multinationals remain stubbornly monocultural. The proportion of foreign-born board members of America's 500 leading companies was 2.1% in 1991, the same as ten years earlier'. There are even fewer foreigners in Japanese companies. [*The Economist, 24 May1995: 'Survey Multinationals', 14*].

5. Among those who maintain that the present international system has been around much longer, see Thomson and Krasner [*1989*].

6. Even though the state remains a controller of its borders and the movement of people across them, the advanced countries seeking 'to police the movement of the world's poor and exclude them ... will not be able effectively to use as a principle of exclusion the claim to cultural homogeneity – for they are ethnically and culturally pluralistic' [*Hirst and Thompson, 1995: 420–21*].

7. Broadly defined, regionalism refers to preferential trade agreements among a subset of nations [*Bhagwati, 1993: 22*]. Lorenz [*1992: 84*] distinguishes, however, between regionalisation, that is, 'the outcome of a natural location phenomenon leading to close economic ties within a region' and regionalism which refers to 'the creation of preferential trading arrangements'.

8. Most international investment house bond dealers and MNC treasurers are not easily persuaded that the current financial order is either unstable or economically inefficient [*Hutton, 1995: 305*].

9. The term global governance does not yet have a fixed meaning. To define it one can use either a Gramscian or a Weberian approach. In the former, global governance consists of the creation of an ideological consensus and its propagation by international organisations so as to secure the reproduction and world-wide extension of industrial capitalism. Amongst the few existing Weberian definitions, the most recent is that adopted by the Carlsson-Ramphal 'Commission on Global Governance' in which global governance is the outcome of a partnership between the agencies of the UN system and the network of world-wide civil society.

10. Although economic integration, to the extent that it occurs, brings greater economic interdependence, the two may not always coincide. Two or more countries may reach a high degree of integration and a low level of interdependence, for example, Australia and New Zealand, and vice versa, for example, the European countries before the development of the EU [*ADB, 1996: 209*].

11. Whereas Bretton Woods established a system – the government-led international monetary system (G-IMS) – 'with a built-in asymmetry between an integrating world market for goods and commodities and domestically insulated, government-regulated financial markets', the rise of international financial markets brought the current market-led international monetary system (M-IMS) which is 'the converse of the preceding one'. Since 'the M-IMS has eroded the power of national central banks and the effectiveness of their instruments', to ensure monetary and financial stability 'a more complete set of policy functions' is required and some institutional

37

requirements that may 'tend to resemble more the framework applying *within* a single nation-state than the loose arrangements applying today *among* nation-states' [*Padoa-Schioppa and Saccomanni, 1994: 264, 237, 240–41, 263, 262*].

12. Lal [*1993: 356*] worries that 'there is a contemporary movement in the West – the global environmentalists – who might trigger another round of imperialism in the name of saving Spaceship Earth', since 'ominous is the Greens' desire to dictate environmental policy to the rest of the world'.

13. To insist that free trade requires that countries have similar labour and environmental standards is like demanding all comparative advantages be eliminated before international trade begins.

14. The term 'trade bloc', or 'trading bloc', is not only ill-defined [*Henderson, 1994: 183*], but its definition is 'problematic' [*Bliss, 1994: 1*] as 'ambivalent has been economists' attitude to this phenomenon' [*Lal, 1993: 349*]. So, while the latter considers all common markets and regional FTAs as trade blocs, for Wolf (quoted by Henderson [*1994: 13*]) there are only two trade blocs: the EU and NAFTA. Bliss [*1994: 6*] thinks that 'the evidence in favour of widespread block formation among the world's trading nations is not as impressive as many accounts would lead one to expect', but in the end recognises that 'trading blocks have come into being and are being developed and extended' [*Bliss, 1994: 136*], while Henderson [*1994: 184*] admits that 'the significance of regional agreements has increased in recent years'.

15. Another reason for LDCs' revived interest in regional integration is to establish 'a defence mechanism to offset some of the costs of even greater isolation resulting from any increase in protectionism in DCs' [*ECLAC, 1994: 11*]. Finally, a reason that applies to both DCs and LDCs is the frustration caused by the slow progress of multilateral trade negotiations under the GATT, although the creation of the WTO may ease this problem.

16. According to Kapstein [*1994: 20*] the major powers may view globalisation 'as being in their national interest'. Yet 'small country firms will see a decline in their relative cost disadvantage and will be the main beneficiaries of the enlargement of the trade bloc', and 'neither the theory nor the data indicate any asymmetric economic gain in favour of large countries as such' [*Casella, 1996: 412*].

17. See the various contributions in De Melo and Panagariya [*1993*]. The World Bank estimated that if the Uruguay Round had collapsed losses resulting from the trade war between rival trading blocs would have amounted to three to four per cent of world output [*WB, 1991: 29*].

18. Among the initiatives that have contributed to the fragmentation of the world market and the movement towards regionalism, Langhammer also includes (i) the Global System of Trade Preferences (GSTP) established since the early 1970s in order to facilitate trade among the developing countries, an arrangement that 'has all the flaws of regional integration schemes plus those of ineffectiveness due to a large membership and problems of "balancing" the concessions in a group of heterogeneous economies'; and (ii) the trade preferences unilaterally offered to developing countries by OECD countries, including several General Systems of Preferences (GSP) [*Langhammer, 1992: 217–23*].

19. Huntington [*1973: 365*] identified this phenomenon more than two decades ago: 'while functional imperatives seem to be making transnational organizations bigger and bigger, cultural and communal imperatives seem to be encouraging political units to become smaller and smaller. "Tribalism" in politics contrasts with "transnationalism" in economics.' That the nation-state and the transnational organisation coexist confirms that 'the existence of one not only implies but requires the existence of the other'. By tribalism is meant 'the retreat by individuals into communities defined not by political association or by the state borders that enclose a political nation, but by similarities of religion, culture, ethnicity, or some other shared experience. The retreat is driven by fear and confusion, and fed by the reassuring "sameness" of others in the group' [*Horsman and Marshall, 1994: x*].

20. 'Deep integration', as opposed to 'shallow integration', refers to an integration process that goes beyond a concern with tariffs to tackle non-tariff barriers to access; it involves a comprehensive, all-embracing approach to liberalisation; and it forces governments to surrender more sovereignty, both in terms of national norms and procedures and of dispute settlement, and to transfer institutions to a supranational level, that is, institutional integration. Monetary union is required more for political union than for economic integration. This is demonstrated in Asia, where even in cases of deep integration as in 'Greater China' and the Singapore-Johr-Riau 'growth triangle' (see later) there is no plan to move towards monetary union because there is no desire to achieve political unity [*Arndt, 1993: 276*].

21. Theoretically, the main reason why blocs may be expected to be more protectionist is that their larger size allows them a higher level of optimal tariff, i.e. to turn the terms of trade to their advantage, although Whalley [*1985: 173, Table 9.6*] has estimated that the optimal tariff for the US, the EU and Japan, assuming no retaliation, is 160, 150 and 175 per cent respectively. That FTAs may not be necessarily inferior, this being dependent much more on their design, is demonstrated by the fact that large-scale economies 'may improve efficiency even if it [the FTA] is predominantly trade diverting' [*Wonnacott and Lutz, 1989: 63*].

22. Furthermore, the nation-state still controls the army and, through taxation, a large share of GDP.

23. According to the 1994 report of the Eminent Persons Group to APEC, open regionalism is a process of regional co-operation, the outcome of which is a reduction of intra-regional barriers and also external barriers to economies that are not part of the regional arrangements. In this sense, open regionalism is consistent with and equivalent to multilateralism and the GATT agreement. Drysdale and Garnaut [*1993: 188*] hope that through open regionalism national governments will enjoy the 'prisoner's delight' of experiencing the beneficial effects of each country's liberalisation on its own trade expansion. Yet since any form of regionalism cannot fail to discriminate in favour of its members, and at the expense of non-members, open regionalism remains a contradiction in terms.

24. Several 'growth triangles', aside from the more formal groupings, are emerging within the region. Particularly suited to countries in transition from a closed and rigid economic system to an open and market-oriented system, a 'growth triangle' is a scheme to promote and rationalise direct investment as well as to build up infrastructure linkages within the area. Although it presents an export-oriented structure, it is not a mechanism solely to promote free trade and it does not imply discrimination as far as a third party is concerned [*Tang, 1995: 19–20*]. The most important of these triangles are 'Greater China' (starting to emerge since the early 1980s) (Southern China, Taiwan and Hong Kong), 'Northeast Asia' (Japan, South and North Korea, Northeast China and Far East Russia), 'Greater Mekong' (established in 1991) (Cambodia, Laos, Myanmar, Thailand, Viet Nam and China's Yunnan Province) and some 'growth triangles' involving localised arrangements including only selected areas of a few countries, like the 'Singapore-Johor-Riau Growth Triangle' (1989) between Singapore and Malaysia's and Indonesia's provinces; the 'Tumen River Area Development' (established in 1991) between North Korea, China and Russia; the 'East ASEAN Growth Area' (established in 1994) between Brunei, Indonesia, Malaysia and the Philippines; and 'Indonesia, Malaysia-Thailand Growth Triangle' (established in 1993).

25. In contrast to the World Bank view, forcefully presented in De Melo and Panagariya [*1993*]), a view is emerging with respect to the possibility of implanting regional integration even in Africa and the least developed countries, using structural adjustment programmes to facilitate the pursuit of integration. Only by reducing its own costs from non-integration, can Africa hope to attract the inflows of foreign investment and technology and cross-border investment on which its development continues to depend [*Robson: 1993: 340*].

26. Intra-firm trade represents 40 per cent of US total trade, a percentage that may rise to 66 per cent if the term 'related party' is more loosely defined [*Ruggie, 1993: fn 14, 149*].

REFERENCES

Alesina, A. and E. Spolaore (1995), *On the Numbers and Size of Nations*, Working Paper No.5050, Cambridge, MA: NBER, March.

Anderson, S. and J. Kavanagh (1996), 'Corporate Power Isn't Discussed', *International Herald Tribune*, 23 Oct.

Arndt, H.W. (1993), 'Anatomy of Regionalism', *Journal of Asian Economics*, Vol.4, No.2, pp.271–82.

Asian Development Bank (ADB) (1996), *Asian Development Outlook. 1996 and 199*, Oxford: Oxford University Press.

Baldwin, R. (1989), 'The Growth Effects of 1992', *Economic Policy*, 9, Oct., pp.247–83.

Bergsten, C.F. (1996): 'Globalizing free trade', *Foreign Affairs*, Vol.75, No.3, May/June, pp.105–20.

Bhagwati, J. (1993), 'Regionalism and Multilateralism: An Overview', in J. de Melo and A. Panagariya (eds.), New Dimension in Regional Integration, Cambridge: Cambridge University Press.

Bienefeld, M. (1994), 'The New World Order: Echoes of a New Imperialism', *Third World Quarterly*, Vol.15, No.1, pp.31–48.

Bliss, C. (1994), Economic Theory and Policy for Trading Blocks, Manchester: Manchester University Press.

Boltho, A. (1996), 'The Return of Free Trade?', *International Affairs*, Vol.72, No.2, April, pp.247–59.

Bolton, P., Roland, G. and E. Spolaore (1996), 'Economic Theories of the Break-up and Integration of Nations', *European Economic Review*, Vol.40, Nos.3–5, April, pp.99–104.

Bressand, A. (1990), 'Beyond Interdependence: 1992 as a Global Challenge', *International Affairs*, Vol.66, No.1, pp.47–65.

Cable, V. (1994), 'Overview', in Cable and Henderson [*1994*].

Cable, V. (1996), 'The New Trade Agenda: Universal Rules Amid Cultural Diversity', *International Affairs*, Vol.72, No.2, April, pp.227–46.

Cable, V. and D. Henderson (eds.) (1994), *Trade Blocs: The Future of Regional Integration*, London: Royal Institute of International Affairs.

Casella, A. (1996), 'Large Countries, Small Countries and the Enlargement of Trade Blocs', *European Economic Review*, Vol.40, No.2, Feb., pp.389–415.

Chen, H. and A. Ho (1994), 'Southern China Growth Triangle: An Overview', in Myo Thant, Min Tang and Hiroshi Kakazu (eds.), *Growth Triangles in Asia: A New Approach to Regional Economic Cooperation*, Oxford: Oxford University Press.

Collier, P. and C. Meyer (1989), 'The Assessment: Financial Liberalization, Financial Systems and Economic Growth', *Oxford Review of Economic Policy*, Vol.15, No.4, Winter, pp.1–12.

Cox, R. (1981), 'Social Forces, States and World Orders: Beyond International Relations Theory', *Millennium*, Vol.10, No.2, pp.126–155.

De Melo, J. and A. Panagariya (eds.) (1993), New Dimensions in Regional Integration,. Cambridge: Cambridge University Press.

Dickey, C. (1995), 'Junk nations', *Newsweek*, 27 Nov.

Drèze, J. (1993), 'Regions of Europe: A Feasible Status, to be Discussed', *Economic Policy*, 17, Oct., pp.266–93.

Drysdale P. and R. Garnaut (1993), 'The Pacific: An Application of a General Theory of Economic Integration', in C.F. Bergsten and M. Noland (eds.), *Pacific Dynamism and the International Economic System,* Washington, DC: Institute for International Economics.

Dunning, J.H. (1993), *The Globalization of Business: The Challenge of the 1990s,* London: Routledge.

ECLAC (1994), *Open Regionalism in Latin America and the Caribbean: Economic Integration as a Contribution to Changing Production Patterns with Social Equity,* Santiago: UN ECLAC.

Featherstone, M. (1990), 'Global Culture: An Introduction' in M. Featherstone (ed.), *Global Culture. Nationalism, Globalization and Modernity,* London:Sage.

Feenstra, R.C. and G.H. Honson (1996), 'Globalization, Outsourcing, and Wage Inequality', *American Economic Review Papers and Proceedings*, Vol.86, No.2, May, pp.240–45.

Frankel. J., E. Stein, and Shang-jin Wei (1995), 'Trading Blocs and the Americas: The Natural, the Unnatural, and the Super-natural', *Journal of Development Economics*, Vol.47, No.1, pp.61–95.

Garofoli, G. (1992), 'Endogenous Development and Southern Europe: An Introduction', in G. Garofoli (ed.), *Endogenous Development and Southern Europe,* Aldershot: Avebury.

Gereffi, G. (1993), 'Global Sourcing and Regional Division of Labor in the Pacific Rim', in A. Dirlik (ed.), *What is in a Rim? Critical Perspectives on the Pacific Region Idea,* Boulder, CO: Westview Press.

Gill, S. (1995), 'Globalisation, Market Civilisation, and Disciplinary Neoliberalism', *Millennium*, Vol.24,No.3, pp. 399–423.

Gilpin, R. (1987), *The Political Economy of International Relations,* Princeton, NJ: Princeton University Press.

Griffin, K. and A.R. Khan (1992), *Globalization and the Developing World. An Essay on the International Dimensions of Development in the Post-Cold War Era,* UNRISD, Geneva.

Henderson, D. (1994), 'Putting "Trade Blocs" into Perspective', in Cable and Henderson (eds.) [*1994*].

Hirst, P. and G. Thompson (1992), 'The Problem of "Globalization": International Economic Relations, National Economic Management and the Formation of Trading Blocs', *Economy and Society*, Vol.21, No.4, Nov., pp.357–96.

Hirst, P. and G. Thompson (1995), 'Globalization and the Future of the Nation State', *Economy and Society*, Vol.24, No.3, Aug., pp.408–42.

Horsman, M. and A. Marshall (1994), *After The Nation-State. Citizens, Tribalism and the New World Order.* London: HarperCollins.

Huntington, S.P. (1973), 'Transnational Organizations in World Politics', *World Politics*, Vol.25, No.3, April, pp.333–68.

Hutton, W. (1995), 'A Postscript', in J. Michie and J.G. Smith (eds.), *Managing the Global Economy,* Oxford: Oxford University Press.

International Herald Tribune (1996), 29/30 June [*IHT*].

Jacquemin, A. and A. Sapir (1991), 'Europe Post-1992: Internal and External Liberalization', *American Economic Review*, Papers and Proceedings, Vol.81, No.2, May, pp.166–70.

Kapstein, E.B. (1994), *Governing the Global Economy,* Cambridge, MA: Harvard University Press.

Kemp, M.P. and H.Y. Wan (1976), 'An Elementary Proposition Concerning the Formation of Customs Unions', *Journal of International Economics*, Vol.6, No.1, pp.95–7.

Krugman, P. (1988), 'La Nueva Teoría del Comercio Internacional y los Países Menos Desarrollados', *El Trimestre Económico*, Vol.40, No.217, Jan./March, pp.41–66.

Krugman, P. (1991), 'The Move Toward Free Trade Zones', in *Policy Implications of Trade and Currency Zones*, A Symposium sponsored by the Federal Reserve Bank of Kansas City, Jackson Hole, Wyoming, 22–24 Aug.

Krugman, P. (1991a), 'Is Bilateralism Bad?' in E. Helpman and A. Razin (eds.), *International Trade and Trade Policy,* Cambridge, MA: MIT Press.

Krugman, P. and Venables A. (1994), *Globalization and the Inequality of Nations*, CEPR Discussion Paper No.1015, London: CEPR, September.

Laïdi, Z. (1995), 'Introduction', in Z. Laïdi (ed.), *Power and Purpose After the Cold War*, Oxford: Berg.

Lal, D. (1993), 'Trade Blocs and Multilateral Free Trade', *Journal of Common Market Studies*, Vol.31, No.3, Sept., pp. 349–58.

Langhammer, R.J. (1992), 'The Developing Countries and Regionalism', *Journal of Common Market Studies*, Vol.30, No.2, June, pp.211–31.

Langhammer, R.J. and U. Hiemenz (1990), *Regional Integration Among Developing Countries*, Tübingen: J.C.B. Mohr.

Lawrence, R.Z. (1994), 'Regionalism: An Overview', *Journal of the Japanese and International Economies*, Vol.8, No.4, pp.365–87.

Ling, L.H.M. (1996), 'Hegemony and the Internationalizing State: A Post-Colonial Analysis of China's Integration into Asian Corporatism', *Review of International Political Economy*, Vol.3, No.1, Spring, pp.1–26.

Lorenz, D. (1992), 'Economic geography and the political economy of regionalization: the example of Western Europe', *American Economic Review*, Papers and Proceedings, Vol.82, No.2, May, pp.84–92.

Lorenz, D. (1993), 'Europe and Asia in the Context of Regionalization: Theory and Economic Policy', *Journal of Asian Economics*, Vol.4, No.2, pp.255–70.

Mittelman, J.H. (1994), 'The Globalisation Challenge: Surviving at the Margins', *Third World Quarterly*, Vol.15, No.3, Sept., pp.427–43.

Ohmae, K. (1993), 'The Rise of the Region State', *Foreign Affairs*, Vol.72, No.2, Spring, pp.78–87.

Oman, C. (1994), *Globalisation and Regionalisation: The Challenge for Developing Countries*, Paris: OECD.

Padoa-Schioppa, T. and F. Saccomanni (1994), 'Managing a Market-Led Global Financial System', in P.B. Kennen (ed.), *Managing the World Economy: Fifty Years After Bretton Woods*, Washington, DC: Institute for International Economics.

Perroni, C. and J. Whalley (1996), 'How Severe is Global Retaliation Risk under Increasing Regionalism', *American Economic Review*, Papers and Proceedings, Vol.86, No.2, May.

Pochih Chen (1994), 'Foreign Investment in the Southern China Growth Triangle', in Thant, Tang and Kakazu [*1994*].

Polanyi, K. (1944/1957), *The Great Transformation: The Political and Economic Origins of Our Time*. Boston, MA: Beacon Press.

Robertson, R. (1990), 'Mapping the Global Condition: Globalization as the Central Concept', in M. Featherstone (ed.), *Global Culture: Nationalism, Globalization and Modernity*, London: Sage.

Robson, P. (1993), 'The New Regionalism and Developing Countries', *Journal of Common Market Studies*, Vol.31, No.3, Sept.

Rodrik, D. (1994), *King Kong Meets Godzilla: The World Bank and the East Asian Miracle*, Discussion Paper Series No. 944, London: CEPR, April.

Rosecrance, R. (1996), 'The Rise of the Virtual State', *Foreign Affairs*, Vol.75, No.4, July/Aug., pp.45–61.

Ruggie, J.G. (1993), 'Territoriality and Beyond: Problematizing Modernity in International Relations', *International Organization*, Vol.47, No.1, Winter, pp.139–74.

Ruggie, J.G. (1995), 'At Home Abroad, Abroad at Home: International Liberalisation and Domestic Stability in the New World Order', *Millennium*, Vol.24, No.3, pp. 507–26.

Schor, J.B. (1992), 'Introduction', in T. Banuri and J.B. Schor (eds.), *Financial Openness and National Autonom*, Oxford: Clarendon Press.

Schwab, K., and C. Smadja (1996), 'Start Taking the Backlash Against Globalization Seriously', *The International Herald Tribune*, 1 Feb.

Sideri, S. (1992), 'European Integration and the Third World', in S. Sideri and J. Sengupta (eds.), *The 1992 Single European Market and the Third World,* London: Frank Cass.

Sideri, S. (1993), 'Restructuring the Post-Cold War World Economy', *Development and Change,* Vol.24, No.1, Jan., pp.7–27.

Sideri, S. (1994), *The Economic Relations of China and Asia-Pacific with Europe,* Milan: ISESAO, Università Bocconi.

Sideri, S. (1995), 'Globalizzazione, Devoluzione ed Integrazione Regionale: la Sfida dell'Economia Mondiale e il Caso Italiano', *Economia e banca,* Vol.17, No.3, pp.261–93.

Sigurdson, J. (1996), 'Globalisation and Corporate Strategic Alliances – A European Perspective', paper presented at the Second International Forum on Asian Perspectives jointly organised by the Asian Development Bank and the OECD Development Centre, Paris, June.

Stokes, B. (1996), 'Divergent Paths: US-Japan Relations Towards the Twenty-First Century', *International Affairs,* Vol.72, No.2, April, pp.281–91.

Streeck, W. and P.C. Schmitter (1991), 'From National Corporatism to Transnational Pluralism: Organised Interests in the Single European Market', *Politics and Society,* Vol.19, No.2, June, pp.133–64.

Tang, Min (1995), 'Asian Economic Co-operation: Opportunities and Challenges', in K. Fukasaku (ed.), *Regional Co-operation and Integration in Asia,* Paris: OECD.

Tang, Min and Myo Thant (1994), 'Growth Triangles: Conceptual and Operational Considerations', in Thant, Tang and Kakazu [*1994*].

Thant, Myo, Tang, Min and Hiroshi Kakazu (eds.) (1994), *Growth Triangles in Asia: A New Approach to Regional Economic Cooperation,* Oxford: Oxford University Press.

The Economist, various issues.

Thomsen, S. (1994), 'Regional Integration and Multinational Production', in Cable and Henderson [*1994*].

Thomson, J.E. and S.D. Krasner (1989), 'Global Transactions and the Consolidation of Sovereignty', in E.-O. Czempiel and J.N. Rosenau (eds.), *Global Changes and Theoretical Challenges,* Lexington, MA: Lexington Books.

UNCTAD (1995), *World Investment Report: Transnational Corporations and Competitiveness,* New York: UN.

UNRISD (1995), *States of Disarray: The Social Effects of Globalization,* London: UNRISD.

Whalley, J. (1985), *Trade Liberalization Among Major Trading Areas,* Cambridge, MA: MIT Press.

Wonnacott, P. and M. Lutz (1989), 'Is There a Case for Free Trade Areas?' in J.J. Schott (ed.), *Free Trade Areas and U.S. Trade Policy,* Washington, DC: Institute for International Economics.

World Bank (WB) (1989), *World Development Report 1989,* New York: Oxford University Press.

World Bank (1990), *World Development Report 1990,* New York: Oxford University Press.

World Bank (1991), *World Development Report 1991,* New York: Oxford University Press.

World Trade Organization (WTO) (1995), *International Trade: Trends and Statistics,* Geneva: WTO.

Yoshida, M., Akimune, I., Nohara, M. and K. Sato (1994), 'Regional Integration in East Asia: Special Features and Policy Implications', in Cable and Henderson [*1994*].

2

Development, Security and World Order: A Regionalist Approach

BJÖRN HETTNE

I. INTRODUCTION

This chapter argues that development theory as a state-centric concern lacks relevance, and, in order to regain its earlier importance, it needs to be merged with International Political Economy (IPE). IPE, on the other hand, would be enriched by the more dynamic and normative concerns central to development theory, particularly Alternative Development Theory (ADT). Such a merger may ultimately strengthen an emerging 'critical political economy', dealing with historical power structures and emphasising contradictions in them, as well as change and transformation expressed in normative terms (development).[1]

The advantages of such a merger would be a two-way traffic. It can be described as filling a theoretical vacuum constituted by at least two problematic gaps. The first is between the growing irrelevance of a 'nation-state approach' and the prematurity of a 'world approach'. The second is between immanence, that is a theorising about development as 'inherent' in history, an approach which tends to generate amoral passivity, and intention, a political will to 'develop', which may breed excessive normativism and unrealistic voluntarism, particularly as development has become globalised and out of reach for the main actor, that is the state.[2]

The first gap corresponds to the transition between what can be termed a 'Westphalian' and a 'post-Westphalian' world order. By 'Westphalian' we imply an interstate system with the following characteristics: the sovereign independence of states; each state motivated in its international behaviour by a consistent national interest; the interstate system regulated by a balance of power among the principal powers.[3] There is a specific political rationality underlying this behaviour, a Westphalian rationality which takes the nation-state as the given guarantee for security as well as welfare. What lies 'outside' the secluded and

This chapter draws on findings from a UNU-WIDER research programme on the New Regionalism of which the author is project director. He wishes to acknowledge contributions from all project participants and also comments on a first draft from Ph.D. students at the IPE-seminar and from an anonymous reviewer. An earlier version was first published in *The European Journal of Development Research* (June 1997, Vol. 9, No.1).

protected nation-state territory is perceived as chaos and anarchy. The disorder, turbulence and uncertainties people experience today come with the realisation that this guarantee can no longer be taken for granted, and the confusion is only magnified when the two political rationalities are mixed, a merger typical of periods of historic transition. Furthermore, the Westphalian political rationality is perverted into forms of pathological Westphalianism, such as irrational bloody wars for pieces of land upon which to build mini-states. A 'post-Westphalian' logic rests on the contrary assumption that the nation-state has lost its usefulness, and that solutions to emerging problems must increasingly be found in transnational structures.

One cause of conflict and turbulence is probably the antagonistic coexistence of the two rationalities. I consider a 'new regionalism' to be a possible way out of this dilemma. The regionalist approach can thus be seen as the compromise between Westphalian and post-Westphalian political rationality, and, in terms of development principles, between territory and function.[4] The world order is increasingly regionalised, and in this process of ongoing global fragmentation, one can discern a core-periphery structure, characterised by 'neo-liberalism' in the core regions, 'open regionalism' in what can be called the 'intermediate regions', and by new experiments with 'security regionalism' and 'developmental regionalism' in the peripheral regions. These experiments are seemingly undertaken to arrest the growing North-South polarisation and may even serve the purpose of avoiding the ultimate collapse of world order.

Clearly, these regionalist trends have a novel quality. Some notable differences between 'old' and 'new' regionalism are that current processes of regionalisation come more from 'below' and 'within' than before, and that ecological and security imperatives as well as economic ones push countries and communities towards co-operation within new types of regionalist frameworks. The actors behind regionalist projects are no longer only states, but a large number of different institutions, organisations and movements. Furthermore, today's regionalism is extroverted rather than introverted, which reflects the deeper integration of the current global economy and the interdependence among its parts. The 'new regionalism' is thus one way of coping (offensively or defensively) with global transformation, as an increasing number of states are realising that they lack the capability and the means to manage such a task on the 'national level'. Finally, one of the defining characteristics of the new regionalism is that it takes place in a multipolar global order, whereas the old regionalism was marked by bipolarity.

The current phenomenon of regionalism has so far been discussed mainly with regard to its impact on the pattern of trade, despite the fact that the new wave of regionalism is often defined by its comprehensiveness and multidimensionality, ranging from shared ecological threats to regional security crises, for which the region, in a world where multilateralism is in deep crisis, has to assume more responsibility. This is due to the ridiculously small (and even diminishing) amount of resources devoted to the unprecedented global problems facing 'world society'. We can, for the sake of argument, assume that there is such a thing as 'world society' with at least an embryonic system of governance, as well as a world population facing a large number of more or less shared problems. What strategies can be conceived of to solve these problems? This question relates to the second gap referred to above: how to intervene in a development process that is no longer national, and on what moral/ethical grounds to do so.

Intervention is often reactive rather than proactive. Karl Polanyi argued that societies which have become completely dominated by the market principle, implying that land, capital and labour have been commodified, are a recent historical phenomenon. Two other economic mechanisms played a more important role in earlier Western economic history as well as in many non-Western cultures: reciprocity and redistribution. The former concept refers to the socially embedded forms of exchange in small-scale symmetrical communities; the latter refers to politically determined distribution in stratified societies marked by a centre-periphery structure. Both modes of distribution were critically undermined by the increasing prevalence of market exchange. However, as the market principle came to penetrate all spheres of human activity, thereby eroding traditional structures and creating social turmoil, redistribution had to be reinvented in order to provide displaced people with the necessary social protection. Polanyi called this phase of market expansion, followed by another phase of reaction on the part of society, the 'double movement'. Protectionism was in this historical perspective not inherently bad, as the conventional economic wisdom described it. Modern society is a result of both market expansion ('the first movement') and the self-protection of society against the disruptive and destabilising effects of the market ('the second movement'). This was the 'Great Transformation' [*Polanyi, 1957*].

Society is continuously being transformed in accordance with the double movement, so that, in its second phase, the economy becomes re-embedded – typically through state action – in society, like the genie who is forced back into the lamp. As market exchange can only be amoral, it falls to the political regime to deal with the social disruptions of an unregulated market. In the Polanyian tradition, the political redistributive logic (historically, the logic of the state) stands out as less destructive than the anarchist logic of the market itself. The preferred alternative to liberal capitalism on a world scale after the Second World War was therefore regionalism and planning.[5] Polanyi developed this regionalist scenario, against what at the time he feared was going to be a new hegemonic world order or 'universal capitalism'. This early and little known argument for a regionalised world system and a 'new protectionism' is still relevant and forms the theoretical hypothesis of this paper. Previously, the protection of society was carried out by the state in accordance with the redistributive logic. The current phenomenon of regionalism could be seen as a manifestation of the second movement, the protection of society, on the level of the macroregion, as a political reaction against the global market expansion which gained momentum in the 1980s. Thus we can speak of a 'Second Great Transformation'.

Owing to the decline of the nation-state, the retreat of the state, and the consequent improbability of a conventional redistributional solution on the national level, the potential of civil society is increasingly often mentioned as a means for the powerless and the poor to protect themselves. The response to globalism will thus contain other elements than transnational redistribution, for instance local solidarity structures based on the principle of reciprocity as new forms of self-protection of civil society. In this paper the focus is on political structures of redistribution in the form of a new regionalism.

II. THE INTERNATIONAL POLITICAL ECONOMY OF ALTERNATIVE DEVELOPMENT

For a decade or more, development theory has experienced a fatal crisis emanating from its exclusive concern with the way nation-states should manage 'their' economies and promote 'their' national developments, as if they were independent universes. In the earlier theoretical phase, dominated by the modernisation paradigm, the external context of development was largely neglected. Development towards ultimate international interdependence was seen by the modernisation theorists as an inbuilt tendency in the market logic. According to this thesis, modern economic history embodied the evolution of the market system, in terms of both vertical deepening and horizontal expansion. Dependency theory, in contrast, did emphasise the role of external structure, and was particularly concerned with its assumed perverting effects on dependent countries, which thereby became 'underdeveloped'. The global economy was in this perspective simplistically analysed as a centre-periphery structure with an inherent polarising tendency between states. This approach did not provide any basis for sound development strategies, which is the ultimate rationale for development theory, concerned as it is with the task 'of developing' (intention). The *raison d'être* of the dependency approach, like development theory in general, was not primarily the exploration of the nature of development (immanence), but rather to intervene in the underdevelopment process in order to achieve 'development' for the periphery.[6]

Modern development theory was from the start both normative and instrumental. Furthermore, it was assumed that development was a process that could be steered by the state. Therefore, development has been a contested concept, and development theory an area of contending schools, modernisation theory, dependency theory and alternative theory being the most influential. The Mainstream model and the Counterpoint critique should be seen as dialectically interrelated, and as the latter is being co-opted by the former, the 'actually existing development' provokes new counter-movements, modifying the direction and pattern of development.

Alternative development theory (ADT) deals with development in terms of how it ought to take place. Such speculative activity is not wasted, since visions of the good society influence actual development, to the extent that development is affected by political actions and human will, rather than being immanent, that is a 'natural history'. What this ultimately involves is the inclusion of the excluded into the development process, shaped by the power structure of society. The pattern of development is a matter of power, and any modification of the pattern of development presupposes some sort of political intervention. Alternative models are thus not born in a vacuum, but derived from negations of existing models, from a critical debate on the reality of development, from incorporating perspectives of 'the excluded', from political struggle, and from utopian traditions. Ethnodevelopment is, for instance, seen as one counterbalance to mainstream development as cultural standardisation. Feminist critique of development theory also gradually enriched this growing tradition of critique of mainstream 'macho' development and provided further ideas for alternative sustainable ends and means.

However, long lists of preferred alternatives, to my mind, do not provide a basis for normative theory. In order to be both coherent and realistic, the alternative concepts should emerge from the fundamental contradictions of mainstream development, such as the unevenness of the development process, the homogenising impact of globalisation on cultural diversity, leading to national and sub-national identity crises, and the finiteness of the resource base. Taking the most challenging problems in contemporary development into consideration, a consistent theory of alternative development should contain the following three principles:

- the principle of *territorialism* as a counterpoint to functionalism;
- the principle of *cultural pluralism* as a counterpoint to standardised modernisation;
- the principle of *ecological sustainability* as a counterpoint to 'sustained growth'.

These three principles overlap to some extent, but nevertheless highlight important dimensions of an alternative pattern of development rooted in space, culture and ecology. They constitute a package supporting each other, and derive from the same basic development philosophy, what I call the 'counterpoint' to the mainstream model. In a dialectical perspective the principles can thus be seen as correctives to the mainstream pattern. The principles are, furthermore, meant to benefit the 'non-elites', in accordance with what was said above about the sources of ADT. In the world of 'actually existing development', 60 per cent of the world's population belongs to a periphery of stagnation, marginalisation and poverty [*Friedman, 1992*]. Alternative development is therefore a cry for visibility, participation and justice, which in the current world order means large-scale (albeit not imminent) structural changes [*Hettne, 1995a*].

The stress on intention, how to design a development process, rather than immanence, the natural history of development, is arguably a major difference between development theory and IPE. The emerging Critical Political Economy is one exception, as it does share some traits with radical development/ underdevelopment theory, in particular the emphasis on transformation and purposeful change.[7] The normative and voluntarist thrust is, however, on the whole conspicuously absent in the most common IPE schools, where structure typically is seen as more important than agency. The scope of action for radical reformists is thus seen as fairly limited.

IPE typically deals with the connection between politics and economics in international relations, and the particular social order which links the two. Its underlying assumption is that an economic system cannot function without a political framework of some sort. From this it follows that development is structured by the social order or, if we are thinking of development in a global context, the world order. Alternative development theory, as described above, is more concerned with 'community' and 'civil society', issues which therefore would also add more flesh and blood to a new IPE, with a higher dose of historicism, holism and normativism.

Development theory in its various manifestations can thus make significant contributions to a new IPE, contributions which are related to normative developmental issues which do not arise from pure considerations of power and welfare. By making distinctions between different paths and strategies of development, the relationship between various domestic situations and different foreign policy outcomes is highlighted. By stressing national development strategy as a special case, it is implied that one can think of other actors than the state as social carriers of development strategies, and other 'levels' of the world system, apart from the 'national', at which these strategies can be carried out by a great variety of actors.

To understand reorientations in the process of development, the study of previously excluded actors is of particular importance. Exclusion can be analysed both in social terms, which means class analysis in a transnational context, and in geographical terms, which means regional analysis. This chapter concentrates on the latter. This perspective opens up a vast field of empirical research, case studies, comparative analysis, and middle-range theorising concerning the role of development actors in the context of a changing IPE and world order, currently affected by the contradictory processes of globalisation and regionalisation. These terms will be further elaborated below.

III. WORLD ORDER AND DISORDER

The study of world order can be regarded as IPE's distinct contribution to social science, and consequently to development theory [*Cox, 1996*]. What is meant by world order? It can be defined as the rules and norms regulating international economic transactions. Disorder consequently refers to the turbulent interregnum between world orders. Polanyi [*1957: 181*] used to warn against what he called the 'hazards of planetary interdependence' associated with global market expansion. His sceptical view on interdependence based on the market corresponds to the contemporary neo-mercantilist view of the market system as a fragile arrangement in need of political control. The post-war world economy was in fact a historic compromise between international economic *laissez-faire* and a certain level of domestic control. This essentially Keynesian approach was abandoned during the 1970s and in the subsequent decade neo-liberal principles became increasingly dominant, a trend that culminated when the socialist world began to disintegrate.

Amongst more radical theorists disorder is therefore often associated with economic globalisation, the crucial question then being the return of 'the political' and the form this return will take. One possibility is regionalism, and another is a variety of alternative or 'new' social movements. These two reactions roughly correspond to the two principles of redistribution and reciprocity mentioned above. The rules in force during the post-war era constituted the Bretton Woods world order, characterised by a compromise between international free trade and domestic regulation (manifested in a milder form in the capitalist countries and a more rigid form in the so-called socialist countries).[8] As long as one particular world order is maintained, the rules of the game are known. This situation generally facilitates the growth of economic interdependence. To the extent that such a situation is widely accepted, it is referred to as 'hegemony', a kind of power based on different but mutually supportive dimensions, fulfilling certain functions (the provisioning of international collective goods) in a larger system lacking formal authority structure, and, consequently, more or less voluntarily accepted by other actors.

The New World Order concept as used in the context of the Gulf War can be seen as a counter-strategy of the declining hegemon against the various challenges, for instance, regionalisation, the rise of aggressive regional powers, and various kinds of 'anti-systemic' resistance movements. Unilateralism is different from hegemony in being conflictive rather than consensual. The leaders of the other two regional blocs, Japan and the European Union, are the only possible hegemonic successors. There are, however, no signs that they are prepared to participate in a bid for hegemony in the foreseeable future. A more likely scenario is a territorial type of fragmentation in the form of regionalisation of the world.

Regionalism and globalism will thus continue to be closely linked, both contradicting and supporting each other. It is therefore important to clarify what is implied by these two processes. Whereas 'regional' has an impressive theoretical tradition behind it, 'global' is a more recent concept in social science, often used in a rather loose and ideological sense. Globalism can be defined as programmatic globalisation, the vision of a borderless world, in which territory has lost all importance and functionalism is predominant. As a process, globalisation indicates a qualitative change in the internationalisation process, thus further strengthening the functional and weakening the territorial dimension.[9] The contemporary concern with phenomena such as 'interdependence', 'world order' or the 'global system' is to a large extent a cognitive phenomenon; that is, it is a matter of how the world is conceived.[10] I see globalisation as a qualitatively new phenomenon. If globalisation simply implies an observed tendency towards a global social system, its origins may be traced far back in history, but one could also argue that the process reached a new stage in the post-Second World War era. The subjective sense of geographical distance is dramatically changed, some even speak of 'the end of geography'. The world is also commonly experienced as one in ecological terms. In the present context we are primarily interested in the economic dimension.

Economic interdependence was made possible by the relative political stability of the American world order, which lasted from the end of the Second World War until the late 1960s or early 1970s. After the breakdown of the compromise of embedded liberalism, political control of the process was abandoned as part of the hegemonic role of neo-liberalism. Globalisation in this period is therefore conceived of as contradictory and 'turbulent' [*Rosenau, 1990*]. It represents the ultimate manifestation of a post-Westphalian logic. It coincides with the neo-liberal doctrine, and is typically articulating the interests of strong economic actors, the big players on the global market, but asserting, in a universalised language, the values of efficiency and competitiveness against corruption and mismanagement, described as 'rent-seeking behaviour' in neo-classical economistic terminology. Thus, globalisation represents the project of the self-regulating market in its ultimate transnational and functionalist form. The basic problem with globalisation is the selectivity of the process. Exclusion is inherent in the process, and the benefits are negatively balanced by misery, conflict and violence. The negative effects are incompatible with the survival of civil society, and thus in the longer run a threat to all humanity.

The New Regionalism, by contrast, represents a territorially based urge for control over financial and economic forces. It is similar to mercantilism, albeit relating to a completely different global context. One can think of the 'new regionalism' as a way of overcoming the contradiction between Westphalian and post-Westphalian rationality. In the era of New Regionalism, regionalisation would be a multidimensional process of regional integration including economic, political, social and cultural aspects which go beyond the free trade market idea, that is, the interlinkage of previously more or less secluded national markets into one functional economic unit. Rather, the political ambition of establishing territorial control and regional coherence cum identity (in Polanyi's terms: protecting regional civil society) is the primary goal. In the Polanyian terms presented above, globalisation, or the rise of the global market, can be seen as the 'first movement' in a second Great Transformation, initiated in the mid-1970s. Consequently we can now observe the beginning of a 'second movement' in terms of popular resistance to globalisation (which can be linked to the principle of reciprocity) and the return of the political (which can be linked to the principle of redistribution), currently in the form of 'the new regionalism'. It corresponds to the concept of ADT in development theory in that it is basically normative (although not utopian). This means that the process of regionalisation is analysed from the point of view of its potential to change the mainstream pattern of development.

Regionalisation occurs in a global situation characterised by multipolarity, but an asymmetrical form of multipolarity. A rough distinction can thus be made between the core and peripheral regions, as well as an intermediate category which I shall call intermediate regions. This is the way countries used to be analysed by the neo-Marxist and dependency tradition in development theory. The core regions are thus politically stable and economically dynamic and organise for the sake of being better able to control the world. The peripheral regions are defined as being politically more turbulent and economically more stagnant; consequently they organise in order to arrest a process of marginalisation. At the same time their regional arrangements are fragile and ineffective. Their overall situation therefore makes 'security regionalism' and 'developmental regionalism' more important than the creation of free trade regimes. In contrast to the core, they strive to change the established pattern of development, simply because they have objective reasons to do so.

The core is made up of regions which are economically dynamic and politically capable, whether this capability is expressed in a formal political organisation or not. So far only one of the three core regions, namely Europe, displays aspirations to build such an organisation, albeit against growing nationalist resistance. The other two, North America and East Asia, are economically strong but still lack a regional political order. All three want a say in world affairs from the point of view of their distinct interests. Accordingly, G7 declarations and co-operation within organisations such as APEC, NATO, and the Organisation for Security and Co-operation in Europe notwithstanding, relations between them are quite tense.

Intermediate regions are those being incorporated into the core, that is, former Eastern Europe, those waiting to join the European Union, Latin America and the Caribbean, those in the process of becoming 'North Americanised', and South-east Asia, Coastal China, the European Pacific (Australia, New Zealand) and the

South Pacific, which are drawn into the East Asian economic space dominated by Japanese capital. South Africa belongs here, as may North Africa, depending on the outcome of the ongoing internal violence and the willingness of the EU to engage itself. Remaining in a peripheral position are thus six regions: the former Soviet Union, the major parts of which are now being reintegrated in the form of the Commonwealth of Independent States, the Balkans, where the countries have lost whatever tradition of co-operation they once might have had, the Middle East, with an unsettled and explosive regional structure, South Asia, with a very low level of region-ness because of the 'cold war' (occasionally getting hot) between the major powers, India and Pakistan, the non-coastal areas of China, and Africa, where in a number of countries the political structures called 'states' are falling apart.

IV. WORLD DEVELOPMENT

The world order provides the context of development. The old world order of 'embedded liberalism' thus meant very different conditions for national development strategies from the neo-liberal new world order or, for that matter, a regionalised world order. Weak and strong states naturally have different stakes in different types of world orders. For instance, in a world conceived of as an international welfare system, authoritative resource allocation would have a different impact from that of allocation based on market exchange, which has now become the general norm [*Strange, 1988: 208*]. There is no political authority accountable for resource allocation and welfare in the global system. To the extent that one can talk of a world welfare system, this is therefore truly embryonic. The same can also be said about the possibilities of an international civil society to sustain such a system. From an IPE perspective, the aid phenomenon is a mechanism of stabilisation and diffusion of strategic world order values from core to periphery. The ongoing controversy over political conditionalities, such as human rights fulfilment, armament levels, type of political system, and type of economic policies shows that norms are in fact being imposed on the dependent regions. This implies a process of homogenisation of the global political space, expressing the hegemonic value system.

More important than aid for the development prospects of the individual developing countries is the nature of the global transaction system and the rules for trade, investment and so on which govern it. This was already discovered by the Latin American dependency school, which took for granted the disruptive impact of the capitalist world economy on the Latin American economies, and therefore urged delinking. As will be discussed below, this perspective is still relevant in a modified form when analysing world regions and their relations. The basic IPE positions regarding development are thus not unfamiliar to development theorists. What is new is the overall perspective, which transcends the nation-state. The liberal paradigm in IPE is closely related to the modernisation perspective in development theory where the gains from the international division of labour are assumed to benefit all. Consequently, outward-oriented development strategies are recommended.

This classical pattern of economically strong states pushing for free trade and 'liberalisation' is repeated in the neo-liberal regionalism among the dominant economic blocs. The crucial development issue in the neo-Marxist tradition is integration into vs. delinking from the world market, or, as the question is posed in more recent contributions, the optimal combination of the two strategies in different conjunctures of the international political economy. This is reflected also in open versus introverted regionalism. The IPE approach to development, derived from so-called realist thinking, is that a national development strategy forms an integral part of the nation-state project. The commitment to 'development' is subsumed under the 'national interest' of state survival, i.e. the modernisation imperative. The outstanding example of this 'realist' or 'mercantilist' approach to development is, of course, Friedrich List. Neo-mercantilism can be seen as transcending the nation-state logic in arguing for a world system consisting of self-sufficient blocs [*Hettne, 1993a; 1993b*]. The external environment of development undergoes continuous changes. What is more, the state operates in an equally shifting domestic context, trying to respond to political challenges from 'the excluded' in a way which optimises its legitimacy and autonomy. The state as such is not a monolithic structure but complex and continuously changing and it will also have to adapt to the international political economy. The current trend is rather the 'internationalisation of the state' [*Cox, 1996*], which means that the state does not so much protect 'its' own population as it is instrumental in its adjustment to global market forces. The main reason for this important transformation of the state is the globalisation process which transfers power from the states to global actors, exploiting the free play of market forces. Against this globalist trend, regionalisation means the return of 'the political', as stressed above. However, different regionalisms carry different political content.

V. NEO-LIBERAL REGIONALISM IN THE CORE

The concept of 'neo-liberal regionalism' is a contradiction in terms, since the universalist liberal doctrine is the antithesis of organised regionalism, whether leftist or rightist. Nevertheless, regional groupings may be instrumental for pursuing different types of goals, in this case non-discrimination in trade and, as is normal for proponents of free trade, access to all relevant markets and the elimination of all kinds of nationalist obstacles. This is not necessarily done in the pursuit of some kind of universal interest, but in the interest of the respective economic bloc, often headed by a rather illiberal government-corporate alliance trying to penetrate the other blocs which are blamed for being protectionist. Free trade has always been an excellent argument for top dogs in asymmetrical relationships, but love of it is seldom blind, not even in the Core. The top dog in question is, of course, the United States which, mainly for security reasons, played an important role in the development of the West European and Asia Pacific regions by 'raising' the two economic giants, West Germany and Japan, often described as 'free riders' under the shield of Pax Americana. With declining US hegemony, these regional great powers are emerging as regional bloc leaders and now challenge even US supremacy on a number of issues, thus establishing what could be described as a trilateral global power structure.

Significantly, the US is active in all regional core organisations. There is perfect compatibility between the ideology of globalism and the strategy of regionalism as far as the core is concerned. Although the blocs in the core accuse each other of being too closed and introverted, none of the three blocs assumes an explicitly protectionist posture. On the contrary, they compete in the praise (if not in the practice) of free trade. Europe has established a single market, but is often described as a 'fortress' by other external actors. For the US, NAFTA was perceived as a step towards free trade – as a natural part of the GATT process and the Uruguay Round.

In Asia Pacific the situation is more complex. According to a World Bank report (Sustaining Rapid Development), East Asia should strengthen regional integration through trade liberalisation and promotion of foreign direct investment within the framework of the multilateral trading system. 'A trading block would more likely foster an inward orientation, impairing the world wide search for market opportunities that has served East Asia so well' (*Bangkok Post*, 15 April 1993, p.25). The preferred regional alternative is thus the 15-member-strong forum for Asia Pacific Economic Co-operation (APEC) which was set up in 1989. It has regional and inter-regional trade expansion as its main goal and in no way implies regionalism of an introverted sort. APEC can thus be compared to 'the Atlantic project' in Europe. It is a transregional network providing a bridge for the US in the area, and therefore supported by US-oriented regimes and opposed by spokesmen for a genuinely Asian regionalism (EAEC) (see below). From the US point of view, APEC – like NAFTA in the Americas – is a continuation of its strategy of bilateralism (that is, pursuing the US national interest).

VI. OPEN REGIONALISM IN THE INTERMEDIATE REGIONS

In the intermediate regions the prevalent economic ideology puts emphasis on 'open regionalism'. In Europe the intermediate region, Central Europe, is more faithful to neo-liberal doctrines than most core countries. The same position is now taken by Australia in the Pacific area. Australia is, of course, desperately anxious not to be left out of the ongoing process of bloc formation. The word 'open regionalism' is often used for regional trade arrangements that do not hurt third parties and thus are 'free trade compatible'. The idea of the slightest kind of more introvert regionalism is on the whole very controversial in the South-East Asian region, being dependent on unhindered world trade. In 1990 Malaysian prime minister Mahathir (in his frustration at the long-drawn-out GATT negotiations) broke this policy line and urged Japan to act as the leader of an emerging East Asian Economic Grouping (EAEG), which would create an East Asian and South-East Asian superbloc with a Sino-Japanese core. EAEG (it has since been modestly renamed East Asia Economic Caucus – EAEC) would be a sort of response to European and North American 'fortresses'.

The EAEC proposal is slowly gaining support among other ASEAN countries, whereas the East Asian countries, particularly Japan and South Korea, have adopted a more sceptical attitude. So, of course, have the US and the World Bank. Thus there are two understandings of regionalism: (i) a way of managing multilateralism, and (ii) a challenge to multilateralism. The first conception predominates in Asia-Pacific. In Latin America the emphasis on the whole is on '*regionalismo abierto*'. This largely neo-liberal interpretation of regionalism appears to be a paradox. According to a 1994 ECLAC document:

> What differentiates open regionalism from trade liberalization and non-discriminatory export promotion is that it includes a preferential element which is reflected in integration agreements and reinforced by the geographical closeness and cultural affinity of the countries in the region. A complementary objective is to make integration a building bloc of a more open transparent international economy [*ECLAC, 1994: 12*].

The concept 'open regionalism' may sound like a contradiction in terms, as having your cake and eating it. To some extent open regionalism is a way of reviving interest in an issue which has been dead for a decade in Latin America, and which in a neo-liberal political context smells of forbidden protectionism and state interventionism. It is also, of course, a recognition of the fact that the global economy in the 1990s is different from that in the 1960s. Finally, it is a cautious strategy, given the high level of uncertainty about the future development of the world economy.

> If a less optimistic international scenario should develop, open regionalism is still justifiable as the least objectionable alternative for dealing with an external environment which is unfavourable to the countries of the region, since it at least preserves the expanded market of the member countries of integration agreements [*ECLAC, 1994: 14*].

In a more negative global scenario, regionalism thus remains a second-best alternative, better than a return to economic nationalism. It is also obvious that MERCOSUR is driven more by political ambitions than by merely trade strategies. Economic nationalism is, however, not on the agenda in Latin America. On the contrary, there are strong convergences both within Latin America and between Latin America and North America.[11]

VII. SECURITY AND DEVELOPMENT REGIONALISMS IN THE PERIPHERY

As an alternative to the scenario of unrestrained globalisation, interventionist regionalism is more attractive to the periphery than to the core. Developmental regionalism and security regionalism constitute a package which, with varying contents, is relevant to all emerging regions, particularly the marginalised areas. Even if 'delinking' is no longer on the agenda, the general orientation may be more or less defensive and introverted.

Security Regionalism

In the field of conflict management and conflict resolution, the idea that conflicts within a certain region are best dealt with directly by the region concerned is not new. In the earlier debate, however, the 'region' was simply thought of as an intermediate level between the global level and the 'floor' of nation-states. The region was not an actor itself, only a 'level' or 'space' of action. With increasing 'regionness' the region becomes an actor in its own right, it is being transformed from object to subject. The crucial criterion for assessing the coherence of a region is therefore its capacity for autonomous conflict management and conflict resolution.

This regional coherence can be described in terms of levels of 'regionness'. We can, with particular reference to regional conflict and conflict management, distinguish five levels. The first level is region as a *geographical* unit, delimited by natural geographical barriers and with limited and sporadic contacts between human groups. Violence is therefore limited and sporadic. The second level is region as a *social system,* which implies more dense translocal relations, constituting some kind of regional complex, what Buzan [*1991*] calls a regional security complex, in which the constituent units (normally states) are dependent, as far as their own security is concerned, on each other. The third level is region as *organised co-operation*, where region is defined by membership of the regional organisation in question. To the extent that the 'formal' region, which may be a *military alliance*, corresponds to the 'real' region (that is, the regional security complex), regional security is enhanced; the contrary would be the case where the region is divided between two military alliances, a common situation in the cold war. The fourth level is region as *regional civil society*, which will take shape when the organisational framework promotes social communication and convergence of values throughout the region, which is thereby transformed into a *security community*. The fifth level is region as *acting subject* with a distinct identity and interest, actor capability, legitimacy, and structure of decision-making in such crucial areas as conflict resolution (between and within former states) and welfare (in terms of social security and regional balance), as well as joint management of ecological problems. A regional organisation capable of handling this range of challenges would be like a state, a region state.

Implied in this sequence of stages (no determinism involved) is the idea that any particular region will increase the level of security and peace by raising the level of regional co-operation and move from security complex to security community (and even more integrated political structures). Paradoxically perhaps, the new type of conflicts, which are internal with respect to a particular state formation (in contrast to the interstate conflicts typical of the Westphalian world order), tend to reinforce regional security co-operation. The reason for this particular outcome is simple. The new conflicts and the 'failed states' create security crises which (in any regional security complex) are impossible to neglect for the states constituting the complex.

To understand how and why a (national) society breaks down, one must understand what makes it peaceful in the first place, that is, how it normally functions. This would be a situation where civil society mediates between the state and the actual and potential 'primary groups'. Civil society (here used as a normative concept) is by definition open, multicultural, and facilitating communication between all groups constituting the national system. The unevenness and selectivity of the globalisation process leads to social (or ethnic) exclusion and increasing social (or ethnic) tensions. The process of erosion can be described as a transfer of loyalties from civil society to the primary group, a concept summing up both 'primordial' and 'socially constructed' groups.[12] This creates a situation in which each single group becomes responsible for its own security [*Posen, 1993*]. This breakdown of civil society leads to a regional security crisis which, if it serious enough, will lead to some kind of intervention from outside.

There is, of course, a need for legitimation in all cases of external intervention because of the sanctity of territorial sovereignty inherent in the Westphalian tradition. There are in the intervention discourse two major varieties of legitimation: (i) a conflict constitutes a threat to international peace, and (ii) the behaviour of the parties to a conflict massively violates human rights. The first has a clear foundation in the UN Charter. The implications of elevating the second variety of legitimation to a general principle are dramatic. There is no international order that will react to all crises in a consistent and uniform way. Therefore *ad hoc*-ism has been the rule, and will probably continue to be. Every case has its own motivations and underlying interests. External intervention can take two major forms, civil and military, with several sub-categories. Civil intervention may be preventive. It may try to influence the parties in the early stages of the conflict, by positive (assistance, encouragement) or negative (sanctions) methods. It may provide humanitarian assistance at a later and violent stage of a conflict, or it may be devoted to reconstruction and peace-building in a post-conflict situation.

There are five different modes of military intervention: unilateral, bilateral, plurilateral, regional and multilateral. The distinctions are not very clear-cut, and in real world situations several actors at different levels are involved, the number increasing with the complexity of the conflict itself. The point to be stressed here is the increasing importance of regional interventions, and the likelihood that a combination of regional and multilateral interventions may be the preferred form in the immediate future, while in the long run the regional mode will be predominant. This implies some form of institutionalisation, which, in turn, means a relative strengthening of regional *vis-à-vis* national structures.

Some illustrations of the various forms of intervention can be given. The US has carried out a large number of unilateral interventions in Latin America, most of them part of the cold war game. Other interventions were made by 'concerned neighbours' (Tanzania in Uganda, Vietnam in Cambodia, India in Bangladesh) as responses to regional security crises. (These interventions may have been multilateral or regional today.) Occasionally such interventions are based on a bilateral agreement (such as India's occupation of northern Sri Lanka). With a stronger SAARC (South Asian Association for Regional Co-operation), this particular operation might have been a regional one (which would have made more sense). Plurilateral interventions are made by military alliances (NATO in Bosnia, or the Organization of Islamic Conference in the case of Mindanao in the Philippines) or other *ad hoc* groupings (such as the 'contact group' also in Bosnia, which is alarmingly similar to the nineteenth century European Concert). They differ from regional interventions by their lack of territorial dimension.

Regional interventions are thus organised by territorially based organisations such as the EU (not yet formed when the crisis in Yugoslavia started). The best example is, somewhat unexpectedly, the ECOWAS (ECOMOG) intervention in Liberia, not particularly successful but nevertheless a good illustration of the dynamics of regional intervention in local conflicts. (In making an assessment it should be kept in mind that some multilateral interventions have been catastrophic.) Multilateral intervention (Cambodia being the most quoted case, although Japan and ASEAN played an important role) is still the norm and, according to many, the only legal possibility. It has therefore been used for authorisation in the case of other types of interventions. To my mind, it will be less frequent and more selective in the future. Regional interventions are necessary and inescapable in deep regional security crises, and there is reason to believe that such interventions lead to more lasting solutions, since otherwise neighbouring countries have to live with the problem and face the eruption of new violent conflicts. The record of regional intervention is recent and the empirical basis for making an assessment is fairly weak. Incidents of national disintegration can both make and break regional organisations, but the more important the regional factor in conflict resolution, the higher the degree of 'regionness' of the region in question.

Developmental Regionalism

The old regionalism was often imposed for geopolitical reasons, and there were no incentives for economic co-operation, particularly if the 'natural' economic region was divided in accordance with the cold war pattern. Attempts at regional co-operation were often inherited from colonial times and did not go far beyond regional trade arrangements. Owing to lack of complementarities, such arrangements were never sufficient to realise the potentials of development regionalism. As the global pattern of uneven development was reproduced within the region, the result was political tension.

The 'new' regionalism, in contrast, is more political. Its approach to free trade is cautious, far from autarkic but more selective in its external relations, and careful to address the interests of the region as a whole, as in the case of management of natural resources or infrastructural development. Benefits with different relevance in different contexts and situations can be found in a number of areas:

(1) In a highly interdependent world the question of size has undoubtedly lost some of its former importance, but regional co-operation is nevertheless imperative in the case of micro states which have either to co-operate to solve common problems or to become client states of the 'core countries' (the argument of sufficient size). In the Caribbean the regional organisation CARICOM (with 13 members) contains less than six million people. There are not more than 32 million people in greater Caribbean. The next step should therefore be to form a Caribbean Basin region which also includes Central America. The small Central American states also have strong incentives for regional co-operation. The change of regime in Nicaragua increased the regional political homogeneity and consequently the scope for regional initiatives. So did the settlement of the border conflict between Honduras and El Salvador and more recently the internal peace agreement in Guatemala. Thus regional conflict resolution is often the first step towards regional co-operation for development. The crucial issue is whether the countries can develop a common approach to the emerging US–Canada–Mexico bloc, or whether they will join NAFTA as individual client states, and thereby become 'North Americanised'.

(2) Self-reliance is an old development goal which rarely proved viable at the

national level. Yet it may be a feasible development strategy at the regional level if defined not as autarky but as co-ordination of production, improvement of infrastructure, and the use of complementarities in order to strengthen the position of the region in the world economy (the viable economy argument). In sub-Saharan Africa there has been little regional integration, simply because there is little to integrate in the first place. The urgent need for a broader and more dynamic concept of development, beyond 'stabilisation', is only possible within a framework of regional co-operation. The 'dynamic approach' to regional integration must be further developed. One important regional initiative is SADC (Southern Africa Development Community), originally created to reduce dependence on South Africa. Recent SADC documents indicate an awareness of the need for political intervention to prevent deepening of regional economic disparities.

(3) Economic policies may be more stable and consistent if they are underpinned by regional arrangements which cannot be broken by a participant country without some kind of sanction from the others (the credibility argument). For external potential investors the country is therefore considered more stable and safe. Political stability is, of course, a wider and more complex concept, as shown in the 1994 Mexican crisis caused by the resurgence of guerrilla activities (first in Chiapas, then in Oaxaca and Guerrero). Being part of NAFTA did not prevent the country from being thrown into a major crisis arising from external speculation. On the other hand, being part of NAFTA did facilitate the salvage programme that followed. For the same reason the Chiapas conflict did not grow worse, and the democratic process has been kept on track. A more recent example (April 1996) of the stabilising role of regionalism was the firm reaction of MERCOSUR countries to an attempted coup in Paraguay. Thus the credibility argument concerns political stability as well as economic policy.

(4) Collective bargaining at the level of the region could improve the economic position of marginalised countries in the world system, or protect the structural position and market access of new successful exporters (the argument of effective articulation). The countries in ASEAN are all outward-oriented, and in various phases of a NIC-type development path. Thus 'open regionalism' is a way to articulate interests from within the region *vis-à-vis* the globalisation process.

(5) Regionalism can reinforce societal viability by including social security issues and an element of redistribution and protection (by regional compensation and development funds or specialised banks) in the regionalist project (the social stability argument). This argument becomes particularly relevant when the degree of regionness is so advanced as to include an element of mutual solidarity among both the constituent states and their sub-national regions. So far, it is at its most embryonic in the peripheral regions.

(6) Few serious environmental problems can be solved within the framework of the nation-state. Some problems are bilateral, some are global, quite a few are regional. Regional problems often relate to water: coastal waters, rivers, and ground water. Of particular importance are the South and South-East Asian river systems. In the field of resource management there are strong interdependences which up to now have been a source of conflict rather than co-operation. They may, however, also be turned into regionalist imperatives (the resource management argument).

(7) Regional conflict resolution, if successful and durable, eliminates distorted investment patterns as the 'security fund'(military expenditures) can be tapped for more productive use (the peace dividend argument). This argument carries special force in the Middle East. Stable peace would open up a completely new world, and for this reason the breakthrough in the Israel–Palestine peace process was particularly important. A regional development process based on the triangle Israel–Jordan–Palestine is essential for the consolidation of the peace process, and again for further development in the whole region.

Here the circle is closed: regional co-operation for development reduces the level of conflict and the peace dividend facilitates further development co-operation. This positive circle must not be turned into a vicious circle, where conflicts and underdevelopment feed on each other. How do these principles fit with an alternative development pattern? On the whole, developmental regionalism forms part of mainstream development thinking, just like dependency theory was a mainstream approach, albeit expressing a Southern viewpoint. However, contradiction is not the same as incompatibility. Along the three axes: territorialism – functionalism; cultural pluralism – standardised modernisation; and ecological sustainability – sustained economic growth, regionalism is to my mind situated closer to the central position than globalism.

VIII. CONCLUSION

I have argued the methodological point that a merger between International Political Economy and development theory, particularly Alternative Development Theory, would reduce weaknesses particular to these social science traditions; in the first, a static amoral concern with power and wealth; in the second, an exaggerated concern with the increasingly irrelevant 'national' space, and failure to take cognisance of the implications of the globalisation of development. A development perspective on IPE would lead to a stronger focus on change and transformation, and an IPE perspective on development would emphasise the global context of development, and the way development is structured by any particular world order.

In more theoretical terms, the chapter has argued (with inspiration from dependency theory) that the emerging world order is regionalised, and constituted by Core, Intermediate regions and Periphery. The new regional order further generates, but also feeds on, the disorder created at the sub-national level in the wake of globalisation. Thus integration and disintegration are simultaneous processes, and order and disorder paradoxically related. This is particularly evident in the peripheral regions. The ambivalent and paradoxical 'open regionalism' of intermediate regions is a contradiction in terms, revealing the completely different structure of interests between Core and Periphery. In this perspective, development should be understood as a reduction of the structural gap between Core and Periphery. The means whereby this could be achieved are Security Regionalism and Developmental Regionalism, which (in contrast with the globalist hegemony established by the Core) necessitate a substantial degree of interventionism. The New Regionalism implies the possibility of a regional formation with a distinct identity and a capacity as an actor. It does not preclude a function for the old nation-state which, for certain limited purposes, could be a useful level of decision-making. However, in many instances, the nation-state often prevents rational solutions, whereas the regional level opens up new ways of solving conflicts that have become institutionalised in the historical state formations.

This chapter was inspired by Karl Polanyi who was a pioneer in the more voluntaristic and development-oriented tradition of IPE. His basic theory about a 'double movement' assumed a return of the 'political', after a phase of market expansion, which according to him is bound to lead to disorder and turbulence. In what I have termed 'the Second Great Transformation', the first phase of market expansion corresponds to globalisation. Regionalism is the major reactive force in the second phase of the contemporary 'double movement'. Regions can only be defined *post factum*, which implies different regionalisms, supported or challenged by different ideological arguments and reflecting various positions in the world economy.

Still within Polanyi's terms, new reciprocal structures in the form of localism, local structures of self-help and solidarity could emerge as a reaction to globalisation and as a supplement to the emerging (if this analysis proves correct) redistributive structures of a new regionalism. It will certainly be a complex system of interacting levels with a stronger role for supranational and sub-national levels, and a diminished role for the nation-state level (post-Westphalianism). This may, again in Polanyi's terms, prevent fascism (linked to a Westphalian mentality) and create 'freedom in a complex society' as the positive alternative to war among civilisations, guerrilla wars without (political) purpose, urban jungles of criminal mafias, tribal wars among motorbike gangs, and other post modern perversions so vividly and usually correctly described in neo-conservative writings, but without much indication of what should be done about it.

Regionalism is one approach to various global problems, but its content will be conditioned by the very nature of these problems. From the point of view of the Core, the function of regionalism is completely different from that of the Periphery. The peripheral regions are peripheral because they are dependent, economically stagnant, politically turbulent and war-prone, and the only way for them to become less peripheral in structural terms would be to become more regionalised, that is, to increase their level of 'regionness'. The alternative is further disintegration and the complete disappearance of the most fragile states, whose territories will be absorbed by stronger neighbours. Developmental regionalism is the appropriate response to the threatening peripheralisation of the poor regions of the world. National strategies will in the end defeat their own purpose, since no country in any particular region can be made immune to a general economic and political regional disease. Without regional co-operation, the only 'power' of these regions is 'chaos power', that is, the capacity to create problems for the Core, thereby providing some kind of engagement. For the poor areas, there are thus strong imperatives in favour of regionalism and alternative development strategies. Such strategies, by their comprehensiveness, provide solutions to a number of problems.

As should be evident from this analysis, development issues cannot be studied apart from issues of security. When a regional security complex moves from largely negative to largely positive interdependences (what is sometimes called a security community), such a process to a large extent coincides with what is usually called development. Conflict resolution is a necessary precondition for development, and development, in turn, reduces the risk of conflicts. Developmental regionalism contains the traditional arguments for regional co-operation, such as territorial size and economies of scale but, more significantly, adds some new concerns and uncertainties in the current transformation of the world order and world economy. Thus security regionalism and developmental regionalism are mutually supportive and together form the only possible strategy to arrest the process of further marginalisation or subordination for the peripheral regions. Alternative development (defined as development for the excluded and marginalised) is not easily reconciled with the strategy of developmental regionalism, since this strategy implies a considerable degree of transnational co-ordination and the development of suprastate institutions. It could, nevertheless, be argued that the counterpoint initiatives are more easily carried out under the protective shield of developmental regionalism, than if they are exposed to the chilly winds of globalisation.

NOTES

1. This problem is raised in Hettne [*1995a*] and was the theme of the special issue of *The European Journal of Development Research*, Vol.7, No.2, Dec. 1995. The concept of 'critical political economy' comes from Robert Cox and is discussed in Hettne [*1995b*]. The discussion on regionalism elaborates earlier analyses in Hettne [*1993a; 1993b*] and Hettne and Inotai [*1994*].
2. The distinction is central to the analysis of development theory in Cowen and Shenton [*1996*].
3. The distinction is made by Robert Cox and summarised in Hettne [*1995b: 12*].
4. This important distinction is elaborated in Friedman and Weaver [*1979*].
5. 'The new permanent pattern of world affairs is one of regional systems coexisting side by side' [*Polanyi, 1945: 87*].
6. For an assessment of this tradition, see Blomström and Hettne [*1984*] and Kay [*1989*].
7. The intellectual father of this still rather tentative 'school' is Robert Cox, whose most important articles are found in Cox [*1996*].
8. Ruggie [*1982*] refers to this compromise as 'embedded liberalism'.
9. Whether this qualitative deepening in the process of internationalisation is significant enough to deserve a new name, that is, globalisation, is debatable [*Hirst and Thompson, 1996*].
10. Is globalisation, for instance, to be seen as a single process or is it made up of more or less interlinked sub-processes or trends? In the UNRISD study, *States of Disarray: The Social Effects of Globalization*, a distinction is made between six 'key trends': spread of liberal democracy, dominance of market forces, integration of the global economy, transformation of production systems and labour markets, spread of technological change, and the media revolution and consumerism.
11. The OAS now appears as less an instrument of US imperialism and more a genuine expression of the interests of most countries in the Americas. This trend towards hemispheric regionalism started in earnest with the 1994 summit of the Americas in Miami.
12. 'Primordial', as used here, does not define particular components of identity, but simply refers to those components which are more persistent and durable.

REFERENCES

Blomström, Magnus and Björn Hettne (1984), *Development Theory in Transition: The Dependence Debate and Beyond,* London: Zed Books.
Buzan, Barry (1991), *People, States and Fear,* Boulder, CO: Lynn Rienner.
Cox, Robert, with Timothy J. Sinclair (1996), *Approaches to World Order,* Cambridge: Cambridge University Press.
Cowen, M.P. and R.W. Shenton (1996), *Doctrines of Development,* London and New York: Routledge.
ECLAC (1994), *Open Regionalism in Latin America and the Caribbean: Economic Integration as a Contribution to Changing Production Patterns with Social Equity,* Santiago: UN ECLAC
Friedman, John and C. Weaver (1979), *Territory and Function: The Evolution of Regional Planning,* London: Edward Arnold.
Friedman, John (1992), *Empowerment: The Politics of Alternative Development,* Cambridge: Blackwell.
Hettne, Björn (1993a), 'The Concept of Neomercantilism', in Lars Magnusson (ed.), *Mercantilist Economics,* Amsterdam: Kluwer.
Hettne, Björn (1993b), 'Neomercantilism: The Pursuit of Regionness', *Cooperation and Conflict,* Vol.28, No.3, pp.211–32.

Hettne, Björn (1995a), *Development Theory and the Three Worlds: Towards an International Political Economy of Development*, London: Longman.

Hettne, Björn (ed.) (1995b), *International Political Economy: Understanding Disorder*, London: Zed Books.

Hettne, Björn and Andras Inotai (1994), *The New Regionalism, Implications for Global Development and International Security*, Helsingfors: WIDER.

Hirst, P. and G. Thompson (1996), *Globalization in Question*, Cambridge: Polity Press.

Kay, Cristóbal (1989), *Latin American Theories of Development and Underdevelopment*, London: Routledge.

Polanyi, Karl (1945), 'Universal Capitalism or Regional Planning', *The London Quarterly of World Affairs*, January.

Polanyi, Karl (1957), *The Great Transformation*, Boston, MA: Beacon Press.

Posen, Barry R. (1993), 'The Security Dilemma and Ethnic Conflict', in Michael E. Brown (ed.), *Ethnic Conflict and International Security*, Princeton, NJ: Princeton University Press.

Rosenau, James N. (1990), *Turbulence in World Politics: A Theory of Change and Continuity*, Princeton, NJ: Princeton University Press.

Ruggie, John Gerard (1982), 'International Regimes, Transactions and Change: Embedded Liberalism in the Postwar Economic Order', *International Organization*, Vol.36, No.2.

Strange, Susan (1988), *State and Markets: An Introduction to International Political Economy*, London: Pinter.

World Bank (1993), 'Sustaining Rapid Development in East Asia and the Pacific (Development in Practice)', Washington, DC: World Bank, March.

3

Intensity Measures for Regional Groups

SHEILA PAGE

I. INTRODUCTION

Traditional economic analysis of regional integration concentrates on trade linkages among the members, and on the trade effects on non-members. This is also the approach now embedded in international trade law. It dates at least from the middle of the nineteenth century, with the acceptance of customs unions as the only permitted exception to the Most Favoured Nation principle. Article XXIV of the GATT followed this precedent, and it was strengthened in the Understanding on it in the WTO. But this approach seems inadequate. It ignores the other types of economic linkage which are increasingly recognised as both explanations and objectives of formal economic regions. It ignores the political and legal approaches to explaining regions. Here we look at other possible forms of integration and motives for it.

There are three reasons for wanting to find a more successful way of measuring regions. The first is to understand why regions form, and why some survive, and become stronger, while others fade, and if possible to predict which of the many new regions of recent years will be effective. A second is to suggest that a broader approach is needed in international regulation. If regions are not entirely (perhaps not even primarily) about trade, regulating them in accordance with their trade policies and effects is inadequate; it may miss other types of effect which they can have on other countries or the international system. A third reason is to encourage analysis of 'diversion' type effects on outsiders of the non-trade linkages. These were extensively studied in analyses of the effects of Europe's move to a single European Market in 1992 on the rest of the world, but have not been well described for other regions.

The definition of 'success' for a region is that it survives, but also that it develops or evolves: it changes its scope; it becomes more closely regulated; it may increase the number of members. The first criterion seems uncontroversial, although judgement can of course only ever be provisional (even the extreme form of the region, the country, can break up). The second may seem less obvious, but the intention is to exclude groups formed for and limited to a single

This research was supported by the Economic and Social Research Council Global Economic Institutions Programme, grant L/20/25/1015.

purpose (in economics, a common infrastructure or environmental objective would be an example; outside economics, it could be anything from a research group to a military alliance). It is precisely those groups which attempt to be more complex than this which are of interest. It is possible to take two 'groups', the WTO itself and the EU, which have survived long enough to have some claim to success and which meet the second condition, against which to measure the others. The regions examined here were chosen as potential successes. They are not a complete list; the main criterion was information. Those chosen are NAFTA, APEC, ASEAN, Australia/New Zealand, SAARC, MERCOSUR, the Andean Group, Central America, CARICOM, SADC, SACU and COMESA (see Appendix).

Two possible approaches to trade analysis of regions are common. The analysis of trade creation and trade diversion, because of the lowering of barriers to imports from within the region and therefore the relative raising of barriers to those outside, measures a single change. It becomes increasingly difficult to apply as production patterns, general trade policies, policies of third countries, etc., all change. As it is argued here that duration and adapting are the tests of a 'successful' region, this measure would be difficult to use. The more flexible measure for a medium- to long-term view is 'intensity'. The conventional ways of measuring the degree of trade integration of regional group members are either by explicitly modelling the effect of distance (economic, geographical, or other) in a trade function, after including all the other conventional variables, or by starting from total trade and studying how the division among partners differs from the world average. This can be used either a priori to measure the degree of integration of a potential group or on a before-and-after basis to attempt to find changes which are the effect of a group which has formed. The intensity measure is subject to all the usual caveats about residual measures. For non-trade integration, as for trade integration, the question that will be asked is: is the integration greater than that of the region with the rest of the world, or, for legal points, than is required by the WTO or other multilateral organisations. A pre-region finding of high intensity might indicate potential for more formal integration; an increase which can be correlated to regional policy might indicate an effect of formal integration.

This chapter will look first at traditional trade intensity measures, but adding also some disaggregation of trade (Table 3.1). It will then look at other types of link (Table 3.2). The obvious next extension is to investment flows. Then there are the broad range of 'trade-related' or new area subjects which are now, or are proposed to be, under the umbrella of the WTO, and some of which may become the next generation of new areas. The actual legal structures of the groups, with respect to their members, to private decision-makers within the countries, and to other groups or countries, is important not only for their obligations in the international system but for the indication this gives of how integrated the group

TABLE 3.1
MEASURES OF TRADE AND INVESTMENT INTEGRATION (%)

Trade	EU	NAFTA	APEC	ASEAN[a]	ANZCERTA	SAARC	MERCOSUR[b]	Andean	CACM	CARICOM	SADC[c]	COMESA	SACU[d]
Intra-region trade/total trade by region													
exports 1990	60.5	41.7	69.3	19.6 (4.6)	7	3.2	8.9 (11.6)	4.1	15.4	8.5	2.6	6	
exports 1994	56.5	48.4	74.4	22.3 (5.0)	8.8	3.7	18.3 (20.4)	8.5	20.2	15	8	6.8	19.2
imports 1990	57.8	33.4	70.6	15.9 (4.3)	7.4	1.9	14.5 (17.7)	5.7	9.6	5.7	4.9	5.3	
imports 1994	54.5	37.4	71.1	19.3 (7.0)	7.9	3.3	16.8 (19.4)	9.3	12.6	6.6	8.3	5.5	21.8
Share of region in world trade													
imports 1994	33.8	21.1	44.4	6.31 (3.92)	1.52	1.09	1.47 (1.78)	0.75	0.23	0.1	0.7	0.41	0.75
exports 1994	34.6	16.8	42.65	6.00 (3.72)	1.41	0.9	1.46 (1.76)	0.78	0.14	0.09	0.77	0.32	0.65
Intensity													
exports 1990	1.46	2.13	1.78	4.32 (1.61)	4.68	2.86	10.44 (10.58)	7.44	81.5	36.3	3.5	12	25.4
exports 1994	1.67	2.3	2.05	3.54 (1.28)	5.79	3.5	12.43 (11.49)	11.31	88.9	150.3	11.5	16.4	
imports 1990	1.44	2.09	1.59	3.92 (1.71)	5.13	2.37	10.72 (10.87)	6.33	75.5	31	5.1	13.4	
imports 1994	1.58	2.22	1.67	3.21 (1.88)	5.59	3.65	11.5 (10.99)	11.92	92.7	72.1	10.7	17.3	33.3

Direct foreign investment (accumulated stocks)

Intra-region as share of total investment

by ASEAN 1980	60
by ASEAN 1993	36
in ASEAN 1980	3
in ASEAN 1993	3

Share in world investment

investment in ASEAN 1993	7
investment by ASEAN 1993	1

Source: IMF, *Direction of Trade, Financial Statistics*; UN, *World Investment Report, 1995*.

Notes: (a) Figures in brackets exclude Singapore; (b) Figures in brackets include Bolivia and Chile; (c) SADC excludes intra-SACU trade; (d) SACU intra-trade
data are derived from estimates by the Swaziland government and probably include some transhipments. They are for 1993.

TABLE 3.2
INTEGRATION BEYOND TRADE AND INVESTMENT

	EU	NAFTA	APEC	ASEAN	ANZCERTA	SAARC	MERCOSUR	Andean	CACM	CARICOM	SADC	COMESA	SACU
Free trade area	yes	planned	proposed	pref.	yes	pref.	with exclus.	with exclus.	pref	pref	proposed	bilat.pref.	yes
Customs union	yes						planned						yes
Clearing system	yes					yes			yes			yes	yes
Labour mobility	yes			some			proposed					proposed	some
Now in WTO													
Technical standards	more	proposed	proposed	yes			limited	limited	limited	limited	proposed	proposed	yes
Company laws	more						yes			some		proposed	
Intellectual property	more	yes						yes			proposed		
Proposed for WTO													
Environment	more	more					proposed						
Labour standards	more	more					proposed						
Public procurement	more												
Direct public access	more				more		more						
Economic policy													
Sectoral policy	yes						limited	(past)		yes	yes	yes	yes
Exchange rates	yes												yes
Monetary policy	proposed											limited	
Macro coordination	proposed												taxes
Financial transfers	yes												yes
Legal powers													
Dispute settlement	yes	yes					not used				yes	yes	
Initiatives from region	yes							limited			proposed		
Negotiating competence	yes		proposed				yes	limited	limited	limited	proposed	limited	yes

TABLE 3.2 (cont.)
INTEGRATION BEYOND TRADE AND INVESTMENT

	EU	NAFTA	APEC	ASEAN	ANZCERTA	SAARC	MERCOSUR	Andean	CACM	CARICOM	SADC	COMESA	SACU
Characteristics of members													
Geographic integration	almost	yes		yes	semi	yes	yes	semi	yes	semi			yes
Size of population	large	large	large	large	middle	large	large	middle	small	small	middle	small	middle
Level of income	middle/high	middle/high	low to high	low/middle	high	low	low/middle	middle	low/middle	middle	low/middle	low	low/middle
One or more large	more	one	more	more	one	more	more	more	none	none	one	more	one
Border integration	yes	yes	yes	yes			yes						

Notes: yes: indicates that the region has some integration in the heading; more: indicates that the region goes further than the WTO.

TABLE 3.3

SUMMARY OF EVIDENCE ON INTEGRATION

	WTO	EU	NAFTA	APEC	ASEAN	ANZCERTA	SAARC	MERCOSUR	Andean	CACM	CARICOM	SADC	COMESA	SACU
Political and social integration														
Responsive elite		yes	partial	yes	some	yes	some	yes	yes	yes	yes	some	yes	no
Business support		yes	yes	yes	yes	yes	yes	yes	yes	yes	yes	some	yes	yes
Popular support		yes	partial	some		yes	yes	yes		yes	yes		yes	no
Authority of govts		yes	no	yes	yes	yes	no	yes	no	some	some	yes	some	yes
Interest grp interaction		yes	some	limited	yes	yes	no	increasing	limited	yes	yes	some	some	some
Common ec.approach		yes	no	no	some	yes	yes	yes	no	no	no	no	no	yes
Motives for forming region														
Trade access		yes	yes	planned	yes	yes	yes	yes		some	yes	yes	yes	yes
Investment access		yes	yes	yes	yes			yes			yes	yes	yes	yes
Development or efficiency		yes					yes	yes	yes	yes				
Reaction to others		yes	yes	yes				yes		yes	yes			
To bargain with others		yes	yes	yes				yes	yes	yes				
Military, security		yes		yes				yes		yes		yes		
Political gesture		yes	yes	yes		yes		yes	yes		yes	yes	yes	yes
Summary indicators (score out of 5)														
Hufbauer, Schott, 1994[a]														
Movement of Goods&Serv	3	5 (4)	4 (4)	3	3	5	2	3 (2)	3 (3)	2 (2)	3 (4)	3	3	5
Movement of capital	4	5 (4)	5 (4)	3	4	5	1	4 (1)	3 (3)	0 (0)	3 (3)	2	2	5
Movement of labour	1	4 (3)	1 (2)	1	1	3	0	2 (1)	1 (1)	1 (1)	3 (2)	1	2	3
Supra-Regional Inst	3	4 (5)	2 (3)	1	2	2	2	3 (2)	3 (3)	3 (2)	2 (2)	2	2	3
Monetary coord.	0	3 (3)	1 (1)	0	0	1	0	0 (0)	0 (0)	1 (0)	1 (2)	0	0	4 (5 ex Bott.)
Fiscal coord.	0	3 (1)	0 (0)	0	0	0	0	0 (0)	0 (0)	0 (0)	0 (0)	0	0	3
Total	11	24 (20)	13 (14)	8	10	16	5	12 (6)	10 (10)	7 (5)	12 (13)	8	9	23

TABLE 3.3 (cont.)
SUMMARY OF EVIDENCE ON INTEGRATION

From this paper	WTO	EU	NAFTA	APEC	ASEAN	ANZCERTA	SAARC	MERCOSUR	Andean	CACM	CARICOM	SADC	COMESA	SACU
Trade integration	5	5	4	4	2	3	1	4	4	4	3	3	1	4
Investment integration	5	5	4	3	4	4	1	3	3	1	2	1	0	3
Trade regime	3	5	4	1	2	5	2	4	3	3	3	2	3	5
Other trade-related	0	5	3	1	2	4	0	3	2	1	2	2	2	2
Economic policy	0	4	0	0	0	0	0	2	1	0	1	1	2	5
Legal powers	3	5	2	1	0	2	2	3	2	4	2	1	2	3
Economic characteristics	3	4	3	2	4	3	4	4	3	4	3	2	3	3
Political characteristics	2	5	3	4	4	5	3	4	3	2	4	2	3	3
Number of motives	3	5	4	4	2	2	2	5	2	2	3	3	3	2
Total	24	43	27	20	20	28	13	32	23	21	23	17	20	30

Note: (a) My score; score by Hufbauer and Schott in brackets.

is or expects to be. Some of these measures are similar to those proposed by Hufbauer and Schott [*1994*] in a ranking system for existing regional groups but these deal with the legal regime, not observed flows or pre-conditions, and the absolute level of barriers, not a comparison with members' normal obligations under the WTO. The conclusions of this chapter will be summarised in that form and compared to theirs (Table 3.3). Then there are the initial conditions, the economic, political, and other conditions and structures, which can be analysed as relatively similar or not. This is closer to the traditional political or historical approach. It is also necessary to look at the declared motives of the members of the groups which have been formed. The conclusion will try to examine whether there seems to be a pattern of links which characterise the more successful groups.

II. TRADE

Three measures, share in world trade, intra-trade, and intensity will be considered in this section. It is clear that the absolute share of intra-trade is an important measure of the importance of the group to each member. This will be important in the interplay of political and economic interrelationships and choices. The share in world trade both measures the potential impact of the region or others and 'scales' the intra-trade measure. The ratio of intra-trade to the share in world trade, the intensity, would be 1 for a region trading no more with itself than do other countries. For a small region, with high intra-trade, it can rise to very high levels (Table 3.1).

The expansion of the GATT, now the WTO, since the early 1980s, plus the applicants now being considered, means that effectively all trade is intra-WTO, giving a share and an intensity of 1. The share would have been lower, but the intensity higher, before this expansion, as there was less trade with the excluded centrally planned economies, and some of the developing countries which had remained outside had done so precisely to restrict their dependence on trade. The liberalisation which has occurred would give it a 3 on a scale of 1 to 5 for free movement of goods and services (Table 3.3) using the scale of Hufbauer and Schott [*1994*]. The objective for the WTO is now full free movement – 5 on the scale.

There is free trade within the EU and it is also a customs union (Table 3.2), giving it a score of 5 now (pre-1994 Hufbauer and Schott gave it 4). The share of EU intra-trade at around 60 per cent for all goods is the highest of the groups (except APEC) (Table 3.1). The EU accounts for a third of world trade, so a high share is not surprising. But intra-EU trade actually fell in the period 1990–94. It is only because the EU's share in world trade also fell that the ratio of the two, the intensity, rose. The range of 1.4 to 1.7 for intensity may seem relatively low compared with the other groups for which it has been calculated, but it is, of course, limited by the high share. (The intra-trade share can also be interpreted as the ratio of actual intensity to the maximum achievable if all trade were intra-group.) Looking at the individual members, the share of intra-trade is always above 50 per cent, with minor exceptions in occasional years for Germany and the UK. This gives intensity measures of at least 1.5.

It is arguable that some types of trade, broadly: natural resource-based, are too driven by supply and fixed technologies to be useful in a measure of the real integration of a region. This would suggest using a measure of intensity of trade restricted to manufactures. Unfortunately, data on trade in manufactures, in particular on its direction, are poor for the developing countries, but it will be possible to give indications for some areas. For the EU, the intensity for manufactures is less, but this is likely to have been influenced by the protection for intra-EU trade in food under the Common Agricultural Policy.

The share of intra-trade in NAFTA is lower than for the EU: it now approaches 50 per cent for exports, after increasing substantially between 1990 and 1994. The region accounts, however, for a smaller share of world trade, about 20 per cent, so that its calculated intensity is greater (and also rising). The share of intra-trade is over 80 per cent for exports and around 70 per cent for imports for Canada and Mexico, but only around 30 per cent for the US. There is little difference for NAFTA as a whole between the importance of intra-trade in manufactures and in all goods. For Canada and the US, manufactures are slightly more important in imports; for Mexico, slightly less. For exports, intra-trade in manufactures is more important for all three countries. On average, therefore, NAFTA seems as integrated, given its smaller share in world trade, as the EU, but the integration is much more asymmetrical than in the EU. Although the objective is free trade, there will be restrictions on some goods, with differential reductions, for at least 15 years from its founding (and services are less integrated), giving it a 4 for trade policy.

The only other group of a comparable size is APEC. It does not offer freer terms for movement of goods or services than the WTO, although it has a target of free trade for the advanced members by 2010, and the developing by 2020. APEC includes NAFTA, ASEAN, and Australia/New Zealand, and its share in world trade was rising rapidly in the 1990s, from 39 per cent to 44 per cent for exports, higher than the EU share. Intra-trade is around 70 per cent, comparable with the highest individual members of the EU. With both world share and intra-trade higher, the intensity is similar to that for the EU, and slightly lower than for NAFTA. Although a few countries are at 50 per cent or just below (notably Chile), for most countries intra-APEC trade accounts for 60–80 per cent of their trade, comparable with the EU countries. Almost all the APEC countries show the same or a higher share for intra-trade of manufactures than for all commodities, the exceptions being Mexico for imports and Chile and Indonesia for exports. Those that are higher, however, have small differences. This provides weak support for the view that manufactures will show a more integrated pattern. On these measures, the integration of the APEC group seems comparable to that of the EU.

The ASEAN countries have now formed the ASEAN Free Trade Area (AFTA). The target is free trade by 2008, but preferences are still very limited, with agriculture excluded. The data for ASEAN suffer from the problem that much trade goes through the port of Singapore, and therefore data for intra-trade may include some goods simply being transshipped. In addition, Singapore does not report trade with Indonesia; these figures have used Indonesia's reported trade with Singapore. For this reason, the figures quoted in Table 3.1 are with and without Singapore. Even including Singapore, the group has only a six per cent share of world trade, although this is much larger than the remaining groups to be considered, which are around one per cent or lower. This means that direct comparison of intensity ratios with the three major groups would be misleading. The share of intra-trade in ASEAN is about 20 per cent, and growing. Intensity, however, appears to be falling (except for imports when Singapore is excluded). For individual members, ASEAN is never more than 50 per cent of trade (it is highest for Brunei's imports, but two-thirds of these are from Singapore). In general, trade with ASEAN, including Singapore, is around 20 per cent for Malaysia and Singapore (again, mainly with each other), and little more than 10 per cent for the others. In manufactures, intra-trade is normally of similar importance, or lower for some countries' imports, but it is more important for Indonesian exports, bringing the share to over 15 per cent.

The Australia–New Zealand agreement covers countries accounting for about 1.5 per cent of world trade. It is a free trade area with only a few exclusions (a score of 5 for movement of goods). Only seven to eight per cent of their trade is intra-trade, and the countries differ sharply: four to five per cent for Australia and around 20 per cent for New Zealand. Even New Zealand is substantially below the levels seen in NAFTA or the EU. For both Australia and New Zealand, however, the share of intra-trade for manufactured exports is about twice as high as for all commodities.

The other group in Asia, SAARC, is not in APEC (data from Khan [*1995*]). This has made little progress on trade liberalisation. Intra-area trade is of the same order of magnitude as for ASEAN without Singapore, although the share of world trade is rather lower. Intensity, therefore, is higher (almost as high as for ASEAN including Singapore), and is increasing. For India, the major member, the shares are low for imports, under one per cent, but comparable to the average for exports, at around three to four per cent. Pakistan shows a similar pattern, with around four per cent for exports and one to two per cent for imports. In contrast, Sri Lanka is much more dependent on the group for imports, at about ten per cent. Bangladesh has a falling share of exports to the group (from nine per cent in 1980, to four to five per cent around 1990, to two per cent in 1992–94. Its share for imports, however, has been growing, reaching 13 per cent by 1994. For manufactures, the Indian share for imports is even lower, while for exports the share is similar. For Sri Lanka, the import share is also around ten per cent, but for exports it is much lower than for all commodities, at under one per cent instead of three per cent. Except for the smallest members, the Maldives and Nepal, with shares of 10–25 per cent, these shares are substantially below those of ASEAN or Australia/New Zealand, and are low for all countries. This could mean that no member would have as strong an interest in preserving or increasing trade in the group.

As Chile and Bolivia became associates of MERCOSUR in 1997, the data show trade with the original four and with six members. MERCOSUR has free trade and is becoming a customs union (with some exceptions, and with special arrangements planned for Chile) (4 for trade policy and free movement; it has kept to its timetable since the low figure of 2 in Hufbauer and Schott) This region shows the most marked increase in the share of intra-trade in Table 3.1. It was mainly for exports: the share for these doubled (to 18–20 per cent), while that for imports, which was already higher, rose only two percentage points (to 17–19 per cent). The region's share of world trade is comparable to that of the Australia/New Zealand group; intensity is around 12. It has risen only slightly because the export share in world trade in particular increased sharply between 1990 and 1994. MERCOSUR is unusual because it had both an increase in world share and an increase in intensity: the EU, NAFTA, APEC, and SAARC saw falls in share with rises in intensity, while ASEAN had an increase in share, but fall in intensity. For the original four members, the share of intra-trade is in the region of 40 per cent for the smaller two, over 20 per cent for Argentina, and just under 20 per cent for Brazil. These are figures approaching those for NAFTA, and similar to those for ASEAN (including Singapore).

Although the figures for Paraguay are erratic, most of the shares have been rising, especially for exports, confirming the association between increased trade within MERCOSUR and the increase in the region's total exports. For Chile, there has been an increase, although smaller, in trade with the MERCOSUR countries, at a time when its share in world trade was rising slightly. Bolivia has seen sharp falls in the share of both imports and exports to the region. For Argentina, there was little difference in the performance for imports of manufactures, and a fall for cars and car parts, one of the principal industries in Argentine–Brazilian trade (Brazil accounts for about half Argentine imports). For exports, however, the share was much higher, rising from 16 to 40 per cent, and for cars from 60 to 90 per cent. For Brazil, in imports the share for all manufactures was lower than for all commodities, but that for cars was rising, from 15 to 30 per cent. As in Argentina, the share for exports of manufactures was higher, and rose from 5 to19 per cent; for cars from 20 to 40 per cent. For Paraguay, manufactures had a slightly lower share of intra-trade for imports and exports. MERCOSUR thus shows a picture of growing integration, particularly for new markets and for exports of manufactures.

In spite of its much longer history, the Andean Group has made less progress on reducing barriers, but its exclusions are a negative list so that its trade policy can be ranked as an intensity of 3. It still had a small share for intra-trade in 1990, but by 1994, this had approximately doubled, to nine per cent. As its share in world trade is about half that of the MERCOSUR countries, this gave it a similar intensity of about 11–12, but there was little change in its share in world trade. Most of the members shared this increase, including Bolivia (in contrast to its performance in its prospective region, MERCOSUR), but Ecuador had falls in the importance of intra-regional trade, and Peru had little change for its exports. But for most, for imports and exports, the shares are only between six and 16 per cent. This is understandable given the low share of the group in world trade, but suggests a limited importance of the group to its members. Exports of manufactures have a high and growing share of intra-trade. On a smaller scale, the performance of the Andean countries is thus similar to that of MERCOSUR.

Although their share of world trade is extremely small, trade among the Central American countries is much higher, at 20 per cent for exports and 13 per cent for imports, and is growing. They offer preferences, not free trade to each other (score 2). This gives extremely high intensity measures (80–90). The highest intra-trade figures are for exports for El Salvador and Guatemala and for imports for Nicaragua, at over 30 per cent. Other flows are around 15 per cent, with some under ten per cent, but no country is extremely high or low for both imports and exports. This means that the average integration may be little different from the Andean Group, although the small size of the markets means that stronger ties are needed to explain this.

The CARICOM countries, which also offer only preferences, but which have a target of a customs union, are a more extreme version of the Central American story. The share of world trade is lower; the share of intra-trade only slightly lower, giving higher intensity measures. It is with areas like these two that the intensity measures become potentially misleading. A ratio of 150 for intra-trade relative to average world trade may look high, but an absolute share of intra-region exports of 15 per cent, while important, does not indicate as much integration as the 20 per cent intra-trade with intensity ratio of only 12 of MERCOSUR (or 60 per cent and 1.7 in the EU). But the increase in the intensity is impressive. The highest figures for shares of intra-trade are not found only in the smaller countries (Barbados has a high share), but Guyana, Jamaica, and Trinidad and Tobago tend to be lower.

The two African groups, COMESA (formerly the PTA) and SADC (formerly SADCC) have a considerable degree of overlap in their membership. Both have programmes of moving towards free trade among their members; there are a variety of bilateral arrangements, but so far trade arrangements are restricted to some commodities. SADC is larger in relation to world trade, similar to the Andean Group, with just under one per cent of world trade. It has also seen a sharp increase in the share of intra-trade, giving an intensity of 11–12 by 1994, on the basis of eight per cent shares of intra-trade. Malawi, Zambia, and Zimbabwe are the countries with the major shares for intra-trade, particularly for imports where the shares reach over 40 per cent (and are rising). For the largest member, South Africa, which also takes almost two-thirds of intra-SADC imports, the share of SADC is only seven per cent for exports and two per cent for imports. This suggests an important imbalance in interest in the region, comparable to the differences observed in NAFTA. This is supported by the trade of Zimbabwe, the second country in the region. Almost all its imports, of manufactures and other goods, come from South Africa. On exports, about half to two- thirds go to South Africa, with the share slightly lower for manufactures. Manufactures are more important in intra-region trade. The intra-trade share for manufactures is substantially higher for Zimbabwe and South Africa than for the others. The greater part of South Africa's exports of manufactures go to the region. Thus manufactures give a more integrated impression, including for South Africa. This role of manufactures makes SADC more like the Latin American regions than like ASEAN, APEC, or the EU. But the pattern suggests that exports of manufactures go from the more to the less developed, and are not the exchange among equals found in the EU, or perhaps MERCOSUR.

COMESA's share in world trade is only half that of SADC (because South Africa is not a member), but in 1990, there was a higher share of intra-trade. The increase in SADC has left COMESA behind, however, and the intensity indices are no longer so much higher than those for SADC. They are greatly below those of Central America (which has a higher share of intra-trade in spite of lower total trade), although they are higher, in share and intensity, than the Andean Group. The countries with relatively high intra-trade are Burundi, Djibouti (possibly entrepôt trade), Kenya and Zimbabwe for exports; Rwanda and Uganda for imports. Some are up to 30 per cent. Tanzania shows a marked increase in imports and exports to the region. Manufactures are important in exports to the region for Zimbabwe and Madagascar. This does not suggest the same integration of the region found in SADC.

Trade figures for intra-trade for the SACU countries are only available for 1993, and are not entirely reliable, as they are not officially compiled by the members. They show a high degree of intra-trade, giving a high intensity measure because of their low share of total trade. As in other groups dominated by a single member, they show serious asymmetry. For imports, South Africa, Namibia and Botswana are all below 19 per cent, while Lesotho and Swaziland are about 60 per cent. For exports, South Africa is five per cent, with the others all over 80 per cent.

On the trade flow measures used here, the regions which seem to be integrated are certainly NAFTA, APEC, MERCOSUR, the Andean Group, and Central America; on a small scale, but fairly interdependent, Australia/New Zealand, CARICOM, SADC, SACU; not particularly integrated ASEAN, SAARC, COMESA.

III. INVESTMENT AND LABOUR MOVEMENTS

Under the WTO, there is now transparently controlled movement of capital, with substantially lower barriers than when the GATT was founded. The situation is approaching that for trade in the early years of the GATT, and therefore offers the same scope for regions to move further ahead, sooner than the world average.

Data on investment flows on a comparable basis and by direction and source are difficult to compile The only international series, by UNCTAD, has detailed figures only to 1990, before the increase either in regions or in foreign investment by many developing countries, and there are only summary and uncertain figures for later years [*UNCTAD, 1995: 53*]. The extreme concentration of all direct investment makes the use of a measure similar to the intensity of trade less useful. The evidence for both the world and the EU is that there are likely to be very uneven flows by different countries, so that we would not expect to find similar ratios among members even in a region with high intensity.

Investment-based integration seems important only in the EU, NAFTA, ASEAN and MERCOSUR. ASEAN's intra-investment is rising rapidly in some countries. By 1991, 12 per cent of investment in Thailand came from other ASEAN countries, double the figure in the 1970s [*Page, 1994*], For the earlier period, 1985–9, where detailed UNCTAD data are available, about four per cent of investment in Thailand came from ASEAN, 12 per cent in Malaysia, six per cent in Indonesia, none in Singapore [*Bannister and Primo Braga, 1996*]. But the UNCTAD data for ASEAN as a whole (using stock figures) can be used to calculate that, although investment in other ASEAN countries accounts for 36 per cent of all ASEAN outward investment, this is lower than the 60 per cent in 1980, and the share of ASEAN investment in total investment in ASEAN has not changed (at three per cent) (Table 3.1).

In 1994, the US and Canada accounted for 60 per cent of the stock of investment in Mexico, but there was a sharp fall in their share of inflows in 1994, to only just above 50 per cent. Within MERCOSUR [*IRELA, 1996*], investment by other members accounted for one per cent of investment in Argentina in the 1980s, and only 1.3 per cent in 1990, but was 5.7 per cent by 1992 (and investment by Chile, which was also negligible in the 1980s, had risen to six per cent). There has been no comparable rise in Brazil. In the new members, MERCOSUR countries account for seven per cent of investment in Bolivia and three per cent in Chile. There is limited intra-region investment in CARICOM, but it is not important in Central America. It is not at present important in SADC or COMESA, although there are expectations of South African investment in SADC. More data are needed to treat investment properly, but there appears to be some support for the view that investment is becoming less regionally oriented, at least in the regions where foreign investment was already important, such as ASEAN, although new investors may start in their own region.

It could be argued that correlation among interest rates would give an indication of integration of capital markets, but there are now few regions where capital flows have been more liberated within the region than with the rest of the world, and in these, internal controls suggest that interest rates are unlikely to move freely. There would also be the usual difficulties of finding comparable rates and ensuring that they were not correlated because of other influences, within or from outside the region. (For these reasons, again as well as data, prices were not used in the measurements of trade integration.) There are a few groups, including SAARC, the Central American Common Market (CACM), and COMESA (and the franc zone in West and Central Africa), which have greater freedom of capital movement among the members than with the rest of the world. For them, this can be considered an important sign of integration. In some others, as in the EU, mobility within the region came earlier than with those outside, although in NAFTA the generalising of Mexico's reforms to its investment law followed almost immediately.

Free movement of labour is still rare in regional groups, and there is no WTO structure with which to compare it. Even the limited types included in the WTO services agreements are restricted to some sectors or types of labour in most countries' offers. Only the EU includes full freedom of movement. There is extensive movement within SACU, and some freedom in Australia/New Zealand and in the CARICOM region; it is a target for MERCOSUR and COMESA.

IV. COVERAGE OF 'NEW' AREAS

This must be a moving indicator, because what is covered at the multilateral level is expanding, leaving fewer new areas and less scope for going beyond the international norm. This is analogous to the problem that lowering MFN tariffs leaves less potential effect from regional preferences or free trade. Table 3.2 indicates where regions are now further advanced than the international norm (or are committed to advance). The EU has taken action on all.

Different national standards became obvious as a potential unintentional barrier to trade when trade linkages increased and products became more complicated and regulated, and then became intentional barriers in the 1980s. The Uruguay Round settlement makes a start on defining international agreement on their setting and recognition. The EU has led on this, with action on all of them, and some of the developing country groups have also made progress, including MERCOSUR and CARICOM: on non-economic types like education; several on customs or other international documentation; and Central America, COMESA (it is proposed for SADC), and Australia/New Zealand on some private standards.

NAFTA had provisions on investment, but they have been extended to non-members by Mexico, and are still subject to dispute between the US and Canada. MERCOSUR gives national treatment for subsidiaries of other member companies which is not available to other foreign investment. The Andean Pact in its early years had arrangements for an Andean company law.

Patent and copyright law have been subject to international agreements for more than a century, but the Uruguay Round brought this into the trade regime. Regions other than the EU which have acted on this include NAFTA and the Andean Group (in its early years); it is proposed for SADC.

Two areas which are now being brought to the fore in the WTO are the environment and labour standards. Protocols on them were added to the NAFTA agreement. Including the environment is a target for MERCOSUR and COMESA, but in general there is little evidence that these are common among regional groups.

External access to public contracts was introduced as a side agreement in the 1980s under the GATT, and extended after the Uruguay Round. It was already accepted in the EU. It is found in the Australia/New Zealand agreement, but is otherwise not generally part of regional agreements (although it is found in some preferential arrangements, like the Lomé Convention).

As regions become more important, it seems plausible for decision-makers and consumers within them to expect direct access to the region, as well as access through member governments. This is being sought in the WTO (there are provisions for consultation in the Uruguay Round agreement), and is embodied in economic consultations in the EU. There are economic groups in MERCOSUR, and provision for access in COMESA.

The step beyond this is to the elements of national economic policy. This is still entirely outside the multilateral regime (except for intervention by the IMF or World Bank). The EU has had direct transfers among member countries since the establishment of the customs union; sectoral regulation, including agriculture, steel, energy, and transport; and exchange-rate co-ordination; it is moving toward monetary union and macroeconomic policy co-ordination. The franc zone (not included here) has considerable monetary and fiscal co-ordination as well as a common currency. The agreements of MERCOSUR and COMESA have provisions for policy co-ordination, and co-operation on infrastructure. SADC also plans such co-ordination. SACU requires the members other than South Africa to follow South African legislation on customs and trade, and provides transfers from South Africa through the allocation of customs revenues. MERCOSUR will need a means of allocating customs revenue.

All the groups go beyond trade in some directions, but Table 3.2 indicates no uniform pattern or sequence for which areas will be tackled.

V. REGIONAL ADMINISTRATION AND RELATIONS WITH OTHERS

The switch from the GATT to the WTO was a formal increase in status, but GATT had been gaining in influence during the previous 10 years. There are still few delegated powers, and policy initiatives and claims in disputes must come from members, not the WTO. But it does have competence to examine, and thus negotiate with, regions among its members and with applicants. The EU has gone beyond this, with competence to act in trade and in some other fields, within the Union and in relations with non-members. It can make proposals for extending the scope of the EU. Although its member states are members of other, non-trade, international groups, they may not join other trade groups without permission. The EU has made bilateral agreements with other countries and some regions, and it is a member of the WTO (in addition to the member states). NAFTA has few of these powers, and there is no assumption that it should be finding new areas of responsibility. Its members are free to join other groups (subject to their NAFTA commitments). It has acted as a negotiating group only informally.

Most of the other groups have none of these powers. MERCOSUR is an exception. It has made at least one international agreement (with the EU), and puts restrictions on members which are members of other groups (although these were relaxed after the first five years of existence). As a customs union it will have to be a negotiating group in any tariff negotiations The CACM and CARICOM, although incomplete common markets, have also made joint trade agreements with other countries in their areas. SACU members have the right to intervene in negotiations by any member with other countries. It is principally, therefore, the regions which have elements of a customs union which have needed to acquire powers. The exception was the Andean Group in its initial existence in the early 1970s, when it was not a customs union but had an industrial planning and development function which led to its taking joint positions relative to the rest of the world.

Some means of settling disputes among members of a group is essential, but there is wide variation in how much there are formal procedures and whether these are used. The strengthening of its procedures was one of the major changes for the WTO in 1994, and since then it has been used at an unprecedented rate (and with acceptance of its decisions).The EU is unusual in having a regularly used procedure, which is immediately applied in the member states. The other groups do not follow this example. NAFTA has an inter-governmental procedure, which has been used, and MERCOSUR has one in principle, but it has not yet been invoked.

VI. CHARACTERISTICS OF THE COUNTRIES

The members of the regions considered here are all geographically contiguous, except in APEC, SADC and COMESA (and the EU has non-member countries within its borders) (Table 3.3). The EU, NAFTA, APEC, ASEAN, SAARC, and MERCOSUR all have large populations (200 million and over), while the Central American Common Market and CARICOM are extremely small. All (except CACM) have wide variations in size and population. The EU, NAFTA, and APEC have significant shares of world output.

For a region to be more than a hegemonic power with supporters, it may be better for it not to have only one major member. The only ones with a dominant member are NAFTA, Australia/New Zealand, SADC, and SACU. Most have large differences in income and stage of development. The EU, SAARC, CACM, and MERCOSUR are relatively uniform, but at very different levels. As was noted in the discussion of trade, absolute size is a potential advantage in making the region significant for its members. A similar level of development may provide common interests, but if this is a relatively low level of development, different growth rates and development paths may destroy the similarity (suggesting that similarity plus low growth may be the appropriate criterion). More direct indications of economic integration are trade and financial infrastructure and sub-regions which cross borders. Both are important in the EU, and can be found in NAFTA (on both US borders, but with no Canada-Mexico equivalent), ASEAN (APEC because of its component regions), and MERCOSUR. They are probably particularly lacking in the Andean Group, COMESA, and SADC. It seems more useful to use these direct measures of integration, along with the trade intensities discussed earlier, than potential measures based on complementary production or trade.

Political similarity or compatibility is more difficult to measure and compare. One set of criteria (developed in detail in Zormelo [*1995*]) is included in Table 3.3. The first three are obvious pre-conditions for support within the member countries: from the political elite, the economic decision-makers, and popular opinion. The need for authority of the member governments has two elements. It is needed for practical implementation, but it can also be argued that governments need confidence in their own authority before being willing to share or delegate it to a regional administration. The EU (with some reservations at some times in some countries, but no more than normal within a country) meets all these, and this is probably also true for Australia/New Zealand. NAFTA and APEC probably have less broad-based support, and the variety of governments in the APEC region make it difficult to assume that all are committed. Popular support may not be essential or ascertainable in ASEAN, but that region meets the other criteria. MERCOSUR and CARICOM probably meet some of the criteria. SAARC has less support, and some of the governments have important problems within their countries which reduce their interest in the region. COMESA has support, but some governments are not fully committed (or wavering between it and SADC). SADC has the same problem, with the additional weakness that its largest member, South Africa, is also trying to establish new ties outside the region with the EU and is inevitably preoccupied with its own development. 'Interaction' within the regions is impossible to measure, except impressionistically, but there are clear examples in the EU, ASEAN, MERCOSUR, CARICOM, and NAFTA of increasingly regular contact by interest groups, economic and non-economic, and there is a long history for Australia/New Zealand. It is probably also true of CACM, COMESA, and SADC, and perhaps the Andean Group. It probably exists on a very limited scale for APEC as a whole.

The importance of a common approach to economic policy depends on the types of integration, as well as helping to explain which are chosen. Similar attitudes towards the extent and form of regulation and intervention as well as the actual choice of policy are at issue. The history of the EU, in particular the most recent moves, has been to require an increasingly common approach, and the pace has depended on countries' willingness to accept this. Both NAFTA and MERCOSUR had moved to more similar economic policies among their members at the time that they were formed than in the past. The Andean Group assumed a common attitude to planning in its first years, and it weakened as policies diverged and changed over its history. Australia/New Zealand probably meet this criterion. The ASEAN countries have important differences, but a strong commitment to economic growth. The other groups have very different policies. The APEC approach, in principle expecting to extend any agreements or liberalisation to all countries, suggests an open attitude to regulation which cannot produce a stable group.

VII. MOTIVES

The intention here is not to analyse why countries form regional groups but to identify the declared or implicit motives. Trade and investment access to other members is the assumed motive in most analysis of regional groups, especially for developed countries. It was important for the GATT and the WTO, of course, and for the EU, MERCOSUR, and ASEAN, and is an important motive for APEC (Table 3.3). Trade without investment is important for most of the others, except perhaps NAFTA where there was substantial access before it was formed. There, investment access may have been more important. An additional (or alternative) traditional motive for developing countries is development: through scale economies, in production, but also in planning and in relations with the rest of the world. This was fundamental to the Andean Group, and important to all the Latin American and African groups. It is an objective of SAARC, but seems less relevant to ASEAN or APEC. It is now the declared motive behind SADC. It is related to the competitiveness motive for the EU's increase in integration through the Single European Market programme, and has been important for some countries which joined it.

Reaction to other groups cannot be a fundamental explanation (at least if there is to be any stability in the system) but has been important, except perhaps in Asia. The scale arguments above can be considered a case of groups reacting to larger countries (the EU to the US and Japan, for example). In addition, bargaining power, bilaterally and within multilateral institutions, has been an important motive: for the EU in multilateral negotiations; for NAFTA against the EU; for MERCOSUR against NAFTA, perhaps for CACM and CARICOM within the western hemisphere; perhaps for Australia/New Zealand in Asia. APEC may be seen in this way by some of its members, such as Japan or Australia, which are left out of the other regions. This reaction motive, however, can only explain timing, not the more fundamental choices of members of a region and the scope of formal integration. It can also be closely related to more traditional security or military alliances. SADC initially had this objective (against South Africa), and the EU and APEC both deliberately include potential political or military opponents in order to make conflict less likely. CACM had elements of this, as did MERCOSUR on the nuclear security side. The EU, MERCOSUR, NAFTA, and SADC (now, with South Africa a member) also cement political alliances and mutual support.

VIII. CONCLUSIONS

The final section of Table 3.3 summarises (judgementally) the strength of the various types of linkage discussed in this chapter. For interest, it also extends (and updates) the similar exercise by Hufbauer and Schott, which looked at a narrower range of links, and gave much greater weight to legal provisions for movements of goods, services, and factors of production. The totals should not be taken seriously: the object of the study is to think about how the links should be weighted. The first two lines measure actual flows. International regulation is found in the third line, the trade regime, while the next three are other matters of integration policy. While the EU and MERCOSUR show high integration on these as well, the other customs unions and full free trade areas do not. Although its scores are perhaps misleadingly high, COMESA is an example of an organisation which has gone relatively far on other policies with less progress on liberalising trade (and very little effective trade integration). NAFTA is the reverse, with unusually little other policy integration and high actual integration, and APEC a more extreme version of this.

The regions with the highest measured trade and investment integration, the EU, NAFTA, APEC, Australia/New Zealand, MERCOSUR, the Andean Group, and SACU are not the same as those with the highest policy integration, namely, the EU by a large margin, SACU, MERCOSUR, Australia/New Zealand, COMESA, and NAFTA, but this comparison identifies five which are in both groups: the EU, MERCOSUR, SACU, Australia/New Zealand, NAFTA. The regions which background characteristics might predict would be the most integrated are the EU and MERCOSUR; then a group including NAFTA, ASEAN (APEC) and Australia/New Zealand; and also CACM and CARICOM. The regions that have a programme and mechanisms for achieving closer integration or new forms are the EU, SADC, COMESA and MERCOSUR. It is possible to identify one attribute which is low or lacking (two or under) in the three groups (other than the EU) which appear most integrated: common macroeconomic policies. Legal powers are also low except in MERCOSUR. The former are the most recent addition to the EU. It is therefore too early to say whether these are a necessary element as groups evolve.

The only attributes which are always at least two are the summaries of political characteristics and motives. There is no group which appears to be formed only for trade and/or investment reasons. This suggests that basing analysis or international regulation only on these could be misleading or potentially distorting.

The groups which are customs unions or free trade areas (or in a WTO-consistent ten-year transition period) are the EU, MERCOSUR and SACU (NAFTA has a 15-year period, beginning pre-WTO). The intention of the new WTO Committee on Regions is to regulate non-conforming regions (there has been effectively no sanction in the past). This could cause the regions to remove or to move forward the trade policy element. But there is no way of regulating the other policy elements, although all of these can also set up barriers to non-member countries, whether actual (meeting a standard or regulation), or relative (a regulation more favourable or familiar to the members; participation in making policy). APEC (with a distant and non-binding trade policy target) might be joined by other non-trade regions which would be outside WTO regulation. This suggests that simply improving the trade-based regulation of regions could be inadequate (or damaging) unless a way is found to incorporate their non-trade elements and objectives and the effects of these on trade and non-trade performance in excluded countries into assessment of the costs and benefits of regions.

REFERENCES

Bannister, G. and C.A. Primo Braga (1996), *East-Asian Investment and Trade: Prospects for Growing Regionalization in the 1990s*, Washington, DC: World Bank.

Fawcett, L. and A. Hurrell (eds.) (1995), *Regionalism in World Politics*, Oxford: Oxford University Press.

Haines-Ferrari, M. (1993), 'MERCOSUR: A New Model of Latin American Economic Integration?' *Journal of International Law,* Vol.25, No.3, summer, pp.413–48.

Harmsen, R. and M. Leidy (1994), M., 'Regional Trading Arrangements', in IMF, *International Trade Policies: The Uruguay Round and Beyond. Vol.II,* Washington, DC: IMF.

Hufbauer, G.C. and J.J. Schott (1994), *Western Hemisphere Economic Integration,* Washington, DC: Institute for International Economics.

Institute for European–Latin American Relations (IRELA) (ed.) (1996), *Foreign Direct Investment in Latin America in the 1990s*. Madrid: Inter-American Development Bank and IRELA.

International Monetary Fund, *International Financial Statistics,* Washington, DC: IMF, monthly.

International Monetary Fund (1995), *Direction of Trade Statistics Yearbook,* Washington, DC: IMF.

International Trade Centre UNCTAD/GATT (1996), *PC/TAS Trade Analysis System on Personal Computer* [CD-ROM]; five-year time series 1990–1994 of international trade statistics with market share and trend analyses by country and product (SITC3).

Khan, A.H. (1995), 'Intra-Regional Trade in South Asia: Problems and Prospects', paper prepared for 'Regional Economic Cooperation (SAARC–ECO): Pakistan's Perspective and Prospects' workshop organised by the Institute of Regional Studies in collaboration with the Adenauer Stiftung, Germany, Islamabad, 4–5 Dec.

Page, S. (1994), *How Developing Countries Trade: The Institutional Constraints,* London: Routledge in association with the Overseas Development Institute.

Thisen, J. (1995), 'Elements of a Model Convention for Subregional Common Markets in Africa', paper prepared for LINK Conference, Pretoria, Sept.

United Nations Conference on Trade and Development, Division on Transnational Corporations and Investment (UNCTAD DTCI) (1995), *World Investment Report 1995: Transnational Corporations and Competitiveness*, New York and Geneva: UN.

Zormelo, D. (1995), *Regional Integration in Latin America: Is MERCOSUR a New Approach?* Working Paper 84, London: Overseas Development Institute, Dec.

APPENDIX
MEMBERSHIP OF REGIONAL GROUPS INCLUDED

EU: European Union. Belgium, Denmark, France, Germany, Greece, Ireland, Italy, Luxembourg, Netherlands, Portugal, Spain, United Kingdom; Austria, Finland, Sweden from 1995 (not included in data).

NAFTA: North Atlantic Free Trade Area. Canada, Mexico, United States.

APEC: Asia Pacific Economic Co-operation. ASEAN members, NAFTA members, ANZCERTA members, Chile, China, Hong Kong, Taiwan, Japan, South Korea.

ASEAN: AFTA: ASEAN Free Trade Arrangement. Brunei, Indonesia, Malaysia, Philippines, Singapore, Thailand, Vietnam from 1995 (not included in data).

Intensity Measures for Regional Groups

ANZCERTA: Australia–New Zealand Closer Economic Relations Trade Agreement. Australia, New Zealand.

SAARC: South Asian Association for Regional Co-operation. Bangladesh, Bhutan, India, Maldives, Nepal, Pakistan, Sri Lanka.

MERCOSUR: Southern Cone Common Market. Argentina, Brazil, Paraguay, Uruguay; Bolivia, Chile from 1997.

Andean Group: Andean Common Market. Bolivia, Colombia, Ecuador, Peru, Venezuela.

CACM: Central American Common Market. Costa Rica, El Salvador, Guatemala, Honduras, Nicaragua.

CARICOM: Caribbean Community. Antigua and Barbuda, Bahamas, Barbados, Belize, San Cristobal, Dominica, Grenada, Guyana, Jamaica, Montserrat, St Kitts and Nevis, St Lucia, St Vincent and the Grenadines, Trinidad and Tobago.

SADC: Southern African Development Community. Angola, Botswana, Lesotho, Malawi, Mauritius, Mozambique, Namibia, South Africa, Swaziland, Tanzania, Zambia, Zimbabwe.

COMESA: Angola, Botswana, Burundi, Cameroon, Djibouti, Ethiopia, Kenya, Lesotho, Madagascar, Malawi, Mauritius, Mozambique, Rwanda, Somalia, Sudan, Swaziland, Tanzania, Uganda, Zambia, Zimbabwe.

SACU: Southern African Customs Union, Botswana, Lesotho, Namibia, South Africa, Swaziland.

4

A New Theoretical Challenge – Regionalism and Institutional Change: The Cases of East Asia and Sub-Saharan Africa

PHILIPPE HUGON

I. INTRODUCTION

Three points are developed in this chapter:

- first, analysis of the asymmetric interdependence between international centres of decision-making in the context of globalisation;

- second, the revival of regionalism and the resulting adaptation of regional economic analysis in such a context;

- and third, the comparison between two opposing regionalisation processes – in East Asia and in sub-Saharan Africa.

II. HIERARCHY AND ASYMMETRIC INTERDEPENDENCE IN THE CONTEXT OF GLOBALISATION

Financial Globalisation and Multilateralism

Financial globalisation and multilateralism result from a number of relatively recent major changes:

- the new rules of world trade, including those for a number of trade-related subjects: the environment and anti-dumping and anti-subsidy initiatives, which result from the WTO;

- the fact that, unlike labour, capital is very mobile. International movements of capital are 50 times greater than the value of international trade. Life-cycles of new products are very short; it is relatively easy for international firms to move production facilities. In 1995, Foreign Direct Investments (FDI) amounted to approximately US$200 billion in comparison with US$40 billion ten years earlier. Countries therefore try to attract international capital;

- the rising share of trade in world output, which increased from 7 per cent to 20 per cent between 1950 and 1995;

- growing understanding that globalisation implies both multilateral changes – that is, liberalisation of multilateral trade and trade policy – and microeconomic, in particular, in the capacity of companies to compete at the global level and to transform their work organisation. Globalisation assumes improved transportation and communication systems and a manufacturing process that can be segmented into multiple partial operations. The need for competitiveness can appear therefore as a constraint on national policy, threatening, for example, countries' social security systems.

Traditional International Economics

Is traditional international economics still relevant in today's context of financial globalisation, multilateralism, linked information networks, or in the new forms of regionalism? And indeed, a number of economists argue that neither the state nor the nation provides a relevant area for analysis. But we must first ask what was meant previously by international economics.

The standard *neo-classical theory*, based on an individualistic and generalistic bottom-up approach, considers that there are no collective centres of decision; there are only individuals and markets. It is impossible to aggregate individual preferences and production functions, and to compare individual utilities.

Holistic analysis considers that the collective centres of decision are either states or nations (the mercantilist and Keynesian schools) or social classes (classical school). The main actor here is foreign trade, in an open macroeconomy; there are not interdependent public and private actors on the international scene, with a dynamic action/reaction process between them.

The *systemic,* the global and top-down, *paradigm* focuses on global markets, global value added and production, the accumulation of capital, and the strategies of transnational firms in a situation of imperfect competition. It does not look at nations or states, or at asymmetric interdependence or hierarchy between actors. Globalisation is a fact, a *deus ex machina,* a constraint for policy-makers; it is not the result of decisions made.

Recent Analysis Adapted to the Context of Globablisation

In the context of globalisation, traditional analysis no longer applies. The following steps can lead to a comprehensive understanding and analysis of the global economic situation.

We must first identify the principal centres of decision-making at the international level. There are different actors, depending on the level considered - local, national, regional or global. They include, for example, international firms, governments, owners of capital or property rights, local firms or governments, international organisations, unions, workers, and so on.

Because of their different positions at different levels, these actors have potentially conflicting interests. Capital, for example, takes different forms, and profits are sought differently by shareholders or pension fund managers. Transnational companies aim for long-term success through technical efficiency and competitiveness, while individuals and workers tend to seek security through social structures such as the family, national, ethnic or cultural networks, etc.

FIGURE 4.1

THREE FORMS OF COMPETITIVE ADVANTAGE

B Territorial competitive advantages

A Transferable competitive advantages (firms and networks)	C Created competitive advantages (public actors and regulations)

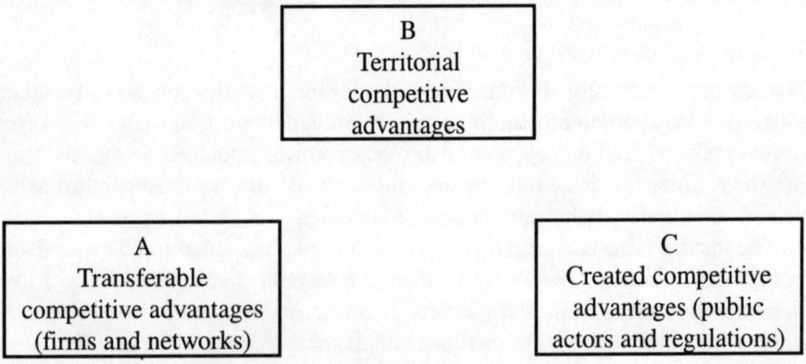

We must then establish different types of comparative or competitive advantages, of which we note three:

(i) the specific and *transferable advantages* internal to multinational firms. This argument is based on organisation theory (transaction costs, non-market co-ordination, etc.) and the theory of imperfect competition;

(ii) the *locational advantages* of local, national, or regional territories (the effects of industrial districts, external economies, agglomeration effects, the supply of factors of production). This argument is derived from the traditional theory of international economics – Ricardo for productivity, and Heckscher/Ohlin for supply of factors – as well as the more recent geographical economics developed, for example, by Krugman. These can look at the advantages of a local and regional activity, as well as national;

(iii) *created competitive advantages* resulting from rules, norms and different economic policies issued by the government. We refer here to the theory of industrial policy as well as to the institutional approach which emphasises the role of regulation and of local institutions in locking in economic policies, reducing uncertainty, and creating credibility and confidence.

Lastly, it is important to note the *asymmetrical dependence between international decision-makers*, of which there are six:

(i) *owners of property rights*. Shareholders often influence company resolutions decisively. They are free to invest their capital on the global market based on risk and profit. Today, investment, distribution of information, and markets including commodity markets, are global;

(ii) *companies and organisations* enjoy specific competitive advantages (permits, modes of organisation, quality, investment for competitivity) which can be transferred to other localities more or less easily. They also have the capacity to influence other firms or decision-makers – by lobbying, financing political parties and so on. Oligopolistic groups organise production globally;

(iii) *local actors* (workers, unions, small business networks) acquire local knowledge and know-how and develop relationships with neighbours, resulting in territorial comparative advantages.

Economic territories are characterised by supplies of natural resource and the effects of economies of scale. Natural resources (land, mineral resources, marine resources, local know-how) are specific local factors. Then, territories compete with one another to attract capital. New cross-border configurations, such as the growth triangles in East Asia, have been emerging recently from multinational projects created by private and public actors. Technological and industrial districts, innovative and creative surroundings and local productive systems at the infra-national level, are absolutely basic to company competitiveness. The more rapid the change in techniques and products and the more flexible the specialisation of industrial units, the greater the possibility for local actors to seize opportunities which appear locally and/or globally;

(iv) *national actors* arise from systems based on culture, education and citizenship which create social ties and reinforce solidarity, and also from common currency. The currency is the expression of national sovereignty; it has legal privileges in the national territory – or regional territory, as in the case of Europe; in the infra- and supra-national contexts, it is accepted because of trust and because of the market. Management of the social system (labour market, labour mobility, wages, social security system, health system, education) is also mostly – and sometimes exclusively – a matter of national territory.

National principles take three main forms: values, including moral and legal norms (rules of action); laws and power (institutional rules); and economic practice (rules of the game). The order and hierarchy of these levels can differ;

(v) *public decision-making centres* (state or local) create competitive advantages by imposing macroeconomic and sectoral policies (in trade, currency exchange, industry). They define the rules of the game and they moderate conflicts by establishing regulations (social and environmental norms, origin and content certification). These state decisions are an expression of the power which operates at the national level and the international level. They follow a logic of intergenerational solidarity and of national cohesion which goes beyond the economic sphere. States are at the heart of the separation between territory and nation. They aim to regulate and to develop national territories, by attracting firms, for example; and they also help national firms abroad through grants, insurances and so on;

(vi) *international organisations* cannot be reduced to either nominal representation or autonomous free-thinking decision-makers. In such organisations, relationships, and in the end, decisions are based on influence, compromise, negotiation, and, in some cases, imposition. For example, decisions made in the WTO – where each state has a vote – differ considerably from those in the Bretton Woods institutions – which suffer from the decisive influence of a few states.

Interactive hierarchy between international decision centres leads back to interdependence between the global, regional, national and local level. While capital, goods and information tend to move about freely, workers, natural resources and infrastructure remain fixed, and executives as well as technology travel in segmented spaces.

III. THE REVIVAL OF REGIONALSIM IN THE CONTEXT OF GLOBALISATION

Within the context of globalisation and of the end of the cold war, and in parallel to national liberalisation processes in developing economies, an important movement towards regionalisation has been taking place. Between 1990 and 1994, for example, the GATT was notified of 34 regional trade agreements. Many of these are in response to the European Union or NAFTA. Regions also discuss and negotiate trade and investment co-operation, as well as social and environmental norms.

While closed regional blocs tend to work against multilateralism, open regionalism does not. In fact, it assists the region to open up, as well as increasing regional interdependence. There is more complementarity than competition between globalisation and regionalisation. Between 1958 and 1993, the share of intra-regional trade in total world trade increased from 40 per cent to more than 50 per cent (from 53 to 70 per cent in the EU).

New Forms of Regionalism in the Context of Globalisation

Different cases of successful integration and co-operation among developing countries have been observed in the past, modelled in most instances on the EU. In Central America, the Central American Common Market was fairly successful for a decade or so, increasing gross trade flows. Other long-standing examples are SACU in Southern Africa and West African Economic Community (CEAO) in West Africa.

Several new forms of regionalism and trade arrangements have appeared recently, from very loose forms to more complex ones, with a number of intermediate arrangements in between:

(i)   the *minimalist form* is the Free Trade Agreement (NAFTA, SAARC, AFTA) which aims to eliminate tariffs between member countries;

(ii)   at the opposite end of the spectrum, the *maximalist form* includes total integration or federation, including transfer of power and the principle of subsidiarity, as in the case of the EU. This includes a common external tariff, special provisions for labour and capital mobility, and macroeconomic policy;

(iii) *intermediate forms* of regional agreements include:

- *custom unions*, such as SACU in Southern Africa, with common external tariffs, partial capital and labour mobility, and compensation mechanisms;
- *common markets*, which are custom unions with full capital and labour mobility and macro-convergence through exchange-rate arrangements;
- *economic unions*, which are common markets with full macroeconomic convergence;

(iv) *other forms* provide, for example, sectoral co-operation – SADC, for example.

The Impact of Liberalisation Policies

We shall now examine the effects of integration on unilateral liberalisation policies and structural adjustment, as well as how these policies, in turn, influence regional processes. The various forms of economic integration and regional co-operation can affect adjustment programmes in terms of their content, rhythm and sequence; and on the other hand, adjustment policies affect economic co-operation and regional integration positively or negatively [*Coussy and Hugon, 1992*].

During the 1980s, structural adjustment programmes (SAPs) aimed to stabilise national finances, reduce the 'distortions' resulting from interventionist policies, open national economies to the rest of the world, and ensure currency convertibility. Reforms sought to reduce or eliminate state trading, price controls on imports, and import-substitution policies. Thus they favoured market-driven integration. Countries adopted 'orthodox' policies which were precisely contrary to those which had been successful in previous periods of industrialisation: financial credibility restraint, free capital movements, abolition of selective trade policies, dismantling of oligopolies (unbundling), reduced protection levels, and liberalised administrative processes and regulatory policies [*Coussy, 1996*].

SAPs were conceived in a country-specific framework; they were initiated at different dates, and with different sequencing for implementing their policies. In some cases, their financial policies ran counter to the financial plans of regional groups.

Unilateral liberalisation (exchange-rate reform, reduced and rationalised protectionist measures, relaxation of various types of restrictions on ownership, etc.) has facilitated regional trade and investment in East Asia, for example. But in sub-Saharan Africa, unilateral liberalisation has often reduced the industrial capacities of the more vulnerable industries – for example, in Cameroon and Zimbabwe – and led to a deindustrialisation of African countries which, in turn, has resulted in cutting regional ties even though currency convertibility exists. Most sub-Saharan countries, for example, are in a process of unilateral liberalisation, in contradiction to regional agreements and efforts to harmonise trade and exchange policies between members of entities such as SADC or COMESA in Southern Africa. example.

Compatibility between Regionalism and the WTO

One of the important debates in liberal circles is whether regional trade arrangements are contrary to the non-discriminatory principle of the GATT/WTO most favoured nation clause [*Bhagwati, 1993*]. For its supporters, regionalism is an answer to globalisation and offers a number of real advantages, such as control over economic and monetary policies, added weight in multilateral negotiations, attraction of investment, greater power to negotiate common social and environmental norms, etc.

We distinguish two basic forms of multilateralism – the universalist and the co-operative form [*Siroen, 1995*] – and three types of regionalism – federal state-driven integration, market-driven integration, and regional networks. Federal regionalism is compatible with co-operative multilateralism but not with the universalist form; on the other hand, market-driven integration is compatible with universalist multilateralism.

Current Economic Analysis

Traditional analysis: Traditionally, the argument in favour of regional economic agreements was that integration should lead to more efficient use of a region's capital, labour and natural resources. It was argued that these potential economic benefits would result from economies of scale, increased specialisation, increased competition, as well as improved terms of trade.

The traditional debate contrasted market-driven integration with state-driven integration:

- In market-driven integration, the aim is free trade, though limited here to a region and to a given period of time. It is the 'second-best' solution, implemented to foster trade creation at the expense of trade diversion (Meade, Viner), to stimulate trade among members of the group, and thus increase their share in world trade. This traditional analysis centres on trade links among members and on the effects of trade on non-members;

- In state-driven integration, the objective is protectionism *vis-à-vis* the world market. The motives for this were that small countries might find it useful as it eases their entry into markets, through initial economies of scale, learning by doing, training, and so on. It strengthens their competitive and comparative advantages in a protected space, the first step towards confronting international competition. It is based on the importance of joint action in an unequal world, creating a stronger bargaining position in relation to the rest of the world and improving terms of trade in this way. Within the protected area, specialisation based on regional comparative advantages helps to avoid duplication of sub-optimal firms.

In reality, however, firms in many developing economies do not benefit from economies of scale as supply constrains them more than demand. Moreover, these countries have often attained different levels of development which makes it even harder to agree on regional protection for the most vulnerable firms.

Recent theories: Several new theories have appeared recently which examine globalisation from different angles.

- For a number of economists, *the role of FDI and of transferable competitive advantages* is crucial. In their view, the determining factor in the context of globalisation is to attract capital and technology. In regions, firms tend to join forces through networks in order to compete with multinationals. In Europe, Asia and Southern Africa the most important effect is probably the role of the private sector and of corporate capitalism in holding back regional processes.

  These conglomerates maintain complex relations with the state and are quite far from the ideal model of 'perfect competition'. Large firms calculate profitability in the long term; they also benefit from economies of scale, new

97

management technology and technical advances. Indeed, in its impact on regions, FDI influences access to technology and accumulation of physical and human capital more than it increases intra-regional trade.

Besides FDI, another transferable competitive advantage should also be considered – the so-called *contagion and imitation effect* in a hierarchical space (Akamatsu, Petri). In East Asia, economic growth has been partly induced by regional contacts and through imitation brought on by such factors as flows of goods, investments, new technology, aspirations, governance, Japanese industrial strategy, and so on. These external ties have been reinforced by the region's focused outward-oriented development strategies [*Petri, 1993*]. In the case of East Asia, it is clear that imitation does not signify duplication but is seen rather as a challenge to overtake.

However, an innovative environment favourable to the creation of enterprises may in some cases reverse comparative advantages. And, indeed, one observes different contagion effects in sub-Saharan Africa and in East Asia.

• *The new geographical economy* (Krugman) examines competitive advantages resulting from localisation in specific territories which engender cumulative effects.

Territorial comparative advantages can cover both industrial districts and new forms of co-ordination and exchange, such as the Chinese network in East Asia, growth triangles (Greater South China, Greater Mekong sub-region) or the Maputo Corridor project in sub-Saharan Africa, for example. These organisations and networks encourage economic growth by widening international contacts and creating agglomeration processes between different regions or countries. Proximity to common resources and well developed transportation and communication systems are all-important factors of competitiveness. At the same time, links between firms and between networks reduce transaction costs. Networking induces economic efficiency in global firms and leads them to evolve from a traditional vertical hierarchy towards more democratic, horizontal models.

The so-called *gravity theory* examines interaction between levels of GDP, diversification of imports and exports, and intensity of regional trade, as well as other factors such as distance, formal and informal cultural blocs, language, historical ties, similar commercial distortion policies, etc. Indeed, trade among Asian countries is characterised not only by economic factors such as resource endowment and relative economic size (GNP, GNP/population), but also by the proximity of neighbouring countries (distance, contiguity).

Frankel [*1991*] has described a regional bloc bias, quite specific to East Asian Economic Caucus (EAEC) countries. In his view, such a regional bloc bias is more important in East Asia than it is in the European Union or in the

Western hemisphere, although the intra-regional base of ASEAN countries diminished during the 1980s.

As for *endogenous growth models*, they include agglomeration effects, information and communication systems, public equipment and infrastructure. 'Spatial capital' can therefore be defined as the sum of localised production capacities which increase the productivity of other factors of production. Concentration of spatial capital in given regions leads to the contrast between centres and peripheries. Centres can be characterised by polarisation effects (as in Southern Africa), or by diffusion effects (as in East Asia); divergence in performance is the result of the initial endowment of spatial capital [*Akanni-Honvo and Leon, 1998; Hugon, 1998*].

Polarised and asymmetrical regional integrations are characterised by disparities in size, concentration of the trade surplus at the centre, net outflows of capital from the centre to the periphery, and migration from the periphery to the centre; specialisation of manufactured industries and advanced technologies at the centre and relegation of primary production to the periphery; centralisation of decision-making.

• In the context of globalisation, the specific *institutional rules and norms* which characterise the international environment play a major role, acting, on the one hand, as a factor of competition and a means of attracting capital, and, on the other, as a new form of protectionism. In order to attract foreign investors, it is necessary to create an atmosphere of confidence and security and a stable environment with credible economic policies. Indeed, one of the important positive results of globalisation for small and developing countries has been their propensity to lock their reforms into those of larger and more developed countries and to take advantage of the credibility thus provided.

This *institutional approach* has led to discussion of other new issues:

(i)   the contrast between federal regionalism, as experienced in Europe, and co-operative regionalism, as encountered in the growth triangles – which could be summarised as co-operation with compatibility of different national interests (game theory);

(ii) the so-called role of 'guarantor' played by developed countries in order to build confidence, ensure that economic policy is credible, and attract foreign capital – which has resulted from vertical integration between North and South (NAFTA, East Asian Economic Caucus);

(iii) de Melo's institutional approach, protecting certain decisions from national lobbies for example, creating institutions, adopting the model of the

Bundesbank for the EU central bank, for example [*de Melo and Panagariya, 1993*];

(iv) the question of institutional transition in a long-term development process characterised by learning periods as well as by trial and error;

(v) the issue of stabilisation and reduced uncertainty, such as would result from regional cereal storage, for example; the trade-off between enhancing trade and regional integration and confronting the risks of market instability.

IV. TWO CONTRASTING REGIONALISATION PROCESSES: THE CASES OF EAST ASIA AND OF AFRICA

East Asia Globalisation and Regionalism Combined

Managed or controlled opening: Between 1960 and 1995, real growth of South-East Asian GDP averaged 5.5 per cent, twice that of sub-Saharan Africa. Economic dynamics require countries to catch up to the standards of living of industrialised nations by accumulating production factors – especially human and material capital resources – by means of high domestic saving rates. In East Asia, investment and saving rates both approach 30 per cent. The area's share in world exports rose from six per cent in 1965, to 17 per cent in 1980, and to 25 per cent in 1994. Today, the openness ratio (exports/GDP) averages approximately 40 per cent.

TABLE 4.1
OPPOSITE SEQUENCES IN AFRICA AND EAST ASIA

a	b	c	d	e
East Asia				
'Good' institutional environment, economic policies	Economic growth	Diversification of industrial structure, change of specialisation	Managed or controlled opening	Regional ties (networks, contagion effect)
Sub-Saharan Africa				
'Bad' institutional environment, economic policies	Economic stagnation	No diversification of industrial structure and specialisation	Marginalisation Aid	Few regional ties 200 regional organisations

In parallel with its opening to world markets, domestic production underwent enormous changes. The volume of intra-firm trade increased and was re-oriented within East Asia (in 1994 the volume of regional trade was 50 per cent higher than for Asia as a whole); and output diversification followed, evolving from light unsophisticated consumer goods to relatively simple capital-intensive products, to more sophisticated technology-intensive goods [*Lautier, 1996*].

Three distinct developments are observed in East Asia: the rapid growth of intra-regional trade, an upsurge in intra-regional investments and the emergence of sub-regional economic areas. Regional trade has increased in consumer goods, services, and low-technology goods, as well as in high-technology and intra-firm trade. The more industrialised countries of the area – Japan and more recently the NIEs – have progressively become the driving forces in regional trade with the development of intra-regional investments and other capital flows, to the point that today intra-regional trade has become more important than extra-regional trade.

With the exception of Malaysia, Thailand and Indonesia, the share of intra-regional trade has increased significantly in this region. ASEAN countries experienced phenomenal growth in trade volume during the 1980s, explained by the combined effects of an acceleration in the tendency towards vertical integration of production, a general trend towards trade liberalisation, an increased level of income in the Asian NIEs, restructuring of the Japanese economy, and, last but not least, the development of China.

Non-programmed open regionalism: Except in ASEAN, no significant regional institutions were set up. Recently, however, some free-trade zones and regional links have emerged, and formal regional trade agreements have been initiated by Australia (APEC) and Malaysia (East Asian Economic Caucus – EAEC).

A combination of several factors has led to this 'open regionalism' or 'informal bloc': the role of Japan in what is a clearly hierarchical process, the role of Chinese networks in a more and more 'Chinese world', and the effect of countries' policies, as well as the strategies of firms, adapting to the necessities of world-wide specialisation. Here, as in other situations, regional processes have resulted from the general economy, growth, and more open policies, but they have also been encouraged by cultural, linguistic, historical and political ties, as well as emerging from pragmatism.

Mixed policies and created competitive advantages: In East Asia, regionalism was not initially planned, nor was it institutionalised, except in the case of ASEAN and, more recently, APEC and the Greater Mekong sub-region. It resulted from a combination of managed outward-looking policies, economic growth and sectoral diversification. The current degree of opening has been all the more effective because it followed support for infant industries. In this region, integration has indeed been able to find a balance between the market economy and state intervention, promotion of exports and import substitution, foreign investment and local saving.

On the one hand, macroeconomic policies were traditional and orthodox *vis-à-vis*, for example, the public sector deficit, inflation, foreign debt, real interest rates and currency levels, i.e. the realignment of exchange rates following the 1985 Plaza Agreement. By opening to the outside world, these countries had access to foreign technologies which they adopted and adapted to their own needs. But it is correct to state that macroeconomic stability was necessary to do this, and that it has been a key factor in the East Asian success story.

On the other hand, industrialisation was encouraged by non-regulatory means. A number of active interventionist policies, protectionist laws, allocations of credit at preferential rates, subsidies for exports and industries in difficulty were available. Governments were able to anticipate economic developments and to offer support.

The role of Japan, of NIEs and of Chinese networks and transferable competitive advantages: Japan, and more recently the NIEs, undertook the role of economic leaders in East Asia. Japan has been a major exporter towards the region and had a net trade surplus – though a change did occur during the latter part of the 1980s. It is also the major investor in the area. Together with the so-called 'New Tigers', Japan has been increasing investment in and transferring production to the low-wage countries and the new emerging markets of the region. This seems to prove the point that regional dynamics are hierarchical and, in a world of imperfect competition, they at least partially follow the theory of product life-cycles and of technological rents (The Flight of the Wild Geese, according to Akamatsu). A similar movement is also visible in the overseas-Chinese trade and financial networks. There is an emergence of innovative circles which reverse comparative advantages. The process resembles shock waves spreading out through concentric circles.

Traditionally, foreign investment in Asian-Pacific developing countries came mainly from Western/developed countries. Because of the changing pattern of comparative advantages and the liberalisation and deregulation processes in different countries, the role of Japan and of the NIES as foreign investors in the region, has become increasingly important in the past few years.

There are four main reasons for this: the hierarchy of comparative, as well as transferable competitive, advantages, the over-evaluation of the yen, Japan's need to increase its surplus, and its will to be present on emerging markets.

Territorial competitive advantages: The increase in trade among Asian nations can be explained by natural proximity and gravity effects resulting from the overwhelming economic growth of Japan and its neighbours. To these, one must add the agglomeration effects due to huge urban areas and the high density of population. Transportation and communication systems in East Asia are extremely dense and high-performing, resulting in low transaction costs; financial and monetary markets are also very dynamic. Moreover, as mentioned earlier, economic actors have created new forms of co-ordination such as the Chinese networks and growth triangles (Greater South China, Greater Mekong sub-region). The formidable result is that EAEC members exchange seven times more goods than if they were not part of the bloc.

Convergence between macroeconomic indicators: Macroeconomic indicators, such as inflation rates, public sector deficits, openness ratios and terms of trade have tended to converge, drawing Asian countries closer to an Optimal Monetary Zone. However, exchange rates are tied more closely to the dollar than to the yen which is not used extensively, either for trade transactions or as a vehicle currency: Asian countries are *de facto* in a dollar zone. This makes them – with the exception of Indonesia – vulnerable to external shocks: indeed, the Mexican crisis of December 1995 led to an attack on the Thai baht and revealed the high degree of currency vulnerability in emerging financial markets. Following this, the ASEAN countries developed monetary co-operation and swap agreements among regional Central Banks.

Marginalisation and Failures of Regional Integration in Sub-Saharan Africa

Economic stagnation and international marginalisation: Sub-Saharan Africa is characterised by long-term stagnation in growth rates, low investment rates (15–20 per cent) and even lower saving rates (10–15 per cent); its debt approaches the level of GDP. With the exception of South Africa, Sub-Saharan Africa still confronts so-called traditional 'colonial problems', including competing primary exports, low levels of industrialisation, and little or no diversification of the economies. There has been no significant long-term increase in productivity.

The integration of sub-Saharan Africa into the world economy is therefore limited. It has lacked the two necessary weapons of 'global competitive strategies', namely, competitiveness and attraction for foreign capital. Until 1990, most countries in the region were less and less integrated into the world economy. Exports grew 1.5 percentage points less than output from 1971 to 1985 and 0.7 per cent less for the period 1986–90. They exceeded output growth by 0.9 per cent for the period 1991–96 [*World Bank, 1995*].

Integration failures: SACU and its associated common monetary area – both established in 1910 – are the most successful examples of institutional regionalism in sub-Saharan Africa. They were set up to meet the needs of the large companies in the region and the interests of corporate capitalism in developing and maintaining strong relations with the state. The monetary integration of the 'Franc Zone' is the other successful integration process found in the subcontinent.

The independence of several African countries brought a 'balkanisation' process which increased the external vulnerability of the world's most fragile subcontinent. However, during the 1970s, East Africa benefited from a customs union, a monetary union, and a number of common services, including higher education, agricultural and medical research, transportation and communication systems. In West Africa, CEAO performed well in terms of intra-group trade flows and other indicators such as a monetary union, financial compensation schemes, etc.

Following the impact of the financial crisis of the 1980s, regional integration in Africa failed for several reasons: the large number of distinct formal integration propositions and inconsistency between them, inadequate compensatory mechanisms, barriers to labour migration, reduction in intra-African trade flows, the magnitude of informal and parallel trade, and also financial crises in the existing regional integration organisations themselves. State-imposed integration doctrines and measures were incapable of holding out, and they consequently collapsed.

Despite the extensive institutionalisation – more than 200 regional organisations have been set up in the area – several factors which had appeared prior to the financial crisis and the SAPs played a role in the failure of the integration process. In Africa, as elsewhere, the disintegration of the colonial empires and the rise of nationalism had extensive implications, leading to political opposition to regions. Certain structural factors, such as the competing nature of primary exports, the low degree of complementarity between economies, and low levels of development were significant. Competition for aid has also impeded regional integration. Regional integration is likely to be easier to achieve when the national productive systems themselves have become coherent and national political integration has been accomplished.

Success and revival of regionalism in the 'Franc Zone': The 'Franc Zone' brought a monetary union among West and Central African central banks in the framework of the West and Central African Economic and Monetary Unions, UEMOA, and CEMAC, together with a fixed exchange rate tied to the French franc, and support for the CFA franc ensured by the French Treasury and a pool of foreign currencies.

In the 'Franc Zone', especially in the UEMOA, regional integration was strengthened after the devaluation of the CFA franc in January 1994 with the simultaneous acceptance of commitment to transform the monetary union into an economic union. Priority was given to legal and institutional unification aspects, such as insurance regulations. A process leading towards a regional monetary and financial market was elaborated, which ensured multilateral supervision of financial indicators and criteria of convergence, with the objective of a common currency without the 'guarantee' of the French Treasury.

Notwithstanding these measures, the 'Franc Zone' has not become an optimal currency area. Interdependence among the economies and intra-regional trade and capital flows have remained limited. External and internal shocks have been important. Investment, especially foreign investment has failed to respond to the new initiatives, and the debt problems of many countries such as Côte d'Ivoire and Cameroon are still serious. Two hopes remain, however: one, the advent of the euro in 1999, and secondly, the possibility of developing monetary co-operation with non-'Franc Zone' countries such as Ghana and Nigeria in the near future.

Success and revival of regionalism in Southern Africa: With intra-regional trade averaging only seven per cent, Southern Africa – with the exception of SACU – is not a well integrated area [*Cassim, 1995*]. Moreover, its two regional entities, COMESA (formerly PTA) and SADC (formerly SADCC) overlap considerably, and there are too many other regional initiatives.

In the path towards the regional integration of the area, South Africa has played an important historical role and also an ambiguous one. South Africa's private sector successfully undertook regional integration by constructing transportation networks which allowed the cross-border migrations of hundreds of thousands of workers towards South Africa, and developing regional trade, transfers of migrants' remittances, and so on. During the 1970s and 1980s, dependence on South Africa was considerable and most Southern African countries suffered from the South African strategy of destabilising its neighbours, politically and economically. Six of the 11 SADCC countries have no outlet to the sea and six share borders with South Africa. In the early 1980s, 90 per cent of all SADCC exports had to use South African ports and routes.

Since 1991, with the advent of political changes in South Africa as well as internal and external liberalisation, immigration has increased considerably. In its relations with other Southern African countries, South Africa's trade and trade surplus have expanded greatly, and intra-regional capital flows have risen rapidly, especially in mining, food processing, and distribution. Transportation is crucial.

Reasons for Africa's lack of competitiveness: Three reasons can explain Africa's lack of competitiveness at both the regional and the international level.

(i) Absence of 'good' economic policies and no created competitive advantages

In contrast to East Asia, and with the partial exceptions of the 'Franc Zone' and

South Africa, macroeconomic policies in Africa have not been orthodox in the areas of public sector deficits, inflation, foreign debt, real interest rates, exchange rates, and so on. At the same time, no long-term industrial strategy has been elaborated. Borders are porous, allowing for smuggling, the degree of real protection is quite constrained, and the institutional framework lacks structure. Instability of economic indicators and policies leads to uncertainty and risks too high for concentrated long-term investment. This, in turn, precludes industrial transformation, adapted to international specialisation and diversification – and primary commodities remain 90 per cent of total exports.

In the 'Franc Zone' and South Africa, macroeconomic management plays a strong role in influencing the external balance of the economy and in developing intra-regional links, but it remains an insufficient condition for successful economic performance.

(ii) *Absence of transferable competitive advantages*

Under the colonial system, Europe was the dominant economy. Following the independence of African countries, Europe remained their main economic partner, though the reverse was never true. Except in the mining and petroleum sectors, foreign direct investment tended to fall. As for aid, it has not necessarily favoured development. In the context of the permanent debt which has characterised Africa for several decades, the continent has been receiving monies in the form of a constant stream rather than a transitory transfusion.

Some African countries – Nigeria or South Africa, for example – could play the role of centre, but the polarisation effect is stronger than the contagion effect. While economic links with South Africa are important for a number of Southern African countries, the reverse is not true. The bulk of South African trade is directed towards Europe, and now increasingly towards East Asia and Latin America.

Although South Africa is the ideal centre in a future regional integration process, it balks at accepting the duties of a 'substitute metropole'. Like other regional hegemons, South Africa explains its accession to SADC as a political move, with motives comparable to those which drove the United States to join NAFTA and the EU to associate with the Maghreb: fear of migratory pressure and of disturbances along its borders, job creation in the periphery, demands for capital from countries in the periphery. However, it is far from clear that South Africa will 'agree to cover the financial costs of other duties assigned to the leader, such as relocating activities, granting financial assistance, guaranteeing financial credibility, reducing the undesirable effects of polarisation, and so on' [*Coussy, 1996: 27*].

(iii) *Lack of territorial competitive advantages*

Although a number of territorial advantages such as natural resources or low wage levels do exist in Southern Africa, other factors – including poor labour skills, lack of agglomeration effects, high transportation and communication costs, weak money and financial markets – reduce the competitivity of its products with the exception of those from South Africa.

It is difficult for countries which export the same primary products to trade and integrate not only in international production markets, but also at the regional level. Transportation costs are generally very high and account for as much as 30–40 per cent of the total value of a given product. To reduce these costs some integration measures have been attempted. The Maputo corridor – a network of five interconnected distinct transportation systems – is an outstanding example. It has succeeded in stimulating economic growth by opening participating countries to the international market and by creating agglomeration effects [*Blanc, 1996*].

Comparison Between These Two Regional Processes

The regionalisation processes encountered in these two parts of the world are manifestly different. In Africa there is an institutional effort to modify international marginalisation and economic stagnation, whereas in East Asia an informal process of open regionalism has led to a situation combining growth and controlled opening. The past histories of these countries, in particular the contrast between the legitimacy of the State in Asia and the role of colonisation in the industrialisation process, explain in part these different attitudes, reactions and results. Japan's role in East Asia differs considerably from that of Europe in Africa – and has for some time.

At the same time, regional processes in East Asia and in Southern Africa share some common history. In both cases, capital accumulation was initially made possible by the existence of a primary export industry sufficient to generate considerable profits which financed new industries, more diversified activities, and, most important of all, import substitution. Asia and Africa have also shared other characteristics including authoritarian regimes, interpenetration of the private and public spheres, corporatism, the invasive role of conglomerates and economic planning.

However, as we have seen, East Asia has been able to offer a large, diversified and competitive industry to the world market, and it reinvests in its own industrial activities. In Sub-Saharan Africa, on the other hand, only South Africa has become competitive, and here again, only in the regional market, with most intra-regional investment concentrated in mining.

The future of regionalism for Africa: Today there are three main regional blocs

107

in the world, with three main centres: the United States, the European Union, and in East Asia: Japan and the Chinese networks. In such a context, Africa has first to consider with which strategic centre it will develop economic and political links in the future. It has then to examine the specific role of South Africa as a secondary centre and as an intermediary between the peripheral African countries and the three main centres.

The future of Lomé IV and the current negotiation of a free trade area between South Africa and the EU are crucial for the future of African regionalism. Europe is sub-Saharan Africa's major partner. It accounts for 40 per cent of South Africa's exports and represents 52 per cent of all foreign investments in the country. In spite of the depreciation of the rand in 1995, South African industries are less competitive than their European counterparts. There have been several discussions in the negotiations on the agricultural products which the EU wishes to exclude from the FTA, as well as the time which will be given to South African industries to adjust to EU products. One of the important effects of the agreement would be to set a framework for South African trade reforms. Moreover, by reducing the level of uncertainty, it would render the country's trade liberalisation programmes more credible and more attractive to foreign investors. On the other hand, the implications of an FTA for South Africa's neighbours could be problematic; the immediate effect would be the loss of customs duty revenues for SACU members. (All SACU members other than South Africa are members of the Lomé Convention.)

V. CONCLUDING REMARKS

In a context of globalisation and regionalism, states have to examine how they will decide to regulate their societies in relation to economic, social and political globalisation and regionalisation. In our view, the objective should be to establish different modes of regulation depending on the local, national, regional or international level considered, either by applying the subsidiarity principle, or, more probably, by elaborating new rules and modes of negotiation between asymmetric powers.

No specific authority deals with international regulation – in its strongest sense – although principles are negotiated, orders are imposed, and intergovernmental institutions do elaborate norms and sanctions with the aim of avoiding systemic risk. In the context of globalisation and regionalisation, one therefore has to address the fundamental issue of adequate regulation *vis-à-vis* the various levels of decision-making. The following two examples refer to the European Union.

In the context of increasing financial globalisation, what authority would be most pertinent to avoid systemic risk? In the EU, globalisation of risk has resulted in a two-way movement, on the one hand, towards decentralising (by subsidiarity) prudential responsibilities, and on the other, towards centralising monetary policy. In order to reduce this contradiction, the role of 'lender of last resort' that the European central bank is supposed to play would therefore be essential [*Aglietta et al., 1990*].

Financial relations between donors can be hierarchic (oligopolies with a leader), co-ordinated (with sharing of competence: co-operating oligopoly), or competitive (with more or less differentiated markets). Relations between donor and recipient countries fall into the categories of tutelage, supervision with conditions, or partnership. Because of the priority given to debt management, the Bretton Woods institutions have developed hierarchic, leader-driven relationships between countries, rather than partnership relations, although certain exceptions do exist. The WTO, on the other hand, has accelerated the liberalisation process and at the same time established its responsibility for negotiation. The decision on the post-Lomé Convention is crucial for regionalism. Will free trade agreements, set in the context of multilateral trade, be elaborated? Or, on the contrary, will commercial and financial proceedings which take account of the asymmetry between countries and the different transition processes towards a market economy, be maintained?

REFERENCES

Aglietta, M. *et al.* (1990), *Globalisation financière: l'aventure obligé*, Paris: Economica.

Akanni-Honvo, A. and A. Leon (1998), 'La naissance endogène regionalisée', *Revue Tiers Monde* 155 (July–Sept.), pp.597–612.

BAD (1993), *Economic Integration in Southern Africa*, Vols.I and II, Oxford: Biddles Ltd.

BAD (1995), *Regional Cooperation and Integration in Asia*, Paris: OECD.

Bhagwati, J. (1993), 'Regionalism and Multilateralism: An Overview', in J. de Melo and A. Panagariya (eds.), *New Dimension in Regional Integration*, Cambridge: Cambridge University Press.

Blanc, M.O. (1996), *The Transport Network in Southern Africa as a Regional Integration Component*, IFAS paper.

Bourginat, H. (1995), *Finance Internationale*, Paris: ThJmis.

Cassim, R., (1994), 'Trade and Industry in Southern Africa', Development Policy Research Unit, University of Cape Town, Report prepared for the Development Bank of Southern Africa.

Cassim, R. (1995), 'Rethinking Economic Integration in Southern Africa', *Trade Monitor*, 10, Sept.

Celimene, Cl. and Cl. Lacour (eds.) (1996), *Intégration régionale des espaces*, Paris: Economica.

Coussy, J. (1996), 'Slow Institutional Progress and Capitalist Dynamics in Southern African Integration: Interpretation and Projects in South Africa and Zimbabwe', in *Transformations*, 29.

Coussy, J. and Ph. Hugon (1992), *Intégration régionale et ajustement structurel en Afrique sub-Saharienne*, Paris: La documentation française.

De Melo, J. and A. Panagariya (1993), *New dimensions in regional integration*, Cambridge: Cambridge University Press.

Dunning, J.H. (1992), *Multinational Enterprises and the Global Economy*, London: Addison Wesley.

Forountan, F. and L. Pritchett (1996), *Intra-Sub-Saharan Africa Trade 'Is Too Little'*, Washington, DC: World Bank.

Frankel, Jeffrey (1991), 'Is a Yen Bloc Forming in Pacific Asia?' *Finance and the International Economy 5,* AMEX Bank Review Prize Essays, Oxford for AMEX.

Gipouloux, (1994), *Regional Economic Strategies in East Asia,* Tokyo: Maison franco-japonaise.

Grossman, G. and E. Helpman (1991), *Innovation and Growth in the Global Economy,* Cambridge, MA: MIT Press.

Hugon, Ph. (1989), *L'économie de l'Afrique,* Paris: la Découverte.

Hugon, Ph. (1996), 'Les séquences inversées de la régionalisation en Afrique sub-Saharienne et en Asie orientale', in Ph. Hugon (ed.), *Le régionalisme comparé en Afrique et en Asie,* Paris: CERED.

Hugon, Ph. (1997), *Économie politique internationale et mondialisation,* Paris: Economica.

Hugon, Ph. (ed.) (1998),' La régionalisation comparée en Afrique sub-Saharienne et en Asie de l'Est', *Revue Tiers Monde* 155, special number (July–Sept.).

Hugon, Ph. and P. Robson (1993), *The Regional Dimension of Structural Adjustment in ACP Countries,* Brussels: CEE.

Kenen, Peter B. (ed.) (1994), *Managing the World Economy: Fifty years after Bretton Woods,* Washington, DC: Institute for International Economics.

Krugman, P. (1991), *Geography and Trade,* Cambridge, MA: MIT Press.

Krugman, P. (1993), 'The Narrow and Broad Arguments for Free Trade', *American Economic Review,* Papers and Proceedings, 83, May, pp.362–6.

Lafay, G. (1996), *La mondialisation,* Paris: Economica.

Lautier, M. (1996), 'Dynamiques des structures industrielles et développement. L'organisation industrielle dans le processus d'industrialisation. Le cas de la Corée du Sud et de Taiwan', thesis, Grenoble University.

Page, S. (1998), 'Intensity Measures for Regional Groups', (this volume).

Pangustu, M. (1995), 'Indonesia in a Changing World Environment: Multilateralism vs Regionalism', *The Indonesian Quarterly,* Vol.XXIII, No.2.

Petri, P.A. (1993), 'Common Foundations of East Asian Success', *World Bank Publications.*

Porter, M. (1990), *L'avantage competitif des Nations,* Paris: Dunod.

Redding, S.G. (1990), *The Spirit of Chinese Capitalism,* Berlin: W. de Ruyter.

Sideri, S. (1998), 'Globalization and Regional Integration', (this volume).

Siroen, J.M. (1995), 'La théorie de l'échange international en concurrence monopolistique: une comparaison des modèles', *Revue Économique,* May.

World Bank (1993), *The East Asian Miracle: Economic Growth and Public Policy,* New York: Oxford University Press for the World Bank.

World Bank (1995), *Global Economic Prospects and the Developing Countries,* Washington, DC: World Bank.

PART II

REGIONS AMONG
DEVELOPING COUNTRIES

5

Regional Integration among Unequal States: The European Union and the Southern African Development Community Compared

STEPHEN F. BURGESS

I. INTRODUCTION

The world's regions are undergoing transitions toward greater co-operation and integration in response to changing global political and economic trends. By 1995, the General Agreement on Tariffs and Trade (GATT) had been notified of 33 new regional trade agreements concluded in the four years between 1990 and 1994 ('The Right Direction', *Economist*, 16 Sept. 1995). In contrast, only 209 agreements were reached in the 46 years between 1948 and 1994. One factor behind the boom in regional integration has been diffusion. The success of the European Union in creating an internal market with uniform product standards between 1987 and 1993, and in boosting intra-regional trade, led other countries to strive to emulate the European model. The long-time hegemon of the West and supporter of global free trade through the GATT – the United States – changed course in the 1980s and began to support regional integration in response to the EU's success and the sluggish pace of the Uruguay Round of trade negotiations. Consequently, the US concluded the Free Trade Agreement with Canada in 1988 and the North American Free Trade Agreement (NAFTA) with Mexico and Canada in 1993. The creation of two powerful regional trading blocs has spurred other countries to accelerate the process of regional integration and to develop their own free trade areas.

Another factor in stimulating regional integration has been the 'globalisation' process of the 1980s and 1990s, featuring the spread of investment capital and manufacturing operations by transnational corporations (TNCs) from developed countries to developing countries. Globalisation led to a manufacturing boom in parts of Asia and Latin America, to the development of competitive advantage in the economies of those states, and to an upsurge in intra-regional trade [*Strange, 1992*]. In turn, these conditions set the stage for the lowering of intra-regional trade barriers and for implementing plans for regional integration. Furthermore, the considerable increase in global capital flows contributed to increased competition for investment and to collaboration by states in order to provide the largest economies of scale and the most favorable terms for TNCs. Subsequently, regional trade barriers were lowered, and prospects for integration increased.

While globalisation flourished in the 1980s and 1990s, bipolar competition came to an end, and Western liberalism triumphed. These seismic changes narrowed the range of economic strategies that developing countries could adopt, ousting socialism, statism and import substitution as acceptable alternative options to neo-liberal capitalism. The spread of neo-liberal economic orthodoxy and proselytisation by major western states, the World Bank and the International Monetary Fund led a growing number of developing countries to embrace privatisation and export promotion strategies, to increase regional co-operation, and to formulate plans for integration. The completion of the GATT Uruguay Round of trade talks in 1993 presaged the further lowering of trade barriers on a broader range of commodities, including agricultural goods and textiles, and this has compelled many developing countries to combine forces to create large enough economies of scale to prevent their industries from being overwhelmed in the face of growing global competition.

The 1990s wave of integration has produced NAFTA in 1993, in which Mexico – a middle-income developing country – joined with Canada and the hegemonic United States. In South America, Argentina and Brazil, along with Uruguay and Paraguay, created MERCOSUR in 1991, which eliminated tariffs by 1994; as a result, intra-regional trade quadrupled, from $2.7 billion to $12 billion over the same period [*Kotschwar, 1995: 15*]. In the 1990s, the Association of South-East Asian Nations (ASEAN) accelerated the process of regional co-operation. The doubling in value of the Japanese yen in 1985 led to a fivefold increase in manufacturing investment in South-East Asia in the 1980s and, combined with recessionary pressures, to the lowering of intra-ASEAN trade barriers and large increases in intra-regional trade. These dramatic changes created greater incentives for regional economic integration [*Stubbs, 1994: 371*]. Intra-regional trade has continued to grow, with a 24 per cent increase to US$110 billion in 1994 alone. In response to a growing regional economy, ASEAN pledged to move forward to an ASEAN Free Trade Area (AFTA) by the year 2003. Recently, the timetable for AFTA has been speeded up from 2003 to 2000, in response to plans for the phased introduction of a free trade area within the Asian Pacific Economic Community (APEC) by 2020 and the prospect of competition for capital and markets from China and India.

The favourable global trends for regional integration have reached Southern Africa in the 1990s. The end of bipolar competition provided advantageous conditions for the resolution of protracted conflicts in Namibia, Mozambique, South Africa and Angola. The destabilisation by apartheid South Africa – the adversarial regional hegemon – of the peripheral Group of Front Line States came to an end. With the end of South African subversion and the four-year struggle to establish an African National Congress-led government, the most basic condition for regional co-operation – peace and stability – became attainable. Subsequently, the prospects of developing normal political and economic relations with a hegemonic South Africa and of increasing interactions with a changing global economy compelled the Southern African states to accelerate the pace of regional integration. Furthermore, their acceptance of neo-liberal orthodoxy has forced them to jettison state-centred economic strategies, diminish protectionism and adopt structural adjustment programme designed to foster free market forces and attract foreign investment.

As a consequence of global and regional pressures, Southern African leaders embraced – tentatively – the principle of economic integration in August 1992, when they transformed the Southern African Development Co-ordination Conference (SADCC) into the Southern African Development Community (SADC) – with the ambitious aims of establishing a free trade area and moving towards an economic community. When South Africa joined SADC in August 1994, the prospect of Southern African integration became realisable. In August 1995, SADC's industry and trade co-ordinator, Abraham Pallangyo, announced that mechanisms to promote a free trade zone were to be in place by February 1996 and signed by August. A feasibility study was to be conducted to assess the effect that lowering tariffs and exposure to international competition would have on the smaller, poorer countries in the region. This study was to be a mechanism to 'compensate countries that stand to lose from the loss of import revenue'.[1]

In the wake of its legalisation and the release of Nelson Mandela in February 1990, the African National Congress (ANC) continued to foster close relations with the Group of Front Line States and SADCC/SADC which it had enjoyed as an observer during the 1980s. In deference to the ANC, most Front Line States and SADCC/SADC members formally refused to remove sanctions against South Africa until the transition to a post-apartheid order was guaranteed. Given this solidarity, it was understandable that President Mandela and the transitional regime committed South Africa to SADC and Southern African regional integration less than four months after coming to power. Clearly, they recognised their political affinities with the SADC leaders. The new South African government also viewed SADC pragmatically – as an organisation with a manageable number of member states and with institutional affinities conducive to integration: 'All SADC states, except for Mozambique and Angola, have similar tax structures, commercial codes, property laws, judicial processes, accounting systems and business styles, as well as a

115

common language'.[2]

In contrast, the new government did not opt to join other regional organisations. It evidently considered the Common Market of East and Central Africa (COMESA) to be too heterogeneous and with too many members to be worth joining. South Africa could not contemplate providing the kind of 'side payments' to more than 20 states which it has been making to Botswana, Lesotho, Namibia and Swaziland in return for their participation in SACU.[3] It has not yet joined the Association of Southern African States (formerly the Group of Front Line States) – a sign that it feels that SADC is a more appropriate body to pursue co-operation in political and security affairs, as well as economic matters. It also chose not to join the African Development Bank, because of serious management problems and the prospect of having to shoulder substantial financial burdens.

The purpose of this chapter is to narrow the range of predictions about Southern African integration and to determine if and when meaningful integration will take place. In making predictions about the future of the European Union, there are 'Euro-optimists' who believe that the adoption of a common currency and central bank will occur and will lead to further integration, as opposed to the 'Euro-pessimists' who believe that the EU cannot sustain further integration. In regard to Southern Africa, the range of predictions varies widely. Optimism first arose in the 1950s, as nationalist movements with a commitment to Pan-Africanist principles emerged throughout the region. In the 1960s and early 1970s, the 'optimist camp' assumed that political solidarity among the liberation movements and independent states would translate into post-independence cooperation and even confederation.

The East African Community (EAC) and the Organisation of African Unity (OAU) provided models of the type of integration which would be a step towards continental unity. Consequently, even the most zealous Pan-Africanist was sobered by the break-up of the EAC in the mid-1970s. In response, the leaders and advisors of the Front Line States – in the process of planning for the Southern African Development Co-ordination Conference (SADCC) – cautioned against excessive integration and the surrender of sovereignty. With the founding of the SADCC in 1979, its supporters praised the project-oriented, division-of-labour approach as more likely to succeed, since it respected the independence of member states [*Thompson, 1985: 273–4*]. The role of the Front Line States in the liberation of Zimbabwe in 1980 led optimists to predict that political and economic co-operation in Southern Africa was on an upward spiral:

> The Frontline States scored a major victory with the independence of Zimbabwe, at great cost to their economies. As they unite for

economic liberation, they will score other victories. The SADCC plans are innovative and daring and could evolve into a programme for alleviating dependent capitalist links [*ibid.: 288*].

As South African destabilisation of SADCC ceased and apartheid came to an end, this optimism was resurrected [*Seidman and Anang, 1992*]. The presumption has arisen that South Africa will act as a 'benevolent hegemon' and provide the capital and build the infrastructure to 'jump-start' the SADC economies and promote the type of integration that will lead to economic growth. In a similar vein, but from a different direction, the World Bank and the International Monetary Fund recommended the establishment of a free trade area in Southern Africa as a means of spurring economic growth [*World Bank, 1989*]. A US official asserted that national interests and trade patterns within the region would converge to create positive conditions for integration:

> With the demise of apartheid, the political justification for SADCC's original objectives will fall away, and more rational trade patterns can and will emerge. Member-states will have more freedom to act in their own national interests regarding South Africa, basing economic decisions on economic rather than political considerations. As a result, South Africa, Swaziland, Botswana, Lesotho, Namibia, and perhaps Mozambique could develop into a closely knit economic zone. A similar relationship already exists or is evolving within the context of the South African Customs Union ... The more likely prospect, however, is that SADCC will eventually evolve into a regional trading bloc or common market along the lines of the European Economic Community [*Arnold, 1995: 194*].

Continuing with this scenario, Arnold envisaged South Africa providing hegemonic leadership and the South African rand serving as the common currency for SADC: 'Although a common currency does not exist, in practical terms the freely convertible South African rand serves a similar purpose in most of these countries' [*ibid.: 194*].

SADC pessimists, on the other hand, maintain that there are no prospects for integration in Southern Africa. They base their arguments on the collapse of the East African Community and on the failure of SADCC to meet its two major goals of lessening dependence on South Africa and promoting regional development. Economic decline and political weakness, as well as South African 'destructive engagement' in Mozambique, Angola and other states, made the SADCC states even more dependent upon South Africa and the West than before 1979. The pessimists have also noted that the Southern African leaders have maintained their state-centric strategies and are avoiding deeper co-operation, because it serves the leaders' interests in accumulating power and wealth [*Davies and Martin, 1992*].

A second strand of SADC pessimism, recently articulated by Jeffrey Herbst (1995), contends that South Africa's interest as a middle-income industrialised state lies in engaging with global markets and capital and in ignoring the backward Southern African hinterland. This line of argument conforms to 'globalisation' theory which contends that regional co-operation and state-directed growth are no longer as important for aspiring newly-industrialised countries (NICs) as linkages with global markets and capital flows [*Drucker, 1989; Stopford and Strange, 1991; Strange, 1992*].

The challenge of inequality: If South Africa's interests lie elsewhere, then it is up to the SADC states to persuade the South African government to pursue integration and to attract TNC investment. However, given the much greater size of the South African economy, most SADC states and their leaders will remain apprehensive about being 'swamped' (even further) by less expensive imports and by takeovers of local industries by investors from South Africa. On the other hand, pressures will build up within the barely viable states of Lesotho and Swaziland to incorporate themselves into South Africa [*Herbst, 1995: 160*].

In between the optimists and the pessimists lie the 'SADC realists' who remain sceptical, though not highly negative, about the prospects for integration [*Hawkins, 1992; Oden, 1993; Rich, 1994; Khadiagala, 1994*]. The source of this scepticism is primarily economic – a free trade area would cause polarisation, with South African manufacturing overwhelming SADC's frail industries. Intra-regional trade – excluding South Africa – remains at below ten per cent of total SADC trade, and comparative advantage remains feeble. Exchange-rate policies make many SADC currencies practically non-convertible and render intra-regional trade cumbersome and integration difficult [*Ostergaard, 1993: 33*]. Also in question are the interests of investors from South Africa and transnational corporations. They may not wish to risk their capital in the SADC states, especially given South Africa's historically high tariff rates, nor will they necessarily take advantage of cheap labour costs to develop industries in Southern Africa which would produce inexpensive goods for South Africa and the world market. Established TNCs might oppose a free trade area with the aim of maintaining their monopolistic positions in the individual SADC countries [*Ravenhill, 1980*]. Finally, the weakness of the private sector and the relative power of the 'state bourgeoisie' and 'neo-patrimonialism' in Southern Africa would make the degree of liberalisation necessary for a free trade area difficult to attain [*Bratton and van de Walle, 1994*].

If the SADC pessimists are correct, Southern Africa will remain disorganised, and the region and the rest of the continent will remain mired in poverty, instability and tyranny. If South Africa chooses to ignore the hinterland, the result will be an increasing flood of immigrants to South Africa and conflicts near its borders. If the SADC optimists are correct, and deep integration does take place, the future of the Southern African states will be more economically secure and politically stable, and democratisation could progress smoothly. If South Africa chooses to serve as the 'Japan of Southern Africa', its capital could be used to stimulate other economies and generate free trade areas. The 'SADC model' could be diffused to the rest of Africa and could, for instance, move ECOWAS in West Africa toward deeper integration. African economies by themselves will remain too small and too poor for the foreseeable future to develop and to compete on their own in the global economy, and regional integration will remain a necessity for them.

II. METHODOLOGY

In this chapter, the range of predictions about SADC is narrowed through comparative case-study analysis, with particular attention paid to the most successful case of integration, the European Union, especially during periods of dramatic progress – 1957–65 and 1984–92. A comparative analysis, focusing on the 'best-case scenario', provides a model from which conditions for integration can be identified. Periods of relative stagnation in the EU, particularly the 1965–84 period, are examined to determine why the integration process stalled. To a similar end, the cases of the ASEAN Free Trade Area (AFTA), MERCOSUR and NAFTA are considered, and the reasons for recent successes explored. From the 1960s to the 1980s, attempts at regional co-operation outside Europe produced nominal integration and little regional free trade. Unsuccessful cases from this period are scrutinised to discover what political and economic conditions were missing. The two overriding problems seemed to be economic nationalism and a low volume of intra-regional trade [*Langhammer and Hiemenz, 1990; Blomqvist et al., 1993*].

Cases of integration efforts in Europe and other regions are examined in order to address the issue of how states 'take off' from nominal co-operation to achieve 'real' integration in the form of a free trade area, customs union, common market and/or economic community with substantial intra-regional trade and effective supranational institutions. Along with appropriate economic and geo-political conditions, it seems logical that a political catalyst has been necessary to bring about change in the successful cases.

The principal issue in this chapter concerns the types of incentives which bring poor and rich countries together in regional integration. Poor countries need to guard against polarisation and further impoverishment. Rich countries must avoid giving too much away to poor countries. In the case of the EU, the inequality can be examined in terms of Germany and the other rich states and the 'poor four' – Portugal, Greece, Ireland and Spain.

A final issue pertains to the development of regional integration, namely, the stages through which integration must pass and the growth of supranational institutions. The EU took more than thirty years to develop into an economic union and still needs to overcome resistance to a common currency and a common monetary policy before true union can be achieved.

In predicting the future of SADC based upon lessons from the EU, questions about the divergent conditions between Southern Africa and Europe need to be answered. The greatest doubts are raised about economic disparities within SADC [*Oden, 1993*]; for instance, a much greater gap exists between South Africa and Mozambique – exacerbated by underdevelopment in the latter – than between Portugal and Germany. Also, the low levels of intra-regional trade in SADC are reminiscent of similar conditions in the 'failed' regional schemes of the 1960s through to the 1980s. The SADC states appear to lack both the comparative and the competitive advantage with South Africa which would justify the creation of a free trade area. The answer to these questions lies in the changing international political economy and, in particular, the transformed behaviour of TNCs [*Strange, 1992*]. With the 1990s and 'globalisation', TNCs are more likely to seek out favourable conditions for competitive advantage in which to invest their capital. Consequently, if Mozambique is stable and can freely export goods to South Africa, TNCs will take advantage of the cheap labour costs and low tax rates to invest there, thereby stimulating intra-regional trade. In conclusion, economic disparities between Europe and Southern Africa are no longer as important in discouraging comparative analysis and inferences as in the past.

III. INTEGRATION 'TAKES OFF'

European integration occurred in fits and starts, with two major leaps forward – from 1957 to 1965 and from 1984 to 1992. The first major initiative brought the European Economic Community (EEC) into existence, eliminating tariff and non-tariff barriers among the member states, creating a common external tariff, liberalising some capital and labour flows, and integrating some economic policies, notably with the Common Agriculture Policy (CAP). The European Commission and other supranational institutions were created – between 1958 and 1970 – to direct the process of economic integration. The plans for a supranational community came to a halt in 1965 and 1966, when President De Gaulle threatened to withdraw France from the EEC.

From 1966 to 1984, the European Community came under inter-governmental control through the Council of Ministers and the European Council (of heads of government). In 1984, the second wave of integration was launched with negotiations for a Single European Act, under which more than 300 product standards of the 12 member states were harmonised in order to establish a barrier-free internal market by 1993. The supranational institutions were given more power, while the power of the individual states and intergovernmental institutions was lessened. In December 1991, the Maastricht Treaty was signed, creating the European Union (EU), with plans for a European currency, central bank, and foreign and defence policy and for the strengthening of the European Parliament. However, momentum towards union was slowed in 1992, particularly by the crisis in the European Monetary System (EMS).

In comparing the European 'take-offs' of the 1950s and 1980s, 'preference convergence' among intergovernmental actors has been found to be the political catalyst [*Keohane and Hoffman, 1991; Moravcsik, 1991; Cameron, 1992; Tsebelis and Kreppel, 1995*]. Preference convergence occurs when governments of the political centre arise, which are influenced by interest groups favouring the free flow of trade, capital and labour and opposed to protectionism. Centrist governments replace protectionist ones, either of the right influenced by small business, or the left by organised labour. Such moves towards the centre occurred in the early 1950s and early 1980s, providing the consensus on integration necessary for take-off. Subsequently, governments that were pushing for integration were able to bargain with less enthusiastic ones and provide 'side payments' to secure success.

In 1955, the foreign ministers of the three smallest states – Belgium, the Netherlands and Luxembourg, members of the Benelux Customs Union – proposed a European Economic Community at a meeting of the European Coal and Steel Community (ECSC). The Benelux countries had conceived of plans for a European customs union during the Second World War and believed that a multi-sectoral trading community would be more effective in developing integration than the coal and steel sectoral framework that had been proposed by the French and embodied in the ECSC. They also felt that an economic community would be less controversial than the type of political or defence integration which had produced several 'failed communities', including the European Defence Community (EDC). In proposing the EEC, the underlying interests of the Benelux countries were to bind West Germany into a confederal arrangement in order to prevent another world war, to strengthen Western Europe against the 'Soviet threat', and to gain access to the larger markets of West Germany, France and Italy [*Urwin, 1995: 74*].

The Benelux proposal was supported by West Germany and Italy. All five countries had Christian Democrat-led governments of the centre which eschewed strong nationalism. Also, the EEC was backed by the hegemonic US as a logical extension of the Marshall Plan and the Organisation of European Economic Co-operation (OEEC) which had stimulated trade and prosperity during the 1950s. The only one holding out was France which, with left-of-centre governments under the Fourth Republic, rejected broad integration and preferred a planned sectoral approach which would allow for protection. The Benelux foreign ministers were able to finesse French resistance to the EEC by agreeing to EURATOM – the European Atomic Energy Agency – which had been a pet French project. The Benelux countries, West Germany and Italy also agreed to make 'side payments' to France in the form of aid to the francophone overseas territories [*Urwin, 1995: 78*]. Also, France was attracted to the EEC by the prospect of further tying West Germany to itself by means of integration – a key national interest.

In the early 1980s, European integration was stalled and drifting in reverse. The French Socialist government was pursuing expansionist and protectionist policies which were undermining the European Monetary System (EMS) and plans for further deepening free trade within the European Community (EC). France was also blocking the applications of Portugal and Spain – two poorer countries which would compete with France in agriculture. Britain was continuing to complain about the size of its annual contribution to the EC, about the CAP and about losing sovereignty to the European Commission. West Germany was refusing to go ahead with the deepening of the EMS and monetary co-ordination until capital controls were liberalised [*Moravscik, 1991: 49*]. Spain and Portugal were apprehensive about joining the EC because of the prospect of having to compete with Germany – a concern shared by Ireland and Greece as members. Finally, the international political economy seemed to be working against the EC, especially with Japanese penetration of the European market and rising unemployment within the Community.

'Euro-sclerosis' was brought to a dramatic end when the Socialist–Communist coalition government of 1981–83 in France was replaced by a more centrist government. In 1984, President Mitterrand quickly reversed the expansionist and protectionist policies and led the EC forward towards the 'internal market'. France agreed to the Single European Act (SEA) under which standards would be harmonised in order to create the internal market, to reforms of the CAP and the reduction of Britain's annual contribution, and to the admission of Spain and Portugal. In response to these concessions and to threats of its exclusion from the EC, Britain agreed to go along with the introduction of majority voting in the Council of Ministers on internal market issues. The 'poor four', including Portugal and Spain, agreed to the SEA in exchange for 'side payments' in the form of greatly increased regional aid – the 'structural fund' – for the development of infrastructure and industrialisation. As the biggest exporter, Germany considered itself to be the main winner, and agreed to increase its annual contribution and to finance most of the side payments.

The Single European Act, the ending of the cold war and the reunification of Germany further propelled the process of European integration forward toward the Maastricht Treaty of December 1991. France, Germany and the European Commission made the argument that the internal market would be unfair to certain member states unless the Community adopted a common currency and established a European central bank which would set monetary policy for all – a move which meant proceeding from an economic community to an economic union. A common defence and foreign policy was proposed, in part because of French anxiety about the future of a united Germany. In negotiating the Maastricht Treaty, France again led the way and made concessions in order to push integration forward. Germany was allowed to house the central bank and to set the course towards monetary union, as well as to map the future confederal development of the European Union (EU) and to strengthen the European Parliament. In return, Germany pledged to stay in the EU and to increase side payments to the 'poor four' including the establishment of a new regional fund. Britain was allowed to delay participation in the monetary union until it felt prepared to join. Since the Maastricht Treaty, the process of integration has again stalled, because of preference divergence. European public opinion had not been convinced of the necessity of integration, and the recession and the cost of German reunification threw the process of monetary integration into reverse.

The two 'take-offs' in European integration occurred primarily because of preference convergence. In the 1950s, the preferences of Christian Democrats converged around the concepts of federalism and supranational planning by the Commission to provide larger economies of scale. The US as hegemon provided resources, both financial and military, for Christian Democrat governments and for the development of regional trade and encouraged the Six to form the EEC. In the 1980s, the convergence was built around a neo-liberal deregulatory programme which was adopted because of changes in the international political economy [*Moravscik, 1991: 71*]. In the 1980s, West Germany and Britain accepted the programme and were joined by the French Socialists when they moved to the political centre. In both cases, the 'take-offs' were intergovernmental initiatives involving prime ministers and foreign ministers (and a French president). Only when the EEC and the SEA came into effect did pressure groups and supranational leaders (for instance, Commission Presidents Hallstein and Delors) become important players.

III. RICH AND POOR STATES

Soon after the founding of the EEC in 1958, poorer countries began to apply for membership and/or associate status. They were attracted by the prosperity of the 'Six' and the early EEC successes and believed that, if they were associated, the prosperity would be diffused. In principle, the EEC held out the prospect of membership to any European country which would be willing to meet its rigorous standards.

In 1973, Ireland became the first poor country to join, largely because its major trading partner – Britain – had joined. At that time, Ireland was an economic backwater, with high unemployment and little industry. Twenty years later, it was prospering, serving as a centre of manufacturing and services and exporting agricultural commodities to the rest of the EU. It benefited from competitive advantage within the EC/EU and from a fairly well-educated population, and was able to avoid marginalisation, probably as a result of conforming to EC/EU standards [*Keatinge, 1993*].

After 20 years as an associate member and after a transition to democracy in the 1970s, Greece was admitted to the EC in 1981. Unlike Ireland, Greece has experienced great difficulties in integrating. Since 1981, the Socialist Party (PASOK) has been in power and has continued to pursue protectionist policies which have often flouted EC/EU regulations. On several occasions, Greece has threatened to leave the Community, and fellow member states have threatened it with expulsion for violating EC/EU rules.

After democratic transitions in the 1970s, Spain and Portugal joined the EC in 1986. During the late 1980s, both prospered, as their less expensive exports to the EC boosted growth [*Marks, 1995*]. Spain became a key player in the Community – just below the level of Germany, France and Britain in importance. However, with the recession of the early 1990s, it experienced a sudden drop in prosperity – with unemployment exceeding 20 per cent. In contrast to Spain, Portugal's lower level of development meant that the economy did not slump so far during the recession [*Lopes, 1993*]. To sum up, in spite of the difficulties experienced, the 'poor four' have remained members of the EC/EU. In general, the benefits which have accrued to the poorer states have not been outweighed by polarisation. While some old industries have been harmed, many have not, and new industries have developed in the poor four to take advantage of this cheap labour and competitive advantage [*Leonardi, 1995*]. In return for meeting membership standards, particularly those imposed by the SEA, the poor EC/EU countries have received 'side payments', in the form of 'structural fund' aid to depressed regions.[4]

Richer countries, such as Germany, have accepted poorer countries, such as Portugal, as EU members, because of established norms and self-interest. From the beginning, EC membership was accessible to all European states which were democratic and were prepared to adhere to the standards of the Community and conform to the rulings of the European Court of Justice and the directives of the Commission. Also, the richer states viewed the poorer members as markets for their industrial exports and a source of less expensive raw materials and light manufactured goods. They were also perceived as an investment opportunity, because of their competitive advantage and cheap labour. In the final analysis, the most important objective for the richer states was stabilising and democratising Europe. EC/EU membership helped guarantee that Greece, Spain and Portugal would not lapse back into authoritarianism. In the coming decade, the Czech Republic, Hungary, and Poland will be admitted – in large part to spread the democratic 'buffer' eastwards and to stem the flow of immigrants that increases with economic and political instability.

IV. STAGES OF INTEGRATION AND SUPRANATIONAL INSTITUTIONS

The EC/EU took 35 years, rather than the initially planned 12, to achieve the goal of a totally free internal market monitored by supranational institutions. In the two periods when it spurted ahead, integration was deepened and the supranational institutions strengthened during periods of preference convergence. In the intervening 20-year period, integration reached a plateau in which a preference for intergovernmentalism predominated. The distinctive feature of European integration has been that supranationalism was accepted at the start in both the ECSC and the EEC. This acceptance reflected the commitment to 'deep' integration of the Benelux foreign ministers and the federalists and planners who wanted to avoid another world war and depression, as well as preference convergence among Christian Democrat governments in the 1950s. Supranational institutions, especially the European Commission, were instrumental in making the common market, the CAP, and other EEC functions work.

Throughout the 'plateau' of the 1970s, the goal of strengthening the supranational institutions was never abandoned. Thus, in spite of neo-liberalism and the 'down-sizing' of government institutions in Europe, preference convergence among EC leaders during the 1980s brought a new wave of deepened integration. As a result, the Commission was strengthened, particularly to implement the internal market, and the powers of the European Parliament were enhanced through the Maastricht Treaty to provide democratic accountability in the EU. The wave of integration in the late 1980s paved the way for the long-sought goal of political co-operation – especially in defence and foreign policy. However, in seeking to fulfil the commitments of the Maastricht Treaty, the EU needs to experience another wave of preference convergence and economic growth – a prospect which seemed remote at the time of writing (1996).

Another distinctive trait of the European integration process has been the promotion of the 'idea of Europe' and the popularisation of a European identity, which helped to weaken the alternatives of right-wing nationalism or revolutionary socialism. The 'idea of Europe' was not exclusionist, though President de Gaulle may have practised exclusion in the 1960s. Besides offering admission to all European countries, which accepted its standards, the Community established good relations with states which opted not to become members immediately. In coexisting with the European Free Trade Area (EFTA), the EC sought to conclude association arrangements which would enhance the free flow of goods. It anticipated EFTA members eventually applying for admission, when they felt the time was right; with the exception of Switzerland, they all joined between 1973 and 1995, although Norway later opted out.

V. RECENT CASES OF 'TAKE-OFF' AND INTEGRATION

The other cases of 'take-off' into integration are not so impressive. In 1991, MERCOSUR was created as the first new customs union – free trade area plus common external tariff – outside of the EU. In the 1980s, Argentina, Brazil, Uruguay and Paraguay all experienced major political changes with the discrediting of military regimes favouring protectionism and import substitution strategies and their replacement by multi-party democracies which favoured liberalisation, privatisation and export-led growth strategies. Preference convergence in the late 1980s was facilitated by the popular demand for democracy and economic stability and an end to inflation. Most important was the rapprochement between the rivals Brazil and Argentina, which resembled the relationship forged by France and Germany in the 1950s. External pressure was applied by the US, the EC, the World Bank, the IMF, and private creditors, which stimulated and in some instances forced the pace of reform. Globalisation touched the Southern Cone, as TNC investment helped to spur industrial growth and intra-regional trade. As a consequence, MERCOSUR became a surprising success, where previous Latin American integration schemes had failed. MERCOSUR has set up a secretariat which monitors free trade and a common external tariff under a customs union [*Kotschwar, 1995*]. However, this does not yet resemble the supranational institutions of the EC/EU, and MERCOSUR still needs to consolidate its status as a customs union before moving on to a common market with free flowing labour and capital.[5]

The EC's success in passing the Single European Act led the United States to propose a free trade agreement with Canada, which was concluded in 1988. In the late 1980s, neo-liberal changes in Mexico and the fast-growing volume of trade between Mexico and the US led to negotiations which were concluded in 1993 with the establishment of NAFTA. The reduction of protectionism in all three countries helped to pave the way for NAFTA, though the hegemonic US supplied most of the incentives in its formation. At the same time, the US's jealous regard for its sovereignty meant that only a free trade area with no supranational institutions could be established. Further integration and EU-style institutions were not a concern for the US. One must therefore conclude that the degree of preference convergence in NAFTA was minor in comparison with that which occurred in the EC/EU and even in MERCOSUR.

The 1980s liberalisation in the ASEAN states and the threat of growing competition from APEC and the EU brought the pledge to form AFTA by the year 2000. However, in comparison with MERCOSUR, democracy and preference convergence have not affected ASEAN as much. Indonesia and Vietnam remain authoritarian and protectionist. Singapore, Malaysia, Thailand and the Philippines all have degrees of authoritarianism and nationalism in their emergent democratic systems. The relatively small level of preference convergence explains why ASEAN has only proposed a free trade area with no supranational institutions of note. Varying degrees of protectionism have ruled out a common external tariff which is the hallmark of a customs union. When AFTA is launched and under way, it will resemble NAFTA more than MERCOSUR.

MERCOSUR, NAFTA, and AFTA have succeeded thus far, while earlier regional integration schemes failed, because of combinations of globalisation and preference convergence. Globalisation of investment by TNCs has provided the means to overcome the problem of intra-regional trade, and the prospect of competition has compelled states to co-operate. Varying degrees of preference convergence have led to the reduction of protectionism and the increased willingness of states to co-operate (see Table 5.1).

TABLE 5.1

INTEGRATION BY PREFERENCE CONVERGENCE

Preference Convergence

	Substantial	*Little*	*None*
Integration	EC 1957-65, 1985-92 MERCOSUR	ASEAN/AFTA, APEC, NAFTA	
No Integration		EC 1970s	ECOWAS, ASEAN, LAFTA, CARICOM

Integration is deepest where preference convergence has occurred. In contrast, the cases of ASEAN/AFTA and NAFTA demonstrate that integration with little preference convergence is shallow and probably will not progress further. In the 1960s and 1970s, the lack of preference convergence and intra-regional trade led to the failure of ECOWAS, LAFTA, and other regional integration efforts. In the 1970s, a weak form of preference convergence existed in the EU, when Chancellor Helmut Schmidt of West Germany and

President Giscard d'Estaing of France forged a close relationship. However, the troubled European economy of the 1970s made efforts to promote deeper integration infeasible.

VI. PREFERENCE CONVERGENCE AND TAKE-OFF IN SADC

Analysis of integration in Europe and other regions demonstrates that preference convergence and intergovernmental bargaining are key factors in determining the trajectory of integration efforts. In the SADC states, conditions for preference convergence have emerged in the 1990s. The liberalisation process has brought significant reductions in protectionism, and the spread of multi-party democracy has led to the emergence of political forces, such as the Movement for Multi-party Democracy (MMD) in Zambia, which profess a commitment to neo-liberalism. At the least, all the SADC states are emerging democracies, and all have mutual political affinities. Nevertheless, serious doubts remain about the depth of commitment to liberalisation and integration and the extent to which preference convergence and intergovernmental bargaining can progress.

All the SADC states are neo-patrimonial, to varying degrees, with governments relying upon patronage to stay in power [*Bratton and van de Walle, 1994*]. Preference convergence and integration would diminish the instruments of patronage at the disposal of leaders. The neo-patrimonialism of the SADC states means that they do not resemble the developed democracies of the EC/EU or the neo-liberal democracies of MERCOSUR, as much as they resemble Mexico and the ASEAN/AFTA states which are more patronage-dependent, nationalist and authoritarian. On the other hand, the political affinities of the SADC states, built up during the independence and anti-apartheid struggles of the 1970s and 1980s, are greater than those among the members of ASEAN/AFTA or NAFTA, and political co-operation has become well-established. To sum up, the chances for preference convergence and fruitful intergovernmental bargaining are greater in SADC than in ASEAN/AFTA, but less than in MERCOSUR and the EC/EU.

While the prospects for preference convergence remain questionable, other factors – such as the rise of South Africa as a legitimate economic and political powerhouse and the spectre of an endless flood of immigrants to South Africa – are driving the ANC government and the other SADC states together. South Africa wants a stable and prosperous Southern Africa so that job-seekers stay at home. The SADC states fear that the fruits of globalisation will be reaped by South Africa and that they will be marginalised. For instance, the South African government is already negotiating a possible free trade agreement with the EU and could do so with other regional organisations and states, and this could pre-empt the benefits of a free trade agreement within SADC. The prospect of a tide of foreign investment capital flowing into South Africa and not into the rest of SADC is compelling the other SADC states to influence South Africa to lower its trade barriers so that TNCs will invest in the region and import goods into South Africa. Of course, it is possible that globalisation may not touch South Africa to any great extent, especially since productivity levels in South African industry remain below those in South-East Asia and the Southern Cone.[6] However, the mere perception that globalisation is approaching provides an incentive for integration. Finally, momentum must count for something. The 1992 conversion of SADCC to SADC, the 1993 GATT Uruguay Round agreement, the 1994 entry of South Africa into SADC, and the 1996 protocol for a SADC free trade area, as well as encouragement from the EU, the US, and the World Bank and IMF, all point towards some progress in integration.

A closer look at each actor in SADC reveals that the impetus toward integration does exist but is weak. In Appendix A5.1, the position on integration, power and salience towards integration of each actor is estimated.[7] In Appendix A5.2, the outcome of bargaining among the various actors is predicted. The South African government, led by President Mandela and the ANC, is obviously the most powerful actor in SADC and could use its power to cover most of the costs of integration, acting as a hegemon.[8] For instance, South Africa could expand the South African Customs Union to include the rest of SADC by offering 'side payments' to the relevant states. However, the salience of South Africa towards integration is not high. While Mandela and the ANC have made statements in favour of integration, they have also cautioned against moving ahead with excessive speed out of a concern that rapid liberalisation might jeopardise South Africa's economic recovery. In fact, the focus of the South African government remains internally oriented on recovery and the Reconstruction and Development Programme, and externally on North America, Europe and the Far East, for the purpose of attracting investment and aid. In addition, powerful interest groups, such as the Congress of South African Trade Unions and domestic manufacturers, fear the consequences of liberalisation for the domestic economy and stand in the way of free trade.

While incentives, such as slowing immigration, exist for pursuing integration more vigorously, there are no interest groups like COSATU within the ANC which are promoting SADC. The Anglo-American Corporation and other regional investors are growing in strength as lobbyists for SADC, but they are not one of the cornerstones of the ANC like COSATU. A sign of the strength of protectionism is the prolonged, seven-year timetable (until 2002) for lowering South Africa's comparatively high tariffs (some as high as 100%) in accordance with the Uruguay Round agreement. As a consequence, SADC cannot expect a free trade area before the beginning of the next century.

If South Africa does not have a high degree of salience towards SADC, then who does? With high salience, the Benelux foreign ministers pressed for the EEC from 1955 to 1957, and President Mitterrand promoted the Single European Act (SEA) from 1984 to 1987 and the Maastricht Treaty from 1990 to 1992. In Southern Africa, the leaders of Zimbabwe, Zambia, Botswana and Malawi appear to have a high degree of salience towards integration in SADC and drawing in South Africa. At the 1995 SADC summit in Johannesburg, Zimbabwe joined with Zambia and Malawi in pressuring South Africa to lower its trade barriers, resolve its trade imbalances and establish preferences for their goods. Zimbabwe's salience stems from a highly disadvantaged trading relationship with South Africa.

In 1992, a preferential trade agreement dating from 1964 expired, and South African tariffs on Zimbabwean goods rose from 30 to 90 per cent. At the same time, Zimbabwe's Economic Structural Adjustment Programme (ESAP) forced a lowering of trade barriers, including those with South Africa. As a result, South African goods flooded into Zimbabwe, and Zimbabwean exports to South Africa slowed. Local industries in Zimbabwe took a pounding and Cone Textiles was liquidated, laying off 6,000 workers. In March 1995, the Zimbabwean government finally persuaded the South African Government to accept, in principle, the necessity of renegotiating the preferential trade agreement, and, in July 1996, initiated a brief 'trade war' to drive the South Africans to take action. However, Zimbabwe sees a SADC free trade area as an opportunity to penetrate the South African market even further, especially now that foreign investment from TNCs is flowing into Zimbabwe.[9] While Zimbabwe has taken bold steps to liberalise and reach out to TNCs and South Africa, neo-patrimonialism and a virtual one-party state remain obstacles to further liberalisation and to integrating with other SADC states.

In moving towards a free trade area, Zambia, Malawi and the other SADC states are trying to correct trade imbalances with *Zimbabwe*, as well as with South Africa. Despite the risk of even greater imbalances and the possibility of polarisation, Zambia, Malawi and Botswana are pressing for a SADC free trade area or even a customs union or common market, as they attempt to attract foreign investment and as they anticipate side payments from South Africa. Of all the SADC states, Zambia has been the most vociferous in favour of free trade and integration. After a steep economic decline from 1973 to 1991, Zambian voters rejected President Kaunda and the one-party state and provided Frederick Chiluba with the mandate to take a new direction. As a result, Zambia has liberalised under a structural adjustment programme and is attempting to attract the foreign investment necessary to rebuild its entire industrial sector and orient it towards exporting.

Malawi, as a recent convert to multi-party democracy, is headed in a similar direction. Botswana and its President, Quett Masire, figure prominently in the integration process, as the site of the SADC secretariat and as a member of

SACU. With consistently high growth rates since the 1960s Botswana is a strong promoter of liberalisation, deregulation, and attracting investment. With improving infrastructure and education and low labour costs, Botswana has begun to attract South African industries to its territory. Mauritius also has a great interest in seeing a SADC free trade area, because of its rapidly growing manufacturing sector and its desire to penetrate the South African market.

Now that the internal conflict has been resolved, Mozambique has a high degree of salience towards SADC. Southern Mozambique possesses the potential to attract industries which will take advantage of the region's lowest labour costs and the proximity to Johannesburg and the largest market in Southern Africa. Furthermore, it would be in Mozambique's interests to promote a SADC common market with free movement of labour so that migrants could move to South Africa for work and send back remittances. A stable and prosperous Mozambique is a goal of South Africa, since Mozambique is the greatest source of immigrants flowing into South Africa. The risk-acceptant attitude of Mozambique stems from having much to gain and very little to lose from integration, and serves as a response to the thesis that the prospect of polarisation precludes integration among rich and poor states.

Within SADC, there are countries with a low degree of salience which will probably accept a free trade area but will not push for it. Namibia, Lesotho and Swaziland accept the *status quo* as members of SACU and the Common Monetary Area (CMA) with South Africa and have not appeared to be important players in the movement towards SADC integration. They already receive substantial side payments from South Africa in the form of customs revenue redistribution and are not as eager as Zimbabwe, Malawi and Zambia to redress trade imbalances or attract investment. In contrast, Tanzania and Angola, are far-removed from South Africa and may opt out of deeper integration. However, increased South African investment in Angola and Tanzania (and, significantly, the Democratic Republic of Congo) may increase their interest in a SADC free trade area.

The SADC secretariat is still limited in its power, but has the highest possible salience and self-interest; consequently, it will keep the integration issue on the agenda of President Mandela and the other SADC leaders and will guide the free trade area towards fruition. The deeper the integration, the greater the chance that SADC will become a supranational organisation with more power and resources at its disposal. As for its 'rival' COMESA (and its backers the UN Economic Commission for Africa and the Organization of African Unity), it lost the battle for South Africa. However, COMESA could seek to become associated with a SADC free trade area, in much the same way as the European Free Trade Area related with the EEC or as Eastern Europe associates with the EU. By 2005 there could be 'concentric rings' of integration, with South Africa in the centre, followed by the CMA, SACU, the SADC free trade area, and, finally, COMESA.

From the preceding analysis of the region as a whole and of individual actors, it is clear that SADC is moving towards becoming a free trade area by 2005. Changes in South Africa and the global economy are forcing the pace of integration. However, the questionable salience of South Africa will force the SADC states with high salience to risk polarisation in order to attract it into the lead in organising the FTA. By 2002, South Africa will have made the necessary adjustments in order to provide leadership and funding. Whether SADC develops any further remains to be seen.

VII. BEYOND A SADC FREE TRADE AREA

The easiest forecast to make is that a SADC customs union will develop, since few obstacles stand in the way of a common external tariff – as long as South Africa agrees to redistribute customs revenue as it currently does with the SACU states. The establishment of a SADC common market with free movement of labour is out of the question, with COSATU standing firm against cheap labour pouring into South Africa. However, the free movement of capital is already becoming a reality, with Zimbabwe removing exchange controls and other states following suit in order to attract foreign capital.

Will SADC ever become a community like the EC? In the area of infrastructure, SADC could be ahead in the game. Moves toward a regional airline, railroad, electric company, banking network, 'telecom' and information super-highway are all under way. However, the 'telephone wars' in Zimbabwe indicate that the neo-patrimonial states are determined to slow the process. In the end, the impetus to modernise backward operations and attract foreign capital will eventually prevail. Through the Group of Front Line States and SADCC, Southern African leaders have already been in the habit of formulating common foreign and defence policies for more than a decade.

On the other side of the ledger, the establishment of a SADC monetary system to stabilise exchange rates and move towards a common currency will prove extremely difficult, as the EU has discovered. The measures needed to stabilise rates – controlling inflation, lowering debt/GDP ratios and reducing budget deficits – require a major 'down-sizing' of government size and expenditures. Few leaders of neo-patrimonial states have demonstrated the willingness to destroy their political base or to further downgrade education, health care and other social services. The ongoing struggle between African states and the World Bank/IMF/structural adjustment crusade stands as witness to the high barrier against currency stabilisation. However, tying SADC currencies to the South African Rand may prove tempting for reformers like Zambia's Chiluba who are not tied to neo-patrimonial states.

The EC/EU experience demonstrates that supranational institutions are crucial to making deep integration work. The establishment of SADC in 1992 brought increased size, importance, and responsibilities for the secretariat in Gaborone. However, there is no sign on the horizon of a SADC 'Commission', with policy-making and regulatory powers, a SADC Court of Justice or a SADC Parliament, and certainly no sign of a SADC central bank. Why not? The SADC states and their leaders are firmly wedded to intergovernmentalism and could not countenance a supranational authority monitoring and penalising them. Obviously, preference convergence in SADC is limited. South Africa would have to cover the costs of supranational institutions, something it is unlikely to do – even if it could move the SADC secretariat to Johannesburg.

Without supranational institutions, recalcitrant states – like Greece in the EC/EU – will not be so easily punished. SADC heads of state and government will be forced to micro-manage the free trade area. And the 'idea of Southern Africa' will not spread so quickly, especially with South Africa acting like the hegemonic United States and the rest of SADC reacting suspiciously like Mexico and Canada in NAFTA. At the pace at which SADC is proceeding, a Southern African Union may take far longer than thirty years to achieve; instead of 2025, perhaps 2075? As for Nkrumah's vision of a United States of Africa, it is probably safe to predict that it will not be realised by 2063 – the centenary of the Organisation of African Unity – even if South Africa acts as the continental hegemon.

VIII. CONCLUSION

Less than a decade ago, a comparative analysis of regional integration would have made little sense for predicting the future of Southern Africa. The SADC states were implacably protectionist, and foreign capital was nowhere on the horizon. However, with globalisation, regional integration has spread rapidly beyond Europe and has sunk roots in Southern Africa, especially with South Africa's accession to SADC. Globalisation and liberalisation have diminished the importance of economic obstacles to integration which have concerned the 'SADC realists', especially the threat of polarisation between rich and poor. The small and poor SADC states have now adopted free trade and have been seeking to attract foreign investment – signs of preference convergence. SADC leaders are compelled to enter into inter-governmental bargaining to preserve their weak economies, and, in particular, they must find a way to attract South Africa into a free trade arrangement with – it is hoped – significant side payments. Under these new conditions of regional liberalisation, the experiences and political configurations of the European Community and, more recently, MERCOSUR and ASEAN/AFTA become relevant.

The changed conditions help to explain why the 'SADC pessimists' – who

133

believed that the organisation would wither – are premature in their evaluations. The pan-Southern African political affinities that had developed among leaders and movements over more than thirty years helped to attract the new South African Government to join SADC so promptly. Political affinities and the growing acceptance of liberalisation by the Mandela government, along with the threat of continued mass immigration and 'trade wars', have provided impetus to the integration process. In the South African private sector, a split has developed between those corporations which are pursuing the prospects for competitive advantage and foreign investment in Southern Africa and those capitalists who are looking more broadly at global markets and not at Southern Africa.

While some preference convergence has occurred among Southern African governments, protectionist and nationalist forces remain in each state and call into question the predictions of the 'SADC optimists' that integration will occur naturally and quickly. The South African government – which will be expected to provide most of the funding and impetus for SADC integration – is slow to look outwards and lower its protectionist barriers, especially in the face of resistance from the unions. In the meantime, penetration by South African goods and capital is taking place and will continue to occur in SADC and Africa – though on a smaller scale than Japanese penetration into ASEAN. Preference convergence among SADC states is still limited, and resistance to supranational arrangements will remain. In the medium term, SADC will integrate and form a free trade area, but it will not establish the depth that Europeans have. SADC states have not reached the level of maturity which is necessary to achieve EU-style integration.

NOTES

1. Feature on the SADC Summit by Gumisai Mutume and J. Mwiinga, Johannesburg, 27 Aug. 1995, Sapa-IPA. Taken from *ANC Daily News Briefing*, 28 Aug. 1995.
2. An assessment by Millard Arnold – later US Department of Commerce minister counsellor to the Southern African region – in March 1991 [*Arnold, 1995: 186*]. A similar statement was made by the South African Foreign Minister, Alfred Nzo, during the SADC summit in Johannesburg in August 1995.
3. The South African government has not proposed expanding SACU and the Common Monetary Agreement (CMA) as some have suggested [*Maasdorp, 1992*].
4. During the 1980s and 1990s, the aid has tended to by-pass national governments, particularly in Spain, and has gone directly to the regions [*Marks, 1992*]. As a consequence, national governments have not been able to target structural aid to counteract the polarising effects of EC/EU membership. The EU has responded by establishing a new fund which goes directly to the national governments of the poorer states.
5. Further research is needed to discover if side payments by Argentina and Brazil have been made to the poorest member – Paraguay.

6. Poor management, high labour costs, poor training, lagging technology and a capital shortage have been blamed for low productivity in South Africa. For instance, labour costs in Zimbabwe and Botswana are estimated to be a quarter of South Africa's. *Information Afrique*, 11 Jan. 1994.

7. The procedure of the estmiation is drawn from a predictive decision-making model developed by Bueno de Mesquita and Stokman [*1992*], Jacek Kugler and others.

8. President Mandela will retire in 1999, and his successor is bound to be less authoritative. This may slow South Africa's integration with SADC.

9. *Economist*, 3 Dec. 1995. Foreign direct investment in Zimbabwe in 1993–4 amounted to US$177 million which was more than for the entire 1980–93 period. TNCs were attracted by the dramatic lifting of exchange controls by the Zimbabwean government and were not deterred by high taxes, interest rates and inflation.

REFERENCES

Arestis, Philip and Eleni Paliginis. (1994), 'Peripherality and Divergence in the EC: The Need for Industrial Policy', in Georgakopoulos, Theodore, Christos Paraskevopoulos, and John Smithin (eds.), Economic Integration Between Unequal Partners, Brookfield, VT: Edward Elgar, pp. 201–9.

Arnold, Millard W. (1995), 'Southern Africa in the Year 2000: An Optimistic Scenario (March 1991)', Helen Kitchen and J. Coleman Kitchen (eds.), *South Africa: Twelve Perspectives on the Transition*, Westport, CT: Praeger for the Center for Strategic and International Studies.

Blomqvist, Hans *et al.* (1993), 'Some Experiences of Regional Cooperation between Third World Countries', in Oden [1993].

Bratton, Michael and Nicholas Van de Walle (1994), 'Neo-Patrimonial Regimes and Political Transitions in Africa', *World Politics* Vol.46, No.4, pp.453–89.

Bueno de Mesquita, Bruce and Frans N. Stokman (eds.) (1992), European Community Decision Making,. New Haven, CT: Yale University Press.

Cameron, David (1992), 'The 1992 Initiative: Causes and Consequences,' in Alberta M. Sbragia (ed.), Euro-Politics, Washington, DC: Brookings Institution.

Davies, Robert and William Martin (1992), 'Regional Prospects and Projects: What Futures for Southern Africa?' in Sergio Vieira *et al.* (coordinators) *How Fast the Wind? Southern Africa, 1975–2000*, Trenton, NJ: Africa World Press.

Davies, Robert (1993), 'Emerging South African Perspectives on Regional Cooperation and Integration after Apartheid', in Oden [1993].

Drucker, Peter (1989), *The New Realities*, London: Mandarin.

French, Howard (1995), 'Out of South Africa, Progress: Apartheid's End is Helping Revitalize a Continent', *The New York Times*, 6 July.

Georgakopoulos, Theodore, Paraskevopoulos, Christos and John Smithin (eds.) (1994), Economic Integration Between Unequal Partners, Brookfield, VT: Edward Elgar.

Hawkins, Anthony (1992), 'Economic Development in SADCC Countries', in Maasdorp and Whiteside [1992].

Herbst, Jeffrey (1995), 'South Africa and Southern Africa after Apartheid', in John Harbeson, and Donald Rothchild (eds.), *Africa in World Politics*, Boulder, CO: Westview Press.

Isaksen, Jan (1993), 'Prospects for SACU after Apartheid', in Oden [1993].

Keatinge, Patrick (ed.) (1993), *Ireland and EC Membership Evaluated*, New York: St. Martin's Press.

Keohane, Robert O. and Stanley Hoffman (eds.) (1991), The New European Community, Boulder, CO: Westview.

Khadiagala, Gilbert (1994), 'Southern Africa's Transitions: Prospects for Regional Security', in

Stedman [*1994*].

Kotschwar, Barbara R. (1995), 'South-South Economic Cooperation: Regional Trade Agreements Among Developing Countries', Cooperation South, New York: United Nations Technical Cooperation and Development Coordination, May.

Langhammer, Rolf and Ulrich Hiemenz (1990), Regional Integration Among LDCs, Boulder, CO: Westview Press.

Leonardi, Robert (1995), 'The Liberalization of Southern Europe via European Integration' (London School of Economics) paper presented at the American Political Science Association AGM, Sept.

Lopes, Jose da Silva (ed.) (1993), *Portugal and EC Membership Evaluated*, New York: St. Martin's Press.

Maasdorp, Gavin (1992), 'Trade Relations in Southern Africa – Changes Ahead', in Maasdorp and Whiteside (1992), Towards a Post-Apartheid Future: Political and Economic Cooperation in Southern Africa, London: Macmillan.

Maasdorp, Gavin and Whiteside, Alan (eds.) (1992), *Towards a Post-Apartheid Future: Political and Economic Cooperation in Southern Africa*, London: Macmillan.

Marks, Michael B. (1992), 'Structural Policy in the European Community', in Alberta Sbragia (ed.), *Euro-politics*, Washington, DC: Brookings Institution.

Marks, Michael B. (1995), 'Influence and Institutions: EU Relations with Spain and Greece', paper presented at the American Political Science Association AGM, Sept.

Moravcsik, Andrew (1991), 'Negotiating the Single European Act', in Keohane and Hoffman [*1991*].

Oden, Bertil (ed.) (1993), *Southern Africa After Apartheid: Regional Integration and External Resources*, Seminar Proceedings No.28, Uppsala: Nordiska Afrikainstitutet.

Ofstad, Arve (1993), 'Will PTA be Relevant in the Post-Apartheid Era?' in Oden [*1993*].

Ohlson, Thomas, Stedman, Stephen John and Robert Davies (1994), *The New is Not Yet Born: Conflict Resolution in Southern Africa*, Washington, DC: Brookings Institution.

Ostergaard, Tom (1993), 'Classical Models of Regional Integration – What Relevance for Southern Africa?' in Oden [*1993*].

Ravenhill, John (1980), 'The Theory and Practice of Regional Integration in East Africa', Christian P. Potholm and Richard Fredland (eds.), *Integration and Disintegration in East Africa*, Washington, DC: University Press of America.

Rich, Paul (1994), 'South Africa and the Politics of Regional Integration in Southern Africa in the Post-Apartheid Era', *The Dynamics of Change in Southern Africa*. New York: St. Martin's Press.

Rima, Ingrid H. (1994), 'Trade Among Partners Who Differ in Their Economic Development', in Georgakopoulos, Paraskevopoulos and Smithin [*1994*].

Seidman, Ann and Frederick Anang (eds.) (1992), *Towards a New Vision of Self-Sustainable Development*, Trenton, NJ: Africa World Press.

Solingen, Etel. (1996), 'Democracy, Economic Reform, and Regional Cooperation', to appear in *The Journal of Theoretical Politics*, Vol.8, No.1.

Southall, Roger (1994), 'The New South Africa in the New World Order: Beyond the Double Whammy', *Third World Quarterly* Vol.15, No.1, pp.121–37.

Stedman, Stephen John (ed.) (1994), *South Africa: the Political Economy of Transformation* (SAIS African studies library), Boulder, CO : Lynne Rienner Publishers.

Stopford, John and Susan Strange (1991), Rival States, Rival Firms: Competition for World Market Shares,. Cambridge: Cambridge University Press.

Strange, Susan (1992), 'Rethinking Structural Change in the International Political Economy', *International Affairs* Vol.68, No.1.

Stubbs, Richard (1994), 'The Political Economy of the Asia-Pacific Region', in Richard Stubbs and Geoffrey R.D. Underhill (eds.), *Political Economy and the Changing Global Order*, New York: St. Martin's Press.

Thompson, Carol B. (1985), *Challenge to Imperialism: The Frontline states in the Liberation of*

Zimbabwe, Boulder, CO: Westview Press.
Tsebelis, George and Amie Kreppel (1995), 'The History of Conditional Agenda-setting in European
    Institutions', paper presented at the American Political Science Association AGM, Chicago.
Urwin, Derek W. (1995), *The Community of Europe*, London: Longman.
World Bank (1989), *Sub-Saharan Africa: From Crisis to Sustainable Development,* Washington,
    DC: World Bank.

APPENDIX A5.1

SADC ACTORS' POSITION ON INTEGRATION, POWER AND SALIENCE

Actor	Position on integration	Power	Salience
SA manufacturers	0	Low (.3)	High (.8)
Jo'burg Stock Exchange	0	Low (.3)	Low (.3)
COSATU	0	Low (.3)	High (.8)
SA Government (President Mandela)	40 (Limited Payments) (Limited Integration)	High (.8)	Moderate (.5)
TNCs in SADC (e.g. Anglo-American Corporation)	40	Low (.3)	High (.8)
SACU (Lesotho, Swaziland, Namibia)	40	Low (.3)	Moderate (.5)
Mauritius	40	Low (.3)	High (.8)
Botswana	50	Low (.3)	High (.8)
Zambia	70 (Substantial Payments)	Low (.3)	High (.8)
Malawi	70	Low (.3)	High (.8)
Mozambique	70	Low (.3)	High (.8)
Zimbabwe	70	Moderate (.5)	High (.8)
Tanzania	70	Low (.3)	Low (.3)
Angola	70	Low (.3)	Low (.3)
SADC secretariat	90 (Major Payments) ('Deep' integration)	Low (.1)	High (1.00)
COMESA	100 (Maximum Payments) ('Wide' integration)	Low (.1)	High (1.00)

Notes: Maximum Side Payments by South Africa = 100; 'Wide and Deep' Integration = 100. No
    side payments by South Africa = 0; no integration = 0.

APPENDIX A5.2

RESOURCES, POSITION AND SALIENCE OF COMPETING GROUPS AND EVALUATION OF BARGAINING WITHIN SADC

Positions

SA govt = 40 (limited side payments), Zimbabwe trade agreement, trade wars, joined SADC, regional stability

Round 1   **Forecast = 70**

South African government concedes to fellow SADC members and agrees to set up a SADC free trade area and to make 'side payments' to Zimbabwe, Zambia, Malawi, Mozambique, Tanzania and Angola. The side payments are similar to those which South Africa makes to SACU members. This round began at the SADC summit in August 1996, with agreement on a SADC Free Trade Area.

Rounds 2 and 3   **Forecast = 42.7**

South African government finds side payments too onerous and retreats to its original position of limited payments and limited integration. Pressure by anti-integration forces in South Africa is also telling. The free trade area is supplanted by bilateral negotiations with Zimbabwe, Zambia, Malawi, and Mozambique.

Round 4 **Forecast = 61.8**

South African government finds bilateral negotiations too cumbersome and commits to reviving the SADC free trade area with slightly smaller side payments in the interest of regional harmony.

Rounds 5 – 10   **Forecast = 42.6, 42.6, 61.8, 42.6, 42.6, 70**

A pattern emerges of receding and expanding co-operation with no equilibrium. South African government is the actor which accounts for much of the fluctuation. Zimbabwe, Zambia, Malawi, and Mozambique 'stand firm' on their position that the South African government should make 'side payments' equivalent to those of SACU members. SACU members, including Botswana, are more reluctant than South African government to see an increase in side payments, fearing dilution.

Analogy: This pattern is similar to the 1970s in the European Community, when Britain, under the Heath government made major side payments to poorer states and then threatened non-co-operation or to withdraw under Labour and Thatcher.

6

'QWERTY Worlds' and South Africa's Preference Formation: Ideas and Policy-Making in Transitional South Africa

JAMES J. HENTZ

I. INTRODUCTION

This chapter examines economic policy-making in transitional South Africa and how it relates to the new South Africa's evolving regional relations. Economic policy-making in transitional South Africa can only be explained by an analytical framework that incorporates domestic and international variables. To this end, a focus on ideas is appropriate and, as it turns out, necessary. The former for two reasons. First, as Emanuel Adler and Peter Haas argue [*1992: 367*], ideas (through the agency of epistemic communities) can 'erase the artificial boundaries between international and domestic politics'. Second, in Arthur Stein's words: 'Changes in the nature of human understanding about how the world works, knowledge, can also transform state interests and therefore the prospects for international cooperation and regime formation' [*Stein, 1993: 49*].

A focus on ideas not only facilitates criss-crossing the international and domestic levels of analysis, but without an understanding of the interplay of ideas across those boundaries transitional South Africa's policy choices would be incomprehensible.

The leadership in post-apartheid South Africa underwent a significant change in its understanding of the mechanics of economic policy, leading it to redefine its interests. This process necessarily impacts on its regional economic foreign policy. In the early transition period, beginning roughly with F.W. De Klerk's 2 February 1990 announcement of the end of the ban on the liberation movement, the release of political prisoners, and his intention to dismantle apartheid, and ending with the April 1994 national elections; the African National Congress articulated a demand-driven economic model of development with a strong focus on redistribution. However, as will be explained below, cracks in the Keynesian edifice were evident prior to the 1994 elections. In the later transition period, between the elections and the South African government's announcement of a new economic plan in June 1996, the new government moved steadily towards economic liberalism. The role of ideas was central to this change, and these ideas

; transplanted from outside South Africa, but found fertile ground in the
loping policy alliance between moderate elements in the ANC and South
African business.

This policy shift will influence South Africa's preference formation for the
institutionalisation of co-operation in southern Africa because domestic political
strategies strongly influence foreign economic policy. Regional relations,
particularly efforts at regional economic integration, can not be separated from
the domestic political forces that shape economic policy. The institutionalisation
of regional co-operation can be expected to reflect the interests of South Africa's
political economy. Ideas that informed the debate over economic policy within
South Africa help shape those interests. Or, more accurately, material and
ideational influences have a recursive relationship. Ideas are the seeds of change,
but without strong material support they will fall on fallow ground. Planted in the
right political economy, on the other hand, they will begin to define, or in South
Africa's case redefine, the landscape.

In transitional South Africa material interests were characterised by the
bifurcation of its political economy pitting the capital-intensive sector against the
labour-intensive sector. The African Development Bank's comprehensive study
on regional integration in post-apartheid southern Africa explained: '...
differences abound [in South Africa], especially in relation to the extent to which
industrial development should be determined by emphasizing labor-intensive
versus more capital-intensive forms of production' [*ADB, 1994: 273*].

This competition was tied to competing ideas over how to promote economic
growth in the new South Africa; capital-intensive interests were linked to the
'neoliberal orthodoxy' of the international financial institutions (IFIs) and labour-
intensive interests to 'Keynesianism'. These sectoral competitions, furthermore,
had explicit and implicit links to South Africa's debate over its regional economic
policy.

Ideas shape preferences. Most of the literature on regional economic co-
operation, including from both neo-realist and neoliberal traditions, ignores
preference formation. Neo-realism and neo-liberalism treat state goals by
assumption [*Baldwin, 1993; Keohane, 1993; Goldstein and Keohane, 1993*].
Because both structural theories and process-oriented theories of co-operation are
rationalist approaches that omit how states' interests are formed,[1] they do not
fully explain the institutionalisation of co-operation. In a situation where more
than one set of co-operative arrangements is possible, neither approach can
explain why one co-operative solution is chosen rather than another.[2] This
chapter will address this lacuna in the concluding section.[3] The focus of this
paper is not on why one solution is chosen rather than another, but on the sources
of those solutions.

First, I challenge the 'rationalist' assumption underlying most co-operation
theory by arguing that co-operation is a stochastic process. In a stochastic process

chance elements are given more weight than systemic forces of change, and there is no automatic convergence on a fixed distributional outcome. This is true of co-operative arrangements because they are a product, first if not only, of domestic competition. The central weakness of most co-operation theory is its lack of domestic political analysis. Domestic politics is the strongest influence on preference formation. Therefore, rather than searching the Pareto frontier for optimal solutions to the problem of co-operation, we use a contextual exploration of South Africa's preference formation.[4] South Africa's policy preferences, driven by the acceptance of new ideas, were an historically contingent process. First, the new paradigm for economic growth, neoliberal economic orthodoxy, was a relatively recent successor to Keynesianism [*Johnson, 1978*]. Secondly, the end of the Cold War and the dominance of the IFIs in developing countries provided the necessary historical moment in which these ideas could take hold [*Bird, 1996*].

Evidence of preference formation being a stochastic process is provided by looking at the role of ideas in South Africa's policy formation. I posit that it was ideas, and not material interest grounded in political rationalities alone, that informed transitional South Africa's economic policy. Ideas, furthermore, were not an instrument for maximising certain interests, but rather redefined interests in post-apartheid South Africa. If ideas were merely a reflection of the dominant interest, then they would not provide the analytical leverage they are given here. I am arguing that ideas, in this case neo-liberal economics policies, are better understood as being refracted through a political economy made up of competing interests. The government's interests were thus redefined. This is not to argue that material interests do not matter; they do. However, I am arguing that the causal arrow can be reversed. Instead of ideas congealing around material interests, the ideas themselves stimulated material interests manifested in new coalitional configurations.

Ideas operate in what Paul David has called a 'QWERTY world' [*David, 1985*]. This is a metaphor for a situation where outcomes cannot be explained by the pursuit, whether conscious or unconscious, of Pareto optimality. In fact, as the story of QWERTY relates, even a decidedly less than optimal solution can evolve. Briefly, QWERTY refers to the position of specific keys on a typewriter/computer keyboard which are less efficient than alternative possibilities. None the less, QWERTY prevailed.[5] In the South African context a Keynesian approach would have been the optimal policy, given the political landscape at the time. None the less, the new ANC government adopted neo-liberal economic policies which created or exacerbated fissures in what had been its core political base.

In a stochastic process, such as that which led to the market dominance of QWERTY, the most important time is the beginning because 'particular sequencing of choices made close to the beginning of the process are key' ivid, 1985: 332]. Robert Axelrod and Robert Keohane opine that international itutions are significant because they 'embody and affect actors' expectations' [*Axelrod and Keohane, 1985: 234*]. However, most co-operation theory, particularly regime theory, has focused on how international institutions *affect* actors' expectations rather than on how institutions *reflect* actors' expectations. While paying tribute to the importance of institutions, co-operation theory typically ignores the initial institutionalisation of co-operation. Because co-operation can be the product of a stochastic process, grounded in large part in domestic political competition, it is important to examine apposite processes of preference formation within South Africa. In transitional South Africa this means first understanding the development of domestic economic policy and then how, in conjunction with other factors, it would influence foreign economic policy.

Regional co-operation in post-apartheid Southern Africa is largely determined, albeit not dictated, by the most powerful state in the region – South Africa,[6] and thus we must understand the development of South Africa's preferences. These are grounded in domestic dynamics, but did not reflect what would typically be considered optimal solutions, at least not in the political sense. Put bluntly, South Africa's leaders did not act in a way that would predict strong political support. They were not being rational. One way to explain South Africa's choice is to give ideas a strong causal role. In Maynard Keynes' famous words: 'The power of vested interests is vastly exaggerated compared with the gradual encroachment of ideas' [*Odell, 1982: 12*]. Ideas are commonly argued to come from external sources [*Nau, 1990: 48*], and in the case of transitional South Africa they came, primarily, if not exclusively, from the international financial institutions.

The argument made in this paper is presented in three parts. First, I briefly reject the rationalist approach to linking ideas and preference formation. Second, I examine the change in South Africa's policy preferences from the early to the later transition period. As noted above, these changes cannot be understood from a purely rationalist perspective. In fact, the South African leadership adopted ideas promoted by the IFIs, which were contrary to its election platform, and that would weaken rather than strengthen its political base. Third, in conclusion I briefly speculate on how South Africa's domestic economic policy interacts with its foreign economic policy (specifically regional relations) to shape co-operative arrangements. This interaction occurs at the material level, but also at the ideational level where international actors, specifically the IFIs, contributed to how South Africa thinks about regional economic integration.

The interaction of domestic and international factors on the ideational plane engender two important processes of what Paul David calls 'Qwerty-nomics'. First, it leads to 'systems of scale economies' where competition leads to standardisation through the predominance of externalities linked to the size of compatible networks [*David, 1985: 335*]. In the present case we can hypothesise that South Africa's domestic policy shift creates externalities that build on new international networks opened to it in the post-apartheid period. Ideas operating on different levels, the domestic and international, interact to create 'scale economies' that would be expected to lead to standardisation. If the logic of scale economies works in this way, it would be difficult for South Africa to have two sets of underlying policy ideas, one for domestic economic policy and another for foreign economic policy. Thus, it would be difficult to adopt economic liberalism at home, and eschew those principles in regional relations.

The standardisation of ideas in domestic and foreign economic policy would be more likely to create positive externalities. Most importantly, South Africa would be more likely to participate in international capital markets. But, also, the formation of policy entails creating political support. Enacting these policies, in turn, strengthens the influence of the groups thus favoured, at once strengthening the base of political support and making backsliding less likely. This ties South Africa's apposite decision to adopt neo-liberal economic policies to David's second process of Qwerty-economics, 'technical interrelatedness'. In the story of QWERTY the dominant key placement was partly due to its association with the Remington typewriter. In the case of South Africa's regional relations the ascendency of neo-liberal economic orthodoxy is not only associated with the IFIs' influence, but is linked to and promotes particular material interests. South Africa's capital-intensive sector was the beneficiary of the ANC's policy shift. As QWERTY's link to Remington strengthened its market dominance, so too does neoliberal economics's link to the capital-intensive sector enhance its position in South Africa's policy debate.

Because the theoretical focus of this chapter is preference formation and the empirical focus is transitional South Africa, I emphasise the competition of ideas and the politics that shape South Africa's bargaining matrix for regional co-operation in post-Apartheid Southern Africa and not the actual outcome of the bargaining process. As with the development of the European Community, regional co-operation in Southern Africa is a process. The unsettled nature of regional relations, and indeed South Africa's own objectives, should not detract from the importance of explaining the process of regional co-operation in Southern Africa any more than the vicissitudes of monetary union in the European Union detract from the study of economic integration in Western Europe. South Africa, like Germany, continues to debate how to institutionalise regional economic co-operation. Finally, like Southern Africa the European Union continues to face a 'choice between the hyper-liberal and the social market forms for future European society' [*Cox, 1997: 28*].

II. IDEAS, INTEREST AND CAUSALITY

While international relations theory accepts that ideas can have causal influence [*Hall, 1989: 4*], there is still a subtle but important debate over how ideas impact

143

on policy. First, part of what differentiates interpretations of how ideas influence policy is the different usages of the term 'ideas'. 'Ideas' as a family of international relations theory has more than one genus, ideas, knowledge, learning, ideology, and causal beliefs, being a few of the most important. As will be explained below, this is more than a problem of taxonomy. Secondly, the relationship between interests and ideas is interpreted in different ways. In some instances ideas are given causal weight because they are married to particular interests [*Goldstein and Keohane, 1993: 4*]; in other instances ideas and interests are separated [*Jacobsen, 1995: 309*].

The central conundrum in most of the ideas literature is how to prove causality [*Goldstein and Keohane, 1993: 11; Garrett and Weingast 1993: 203; Yee, 1996: 70*]. This, in turn, creates the challenge of how to show that ideas are more than mere hooks that competing elites use to legitimise and promote their interests. In other words, as Geoffrey Garrett and Barry Weingast state:

> The problem is that invariably the events in question can be explained in numerous other ways that assign the ideas an ancillary role: that is, the ideas are epiphenomenal and some other variables – such as material interest – ultimately bear the causal weight [*Garrett and Weingast, 1993: 203*].

Explaining causality demands clearly stating the genus of the idea generating the effects being explained, and a precise specification of the policy results that are affected [*Yee, 1996: 69*]. To do this we must first be clear on what we mean by ideas.

It is necessary to distinguish among the many apparent meanings of the term 'idea' because they have implications for the causal force of ideas. The allusive notion of causality, unfortunately, is at times nested within the interaction of different aspects of what comes under the general family of 'ideas'. The two key terms (genus) that need to be distinguished are causal ideas and learning. As Ernst Haas stated: 'learning is but one other word for reinterpreting one's interest' [*Haas, 1990: 370*]. Learning is stimulated by the introduction of new ideas, but not just any kind of idea will suffice.

Goldstein and Keohane [*1993*] distinguish among three types of beliefs (ideas): world views, principled beliefs, and causal beliefs.[7] The first two could be included in what Jacobson calls 'consensual beliefs' which, he argues, shape the legitimate ends of economic activity [*Jacobsen, 1995: 287*]. Jacobson argues that causal beliefs, which would include what he called economic ideas, are the means to achieve socially approved ends. In this process economic ideas, or in more general terms 'stated causal beliefs' [*Goldstein, 1993: 11*], are instrumental for pursuing particular ends defined as 'consensual beliefs'. This is a murky conceptual path because the cause and effect are both contained within the single family-beliefs (ideas).

Imputing causal significance to ideas demands separating independent and dependent variables and thereby more clearly explaining cause and effect. Ideas can do much more than help achieve predetermined goals. They can redefine the socially approved end being pursued. Making this distinction is important for demonstrating causality. If ideas are merely one way among others to promote particular interests, they do, indeed, belong in a rationalist paradigm. In this case, they are either weapons used by competing elites, or one set of interests among others that powerful groups are promoting. The causal power of ideas, however, rests in their ability to redefine state interests. Interests, therefore, must be a legitimate dependent variable that does not co-vary with the independent variable – the idea (causal belief).

Ikenberry and Kupchan's typology can help us out of this morass. They distinguish among norms, value orientations, interests and preferences. The latter two terms are key for defining our independent and dependent variables. Preferences are the ordering of alternative courses of action; interests are the broad objectives of policy. Ideas, defined precisely as causal beliefs, are tied to alternative courses of preferences. Political actors propagating certain preferences are the intermediaries through which interests are redefined. Ideas have causal power precisely because of their consanguinity with particular preferences [*Ikenberry and Kupchan 1990: 285*]. This is true whether or not this relationship is known beforehand. In other words, ideas (neo-liberal economics) could come from external sources (the IFIs) but find strong blood ties (South African business) in the host country. If, returning to Haas's dictum, 'learning is but one other word for reinterpreting one's interest', what we want to know is what ideas triggered such learning and how (if) those ideas have defined or redefined a state's interests – its broad objectives of policy.

Although ideas have been used in international relations theory to explain preferences, it has typically been done within the rationalist paradigm. The focus is on how ideas promote particular interests. They do, but not necessarily in the way scholars traditionally explain. The coalitional approach, for instance, argues that policy preferences are used by groups to build coalitions for political support.[8] The literature on epistemic communities can also be, somewhat deceptively, rationalist. For instance, Emanuel Adler and Peter Haas state that the epistemic community literature provides the prerequisite for rational choice by explaining where payoffs come from. This is because, as they later state: 'Leaders tend to align with ideas which "implicitly align" with their own preexisting political agenda ... ' [*Adler and Haas, 1992: 386*]. Although this obviously does occur, there are two conceptual problems with linking this process to an argument of causality. First, it remains a rationalist explanation binding ideas to interests. Secondly, it leads to an overdetermined result. It is difficult to grant ideas separate causal weight because they are chained to a particular interest; ideas remain epiphenomenal.

One way out of this analytical cul-de-sac is to show that leaders can initially accept one set of ideas and later adopt new ideas that cause a realignment of interest. This is what happened in transitional South Africa, where the ANC aligned with ideas which seemingly redefined its political agenda. The leaders, through the influence of what could be called an epistemic community (the IFIs' policy advisers), reshaped their political agenda. South Africa went from promoting 'redistribution with growth', with the accent on the former, to a policy of growth. This switch was not caused by the political calculation (domestic) that such a policy would be propitious for forming a coalition, but rather was the natural concomitant to a switch from Keynesian to neo-liberal policy prescriptions.

As Henry Nau argues, the policy process is more than interest (society) and institutions (state). There is a competition within what he calls a 'cocoon of non-governmental actors'. He continues, ' ... ideas mix with politics to influence outcomes in a struggle that is not predetermined by deep-seated interests, institutions or politics' [*Nau, 1990: 44, 49*]. Ernst Haas has a similar understanding:

> The knowledge available about 'the problem' at issue influences the way decision makers define the interests at stake in the solution to the problem; political objectives and technical knowledge are combined to arrive at the conception of what constitutes one's interest [*Haas, 1990: 9*].

The following section looks at competing policy ideas about how to promote economic growth in post-apartheid South Africa. The competing policy ideas were articulated by the ANC and the National Party (NP) and were tied to the material interests of particular groups, respectively labour and big business. However, the winning idea was inconsistent with the original configuration of the policy/interest alignments. The ANC, once in power, rejected the policy ideas that were consistent with its material base (labour).

III. POLITICS, IDEAS AND COMPETING POLICIES: CHANGING INTEREST IN TRANSITIONAL SOUTH AFRICA

This section compares two periods in South Africa's transition. During period one, from De Klerk's unbanning of political opposition to the 1994 elections, the ANC (and the 'democratic movement') promoted demand-led growth as its economic model for post-apartheid South Africa. This preference was tied to a broad policy objective that was labelled 'growth with redistribution'. The material interest that was tied to this policy objective was labour, most forcefully represented by the Congress of South African Trade Unions (COSATU), and the black majority. After the April 1994 elections the ANC, now the dominant political partner in the transitional unity government, changed its preferences. Its broad policy objectives also changed. The ANC went from a strong Keynesian approach to a neo-liberal approach, and from a broad policy objective of redistribution to a focus on growth.

The material interest tied to this policy was primarily big business. This was surprising, if not completely unexpected, for two reasons. First, as Peter Hall notes, Keynesian ideas are a potent weapon against *laissez-faire* economics [*Hall, 1989: 366*] which had been anathema to the ANC and its allies ever since the publication of its 'Freedom Charter' in 1955. Secondly, the logic of South Africa's electoral politics was more consistent with Keynesianism. The same constituency that had shaped the ANC's earlier preferences, and remained as its political core, reacted negatively to the ANC's apparent shift.[9] This shift cannot be explained by material interest alone. A change in understanding, causal beliefs, triggered by the steady flow of external ideas led to a new ordering of alternative courses of action.

This section will examine this change diachronically. First, I outline the policy debate in South Africa during the earlier transition period, with a focus on three political groups/alignments, the ANC/'democratic movement', the NP and its policy allies, and the international financial institutions.[10] Secondly, I look at the shift in the ANC's policies and the reconfiguration of the inside-outside policy alignments. Finally, I posit that ideas (causal beliefs) and not material interests led to a redefinition of broad policy objectives. These redefined interests, furthermore, are a political liability for the ANC.

The dialogue over the appropriate economic policies for post-apartheid South Africa had three major participants, the National Party (NP) (the ex-government), the African National Congress (ANC), and the IFIs, specifically the World Bank and the International Monetary Fund. Prior to the April 1994 elections, each produced blueprints for South Africa's post-apartheid economic development. In March 1993, the Central Economic Advisory Service (CEAS), in consultation with the South African Reserve Bank and government departments, co-ordinated by the Special Economic Adviser to the Minister of Finance, published the comprehensive study, *The Restructuring of the South African Economy: A Normative Model Approach* (NEM). Although the authors did not intend it to be an NP platform, the NP in fact acted as if it were.[11] Derek Keys, Finance Minister at the time, claimed that South Africa had only one model for economic growth on the table – the NEM (*Business Day*, 1 Dec. 1993).

The ANC's economic policy platform, released just prior to the April 1994 election, was revealed in two documents: the *Reconstruction and Development Programme (RDP)*, and *Making Democracy Work: A Framework for Macroeconomic Policy in South Africa* (the MERG Report). The former had gone through several drafts and was stated to be official ANC policy. The latter was drafted by officials who were aligned with the ANC and, while left-leaning, included many key ANC officials who would obtain high-level government positions in the first ANC government.

Both the IMF and the World Bank were active in the debate over how to structure the post-apartheid economy.[12] For example, the preface to an IMF study stated:

> Within this context [transitional South Africa], a debate has begun on the appropriate economic policies to be pursued in a new South Africa to address the country's acute socioeconomic backlogs. This study aims at making a contribution to that debate [*Lachman and Bercuson, 1992: vii*].

A World Bank study related:

> This paper is a synthesis of some informal studies on different aspects of the South African economy prepared by the World Bank. The studies have been discussed with a wide range of South Africans, and have benefitted from South African ideas and inputs [*World Bank, 1993*].

In essence the policy debate during the first part of South Africa's transition divided into two camps, the ANC/'democratic movement' and the government and the IFIs. The ANC not only rejected the IFIs' policy prescriptions for South Africa, but painted a picture of an unholy alliance between the IFIs and the government. Both the RDP and the MERG Report, in fact, took explicit stands against the IFIs' policies.

> [T]he MERG analysis of the causes of this failure, and its policies to address the crisis differ radically from those promoted by the government and the Washington-based international financial agencies. The differences start at the theoretical level. The MERG view is that government, IMF and IBRD conclusions are analytically incoherent, coloured by an ideological anti-worker bias, and unsupported by the available empirical evidence [*World Bank, 1993: 152*].

Whereas the ANC rejected the IFIs' prescriptions, the NP built its platform on those same prescriptions. Alan Hirsch, who became a top trade official in the first ANC government, pointed out that discussions with the World Bank had strongly influenced the writing of the NEM [*Hirsch, 1993: 54–55*]. The NEM stated, for example: 'This model is compatible, not only with a post-apartheid dispensation, but also with virtually all macro-economic stabilization and structural adjustment programmes in developing countries during the 1980s' (*Business Day*, 1 Dec. 1993). As the MERG Report stated, the conclusions of the IMF were virtually identical to those outlined in the NEM, establishing a consensus between the NP and the IFIs on economic policy for post-apartheid South Africa [*MERG Report, 1993: 152–3*].

The divide between ANC and NP policy was revealed by their conflicting positions over three issue areas central to the IFI's economic reform programmes: privatisation, budget deficits, and inflation. The NP had promoted the privatisation of South Africa's extensive parastatal sector even prior to the elections. However, in anticipation of relinquishing the reins of power to the ANC, privatisation was accelerated. This was consistent with the World Bank's call for a reduced role for the state. The World Bank argued that re-investment in South Africa's parastatals was poor policy because: '[T]he productivity of capital (that is, the output-to-capital ratio) is higher in the private sector than in parastatals' [*World Bank, 1993: 10*]. Higher investment in sectors with lower productivity would depress the level and the rate of growth in GDP. The NEM followed lock step with this conclusion. The ANC, however, argued that parastatals could be used for Black empowerment. This line of argument was present in earlier drafts of the MERG Report written in part by Tito Mboweni (Labour Minister in the new government). Mboweni cautioned against rapid anti-trust moves by the government, and did not argue for forced unbundling (*Business Day*, 6 Dec. 1993). The RDP even stated that 'The democratic government will reverse privatisation programmes that are contrary to the public interest' [*RDP: 46*].

The NP and ANC blueprints for the post-apartheid economy had distinct implications for South Africa's budget. The NEM's proposal was based on monetarist prescriptions which were consistent with the IFIs' policies. In contrast, the RDP and MERG Report were essentially Keynesian models of economic management. The MERG Report stated: 'The starting point for the calculations is the principle that in order to overcome a major failure of policy in the recent past, the relative size of public sector investment needs to be increased' [*MERG Report, 1993: 25*]. The long list of government-funded projects found in both the RDP and the MERG Report reflected their philosophy of demand-led growth.

The NEM and the IFIs' strong commitment to budgetary restraint was tied to their commitment to maintain low levels of inflation. Both the IMF and the World Bank cautioned against high inflation. For the IMF, commitment to low inflation was a working assumption: ' ... it is assumed that monetary policy will continue to be used to bring inflation under control ... ' [*Lachman and Bercuson, 1992: 14*]. The World Bank stated: 'Any significant increase in inflation, however, would be destabilizing and foster greater social discontent' [*World Bank, 1993: 6*]. The NEM had a strong anti-inflation stance and directly linked the rate of inflation to domestic savings. Furthermore, in order to keep inflation under control both the NEM and the IFIs argued for wage constraint.

The ANC countered that the emphasis on inflation was misplaced. The MERG Report, for instance, argued that the government had focused far too much on inflation in the past. South Africa's fifteen years of economic decline were, in fact, blamed on too little government spending.

The contending political parties adopted clearly distinct economic blueprints for the new South Africa. The NP's was consistent with the neo-liberal orthodoxy of the IFIs and the ANC's with the traditional Keynesian paradigm. Their respective economic models made political sense. The ANC's constituency was the newly enfranchised Blacks, represented most importantly by organised labour. Both parties acted in their own best political interests during the election campaign. The ANC, in an open alliance with COSATU and the South African Communist Party (SACP), campaigned for a Keynesian programme of demand-driven economic growth. The NP campaigned for a free market-driven strategy of economic growth with limited state involvement.

In February 1994 Nelson Mandela argued that job creation was the ANC's highest priority. He also argued: 'We are convinced that, left to its own devices, the South African business community will not rise to the challenges that face us' (*Business Day*, 21 Feb. 1994). In the same month he told workers at a National Union of Mineworkers conference that the ANC-led government would wrest mineral rights from the mining houses and place them in the hands of the state (*The Star*, 12 Feb. 1994).

Labour was aware of the conflict between the IFIs' policy prescriptions and the promotion of their own interest, and lobbied long and hard against those prescriptions. COSATU General Secretary Sam Shilowa stated, 'SA's militant and organized workers will not accept a formula for economic growth based on their exploitation' (*Business Day*, 2 Dec. 1993, p.4). He opposed an IMF loan of $850 million because the IMF was on record as favouring wage constraints in South Africa, and argued that the 'much-vaunted Asian tiger' scenario would lead to widespread social and industrial conflict,[13] an implicit stab at the IFIs. Furthermore, it was reported that COSATU reacted 'swiftly and angrily' to bankers' criticism of the RDP (*The Star*, 4 Feb. 1994). Tony Ruiters, a member of the COSATU national economics task force, also argued against 'IMF adjustment plans', stating that there was 'scope for government intervention in business beyond an enabling role', another quiet jab at the IFIs [*Business Day*, 22 Nov. 1993].

The NP's key constituent was big business. South African business criticised the RDP and the MERG Plan. For instance, a book edited by Ben Vosloo, managing director of the Small Business Development Corporation, painted the ANC policy as 'a grim picture of the growth of the public sector in SA to the detriment of the private sector', and pointed to the Asian newly industrialised countries as a model for future South African policy (*Sunday Times, Business*, 6 March 1994).

Only months after winning close to two-thirds of the seats in Parliament, however, the ANC signalled a paradigm shift that strained its relationship with its core political ally – labour. A cautionary note is necessary at this point.

Although there was a discernible break in the ANC's economic policy prescriptions after the election, it was never as completely committed to statist policies as the rhetoric of the election period might have indicated. In fact, during South Africa's transition, new domestic alignments had evolved beneath the veneer of ANC–labour solidarity.[14] A month before the elections, *The Star* reported: 'The underlying message from the ANC delegation was that they were looking for a partnership with business' (*The Star*, 31 March 1994, p.1). This shift in domestic political alignments was at once reinforced by, and a response to, the importance of foreign capital. None the less, although the lines might not be as sharp as the diachronic structure used here may imply, the ANC's economic polices had changed.

Immediately after the April 1994 elections South Africa was racked by labour unrest. By July 1994 there had already been more work stoppages than in any year since 1987, and they were spread evenly throughout the economy. COSATU leader, Sam Shilowa, expressed the common labour jeremiad, 'Why is there no improvement in my paypacket?' (*Reuters*, 22 July 1994). As a symbolic close to a summer of labour discontent the annual COSATU convention in September 1994, attended by 1,700 delegates, was marked by strong anti-government rhetoric. Even the future of the ANC–COSATU alliance was challenged. None the less, in the face of political opposition, the ANC moved away from its Keynesian paradigm, and away from labour interests.

The characterisations of the ANC leadership early in the ANC's first government reflected its acceptance of neo-liberal economic policies. Jay Naidoo, the former head of COSATU, and the new government's minister in charge of implementing the RDP, was once described as 'looking like Satan, sounding like Marx, and acting like Mephistopheles'. As minister, however, he was described as 'a figure of flawless economic orthodoxy' (*Financial Times*, 18 July 1994). Alec Erwin, the new government's deputy Minister of Finance, an ex-unionist, was labelled a convert to economic orthodoxy.[15] In Mandela's first 'State of the Union' address to Parliament, he was described as being as intent on 'soothing' the fears of foreign investors and domestic business as on pleasing his traditional supporters. In the opening session of the World Economic Forum in Cape Town on 9 June 1994 Mandela stressed that his government would adhere to Western economic policies rather than the socialist policies the ANC had advocated as a banned liberation movement. The ANC had moved towards the IFIs' positions on the three central issues of economic reform, privatisation, the budget, and inflation.

The ANC had backed away from its strong line against privatisation. Jay Naidoo, minister without portfolio responsible for the 37.5 billion rand ($10.5 billion) five-year RDP, stated that underutilised properties might be sold (*Reuters*, 27 Aug. 1995). The *Economist* reported:

Though too coy yet to use the word 'privatisation' openly, the government is putting the finishing touches to a plan that amounts to nothing less: the sale of stakes in state-owned corporations that together are worth at least 64 billion rand ($18 billion) (*The Economist*, 6 May 1994).

In late June 1994, the new government announced its first budget, described by Trevor Manuel, then Minister of Trade and Industry in the new government (also once a labour leader), as an 'investors' budget'. The IMF, in fact, reported positively on this first budget: 'The budget helped to allay fears that the Government's Reconstruction and Development Program, which promised reform in critical areas such as housing, education, health and landownership, would lead to financial instability' [*IMF, 1995*].

The ANC's first budget only foreshadowed its conversion to economic liberalism.[16] The tug-of-war between competing economic policies pitting business against labour continued to tear at the new government's stated policy of redistribution with growth. Labour continued to call for worker protection and state-sponsored job creation; business continued to call for slimmed-down government and liberalisation of the markets. It was reported in 1995:

> The tension in government between neoliberal economic policy and a prolabor orientation poses difficult practical decisions for many on the left. COSATU, SANCO and the SACP were all part of the coalition that ousted the old apartheid regime; they all foresaw economic as well as political and 'racial' change as part of their objective ... Thabo Mbeki, often spoken of as Mandela's successor in the ANC and Deputy President, has suggested that the ANC might split up by the next election in 1999 [*Marcuse, 1995*].

As one ANC MP, and a member of the ANC executive committee, stated, commenting on the first budget: 'It's going to be hard to sell this budget [1994] in the townships' [AP, 14 Sept. 1994].

In the following year both business and labour published position papers on South Africa's economic policy. The business perspective was promoted in the document drafted by the so-called Brenthurst Group (named after mining magnate Harry Oppenheimer's home) in March 1996, 'Growth for All'. COSATU, the Federation of South African Labour Unions (Fedsal) and the National Council of Labour Unions (NACTU), the three main labour unions, responded with their own manifesto, 'Social Equity and Job Creation'.

The culmination of the government's conversion to neo-liberal orthodoxy was signalled by the apparent demise of the RDP on 28 March 1996 and its replacement with a new economic blueprint, the 'macroeconomic framework', in June 1996. The RDP was not dismantled, but the RDP portfolio was closed and the RDP fund re-allocated to the Department of Finance and the Office of

Deputy President Thabo Mbeki. There is, of course, more than one interpretation of this move.[17] None the less, Mandela's Spring 1996 Cabinet reshuffle, scrapping Jay Naidoo's Reconstruction and Development portfolio while raising Mbeki to the position of South Africa's 'growth czar', symbolised the ANC's shift in policy emphasis from development to growth. Mbeki was reported to have been 'deeply skeptical at the outset about the RDP; he knew the government's delivery promises would lead it up a dead-end' [*Issues, 1996:5*].[18] Further evidence of the ANC's shift was Pallo Jordan's replacement as Minister of Posts, Telecommunications and Broadcasting by Jay Naidoo. Jordan was possibly the most powerful proponent of the ANC's Keynesian wing, and reportedly clashed frequently with Mbeki.

The 'macroeconomic framework' was the ANC's first comprehensive economic plan since its election in 1994. Nico Czypionka, chief economist at Standard Bank, stated that the 'debate appeared to have shifted in favor of a free market approach despite accusations from labor and some in the ANC of such an approach as "Thatcherite"'. The 'macroeconomic framework' had three main tenets, each signalling a move away from what South African business leader Edward Osborn called the 'slick neo-Keynesian notion' of demand-led growth (*Reuters*, 12 March 1996). The South African budget was to be reduced from 5.1 per cent to 3 per cent of GDP by 2000; it called for tight monetary policy, with inflation to be kept to an average of 8.2 per cent until 2000 and it called for accelerated privatisation of the parastatal sector.

The 'macroeconomic framework' was announced despite strong labour opposition. COSATU's '1996 Mission Statement' argued that unemployment was still too high due to 'bad or non-existent policies from the Ministers of Trade and Industry and Finance'. The title of COSATU General Secretary Sam Shilowa's address to the World Economic Forum meeting in Cape Town on 23 May 1996 was 'Why is COSATU concerning itself with the proposed restructuring of South Africa's enterprises?', and COSATU organised a general strike for 16 January protesting against the 'piecemeal privatisation' supported by the government. In June 1996 COSATU also repeatedly lobbied against tight monetary policy by calling for lower interest rates.

South Africa's shift may have made economic sense, but it did not make political sense. The change in the ANC's economic policy caused serious strains in the alliance between the ANC and COSATU. With 3.5 million members, or approximately 26 per cent of the economically active population, organised labour in South Africa is a force to contend with. Rather than shoring up its alliance with labour, the government continued to reject the Keynesian paradigm backed by labour in favour of the IFIs' neo-liberal orthodoxy. Meanwhile, COSATU continued to question the appropriateness of the IFIs' policies for South Africa. John Gomomo, the COSATU President, in his address to the 1996 World Economic Forum stated that the IMF and the World Bank had had a 'devastating' impact on the lives of many people [*Gomomo, 1996*].

Transitional South Africa's change of economic models, essentially trading a Keynesian one for the neo-liberal orthodoxy of the IFIs, did not make political sense. This is not to say that material interests did not matter. A powerful counter-factual argument could be made for a state-centric explanation for the policy shift. For instance, a strong central bank can lead to tight monetary policy. In South Africa the head of the Reserve Bank, Chris Stals, one of only two top officials to survive the transition with his position intact (the other being, briefly, Derek Keys), was a powerful influence. The question remains, however, why, when the ANC came to power, the autonomy of the Bank was not abraded, as it had so often threatened to do during the election campaign. Both the RDP and the MERG Report argued for tighter government control over the Federal Reserve Bank. Nor should the technocratic element in the administration be credited with undue influence. Although part of the transitional bargain was the protection of civil service jobs, as Peter Hall notes [*Hall, 1989: 375*] the influence of the bureaucracy increases during normal periods. The transition was not such a time.

The strongest materialist counter-factual would be to argue that South Africa was intent on attracting investment and therefore needed the 'good housekeeping seal of approval' from the IFIs. This is correct. The power of the ideas promoted by the IFIs is certainly linked to their influence at the historical moment when South Africa accepted neo-liberal orthodoxy in place of Keynesianism. However, the IFIs' influence was nonetheless more ideational than material.

First, the ANC was acutely aware of the IFIs' material base of influence and went to great lengths to avoid it. The RDP stated:

> Relationships with international financial institutions such as the World Bank and International Monetary Fund must be conducted in such a way as to protect the integrity of domestic policy formation and promote the interests of the South African population and the economy. Above all, we must pursue policies that enhance national self-sufficiency and enable us to reduce dependence on international financial institutions [*ANC, 1994: 60*].

Once in power, the ANC adopted the IFIs' policy prescriptions while nonetheless trying to control their influence. As late as the autumn of 1995 *The Economist* reported:

> The Bank [World Bank] opened an office in Johannesburg, wrote lots of reports on the country and is ready to lend. Lo, South Africa says it is not yet interested, and will call the Bank when it is. Jay Naidoo, the minister in charge of aid projects refuses to be bullied by aid givers. 'There has been an insistence from foreign governments that we slip into a dependence relationship', he says. 'But we will continue to insist

that overseas aid, while welcome and valuable, must fit in with existing programmes and priorities' [*The Economist*, 28 Oct. 1995].

Not only was South Africa sensitive to the IFIs' influence, but it was not susceptible to their direct influence. Graham Bird explains:

> The IMF exerts an important influence over the design of economic policy in countries that turn to it for financial assistance. This influence is at its strongest in areas where the IMF stipulates preconditions and prior actions or where there are quantified performance criteria [*Bird, 1996*].

South Africa is not included in the IMF's 1996 listing of 'Member Countries' Use of Fund Facilities'. In fact, according to the World Bank tables, South Africa is categorised as 'less-indebted middle-income'.

There were numerous meetings between the IFIs and ANC officials prior to the 1994 elections [*Gordhan, 1991: 9*], including between Nelson Mandela and the World Bank during his visit to Washington in February 1990. The Bank, furthermore, was ' ... showing great sophistication, and most progressive South Africans who have met with Bank missions have been impressed with how willing Bank staff appear to work with what might be viewed as an ANC government-in-waiting' [*Bond and Swilling, 1992: 31*]. The World Bank, to its credit, was cognisant of its reputation in Africa, particularly in neighbouring countries such as Zambia where many of the exiled ANC leaders had lived, and it therefore adopted a more subtle approach to influencing economic policy in transitional South Africa.

Ideas mattered in transitional South Africa. The ANC leadership adopted neo-liberal economic policies, which may have been economically rational but were of questionable political utility. In fact, economic policy-making is as much a stochastic process as a rational choice. Paul David's QWERTY-nomics would, then, be one way to build analytical linkages between South Africa's domestic and regional economic policy.

IV. LEARNING IN A 'QWERTY WORLD' AND REGIONAL RELATIONS IN POST-APARTHEID SOUTHERN AFRICA

Ideas, specifically causal beliefs, were the catalyst for the ANC leadership's reinterpretation of its interest; external ideas were responsible for new learning. The process, however, was not rational in the political sense of using ideas around which to build a coalition. It was, rather, a stochastic process. This has logical ramifications for South Africa's foreign economic policy, including regional economic co-operation.

Three elements of the stochastic process in Paul David's 'QWERTY World' affect South Africa's regional relations: the emphasis on the beginning of a process; the effect of scale economies; and technical interrelatedness. Furthermore, each should be considered not as separate process but rather as reinforcing and interdependent with the other two.

In transitional South Africa there was general agreement that regional co-operation should be pursued. As Tony Hawkins put it: 'The issue has become not whether the region should integrate economically but the logistics – who, how and when.' [*Hawkins, 1994*] The 'how' was debated within and outside South Africa. Rob Davies stated at the time:

> ... significantly different perspectives have, in fact, emerged between different forces in South African policy on the terms, principles, and approaches to govern a programme of closer regional economic cooperation and integration after apartheid [*Davies, 1992: 75*].

Three general forms of regional co-operation were discussed: 'developmental co-operation', 'market co-operation' and '*ad hoc* co-operation'.[19] Developmental co-operation promotes sectoral and cross-sectoral agreements and incorporates corrective measures within the regional co-operation scheme to deal with the natural inequalities accompanying economic integration among developing countries.[20] It is argued that the most advanced of the developing countries reap a disproportionate share of the integrated region's aggregate gains because of the effects of 'backwash' and 'polarisation'. This model of regional co-operation was promoted by the Southern African Development Community (SADC). Market co-operation focuses primarily on trade and, possibly, monetary co-operation and in southern Africa was best represented by the Southern African Customs Union (SACU).[21] *Ad hoc* co-operation refers to bilateral co-operation in both trade relations and infrastructural projects (in this context also called functional co-operation). This form of co-operation was actively promoted by big business in South Africa.[22]

Decisions on domestic economic policy, in conjunction with the IFIs' emphasis on national initiative, implied a path dependency for South Africa's foreign economic policy. Thus, the importance of the beginning in a stochastic process was reinforced by the interaction of ideational and material forces across domestic and international boundaries. The IFIs' domestic policy prescriptions for South Africa not only supported and strengthened the capital-intensive sector, but also supported big business's policy on regional co-operation. The direction of South Africa's economic policy, the apposite policy decision, strengthened the material base of business relative to labour. The IFIs' notion of regional economic co-operation following national initiatives would naturally favour the actor most capable of taking the initiative – business.

Debating the future of Southern Africa became a virtual cottage industry in transitional South Africa, in which the IFIs actively participated. SADC's Macro-Framework Study Report, for instance, stated that the World Bank had established a firm presence among 'opinion leaders' in South Africa on regional issues [*SADC, 1993: 33*]. As related above, 'systems of scale economies' are where competition leads to standardisation through the predominance of externalities linked to the size of compatible networks. In the sense that David uses the term, therefore, the competition among the competing forms of regionalism would be expected to lead to standardisation, in this case a regional policy consistent with neo-liberalism. This in turn, would lead to positive externalities in the form of expanding networks.

Fantu Cheru noted that the World Bank's vision was fundamentally different from that informing most African integration schemes. The World Bank, in a series of studies, generally supported regional integration in Southern Africa that is outward-looking. Rather than pulling away from the international economy, the Bank saw regional integration as a way to reintegrate Africa into the global economy [*Cheru, 1992: 2*]. Supporting regional co-operation was part of the larger process of liberalising trade and removing controls on the flow of capital across borders [*Davies, 1991: 241*]. The liberalism that informed the World Bank's economic policies, in general, was also expected to encourage regional integration in Africa. The Bank's approach relied on the private constituencies that would benefit from economic integration to lobby for regional integration and, thus, enhance the prospects of success [*World Bank, 1990: iv–v*]. This mirrors the logic underwriting the IFIs' structural adjustment programmes in Africa. Adjustment creates winners and losers, the former being those around which a constituency for reform is built.

The technical interrelatedness is tied to the path dependencies created by neo-liberal domestic policies, and is reinforced by economies of scale. The importance of the domestic sources of regional co-operation and integration are reflected in the *Desk Study on Regional Integration in Eastern and Southern Africa: Constraints to Intra-Regional Payments, Trade and Investment*, partially attributable to the IFIs. The *Concept Paper* that accompanied this study stated:

> The underlying hope is that the private sector will no longer feel constrained to the national market, rather it will consider widening opportunities of a subregional rather than a national market, and develop and investor culture to exploit such opportunities [*World Bank, African Development Bank, IMF, CEC, 1993*].

Most importantly, the study's focus was on 'national selection' and 'self selection'. In other words, although the aim of the study was to find ways to promote regional co-operation and integration, specifically cross-border trade and investment, the process that would accomplish this was argued as beginning at the national level.

The private sector, however, is more accurately described as the private sectors, and the competing sectors in South Africa had different visions of how to institutionalise regional economic integration. Therefore, if, as the *Concept Paper* expects, the private sector that benefits from the process promotes integration, each sector should promote the form of co-operation from which it accrues the greatest benefits. The support for neo-liberal polices, in both domestic and regional policy, would thus have the advantage.

The labour-intensive sector, backed by COSATU, supported the SADC approach, while big business strongly supported the ad hoc approach, and to a lesser extent the market approach. The co-operation process which SADC encouraged envisaged multilateral negotiations in 'baskets' of issues to facilitate trade-offs in such areas as trade, labour mobility, industrialisation, and water and energy [*SADC Secretariat, 1994: 9*]. Such an approach would allow a country to protect a relatively weak sector, that is, the labour-intensive sector in South Africa, through linkages across issue areas. *Ad hoc* co-operation, and to a lesser extent market co-operation, is driven by the logic of the free market. *Ad hoc* co-operation, as promoted by big business in South Africa, would have a thin institutional veneer allowing for the market to pick winners and losers.

The logic of QWERTY-nomics would point to a process of regional economic co-operation in post-apartheid Southern Africa that would have strong neo-liberal undertones, and would most likely reflect business interests. Although it is still early days, the new South African government has, in effect, pursued regional ties through stages under the auspices of SADC which it joined in the autumn of 1994. But the first steps were along functional lines. The communiqué signed by the Heads of State after the SADC 1995 meeting in Johannesburg reflected this balance. The tangible progress towards greater regional co-operation made at the summit was reflected in the protocol on 'Shared Watercourse Systems', functional co-operation under the auspices of SADC.

In transitional South Africa ideas have power. This does not necessarily come from their association with particular interests. Ideas are also a source of interest. In transitional South Africa the power of ideas was not linked to strong material interests and thus should not be considered epiphenomenal. As Hirschman argued in the context of the spread of Keynesian ideas: ' ... it is possible to see new ideas in a more activist role: apparently they can become leading actors in the political process as they shape new policies and political arrangements' [*Hirschman, 1978: 356*].

NOTES

1. For discussions on this problem, see Sandholtz [*1993*]; Wendt [*1992*]; Jervix [*1988*]; Cohen [*1990*].
2. For an explanation of how alternative co-operative arrangements (which for instance the 'folk theorum' points out are likely), are ignored in much of the literature, see Garertt and Weingast [*1993: 157–7*].
3. For a thorough explanation of this issue in the context of regional co-operation in Southern Africa, see Hentz [*1997*].
4. This is similar to Albert Hirschman's argument that the spread of Keynesian ideas after the Second World War was due to unique circumstance and that 'the next time around, we may have to look for a very different combination of circumstances to explain (promote) the acquisition of political influence by an economic idea' (Hirschman, in Hall [*1989: 351*]).
5. Similar stories are told about the apparent victory of Microsoft over Apple, and of Matsuchita's VHS over Sony's Betamax.
6. The notion that the most powerful state is the key influence in the institutionalisation of co-operation is generally accepted. See Kahler [*1995*]; Keohane and Nye [*1977*].
7. These distinctions mirror the commonly made distinctions. For instance, John Odell distinguishes between specific beliefs (causal) and general beliefs (ideology) [*Odell, 1982: 62*].
8. The classic example of this approach is Gourevitch, 1986. For his use of this approach to explain the adoption of Keynesian policies in the post war era see Gourevitch [*1989*].
9. Peter Hall also argues that Keynesian ideas were particularly well situated for building political coalitions [*Hall, 1989*].
10. There are important differneces between the IMF and the World Bank and they may develop different relationships with the South African government. However, they generally promote a similar orthodoxy (although the World Bank's distinct mission, at times, leads to a more state oriented policy), but possibly more important, in transitional South Africa they were typically lumped together.
11. Interview, T. Malan, economist: CEAS, 18 March 1994. Malan pointed out that, in fact, the document was accompanied with a disclaimer staing that it was not an NP policy document.
12. For a general review of the early debate in South Africa over the appropriate role of the IFIs in post-Apartheid South Africa see Lipschitz [*1993: 212–17*].
13. The 'Asian tiger' scenario has, in the mainstream, been associated with the neo-liberalism of the IFIs and this acts as a code-word for IFI policy.
14. This is not to argue that the relationship between South African business and the ANC began with the transition. Robert Price has chronicled what he called 'The Trek to Lusaka', which was largely South African businessmen meeting with ANC officials a decade before the transition began [*Price, 1991: 240*].
15. Erwin, who represented COSATU on the National Economic Forum (NEF), and became Deputy Finance Minister in the new government, had earlier stated: 'We do not accept a simple macroeconomic formula, such as the IMF's labour elasticity model, in assessing job growth in SA' (*Sunday Times/Business Times*, 27 March 1994).
16. The 1996/97 budget was similar. 'The key thrust was keeping the deficit down. Social welfare remains severely underdeveloped. Poverty relief for the unemployed and the destitute remains minimal.' [*AIA, 1996: 1*].
17. Professor Willie Esterhuyse [*1996*] of the University of Stellenbosch has argued, for instance, that it was just a necessary administrative move for greater efficiency.
18. This policy shift was evident as early as mid-1995 when Mbeki and others had concluded that economic growth was more important than growth and redistribution [*Esterhuyse, 1996: 2*].

159

19. These are often offered as the possible forms for regional co-operation in Africa. For instance, John Ravenhill stated that the three possible forms were: 'largely unregulated unions/common markets', 'common markets with industrial planning with possible explicit counter-dependency objectives' and 'functional co-operation' [*Ravenhill, 1986: 97*].
20. For explanations of how developmental co-operation/integration is expected to deal with this problem see Mytelka [*1975*]; Axline [*1977*].
21. SACU includes Botswana, Lesotho, Namibia, South Africa and Swaziland.
22. SACOB 1992 was prepared for SACOB by the Africa Institute in Pretoria by Dr. Erich Leistner. The SACOB official dealing with regional trade relations largely echoed the conclusions of the report (Interview (Johannesbury), SACOB, Bess Robertson, 14 Feb. 1994).

REFERENCES

African Development Bank (ADB) (1994), *Economic Integration in Southern Africa*, Abidjan: ADB.
Adler, Emanuel and Peter Haas (1992), 'Conclusion: Epistemic Communities, World Order, and the Creation of a Reflective Research Program', *International Organization* 46.
African National Congress (ANC) (1994), *Reconstruction and Development Program – Draft*, Johannesburg: ANC.
AIA (1996), *Southern Africa Chronicle* 9, April.
AP (1994), various.
Axelrod, Robert and Robert Keohane (1985), 'Achieving Cooperation Under Anarchy: Strategies and Institutions', *World Politics* 38.
Axline, Andrew (1977), 'Development, Dependence and Integration: The Politics of Regionalism in the Third World', *International Organization* 37.
Baker, Pauline, Boraine, Alex and Warren, Krafchik (eds) (1993), *South Africa and the World Economy in the 1990s*, Washington, DC: Brookings Institution.
Balassa, Bela (1961), *Theory of Economic Integration*, Homewood, IL: R.D. Erwin.
Baldwin, David (1993), 'Neoliberalism, Neorealism, and World Politics,' in David Baldwin (ed.), *Neoliberalism and Neoliberalism: The Contemporary Debate*, New York: Columbia University Press.
Bird, Graham (1996), 'The International Monetary Fund and Developing Countries: A Review of the Evidence and Policy Options', *International Organization* 50.
Bond, Patrick and Mark Swilling (1992), 'Can the Bank be stopped?' *Work in Progress*, Vol.82, p.31.
Business Times (1993), Johannesburg, 31 Oct.
Business Day (1993 and 1994), various, Johannesburg.
Central Economic Advisory Service (CEAS) (1993), *The Restructuring of the South African Economy: A Normative Model Approach*, Pretoria: CEAS.
Cheru, Fantu (1992), 'The Not So Brave New World: Problems and Prospects of Regional Integration in Post-Apartheid Southern Africa', *The Bradlow Series* No. 6, Johannesburg: SAIIA.
Chipeta, Chinyamata and Davies, Rob (1993), *Regional Relations and Cooperation Post-Apartheid*, Gaborone: SADC.
Cohen, Benjamin (1990) 'The Political Economy of International Trade', *International Organization* 44.
Cox, Robert W. (1997), 'A Perspective on Globalization', in James Mittelman (ed.), *Globalization: Critical Reflections*, Boulder, CO: Lynne Rienner.
David, Paul (1985), 'Clio and the Economics of QWERTY', *The American Economic Review* 75.
David, Paul (1986), 'Understanding the Economics of QWERTY: the Necessity of History', in

William Parker (ed.), *Economic History and the Modern Economist*, New York: Basil Blackwell.

Davies, Robert (1991), 'South Africa Joining SADCC or SADCC Joining South Africa? Emerging Perspectives on Regional Cooperation After Apartheid', in Anthoni van Nieuwkerk and Gary van Staden (eds.), *Southern Africa at the Crossroads: Prospects for the Political Economy of the Region,* Johannesburg: SAIIA.

Davies, Robert (1992), 'Emerging Perspectives on Regional Cooperation and Integration after Apartheid', *Transformation* 20.

The Economist (1995), various.

Esterhuyse, Willie (1996), 'What Happened to the Reconstruction and Development Programme?' mimeo.

Financial Times (1994), various.

Garrett, Geoffrey and Barry Weingast (1993), 'Ideas, Interests, and Institutions: Constructing the European Community's Internal Market', in Goldstein and Keohane [*1993*].

Goldstein, Judith (1993), *Ideas, Interests, and American Trade Policy,* Ithaca, NY: Cornell University Press.

Goldstein, Judith and Robert Keohane (1993), *Ideas and Foreign Policy: Beliefs, Institutions and Political Change,* Ithaca, NY: Cornell University Press.

Gomomo, John (1996), *Address to the World Economic Forum,* Cape Town, 23 May.

Gordhan, Ketso (1991), 'Should South Africa Get Involved with the International Monetary Fund and the World Bank?' in Symposium 'What Has the IMF in Store for South Africa', Johannesburg: Institute for African Alternatives.

Gourevitch, Peter (1986), *Politics in Hard Times,* Ithaca, NY: Cornell University Press.

Gourevitch, Peter (1989), 'Keynesian Politics: The Political of Economic Choices', in Hall [*1989*].

Haas, Ernst (1990), *When Knowledge is Power,* Berkeley, CA: University of California Press.

Hall, Peter (ed.) (1989), *The Political Power of Economic Ideas*, Princeton, NJ: Princeton University Press.

Hawkins, Anthony (1994), paper at Africa Regional Workshop on Economic Integration, Cape Town, 2–4 March 1994.

Hentz, James (1997), 'Regional Cooperation: Politics, Policy and Preference Formation in Transitional South Africa', unpublished.

Hirsch, Alan (1993), 'Trading Up: Towards a Trade Policy for Industrial Growth in South Africa Industrial Strategy Project', Draft Final Report, Aug. pp.54–5, Development Policy Research Unit, University of Cape Town.

Hirschman, Albert O. (1958), *The State of Economic Development,* New Haven, CT: Yale University Press.

Hirschman, Albert O. (1978), 'How the Keynesian Revolution Was Exported from the United States, and Other Comments', quoted in Hall [1989].

Ikenberry, John and Charles Kupchan (1990), 'Socialization and Hegemonic Power', *International Organization* 44.

IMF (1995), *IMF Annual Report, 1995,* Washington, DC: International Monetary Fund.

Issues: A View of South African Political Trends (1996), Johannesburg: Communications Services, June 1996, p.5.

Jacobsen, John Kurt (1995), 'Much Ado about Ideas: The Cognitive Factor in Economic Policy', *World Politics* 47.

Jervis, Robert (1988), 'Realism, Game Theory, and Cooperation', *World Politics* 40.

Johnson, Harry (1978), 'The Keynesian Revolution and Monetarist Counter-Revolution', in Harry Johnson and Elizabeth Johnson (eds.), *In the Shadow of Keynes,* Oxford: Basil Blackwell.

Kahler, Miles (1995), *International Institutions and the Political Economy of Integration,* Washington, DC: Brookings Institution.

Keohane, Robert (1993), 'Institutional Theory and the Realist Challenge after the Cold War', in David Baldwin (ed.), *Neoliberalism and Neoliberalism: The Contemporary Debate,* New York:

Columbia University Press.

Keohane, Robert and Joseph Nye (1977), *Power and Interdependence: World Politics in Transition*, 2nd Edn, Boston, MA: Little, Brown.

Lachman, Desmond and Kenneth Bercuson (1992), *Economic Policies for a New South Africa*, Occasional Paper 91, Washington, DC: International Monetary Fund.

Lipschitz, Leslie (1993), 'Review of the Debate on the Prospective Role of the IMF and World Bank in South Africa', in Pauline Baker *et al.* (eds.), *South Africa and the World Economy: A Normative Model Approach*, Washington, DC: Brookings Institution.

Marcuse, Peter (1995), 'Transitions in South Africa: To What Questions Arise Over the New Direction of the Government', *Monthly Review* 47.

MERG Report (1993), *Making Democracy Work: A Framework for Macroeconomic Policy in South Africa*, Cape Town: Centre for Development Studies.

Milner, Helen (1992), 'International Theories of Cooperation Among Nations: Strengths and Weaknesses', *World Politics* 44.

Mytelka, Lynn (1975), 'Regional Integration in the Third World: Some Internal Factors', in *International Dimensions of Regional Integration in the Third World*, Ottawa: University of Ottawa Press.

Myrdal, Gunnar (1957), *Economic Theory and Underdeveloped Regions*, London.

Nau, Henry (1990), *The Myth of America's Decline*, New York: Oxford University Press.

Odell, John (1982), *U.S. International Monetary Policy: Markets, Power and Ideas as Sources of Change*, Princeton, NJ: Princeton University Press.

Price, Robert (1991), *The Apartheid State in Crisis: Political Transformation in South Africa, 1975–1990*, New York: Oxford University Press.

Ravenhill, John (1986), 'Africa's Continuing Crisis: The Elusiveness of Development', in John Ravenhill (ed.), *Africa in Economic Crisis*, New York: Columbia University Press.

SACOB (1992), *South Africa's Options for Future Relations with Southern Africa and the European Community: Discussion Document*, Johannesburg: SACOB.

SADC (1993), *Regional Relations and Cooperation: Post-Apartheid South Africa*, Gaborone: SADC.

SADC Secretariat (1994), 'Regional Relations and Cooperation Post-Apartheid: A Strategy and Policy Framework', mimeo, SADC, Gaborone.

Sandholtz, Wayne (1993), 'Monetary Politics and Maastricht', *International Organization* 47.

Stein, Arthur (1993), 'Coordination and Collaboration: Regimes in an Anarchic World', in Baldwin [*1993*].

Wendt, Alexander (1992), 'Anarchy is What States Make It', *International Organization* 46.

World Bank (1990), 'Intra-Regional Trade in Sub-Saharan Africa', mimeo, Economics and Finance Division, Technical Division, Africa Region, World Bank, Washington, DC.

World Bank (1993), *An Economic Perspective on South Africa*, Southern Africa Department, Washington, DC, May.

World Bank, ADB, IMF and the Commission of the European Communities (1993), *Concept Paper: Initiative to Facilitate Cross-Border Private Investment, Trade and Payments in Eastern and Southern Africa*. Washington, DC: World Bank.

Yee, Albert (1996), 'The Causal Effects of Ideas on Policy', *International Organization* 50, p.70.

7

APEC and the World Trade Organization: Does Regional Integration Strengthen the Global Trade Regime?

HERIBERT DIETER

I. INTRODUCTION

In recent years, the collapse of the USSR and growing globalisation have wrought fundamental changes in the world economy. To put it simply, the change is taking place on three levels (i) At the core of the world economy the trend towards Triadisation continues: some four-fifths of the merchandise and capital flows in the world economy take place between the three poles Europe, North America, and East Asia. (ii) The post-1989 new world order is a challenge for actors in the Third World. For the first time, all regions are integrated into the capitalist world economy. Whereas in the past many developing countries endeavoured to find alternatives and 'third ways', the only issue today is the most efficient way to enter the world economy. (iii) Finally, completely new actors have come on to the scene – the transition economies. Although these countries are experiencing considerable difficulty transforming a planned economy into a market economy, both industrial and developing countries often regard the new competition as a threat.

One reaction to these developments is the proliferation of new projects for regional integration[1] among independent countries, which have experienced an astonishing renaissance in the 1990s. Although the economic order that has established itself throughout almost the entire world follows a neo-classical model, regional integration projects are nevertheless being created.[2] This is obviously a contradictory development. From a neo-classical point of view, the trend towards regionalisation is neither useful nor desirable [cf. *Krugman, 1991a: 26; Bhagwati, 1993: 29ff*]. The question is why a model that has proved its worth at the national level is not extrapolated to the global level. Why does the multilateral trading system attract muted support in the age of globalisation?

Today it is clear that regional integration projects were not only initiated to safeguard against the possible failure of the GATT Uruguay Round; they have established themselves as an independent form of economic co-operation.[3] This 'second wave' of regional integration is by no means restricted to minor actors.

The United States and the European Union are particularly active initiators of such projects. Concrete negotiations are now under way not only on major integration projects like Asia Pacific Economic Co-operation (APEC) or the Free Trade Area of the Americas (FTAA) stretching from Alaska to Tierra del Fuego; there are more and more proposals for interregional projects, for example between the EU and MERCOSUR, or between the EU and the United States or NAFTA in the context of a Transatlantic Free Trade Area, TAFTA [cf. *Reinicke, 1996; Prestowitz et al., 1996*].

Among these developments, the Asia Pacific Economic Co-operation forum APEC is of particular importance. First, because APEC is by far the largest project, covering more than 40 per cent of world trade and about half of world output. A second reason is that APEC is the first international organisation encompassing a number of Asian countries still involved in unresolved conflicts.[4] Finally, one of the most pronounced characteristics of APEC is the strong diversity among member countries. Both in economic performance and in economic structure, the APEC countries differ to an extraordinary degree. No other integration project has so heterogeneous a profile.

The development of more and more regional integration projects is not without risk for the world economy and the world trading system. If the trend towards creating regional economic areas continues unabated, the existing world economic order could find itself in danger. The restructuring of the world economy into a small number of major blocs could permanently weaken the multilateral trading system and encourage protectionist tendencies [cf. *Krugman, 1991a: 16f*].

On the other hand, it would be wrong to see all integration projects only from the point of view of potentially unfavourable consequences for the world trading system. Especially for the developing and transition countries, regional integration can be a component in a useful development concept. The establishment of a larger economic area can allow economies of scale in production to be achieved, and can enhance the attractiveness of the area concerned for investors [cf. *Langhammer and Hiemenz, 1990: 5*]. Moreover, regional integration can have a favourable impact on the foreign policy salience of a region, as ASEAN and MERCOSUR have demonstrated.

In assessing the regionalisation of the world economy, two types of regional integration must therefore be distinguished. In the first place there are the major integration projects that have been initiated or prepared since the end of the 1980s, involving the largest economies in the world. Besides the European Union, they include Asia Pacific Economic Co-operation (APEC), the North American Free Trade Agreement (NAFTA), and the already launched Free Trade Area of the Americas (FTAA). A further major project, the Asia Europe Meeting (ASEM) emerged in 1996; in March there was a meeting of heads of state and government in Bangkok, but no decisions were made on the creation of an integration area. The debate on a 'Transatlantic Free Trade Area' (TAFTA) has also failed to produce agreement on a free trade pact. An East Asian bloc has been proposed time and again in the form of an 'East Asian Economic Caucus' (EAEC), but no formal foundation has yet taken place.

Only these large-scale projects could affect the world trading system. Smaller integration projects among developing countries must be seen differently. The increase in the number of such undertakings is doubtless no threat to the existing multilateral system.

This chapter addresses four main issues:

(i) First, what factors cause regionalisation of the world economy? The prime focus will be on macro-regionalisation, i.e., above the level of the individual country [cf. *Cox, 1987*]. What have been the motives for regional integration since the conclusion of the Uruguay Round?

(ii) Secondly, the economic basis for regional integration in the Pacific Rim is considered. Is a region as heterogeneous as the Pacific Rim able to implement a classical integration scheme?

(iii) In the third section the relationship between APEC and the WTO will be analysed. Does APEC contravene the rules and the spirit of the GATT and the World Trade Organization? At first glance the agreement to create an Asia Pacific Free trade area appears to violate specific WTO rules on the setting up of free trade areas and customs unions. Secondly, an APEC free trade area granting preferences on a basis other than that of most-favoured-nation treatment is in striking contradiction with the spirit of the GATT. APEC includes so great a part of the global economy that Asian Pacific integration within this framework could develop into an alternative to liberalisation in the WTO context.

(iv) Finally, the development of a polarised world economy will be considered. The question is whether the global economic order is threatened with destabilisation through competing systems of trade liberalisation. Are we moving towards hostile blocs or can the current development be understood as the attempt to organise international economic co-operation in a post-hegemonial environment?

II. MOTIVES FOR REGIONAL INTEGRATION IN THE AGE OF GLOBALISATION

In regional integration, policy-induced and market-induced processes need to be distinguished [cf. *OECD, 1995: 13*]. Policy-induced processes are arrangements based on treaties. Governmental actors agree to set up a certain economic framework and fix it by treaty. In the case of market-induced integration, by contrast, increasing economic interdependence produces a regionalisation trend in the economy driven not by governmental but by private actors.

But let us take a closer look at the underlying conditions for the world economy in the mid-1990s. The 'megatrends' of globalisation and regionalisation are playing an ever greater role in the development of the world economy [cf. *Altvater, 1996*]. The two terms describe overlapping processes. Globalisation is a phenomenon that has a strong impact at the micro-level, causing an increase in competitive pressure in many sectors. At the same time, global political regulation is being attempted in a few fields, for example in co-ordinating macroeconomic policy [cf. *Reinicke, 1996: 27ff*].[5] At the regional level, by contrast, we find both an integration tendency among companies and political regulatory endeavours.

In the debate on development and foreign trade, it is striking that the slogan 'globalisation' appears to have displaced the concept of interdependence [*Jones, 1995: 3*]. Globalisation serves to justify unavoidable, intensified competitive pressure, in other words, the world market is taken to be a phenomenon that affects national economies as an 'inherent necessity' [cf. *Altvater, 1987*]. Globalisation trends reduce both national autonomy and economic actors' scope for action. As the functions of the state diminish, problems must increasingly be tackled at the supranational level, where the approach can be both global and regional [cf. *Hettne, in this volume*; *Messner and Nuscheler, 1996: 6ff*].

Regional integration can thus be seen as a reaction to the increasing globalisation of the economy, but also as a reaction to growing problems in other policy areas. In periods when societies are increasingly pervaded by apparently inevitable, world-market-induced economic policies, regional integration represents, among other things, an attempt to strengthen the autonomy of the actors involved. Regional integration can be interpreted as an endeavour to exploit the advantages of free trade and larger markets without renouncing the ability to act, for example, in shaping social security systems, in environmental policy, or in national labour market policy [cf. *Altvater, 1996: 80ff*].

The 'second wave' of regional integration differs considerably from the 'first wave' of the 1960s and 1970s, in which the (failed) strategy of import-substituting industrialisation played an important role [*de Melo and Panagariya, 1992: 1*]. The new regionalism involves more actors; the entire process is more strongly market-induced than policy-induced, and both ecological and security motives are more salient [OECD, 1995: 25]. The actors no longer include only national governments but also numerous private, non-governmental entities. Unlike in the first wave, the trade strategies of integration projects are not directed towards substituting imports, but towards the world market [cf. *Hettne in this volume; Koopmann, 1994: 136*].

In both the first and second waves of regional integration, the distribution of welfare gains from the integration process has been a central issue. The theoretical discussion continues. From a neo-classical point of view, welfare can be expected to increase in the long run throughout an integration project.[6] A more critical view, taken, for example, by Harry Johnson and Gunnar Myrdal, is that integration can be expected to cause concentration at the centre to the disadvantage of the peripheral ('backwater') regions [de Melo and Panagariya, 1992: 18].[7] Machlup points to the importance of distributing economic utility: 'Since all plans for more extended economic integration assume that gains will be derived from it, it will be necessary to make clear ... which parts of the world will be major beneficiaries, which minor beneficiaries, and which possibly losers' [Machlup, 1977: 30].[8]

Analysing the internal dimension of regional integration projects is not enough, however. The change in underlying conditions from a bipolar to a multipolar world must be taken into account (see Hettne, this volume). Although the motives for creating regional integration projects are in large measure economic, it should not be forgotten that there is a link between the collapse of the USSR and the end of confrontation between competing systems. It should also be borne in mind that new conflict patterns could emerge following the end of East–West confrontation [Rotte, 1996: 43]. The OECD points out that, with the end of the cold war, trade policy has lost its function of stabilising the Western world, and has now become an element in the endeavours to find a new world order [OECD, 1995: 20].

It is not clear to what extent international policy co-ordination requires a hegemon [cf. Krugman, 1991a: 28f], but there can be no doubt that the United States has played a central role in the creation of a new world order. In this connection, the lack of coherence in American foreign trade policy has been counterproductive. The United States, which can now assert its leading position without contradiction, is less and less willing and able to assume the leadership of the world economic order [cf. Bierling, 1996: 29f; Bhagwati, 1993: 29]. Bergsten notes that both the economic basis for the continuance of American hegemony and common security interests are now lacking. Neither Europe nor Japan still need the American 'security blanket' [cf. Bergsten, 1991: 44f].

The weakening of the American hegemonic position has not contributed to stabilising the world economic system. Unlike in the period from the end of the Second World War to the mid-1980s, the US is no longer championing liberalisation of world trade in the GATT or WTO context, but is itself an increasingly frequent participant in regional integration projects (NAFTA, APEC, FTAA). This is not a sign of strength but rather a reflection of reduced American trading options [cf. Dieter, 1996c].[9] Declining American support for the multilateral trading system is surprising from the historical point of view.[10] The efforts by Germany and Japan to obtain economic control of their regions led to the post-war development of explicitly global institutions. Kahler notes:

> The experience of regional blocs organised by imperial powers
> produced a sharp reaction immediately after World War II. Post-war
> economic institutions were explicitly global; the United States enforced
> its own hostility to the continuation of imperial blocs and regional
> organisations of the world economy [*Kahler, 1996: 1*].

Despite its professed support for multilateral liberalisation in the WTO context, the United States is today also promoting several regional projects. It is participating in APEC; it is pushing the implementation of the Free Trade Area of the Americas (FTAA) by 2005; it is practising regional integration in NAFTA; and it is discussing the creation of a transatlantic free trade area or a transatlantic market with the EU [cf. *Reinicke, 1996; WTO, 1995a, 1*].[11] The lack of leadership causes uncertainty about the future of the multilateral trade regime and consequently encourages the creation of new integration projects.

III. FREE TRADE IN APEC

APEC's development since 1989 has already been well documented elsewhere [e.g., *Soesastro, 1995*]. From the beginning, APEC suffered from a lack of a precisely defined agenda on trade issues. Although there was consensus that APEC should be concerned only with economic questions, surprisingly little is known about the way to achieve economic liberalisation.[12] However, the principles of the APEC trade liberalisation process were set during the first ministerial meeting in Canberra in November 1989, when it was declared that APEC should support an open multilateral trading system and should avoid becoming an inward-looking trading bloc [*ibid.: 479*].

The subsequent ministerial meetings in Singapore, Seoul, Bangkok and Seattle dealt mainly with questions of membership as well as organisational and procedural affairs. However, at the fifth summit in Bogor, Indonesia in November 1994, the APEC heads of state and government decided on the creation of a free trade zone with unrestricted investment, by the year 2010 for the more developed countries and by 2020 for the developing countries in the region [cf. *APEC, 1995a, 1994*]. Four points need to be examined here. First, the question of whether the decision to establish a free trade area was the outcome of a wise and coherent strategy. Secondly, whether the establishment of a two-stage integration process (2010/2020) will suffice to balance out the differences in development levels and to motivate the less developed countries to take part in the integration process. The third question concerns the motives for deciding to create a free trade area. And as a final question, we must ask whether the Bogor liberalisation resolutions amount, not to the creation of a classical free trade area, but to a new form of integration that could be referred to as 'open regionalism'.

Before discussing the positive as well as negative elements of a free trade area, a point of clarification seems necessary. The term free trade area is not used in official statements on the Bogor meeting. These only emphasise that free trade and unrestricted investment are to prevail within APEC. This (deliberate) conceptual vagueness does not, however, conceal the fact that the resolutions point in a certain direction. If the participating countries do not intend to alter their foreign economic policy radically and completely abolish external tariffs, the outcome will be a classical free trade area.

A similar point is made by Soesastro. He argues that a definition of the term 'free and open trade' is necessary [*Soesastro, 1995: 488*]. Without such a definition, both a broad and a narrow interpretation of the term are possible. A broad interpretation would be to expect all tariffs and non-tariff barriers in intra-regional trade to be eliminated by 2010/2020. A narrower interpretation would be to read the Bogor declaration as a purely rhetorical statement: if that were the case, one would have to question the practical relevance of this vision.[13]

In the classical multi-stage plan we distinguish five forms of integration: free trade area, customs union, common market, economic and monetary union, with complete political integration as the fifth stage [cf. *Balassa, 1987: 43*]. The terminology often leads to confusion. Customs unions represent a higher stage of integration than free trade areas, since the former have common external tariffs for the area whereas the latter waive agreement on this. The differences in external tariffs among the participating countries constitute one of the greatest disadvantages of free trade areas. To prevent importers exploiting or evading differences in tariff rates, products to be traded within the free trade area have to be issued with certificates of origin. Rules of origin are used to ensure that the advantages of liberalisation accrue only to parties to the agreement and to third countries that have accepted a commitment to reciprocity [*OECD, 1995: 71*]. In a free trade area, criteria must accordingly be agreed on how to define goods produced within it.[14] Rules must then be found for handling certificates of origin, and the customs authorities in member countries have to inspect these certificates in intra-regional trade.[15]

This arduous and bureaucratic procedure no longer applies in a customs union. A product on which duty has been paid at the external borders of a customs union can be freely traded within it.[16] By comparison the free trade area is not a convincing approach. The bureaucratic obstacles involved in the exchange of goods within a free trade area must be regarded as extremely detrimental to the intensification of economic relations. This is one of the main reasons why, from the beginning of European integration, the countries involved concentrated on creating a customs union, which was completed in 1967.[17]

Experience with free trade areas in other parts of the world has also shown that such arrangements are very problematic, especially between countries with widely differing international economic strategies. In past years, several attempts have been made in ASEAN to intensify intra-regional trade, but they have met with only mediocre success. At least to date the ASEAN free trade area AFTA has not come up to expectations. Among the main reasons have been that many firms have found markets outside AFTA to be more lucrative, and in particular, that high bureaucratic barriers have continued to hamper intra-regional trading.[18]

Against this background the Bogor decision to introduce free trade in the region by stages is far from convincing. No thoroughgoing improvement over previous trade regimes is apparent. Tariffs, the principal starting point for a free trade area, no longer represent the most formidable impediments to trade between industrial countries [*Frenkel and Radek, 1996: 18*].[19] This applies even more with respect to the Pacific region. The most important conflicts there are concerned not with tariff levels but with non-tariff and other structural barriers to trade, especially between the United States and Japan.

For this reason a customs union appears to be the fundamentally more sensible approach. It should be remembered, however, that the divergence between the individual APEC economies does not provide a good basis for a customs union. Agreement on common external tariffs would presumably be extremely difficult to reach. Countries with very open economies like Singapore and others like South Korea, with high protective tariff duties on individual products, would have to agree. In other words, agreement on common external tariffs between countries with very different levels of tariff protection is difficult, and from the present perspective, hardly feasible in APEC. The Bogor resolution may have taken this into account.[20]

Another question is whether stretching out the integration process will suffice to take account of the differences in development level between countries. At the same time, one must ask what effects are to be expected from integration. An observer with a neo-classical view of the subject would expect regional integration to lead, at least in the long term, to an approximation of development levels among the countries involved. Accordingly it would be expected, on the basis of Heckscher/Ohlin assumptions, that factor costs will approximate in an integrating economic area. However elegant this idea may be in theory, there is little empirical evidence to support it. The failure of most integration projects in the past is to be attributed to the disadvantages suffered by less developed regions and the more dynamic development in the economic centres, even if not in entire countries. Experience shows that a similar level of development is an indispensable precondition for success in an integration process [*de Melo and Panagariya, 1992: 18*]. Development processes tend to concentrate at the centre and not on the periphery. This is true both for individual countries and for integration projects, as we have been aware since the issue was discussed in the 1950s by Gunnar Myrdal and others.

The strong diversity among APEC economies also played a role in the decision to opt for a ten-year supplementary adjustment phase. Although it is difficult to judge from the present perspective which APEC countries will have attained what level of development by 2020, marked differences in competitiveness will certainly persist among the countries in the region. Experience with European integration has shown that simply trusting in the dynamics of integration is not enough to bring the less developed parts of the community up to the level of the more highly developed areas. The European process has demonstrated that, despite costly support programmes, the gap between poor and rich regions cannot be narrowed. In APEC, where the gap between rich and poor is far wider than in Europe, attention will have to be given to ways and means of protecting the less competitive countries and regions if a loss of political support for integration is to be avoided. These concerns are shared in particular by the ASEAN countries. They are concerned that the vastly differing levels of economic development, together with greatly differing levels of technology and human capital, could lead to asymmetrical dependence and a North–South polarisation in APEC [*Soesastro, 1995: 483*].

The third question concerns the motives behind efforts towards regional integration in the Pacific area. In the light of the positive experience, especially of the world market-oriented Asian APEC countries, with the existing global trading system, there is for the moment no urgent motive for such countries to establish a formalised integration project in the Pacific region [*Nunnenkamp, 1993: 178*]. The Uruguay Round having been brought to a successful conclusion, interest in protecting the international trading system appears to be satisfied [*Borrmann and Koopmann, 1994: 368*]. It is therefore difficult to assess Asian motives for intensifying co-operation. *De facto* integration through the increasing flow of trade and investment certainly supplies a strong motive for expanding the dialogue in the region. But it was unnecessary to decide on a free trade area in order to do this. It would have been enough to conform to WTO rules and possibly to set up an additional regional forum for trade and investment-related issues.

As for American motives, three factors may have played a role. The US government's first reason must have been the fear of exclusion from an Asian integration project, namely, the East Asian Economic Caucus. Second, the US has a vital interest in opening up further the markets of its Asian trading partners. The high US balance of payments deficits are largely the outcome of trade with Japan and the Asian newly industrialising countries. Thoroughgoing, successful liberalisation in the Pacific region would be in the interests of the United States [*Bergsten, 1996: 71*].[21] The third factor might have been the assumption that it was advisable to seek a formal integration agreement with America's main trading partner, Japan. Whereas the first two of these reasons appear plausible, the third needs to be examined more closely. If one calls to mind the more or less open conflicts between the United States and Japan on trade and investment issues over the past decade and more, it is obvious that any hope of settling disputes within a regional framework is illusory.

The most recent example of trade disputes between the US and Japan has been the car dispute, which made headlines in June/July 1995. The policy followed by the US administration has been criticised for two reasons. First, it pursued aggressive unilateralism. Secondly, it demanded 'voluntary import expansions' [*Bhagwati, 1996: 261*]. The outcome of the car dispute was not only harmful to US–Japanese relations, but also to the future of the multilateral system. In Bhagwati's words:

> These bilateral negotiations tied down to a one-way stream of demands, in which the United States casts itself simultaneously as complainant, jury and judge, constantly yelling at the Japanese, seeking concessions and offering none, contain absolutely no element of the reciprocity and symmetry that define virtually all other successful negotiations among trading nations [*ibid.: 279*].

The United States and Japan have hitherto been incapable of finding a lasting settlement of their differences, either in the GATT context or in bilateral talks. Why should it be easier to solve these problems within the APEC framework? On closer consideration it is clear that settling bilateral conflicts between the United States and Japan is the *precondition* for successful integration in the Pacific region. If this cannot be achieved, the feud will merely continue with a shift of venue.[22]

Apart from the motives of the US administration, the question remains whether the United States is willing to support APEC integration comprehensively and with perseverance. Indications to the contrary are that, despite all the rhetoric in support of the APEC process, the US has certain reservations. As we know from the domestic debate on the passage of the NAFTA agreement, there is considerable opposition in Congress to intensifying regional integration. It is not to be expected that domestic opposition to a regional integration project with the countries of East and Southeast Asia will be less significant than on the question of whether an agreement should be concluded with a country that is not very competitive, like Mexico.

The fourth question is whether the APEC integration process differs structurally from other integration projects. This is claimed by apologists for the APEC process who prefer to describe the form of integration in the Pacific as open regionalism. The EU, which, in contrast to APEC, has proved to be an inward-oriented integration project, is often cited as a model to be avoided.

Open regionalism is taken to mean that there should be no discrimination against third countries [*OECD, 1995: 45*]. There are two conceivable approaches.

APEC can be open to all interested countries – the standpoint taken by Fred Bergsten, for example, chairman of the APEC's top advisory body (eminent persons group) from 1992 to 1995. Bergsten suggested that the action agenda to be adopted by the APEC summit in the Philippines should be opened to all interested parties to the WTO agreement who would be prepared to take the appropriate steps.[23] He pointed out that, only a few weeks after the APEC summit, the first WTO ministerial conference met in Singapore. The APEC action agenda to be adopted in the Philippines should not only demonstrate the progress in liberalisation being achieved in the region but also be open to WTO members:

> It can then bring that programme to Singapore, leading both by example and by offering to extend the benefits of its new cuts in tariffs and non-tariff barriers to all countries that are willing to move correspondingly. It is hard to imagine that the rest of the world, offered an opportunity to participate fully in enhanced access to the world's largest and most rapidly growing market, would opt instead to face new discrimination [*Bergsten, 1996: 71*].

Bergsten's arguments should be viewed with a critical eye for two reasons. First, if APEC had followed Bergsten's proposals, it would have begun to develop into a mini-WTO or a rival system for the liberalisation of economic co-operation. We shall go into this issue in greater detail in the following section. On the other hand, Bergsten's statement invites the conclusion that progress in liberalisation is to be ensured on the basis of reciprocity, that is, third countries could profit from APEC liberalisation measures if in exchange they grant APEC countries preferential treatment. This would not only be in violation of the GATT most-favoured-nation clause but would also introduce an element of bilateralism to trade relations [*OECD, 1995: 71*].

A second possibility for practising open regionalism would be for APEC countries to liberalise trade in accordance with GATT/WTO rules. In APEC-speak this is called 'co-ordinated unilateral liberalisation'. The question would then be why APEC is necessary, because co-ordinated, unilateral liberalisation already poses no problem within the GATT context. This variant of open regionalism, too, would overlap considerably with the work done by WTO.[24]

To evaluate the willingness of countries to liberalise unilaterally, it is not too far-fetched to take a look at the experience with the countries concerned in the multilateral system. In both the multilateral trading system and in a regional integration project, the final object is to grant partner countries advantages in exchange for increasing one's own benefits. In this connection it is necessary to remember the restrictive import policies espoused by many Asian countries, particularly Japan and South Korea. Openness is often understood as openness for exports, not, however, for imports. This manifests itself in the chronic trade and current account surpluses of these countries.

Since 1985, for example, Japan has earned a surplus on current account of more than US$700 billion. As a consequence of the strong external value of the yen, the surplus is slowly shrinking, but in 1993 it was still US$131.5 billion. The reduction of surpluses in the Japanese balance of trade has also been far from dramatic. Although the trade surplus dropped from US$144.4 billion (April 1994–March 1995) to US$125.1 billion (1995–96 estimated), even the latter total remains a heavy burden for Japan's trading partners to bear.[25] When one considers that these surpluses mean deficits in other countries, it becomes clear that Japanese surpluses have made a considerable contribution to destabilising the world economy. There is no reason to assume that the behaviour of Japan and other countries with surpluses in a regional integration project would differ essentially from their behaviour in the multilateral trading system.

The concept of open regionalism does not adequately justify APEC. If countries that still maintain comprehensive barriers in economic co-operation wish to dismantle them, they can do so without APEC.

IV. APEC AND THE WTO

One of the most important aspects in assessing the second wave of regional integration, and possibly the most interesting aspect of APEC, is the relationship between multilateral and regional trade policy, in other words the compatibility of APEC and the World Trade Organization. In the words of the OECD:

> A question of fundamental importance for the future is whether regional integration – or trade agreements – will result in the evolution of divergent, competing regional approaches to international commercial relations and thus threaten the long-term viability of a common multilateral approach [*OECD, 1995: 14*].

It has to be asked whether a regional integration project with the dimensions of APEC could represent a danger to the multilateral approach, in other words, whether other, competing ways to liberalise economic relations could develop. This question will be discussed in detail in the next section. A brief look at the history and terms of the General Agreement on Tariffs and Trade will enable us to understand better the tensions that exist between APEC and WTO.

Article XXIV of the GATT is of crucial importance in considering this issue. When the GATT was concluded in 1947, a provision was included under Article XXIV regulating the relationship between GATT and free trade areas and customs unions. Article XXIV contains the only important derogation from Article I, the unconditional most-favoured-nation principle [*Bhagwati, 1993: 25;*

Lemper, 1994: 9].[26] In other words, preferential trade agreements between two or more countries under Article XXIV did not automatically have to be made accessible to the other contracting countries. One of the reasons for this arrangement was that regional integration was understood as a contribution to world-wide liberalisation [*Senti, 1994: 131; Bhagwati, 1993: 25*].

Article XXIV of the original GATT contained a non-specific provision on the time scale for implementing integration projects. It laid down that a project was to be realised within a 'reasonable length of time' [*WTO, 1995b: 523*]. In the Uruguay Round this provision was made more specific. The amended Article XXIV still allows free trade areas and customs unions, but requires them to be implemented within a period of ten years, with exceptions needing approval by the WTO.[27]

As far as the timetable for the APEC free trade area is concerned, both the 16-year phase-in period for industrial countries and the 26-year period for developing countries quite clearly violate the provisions of Article XXIV. At the very least, the WTO would be required to approve the extended period.[28] Far more relevant than this rather technical point is the question of whether an APEC free trade agreement violates the spirit of the GATT. As we have already mentioned, all free trade areas and customs unions are departures from the GATT unconditional most-favoured-nation clause. Article I of the GATT lays down that all trade preferences granted to a member country must automatically be conceded to all other members. This provision has rightly been described, time and again, as the heart of the GATT [e.g., *Bhagwati, 1993: 25; Lemper, 1994: 3f*].[29] The idea behind Article XXIV being included was to give developing countries the opportunity to use the advantages of larger internal markets and stronger competition. It was also assumed that regional integration projects among developing countries would offer them the benefits of economies of scale without their having to open up their markets immediately to competition from industrial countries.

With APEC, however, integration is envisaged in quite different dimensions. In 1994, more than 55 per cent of world economic output was produced by APEC members and more than 40 per cent of world trade took place within the APEC region. An integration project involving the two largest economies in the world can hardly invoke an exceptional provision designed to accommodate developing countries. APEC would be a system in competition with others in its efforts to liberalise economic co-operation. It is obvious that the existing organisations promoting the liberalisation of world trade, especially the WTO, would be permanently weakened by such competition. The WTO would not be able to tolerate an APEC not operating under the principle of most-favoured-nation treatment. It would either lose what it still has in the way of credibility or the APEC integration project would have to create structures conforming to the GATT, thus putting the need for its existence in doubt.

This chapter has concentrated so far on analysing the prospects for the APEC process with regard to liberalising regional trade. Taking into account the numerous obstacles facing integration, one must continue to be sceptical about the chances of success. But one should also remember that there is a second side to the APEC process that has attracted less public scrutiny, namely, the dialogue mechanisms in APEC. Against the background of the regional heterogeneity we have described, measures to establish a permanent dialogue among the elites of the Pacific Basin are an eminently important move. The creation of intra-regional policy networks is at least as important as the trade policy measures to be taken [*Higgott, 1996: 4ff*]. In the Pacific region, these confidence-building measures are indeed the precondition for successful co-operation and integration. The individual working groups on subjects like telecommunications or transport seldom hit the headlines, but they are doubtless steps in the right direction.

It was agreed in Osaka in November 1995 that, taking account of the autonomy of the participating economies, three forms of co-operation in specific fields should be sought. First, the development of common, although not binding policy concepts; second, the implementation of joint projects; and, third, the intensification of the policy dialogue [*APEC, 1995c*]. Economic and technical co-operation was decided on for the following 13 specific fields: human resources development; small and medium-sized enterprises; energy; telecommunications and information; trade and investment data; marine resource conservation; agricultural technology; industrial science and technology; economic infrastructure; transportation; tourism; trade promotion; and fisheries [*ibid.*].

There is a further argument for the importance of APEC dialogue mechanisms. The principal goal of free trade areas and customs unions is to reduce tariffs between member states. The problem is that – particularly for trade between industrial countries – tariffs are less and less important, especially since the conclusion of the Uruguay Round. A wide spectrum of non-tariff barriers to trade constitutes a far greater problem than tariffs. In today's global economy, tariffs play an important role at most in developing countries and in a few sectors in industrial countries. Developed countries protect their markets with far more subtle means than tariffs. There are good examples of such policies to be seen in South-East and East Asia, where foreign importers are frequently obstructed by means of administrative impediments. In the discussions of recent years between the United States and Japan, for example, tariffs have played no role. The Americans have complained about the existence of structural trade barriers in Japan. Accordingly, liberalisation of trade in the Pacific region requires comprehensive changes in internal economic structures, especially in a number of Asian countries, the preparation of which will require intensive discussion among the trading partners of the region.

V. IS THE WORLD ECONOMY THREATENED WITH POLARISATION?

In recent years, numerous new integration projects have been decided or implemented. The most important of these are:

- Sweden, Austria and Finland joined the EU on 1 January 1995.

- Poland, Slovakia, Bulgaria, Romania, Lithuania, and Estonia have applied to join the EU. Further Eastern European countries are expected to apply.

- The EU has concluded a customs union with Turkey, is negotiating association status for Mediterranean countries, is preparing an inter-regional free trade area with MERCOSUR, and is negotiating with Russia on trade concessions.

- In November 1994, APEC decided to create a free trade area in two stages by 2010/2020.

- The agreement on the creation of NAFTA was concluded in 1992.

- In Miami in December 1995 it was decided to set up a pan-American free trade area (FTAA) by 2005, including all American countries except Cuba.

- Since the beginning of 1995, proposals have been under discussion on the creation of a Transatlantic Free Trade Area (TAFTA) or a Transatlantic Economic Space.

In examining the future relationship between regional and multilateral trading systems, the distinction mentioned above must be taken into account. Regional integration projects of smaller actors do not pose a threat to the multilateral system. The latter can be at risk only if one of the three poles of the world economy participates in a project. The existence of a threat to the multilateral order depends on whether there is an alternative to the WTO. Only if it is conceivable to organise world trade and to exchange direct investment outside the WTO structures can one speak of a potential danger to the WTO.

On the basis of this distinction, the major integration projects initiated in the 1990s could put the WTO at risk.[30] It is therefore a question of what prospects there are for APEC, for the American free trade area FTAA, the European Union, a possible East Asian bloc, and the still young projects of a transatlantic free trade area TAFTA and European-Asian co-operation in the 'Asia-Europe Meeting' (ASEM). In particular, the projects including two of the three poles of the world economy (APEC, TAFTA, ASEM) are of such importance for the world economy that they could develop into alternatives to the WTO.[31]

Hitherto, the World Trade Organization has adopted a wait-and-see attitude on both the number and dimensions of regional integration projects, without taking a definite stand. Whilst it has recognised that the multilateral trading system could be threatened by the development of competing systems [*WTO, 1995a*], its scope for action is limited, since any attempt on its part to prevent regional integration projects could bring it into conflict with the EU and the United States. These two poles of the world economy are crucial in the potential instability of the world trading system. Precisely because the major actors in the world economy, the United States and the EU, have left the path of multilateral trade liberalisation, conflicting regional blocs could come into being [*Dieter, 1996c*].

The discussion about the transatlantic free trade area illustrates the problems that are involved with these major integration projects. Incorrect assumptions are often made. Prestowitz *et al.*, for example, express their surprise that there is not yet a free trade pact between Europe and North America [*1996: 183*]. They overlook that the GATT arrangements have hitherto been perfectly adequate [*Piazolo, 1996: 113*].[32] Only if the functioning of the GATT/WTO were to be impaired would it be necessary to think about setting up a TAFTA.

Prestowitz *et al.* demand not only the creation of a TAFTA but also suggest using the European–American coalition to discipline East Asia in order to prevent that region from exerting too great an influence [*Prestowitz et al., 1996: 184*].[33] At first glance, this proposal can naturally be justified by the high deficits run by the United States in trade with East Asia. Between 1980 and 1994 the accumulated current account deficit of the US amounted to $882 billion [*ibid.*]. Far more important, however, is the fact that shifting coalitions can produce a problematic situation in which not only are the interests of third countries disregarded but the goal of creating a universal economic order is neglected [*Dieter, 1996a: 285ff*].

Three variants of shifting coalitions between the three poles of the world economy are conceivable: Americans and Asians (APEC), Americans and Europeans (TAFTA), Asians and Europeans (ASEM) [*Dieter, 1996b*].[34] These coalitions have already been addressed in the literature. Prestowitz et al. [*1996*] propose a coalition of Western market economies. Bergsten calls for an APEC initiative to oblige the Europeans to revise their trade policy [*Bergsten, 1996*]. Although Nesadurai does not demand an Asian-European alliance, in the event of a trade threat from the United States she does expect a decline in direct investment in East Asia should a trade dispute cause a shift to European technology and investment [*Nesadurai, 1996: 43*].

The trend towards forming large regional blocs received what could prove decisive impetus in 1994. The APEC decision of November 1994 and also the resolution of 34 countries in Miami to establish a pan-American free trade area by 2005 have to be considered in this context.

From a European perspective, this scenario was not very welcome. Within a few years, the Europeans would have found themselves confronted with an

Asian-American bloc and would have had to fear restricted trade options. This prospect induced the European Union to become active at two levels. First, proposals multiplied for an EU transatlantic initiative, for example, by the French foreign minister Alain Juppé on 6 February 1995.[35] Second, greater efforts were made to intensify the dialogue with East Asian countries. The first outcome was the summit meeting of heads of state and government of the 15 EU countries and 10 East Asian countries in the context of the 'Asia-Europe Meeting' on 1 and 2 March 1996 in Bangkok. ASEM is envisaged as counterbalancing APEC [*Camroux and Lechervy, 1996: 442ff; Rüland, 1996: 74*]. It is certainly no accident that the ten Asian countries in ASEM (the ASEAN countries, Japan, China, South Korea) are not only the strongest national economies in Asia but are also the countries that form the 'East Asian Economic Caucus' propagated by the Malaysian prime minister Mahathir since the late 1980s [*Camroux and Lechervy, 1996: 448*]. Through the ASEM and transatlantic initiatives, the EU was able to prevent what was from its standpoint a menacing situation. Today all three poles of the world economy are involved in dialogue with one another, and the isolation of Europe has been checked for the foreseeable future.

Although this can be seen as a success for Europe, the consequences for the WTO are still an open question. For, with the establishment of projects between the three poles of the world economy – which cannot as yet be considered unqualified regional integration projects, since to some extent only co-operation is envisaged – the issue of compatibility with the WTO takes on a new urgency. The possibility of regulating commercial relations in the framework of APEC, ASEM, and TAFTA reduces the need to find a solution in the WTO.[36] If a new liberalisation initiative for the world economy is wanted, it ought to be realised within the WTO *context* [*Dieter, 1996a: 287; Reinicke, 1996: 17*].

Although hitherto there has been no statistical evidence on the development of three closed trading blocs, the main issue remains whether these discussion forums serve to avoid trade disputes that would otherwise fall within the purview of the WTO, or whether, possibly in shifting coalitions, they augment controversy between the poles of the world economy. In a world economy characterised by regional blocs, is it easier to eliminate trade disputes?

It is also unclear what effect the existence of large blocs will have on their trade policy. Do regional blocs lead to trade liberalisation? The OECD, for example, points out that regional integration in Europe has greatly eased trade. Approval and licensing procedures now have to be gone into only once to permit export of a product to 15 EU countries [*OECD, 1995: 68*].[37]

Furthermore, the future relationship between regional blocs and the WTO is still open. If the multilateral trade system is not to be weakened by the development of regional blocs, arrangements must be found to ensure that the two dovetail better and support one another. The WTO must discipline and regulate integration projects [*OECD, 1995: 90*]. Although the Uruguay Round has tightened up Article XXIV, integration projects still need to be better monitored [*OECD, 1996: 16; Koopman, 1994: 131*]. For example, the WTO is considering improving the operation of the 'working parties' that examine the integration projects notified pursuant to Article XXIV, tightening up its provisions, and supervising existing free trade areas and customs unions more closely [*WTO, 1995a: 4*]. The provision that free trade areas and customs unions have to cover 'substantially all the trade' is now given very generous interpretation. The planned free trade area between South Africa and the EU, for instance, would place restrictions on 38 per cent of South African exports, but the EU still considers this to conform with Article XXIV.

It is not only APEC, of course, which threatens the WTO. All the big integration projects currently envisaged or already implemented (EU, NAFTA, FTAA, TAFTA, APEC) call into question the existence of the WTO. Such large blocs lead to the creation of economic communities often with very specific markets and a degree of harmonisation in economic policy. All the integration projects currently planned embrace more than classical trade issues, evidencing at least a trend towards shallow integration. These forms of integration pose risks for non-members, for example through the erection of non-tariff trade barriers and especially by reducing the necessity for a multilateral trading system [*Senti, 1994: 147ff; Devos, 1995: 7*].

However, there are two patterns of argument on this issue. Regional integration is interpreted by some observers as a procedure for regulating multilateralism, while others see it as a challenge to multilateralism [Hettne in this volume; *OECD, 1995: 61*]. This is demonstrated by a controversy between Paul Krugman and Fred Bergsten. Although, because of theoretically possible trade diversion, Krugman regards integration projects as potentially detrimental and apt to reduce welfare, he concludes that they are 'wrong in theory but right in practice' [*Krugman, 1991a: 33*]. Bergsten claims the opposite: free trade areas and customs unions are not only inferior to theoretically global free trade, but are also to be rejected because they could be seen as alternatives to a global trading system [*Bergsten, 1991: 43*].

If the world economy is organised in a small number of regional blocs, this could have two advantages. First, regional integration can be taken as a preliminary step towards, and test of, multilateral liberalisation. Rules and procedures can be tried out in the regional context and modified if need be, before being applied in the multilateral context [*OECD, 1995: 62ff*]. Secondly, negotiations on global liberalisation might be facilitated in a world economy organised in regional blocs. Whereas under GATT a balance has to be found among the interests of a multitude of contracting parties, it might prove very much easier to reach a compromise where fewer actors are involved [*Lemper, 1994: 11ff; OECD, 1995: 61; WTO, 1995a: 55ff*].[38] But even if we assume that regional integration and global liberalisation in the WTO are mutually beneficial, the increase in the number of integration projects requires strengthening WTO regulations on such projects. The need for regulatory reform is underlined by the fact that, of the 69 working parties of the GATT that completed their work on integration projects by December 1994, only six showed evidence of compliance with the regulations of Article XXIV [*WTO, 1995a: 3*].[39]

As mentioned above, today we can follow the development of international regimes between the three poles of the world economy. With the first Asia-Europe Meeting between the 15 countries of the European Union and ten Asian countries we have seen the completion of a triangular arrangement. The three poles of the world economy, East Asia, Europe and the US, have established a system of dialogue mechanisms with each other: the EU and the US in TAFTA, the EU and East Asia in ASEM, and the US and East Asia in APEC.

FIGURE 7.1

RELATIONS AMONG THE THREE POLES

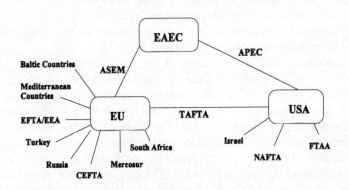

APEC:	Asia-Pacific Economic Cooperation
ASEM :	Asia Europe Meeting
CEFTA:	Central European Free Trade Agreement
EAEC:	East Asian Economic Caucus
EEA:	European Economic Area
EFTA:	European Free Trade Association
FTAA:	Free Trade Area of the Americas
NAFTA:	North American Free Trade Agreement
TAFTA:	Transatlantic Free Trade Area

The validity of the above scenario very much depends on the future of the East Asian Economic Caucus. At this stage, only Japan could provide sufficient leadership for the EAEC and it has already been encouraged to do so by Malaysian politicians [*Nesadurai, 1996: 48*]. However, a thorough reorientation of its foreign policy would be necessary. Although it acts as the engine and model of economic development for the Asian NICs, this has not abated reservations about Japan. There are, of course, historical reasons for this attitude. The memory of its aggressive, imperialist policy in the Second World War and the attempt to set up a 'Greater East Asian Co-Prosperity Sphere' are still very much alive in the region. The refusal of the Japanese government to acknowledge responsibility for war crimes committed during the war has nurtured wariness towards Japan among its neighbours.

Leaving aside these questions, Japan would have to revise its foreign economic policy if it were to assume the task of regional hegemon. Its still mercantilist international economic policy is contradictory to the function of benign hegemon. A clear indication of a break with the policy hitherto embraced would be to reduce the Japanese current account surpluses. As long as Japan is not prepared to do this, high Japanese surpluses mean deficits in other countries, in the region as well. Japan thus accepts the risk of destabilising individual economies through balance of payments crises. Both the manifestation of its willingness to pursue a responsible international economic policy and convincing acknowledgement of its responsibility for war atrocities are preconditions for a leading political role for Japan in the region.

The consequences of the formation of the tripolar arrangement described above cannot yet be predicted precisely. But when the increasing disputes between the three poles of the world economy are taken into consideration, a sceptical note is appropriate. In particular, the US in the last 18 months has caused friction in its relations with both East Asia and Europe. Its showdown with Japan in the car dispute, called the car war by some observers, has been a highly negative example of how the future relationship between the three poles of the world economy might be shaped. More recently, US legislation on commerce with Cuba and Iran/Libya and the subsequent tensions between the US and Europe underline the fact that we may well see less harmonious economic relations in the future. Since its foundation in January 1995, however, the WTO has failed to play a significant role in the solution of these conflicts. So long as it is unwilling to call its major participants to discipline themselves, it will reduce the need for multilateral negotiations. The WTO as a 'peacekeeping force' in world trade needs a much more decisive profile.

Whilst EU and US policy appears to be to participate in as many integration projects as possible, other actors must ask what strategy they are to adopt in response to the regionalisation trends described. The OECD lists five options:

(i)   to wait and see without reacting or developing a strategy of one's own;
(ii) to attempt to strengthen the multilateral trading system and the WTO;
(iii) to participate in an integration project;
(iv) third countries could conceivably seek to contain the detrimental effects of

regionalisation by making bilateral arrangements;

(v) to set up a bloc of one's own to counterbalance existing groupings [*OECD, 1995: 79ff*].

In practice, we are seeing a combination of these options. It is certainly striking that interest in the WTO has strengthened especially in Eastern Europe and in some developing countries. Whereas some years ago the GATT was considered an industrial countries' club, developing countries, fearing any further increase in the trend towards regionalisation among industrial countries, and not unjustifiably concerned that this could further marginalise the South, are displaying greater commitment to the WTO.[40] The OECD also addresses this surprising development: 'Paradoxically, these developments strengthen the multilateral trading system at a time when its former champions have moved to regional approaches' [*OECD, 1995: 80*].

VI. CONCLUSION

From the current perspective it is impossible to predict with any precision what the future holds for APEC or how the multilateral trading system will fare. Scepticism now tends to predominate on APEC's prospects. Differences between systems are too great, the gap between poor and rich countries is too wide, and conflicts between important actors like Japan and the United States are too far from settlement. However, one qualification should be made. APEC has an important role to play in intensifying dialogue in the region and in creating regional networks. Important preconditions for further development could be in the making here.

If, contrary to expectations, APEC does indeed integrate successfully and comprehensively, this would permanently affect the multilateral trading system and the WTO. Synergies between the two projects are likely to be strictly limited. The prospective development of new, large integration projects (FTAA, TAFTA) and the integration dynamics of the European Union jeopardise the current world economic order.[41] The victims of such a development would doubtless be the non-participant third countries, which would face further marginalisation. The WTO in its present form would then be relatively superfluous. Nevertheless, an international regime would continue to be needed, since the regional blocs would require a forum in which to discuss inter-regional relations and settle disputes.

The developments we have been describing constitute a danger for the WTO that should not be underestimated. In future much will depend on the credibility of the WTO. Only a short time after the multilateral trading system has been institutionally fortified with the establishment of the WTO, the system is facing one of the greatest challenges in its history. In particular, the WTO faces the question of how it is to bring regional arrangements into line with WTO rules, and how it is to exercise a regulatory and disciplinary influence on integration projects.

Unfortunately, precisely those actors that fuel the development of regional blocs, the US, the EU and to a lesser extent East Asia, are the ones that could bring the multilateral regime back on track. Whereas America and Europe would have to stop the development of new integration projects, East Asia's contribution would need to be a substantial reduction of existing trade surpluses. If the three big actors in the world economy continue their departure from the multilateral route, we may gradually slide into a world economy increasingly characterised by confrontation.

NOTES

1. Regional integration is to be defined as the gradual elimination of political and economic barriers between the participating countries. Political integration means the transfer of national sovereignty to a supra-national organisation. Economic integration aims first to reduce tariff and non-tariff barriers to trade, whereas more advanced stages of integration represented by economic and monetary union demand the establishment of jointly operated institutions. In contrast, co-operation is a process that renounces the transfer of sovereign rights, and is concerned only with specific areas of common interest. Its scope is therefore much narrower than that of integration.

2. 33 new integration projects were notified to the GATT between 1990 and 1994 [cf. *WTO, 1995a:1*].

3. Bhagwati, too, assumes that the trend towards creating integration projects will not be a flash in the pan [cf. *Bhagwati, 1993:31*].

4. APEC has been the first forum to include the three Chinas (People's Republic of China, Taiwan, Hong Kong) on an equal footing. However, as indicated by the escalating conflict in February/March 1996, tensions between the People's Republic and Taiwan in particular are far from resolved. Japan and South Korea furnish a further example. Not only Japan's imperial past but also current conflicts, for example, over the Tokda archipelago claimed by both countries, cause not inconsiderable tension between the two countries.

5. Messner and Nuscheler [*1996*] therefore demand a sort of 'global governance' to permit adequate reaction to the challenges of globalisation.

6. However, even liberal economists admit that where there are differences in levels of development, polarisation in favour of the stronger countries can occur [cf. *Langhammer and Hiemenz, 1990: 15*].

7. Pelkmans and Egenhofer stress the convergence problems in the EU. Despite comprehensive measures, no success worth noting has been achieved in reducing regional disparities [cf. *Pelkmans and Egenhofer, 1993: 335–40*].

8. Kahler also points to the problem of measuring welfare effects. The difficulty is to assess the development of fictional scenarios: on the one hand, developments where the integration project is implemented, and on the other, developments without regional integration. It is wrong to assume that regional integration always has a positive, welfare-enhancing impact [*Kahler, 1996: 11*].

9. Thurow asks why the United States ought still to have an international perspective after the collapse of communism, and expects a further retreat to internal politics [*Thurow, 1996: 23*].

10. Krugman emphasises the role of the United States in the establishment of GATT after the

Second World War. From its position as hegemon, the US was able to discipline free riders: 'The United States could and did both twist arms and offer system-sustaining concessions as a way of helping the GATT process' [*Krugman, 1991a: 28*].

11. The fact that the United States is taking part in the Asia-Pacific integration project and also promoting a transatlantic free trade area is attributable in part to the dual structure of the US economy, which is oriented towards both the Pacific and the Atlantic.

12. The lack of accuracy is not limited to trade policy, but is mirrored in the name APEC itself. According to the former Australian foreign minister, Gareth Evans, APEC is four attributes in search of a noun [cf. *Soesastro, 1995: 479*].

13. The concerns of Malaysia reflect the differences in interpretation. Malaysia's interpretation, for instance, was that the time frames of the Bogor declaration were purely indicative and not binding [*Soesastro, 1995: 489*].

14. Certificates of origin look at the alteration of a product during the production process and apply a combination of value-added indicators, changes in customs classification, and process-induced indicators to establish the origin [*OECD, 1995: 40*].

15. The complexity of certificates of origin may lead to a situation where they constitute complex barriers to trade, rather than facilitating it [*WTO, 1995a: 53*].

16. In a customs union there are, of course, non-tariff and other barriers to trade, for example, different standards in the participating countries.

17. In the first proposals for a General Agreement on Tariffs and Trade only customs unions were to be permitted under Article XXIV. In March 1948 Syria and Lebanon proposed the inclusion of free trade areas. With the support of France, the proposal was accepted [*WTO, 1995a: 8*].

18. Despite all policy-induced attempts to make a success of the regional integration project, the share of intra-regional trade in ASEAN over the past three decades has only amounted to between 18 and 22 per cent, of which 80 per cent is accounted for by trade with Singapore [*OECD, 1995: 30*]. In 1995 and 1996, however, intra-regional trade in ASEAN has increased significantly.

19. After implementation of the Uruguay Round resolutions, the average tariff level for imports of industrial products in the developed countries is 3.9 per cent [*Frenkel and Radek, 1996: 18*]. In other words, classical free trade associations contribute only to solving a problem that is becoming less important anyway.

20. In theory, the establishment of a free trade area without rules and certificates of origin is possible. However, this would substantially weaken the ability of the participating countries to determine their own external economic policies.

21. Critics of the US participation in APEC argue that the US may try to use APEC as a tool for forcing the Asian countries to adopt liberal economic policies [*Nesadurai, 1996: 32*].

22. The parallel to relations between France and Germany comes to mind. Reconciliation between the two arch enemies was both the precondition for and the aim of European integration.

23. Open access to all interested countries is not an APEC invention. The EU has grown from the original group of six to its present membership of 15, soon to be 20. And GATT is a system open to all countries wishing to join, which has seen its membership proliferate since 1947. With or without restriction to a region, open access is a widespread phenomenon.

24. The OECD correctly doubts whether some APEC countries are willing to sanction progress in liberalisation on the basis of most-favoured-nation treatment [*OECD, 1995: 82*].

25. The phenomenon of persistent current account surpluses cannot be explained in terms of conventional neo-classical theory. A high current account surplus ought to have caused a rapid marked rise in the external value of the yen. For example, the sale of US dollars earned in the dollar area should have led to stronger demand for the yen and thus to a rising exchange rate. Although this process could not be completely halted, it was nevertheless postponed by the investment abroad of the earnings underlying the current account surplus. It was not a matter

of isolated decisions by individual actors. Both numerous private investors and many managers of Japanese companies decided to invest in the United States although fully aware that the US dollar was overvalued. This collective decision cushioned the impact of the current account surplus, permitting Japanese firms to retain their competitive edge and allowing all exporting firms to adjust gradually to the new conditions.

26. Critical neo-classicists point out that GATT made mistakes in its treatment of integration projects in the 1950s. The tacit acceptance of the EEC created a double precedent. First, GATT accepted an integration project between industrial countries. Secondly, exceptions were allowed, for example, for agricultural products, in contradiction of Article XXIV. In connection with acceptance of further preferential trade agreements, the legal discipline in GATT was weakened [*Bhagwati, 1993: 26; Nunnenkamp, 1993, 184; Borrmann and Koopmann, 1994: 371*].

27. The provision is worded as follows: 'The "reasonable length of time" referred to in paragraph 5 (c) of Article XXIV should exceed 10 years only in exceptional cases. In cases where Members parties to an interim agreement believe that 10 years would be insufficient they shall provide a full explanation to the Council for Trade in Goods of the need for a longer period' [*WTO, 1995b: 32*].

28. If APEC really is a process characterised by co-ordinated unilateral liberalisation, such approval by WTO would not be needed.

29. See WTO [*1995b: 986ff*] on the individual provisions of the 1947 GATT.

30. The WTO itself considers the number of integration projects as less of a danger to the world trading system than the creation of two or three large blocs [*WTO, 1995a: 27*]. The Director General of the WTO, Renato Ruggiero, estimates that the multilateral system could be endangered by two or three trade blocs [*Camroux and Lechervy, 1996: 450*].

31. In 1991 Bergsten regarded the prospects for co-operation between the three poles of the world economy quite critically: 'Economic (and other) issues are now much more likely to produce conflict among the Big Three because of the onset of equal tripolar economic power and the elimination of the cold war glue that bound the allies together' [*Bergsten, 1991: 45*]. Since 1991, there have been both favourable developments, especially the conclusion of the Uruguay Round, and strident confrontation between the three poles, for example, the 'car dispute' between the United States and Japan and tensions between the United States and the EU caused by American laws affecting European companies (Helms-Burton, D'Amato).

32. Piazolo notes that the multilateral approach would be threatened by the creation of a transatlantic free trade area [*Piazolo, 1996: 113*].

33. Krugman: '... the great advantage of regional pacts is that they can exclude Japan' [*1991a: 31*].

34. Krugman brings up interesting questions on what impact the number of trade blocs has on global welfare. Estimations of welfare effects indicate that three blocs would have the greatest negative impact [*Krugman, 1991a: 38ff*].

35. For a comprehensive record of all proposals advanced on both sides of the Atlantic, see Reinicke [*1996: 73ff*].

36. The three large co-operation or integration projects, like the WTO, are not exclusively concerned with trade issues. They also seek, among other things, to regulate direct investment, crossborder services, and industrial property rights (see Wartenweiler [*1994: 87*] on the functions of the WTO). Both the WTO and the three projects mentioned have at least shallow integration as their goal. Senti sees a risk that policy co-ordination in various fields could give rise to very specific markets to the disadvantage of third countries [*Senti, 1994: 147f*].

37. However, it should also be remembered that the EU is not a free trade area in which certificates of origin are required. In individual cases, the certificate of origin can be used to hinder rather than facilitate trade.

38. Tinbergen also assumed that it would be easier to organise the world economy in a small number of regional blocs than in a world determined by individual countries [*Tinbergen, 1962: 143*].

Senti, by contrast, expects bloc formation in Europe, North America, and Asia to threaten the existence of GATT/WTO: 'The concept of open markets based on the most-favoured-nation principle and equal treatment for domestic and foreign trading partners is incompatible with the economic groupings now coming into being' [*Senti, 1994: 132*].

39. Since four of these ceased to be operational, today only the Caribbean Common Market (Caricom) and the Czech/Slovak customs union fulfil the conditions of Article XXIV [*WTO, 1995a: 16*].

40. A quote from Joan Robinson illustrates this concern: 'The misery of being exploited by capitalists is nothing compared to the misery of not being exploited at all' from Penrose [*1992: 247ff*].

41. The OECD, too, admits that there is a danger of competing systems coming into being [*OECD, 1995: 64*].

REFERENCES

Altvater, Elmar (1987), *Sachzwang Weltmarkt. Verschuldungskrise, blockierte Industrialisierung und ökologische Gefährdung: Der Fall Brasilien*, Hamburg: VSA-Verlag.

Altvater, Elmar (1996), 'Die Regionalisierung des Weltmarktes', in Heribert Dieter (ed.), *Regionale Integration in Zentralasien*, Marburg: Metropolis-Verlag.

Altvater, Elmar and Birgit Mahnkopf (1996), *Grenzen der Globalisierung: Ökonomie, Ökologie und Politik in der Weltgesellschaft*, Münster: Westfälisches Dampfboot.

Asia Pacific Economic Co-operation (APEC) (1994), *The Economic Leaders' Declaration of Common Resolve*, Bogor, 15 Nov.

Asia Pacific Economic Co-operation (1995a), *APEC Economic Leaders' Declaration for Action*, Osaka, 19 Nov.

Asia Pacific Economic Co-operation (1995b), *The Osaka Initial Actions*, APEC 1995 Osaka Official Information.

Asia Pacific Economic Cooperation (1995c), *The Osaka Action Agenda*, Implementation of the Bogor Declaration, APEC Osaka Official Information.

Balassa, Bela (1961), *The Theory of Economic Integration*, Homewood, IL: Richard Irwin.

Balassa, Bela (1987), 'Economic Integration', in John Eatwell, Murray Milgate and Peter Newman (eds.), *The New Palgrave: A Dictionary of Economics*, Vol.2 (E to J), London: Macmillan.

Bergsten, Fred (1991), Commentary: 'The Move Toward Free Trade Zones', in *Policy Implications of Trade and Currency Zones* (A Symposium Sponsored by the Federal Reserve Bank of Kansas City, Jackson Hole, Wyoming), Aug.

Bergsten, Fred (1996), 'An Asian Push for World-Wide Free Trade', *The Economist*, 6 Jan., pp.70–71.

Bhagwati, Jagdish (1993), 'Regionalism and Multilateralism: An Overview', in Jaime De Melo and Arvind Panagariya (eds.), *New Dimensions in Regional Integration*, Cambridge: Cambridge University Press.

Bhagwati, Jagdish (1996), 'The US–Japan Car Dispute: A Monumental Mistake', *International Affairs*, Vol.72, No.2, pp.261–79.

Bierling, Stephan (1996), 'Amerikanische Außenpolitik im neuen Zeitalter', *Internationale Politik*, 5 pp.27–32.

Borrmann, Axel and Georg Koopmann (1994), 'Regionalisierung und Regionalismus im Welthandel', *Wirtschaftsdienst* (Hamburg), VII, pp.365–72.

Camroux, David and Christian Lechervy (1996), 'Close Encounter of a Third Kind? The Inaugural Asia–Europe Meeting of March 1996', *The Pacific Review*, Vol.9, No.3, pp.442–53.

Cox, Robert (1987), *Production, Power and World Order: Social Forces in the Making of History*,

New York: Columbia University Press.

de Melo, Jaime and Arvind Panagariya (1992), *The New Regionalism in Trade Policy: An Interpretive Summary of a Conference*, Washington, DC: World Bank.

Devos, Serge (1995), 'Regional Integration', *The OECD Observer*, 192 (Feb./March), pp.4–7.

Dieter, Heribert (1993), 'Probleme der Kooperation zwischen asiatischen und angelsächsisch geprägten Ländern im asiatisch-pazifischen Wirtschaftsraum', *PROKLA* (Berlin), Vol.23, No.90, pp.94–128.

Dieter, Heribert (1994), *Australien und die APEC. Die Integration des fünften Kontinents in den asiatisch-pazifischen Wirtschaftsraum*, Hamburg: Institut für Asienkunde 1994 (= Band 240 der Mitteilungen des Instituts für Asienkunde).

Dieter, Heribert (1995a), 'APEC Free Trade May Break the WTO Rules', *The Australian Financial Review*, 14 July 1995, p.19.

Dieter, Heribert (1995b), 'US Holds Key to World Economic Order', *The Australian Financial Review*, 9 Nov., p.19.

Dieter, Heribert (1996a), 'Asiatisch-pazifische Wirtschaftsgemeinschaft und Welthandelsorganisation', *Aussenpolitik* (Hamburg), Vol.47, No.3, pp.275–87.

Dieter, Heribert (1996b), 'Regional Blocs: A Help or Hindrance to the WTO?' *Asia Times*, 19 Aug.

Dieter, Heribert (1996c), 'Bleibt der Internationale Freihandel auf der Strecke? Regionale Wirtschaftskooperation oder Blockbildung', *Internationale Politik*, Vol.51, No.6, June, pp.7–14.

Frenkel, Michael and Dieter Bender (eds.) (1996), *GATT und die neue Welthandelsordnung*, Wiesbaden: Gabler.

Frenkel, Michael and Karin Radek (1996), 'Die Beschlüsse der Uruguay-Runde: Hintergrund, Inhalt und Bewertung', in Michael Frenkel and Dieter Bender (eds.), *GATT und die Neue Welthandelsordnung*, Wiesbaden: Gabler.

Higgott, Richard (1993), 'Economic Cooperation: Theoretical Opportunities and Practical Constraints', *The Pacific Review* (Oxford), Vol.6, No.2, 103–117.

Higgott, Richard (1994), 'Ideas, Identity and Policy Coordination in the Asia-Pacific', *The Pacific Review* (Oxford), Vol.7, No.4, pp.367–79.

Higgott, Richard (1996), 'Regional Integration, Economic Cooperation or Economic Policy Coordination in the Asia-Pacific? Unpacking APEC, EAEC and AFTA', mimeo.

Jones, R.J. Barry (1995), *Globalisation and Interdependence in the International Political Economy: Rhetoric and Reality*, London: Pinter Publishers.

Kahler, Miles (1996), 'The New Regionalism and its Institutions', paper presented at the conference 'Regionalization and Economic Integration: Processes and Institutions Compared' in Buenos Aires, 29 Nov., mimeo.

Koopmann, Georg (1994), 'Regionale Zusammenschlüsse und das GATT', *Nord-Süd Aktuell*, Vol.8, No.1, pp.131–7.

Krugman, Paul (1991a), 'The Move Toward Free Trade Zones', in *Policy Implications of Trade and Currency Zones* (A Symposium sponsored by the Federal Reserve Bank of Kansas City, Jackson Hole, Wyoming), Aug.

Krugman, Paul (1991b), 'Is Bilateralism bad?' in E. Helpman and A.Razin (eds.) *International Trade and Trade Policy*, Cambridge, MA: MIT Press.

Langhammer, Rolf J. and Ulrich Hiemenz (1990), *Regional Integration among Developing Countries: Opportunities, Obstacles and Options*, Kieler Studien No.232, Tübingen: J.C.B. Mohr.

Lemper, Alfons (1994), 'Die Zukunft des multilateralen Handelssystems', *Berichte des IWVWW* (Berlin), Vol.4, No.29, Dec., pp.1–14.

Machlup, Fritz (1977), *A History of Thought on Economic Integration*, London: Macmillan.

May, Bernhard (1993), 'Sieben Illusionen der Uruguay-Runde', *Europa-Archiv* (Bonn), Vol.48, No.16, pp.463–470.

Messner, Dirk and Franz Nuscheler (1996), *Global Governance*, Bonn: Stiftung Entwicklung und Frieden, Policy Paper 2.

Nesadurai, Helen E.S. (1996), 'APEC: A Tool for US Regional Domination?' *The Pacific Review* (Oxford), Vol.8, No.1, pp.31–57.

Nunnenkamp, Peter (1993), 'The World Trading System at the Crossroads: Multilateral Trade Negotiations in the Era of Regionalism', *Außenwirtschaft*, Vol.48, No.2, pp.177–201.

OECD (1995), *Regional Integration and the Multilateral Trading System: Synergy and Divergence*, Paris: OECD.

OECD (1996), *Regionalism and Its Place in the Multilateral Trading System*, Paris: OECD.

Pelkmans, Jacques and Christian Egenhofer (1993), 'Defizite in den Politikfeldern der EG-Integration', in Cord Jakobeit and Alparslan Yenal (eds.), *Gesamteuropa*, Bonn: Bundeszentrale für politische Bildung.

Penrose, Edith (1992), 'Economic Liberalization: Openness and Integration – But What Kind?' *Development Policy Review*, Vol.10, No.3, pp.237–54.

Piazolo, Daniel (1996), 'Die Pläne für eine transatlantische Freihandelszone: Chancen, Risiken und Alternativen', *Die Weltwirtschaft*, Vol.1, pp.103–16.

Prestowitz, Clyde V., Chimerine Lawrence, and Andrew Szamosszeg (1996), 'The Case for a Transatlantic Free Trade Area', *Internationale Politik und Gesellschaft*, 2, pp.183–8.

Reinicke, Wolfgang H. (1996), *Deepening the Atlantic: Towards a New Transatlanic Marketplace?* Gütersloh: Bertelsmann Foundation Publishers.

Rotte, Ralph (1996), 'Die Politische Reorganisation der Weltwirtschaft', *Aussenpolitik*, Vol.47, No.1, pp.43–52.

Rüland, Jürgen (1996), *The Asia-Europe Meeting (ASEM): Towards a New Euro-Asian Relationship?* Rostocker Informationen zu Politik und Verwaltung No.5.

Senti, Richard (1994), 'Die Integration als Gefahr für das GATT', *Außenwirtschaft*, Vol.49, No.1, pp.131–50.

Soesastro, Hadi (1995), 'ASEAN and APEC: Do Concentric Circles Work', *The Pacific Review*, Vol.8, No.3, pp.475–93.

Thurow, Lester (1996), 'Rückzug aus der Verantwortung? Eine multipolare Welt braucht keine Einzelmacht', *Internationale Politik*, 5, pp.20–26.

Tinbergen, Jan (1962), *Shaping the World Economy: Suggestions for an International Economic Policy*, New York: The Twentieth Century Fund.

Wartenweiler, Roland (1994), 'Ein Markstein in der Weltwirtschaftsgeschichte. Zum Verhandlungsabschluß der Uraguay-Runde', *Vereinte Nationen*, Vol.42, No.3, pp.87–92.

World Bank (1995), *World Development Report*, Washington, DC.

World Trade Organization (1995a), *Regionalism and the World Trading System*, Geneva: WTO.

World Trade Organization (1995b), *The Results of the Uruguay Round of Multilateral Trade Negotiations: The Legal Texts*, Geneva: WTO.

8

EU–APEC Foreign Direct Investment: A Case of Interregional Relations

SIEGFRIED SCHULTZ

I. INTRODUCTION

Since the beginning of the 1980s, the global surge in foreign direct investment (FDI) has transformed world economic relations, as FDI has become an essential element in today's complex corporate production strategy. Reflecting the globalisation of business activity, the world-wide FDI network is becoming tighter; interregional relations are of growing importance.

The purpose of this chapter is to shed some light on the status of APEC–EU linkages in the field of FDI. The interrelation of APEC and the EU will be discussed with the emphasis on East Asia *vis-à-vis* western Europe, while keeping an eye on trends at the global level. The motivations of potential investors and their choice of location within Europe will be touched upon briefly. The final section deals with the extent to which the regional and the multilateral approach of organising world trade and FDI may be reconciled.

II. THEORETICAL BACKGROUND AND RECENT TRENDS

FDI in Economic Theory

Measured against the importance of foreign direct investment over the last three decades, the contribution from economic theory 'explaining' why, when and where foreign investment takes place is quite meagre. Although there have been diverse approaches from different points of departure (macroeconomics, strategic marketing, organisational behaviour, theory of the firm, and so on), no convincing explanation has been provided that receives majority support from the research community [*Meyer, 1996*]. Instead, a variety of different trains of thought have been taken, among which the following are worth mentioning:

- In the *capital markets approach* it is assumed that multinational enterprises follow differentials in the rents of international capital markets. Companies allegedly fund themselves in countries with good capital endowment and thus relatively low interest rates, and act as investors where capital endowment is poor and remuneration is supposedly high. In other words, FDI is interpreted as one form of international capital arbitrage. Empirical facts do not lend much support to this kind of approach since FDI flows do not show the same characteristics as international portfolio capital flows [*Graham and Krugman, 1995*]. In particular, the levelling-off of barriers to capital transactions has progressively facilitated investment among highly developed countries, which makes up the bulk of world-wide FDI.

- *Geographical proximity* may be a relevant determinant because a high proportion of crossborder investment takes place between neighbouring countries or countries linked together in regional integration schemes. The research interest in this field is focused on the agglomeration effects which can be attributed to the utilisation of increased returns to scale. FDI can be interpreted [*Krugman, 1992*] as the international allocation of mobile capital in the presence of immobile workers and complex barriers to trade. However, the argument can easily end up in some kind of circular causation because existing industrial complexes turn out to be the major determinant of further FDI.

- In the framework of *institutional analysis,* research attention has been focused on the legal and institutional conditions faced by potential foreign investors; supplementary factors are the social and general policy environment (*Ordnungspolitik*). At the same time, public authorities at the national, regional and local level offer incentives to attract potential investors to their country, area or community respectively. Although it is quite common to allocate public funds to this kind of competition, in substance its effect, at best, boils down to bringing about a decision to relocate the planned site among regions of a targeted country. In fact, it has a strong element of partial 'free-riding' for the investor as his basic decision is only marginally affected. Obviously tax allowances and other fiscal incentives rank lower than the general policy framework, that is, openness of the economy, extent of 'red tape', environmental legislation and the stipulations of local authorities. A specific aspect of the institutional approach is political risk. To keep such risks in check publicly supported guarantee and/or insurance schemes have, of course, been implemented. However, empirical evidence does not support the assumption that serious country risk can be successfully (over)compensated by inserting public funds.

- Finally, we should mention the notion that economically leading countries, while qualifying for higher ranking in the international division of labour, systematically give up production lines and positions in foreign trade in favour of neighbouring countries or members of the same regional grouping, thus providing guidelines for a future pattern of FDI. An alleged relationship of this kind can be found in the literature on key elements of the 'Asian miracle' under the catchword of *'flying geese'* [*Akamatsu, 1962; Tanaka et al., 1983*]. However, on considering the 'explanatory' components of this approach, it seems to be a neat metaphor, with undeniably strong graphic elements, rather than a testable hypothesis for empirical research.

The most commonly used interpretation of investors' behaviour in cross-border investment makes use of three core components: the sources of firm-specific advantages, the location of production, and the reasons to integrate different business units into one firm, known as the 'ownership-location-internalisation' paradigm [*Dunning, 1981, 1988, 1993*]. According to the *'eclectic paradigm'* entrepreneurial activity in a foreign country will be undertaken if (i) the potential investor has ownership-specific advantages which exceed the costs of serving a foreign or remote market with exports, (ii) the potential host country offers location-specific advantages (low wage level, established infrastructure, public support, etc.) and (iii) there are advantages of internalisation that accrue to the investor and which more than compensate for the transaction costs of alternative solutions (export, leasing, etc.). Although there were mono-causal explanations before (theory of location, transaction cost approach), it was Dunning who, in various extensions, pulled together all three prerequisites ('O-L-I') to formulate the necessary and sufficient conditions to explain FDI.

With reference to the empirical evidence, most studies on the motivational structure of investors' decisions have concluded that opening-up, penetrating and securing the market are the principal driving forces behind entrepreneurial activity in the form of equity investment. Market size and growth are commonly proxied by GDP and its change over time. The preoccupation in some political and academic quarters with low labour costs, allegedly the most important single determinant because of their immediate impact on reducing the costs of production, is not properly reflected in empirical findings (see, *inter alia*, Wilhelm [*1996*]). Rather, most research results tend to confirm the predominance of market orientation among the entrepreneurial considerations in the context of investing abroad.

Availability of Data and What They Tell Us

International comparison in the field of direct investment is cumbersome and may even be misleading. This is because foreign direct investment and direct investment abroad are not properly reflected in the statistics. Not only are there differences in the definitions employed but the recording rules and reporting systems differ substantially between countries. While some countries enjoy several sources of data, reflecting existing structures and trends in direct investment, others still suffer from a lack of minimum standards as defined and recommended by international agreement [*OECD, 1992*]. In this context, however, it should be mentioned that even industrialised countries do not automatically belong to the group of countries whose documentation corresponds to the agreed rules. To give an example: In its 1995 report on direct investment the EU Statistical Office concludes with the verdict that in 1993 the overall discrepancy resulting from the inaccurate accounting procedures of intra-EU flows amounted to 23 per cent of this investment. In 1992, this gap was 40 per cent [*Eurostat, 1995*].

What are the reasons behind these discrepancies? The main causes are the insufficient geographical allocation of FDI and the use of different collection systems. While some data are based on bank settlements, others refer to partial inquiries using enterprise panels, or a combination of both. With regard to the new questionnaire - now used jointly by OECD and Eurostat - it may be added that none of the EU member states is as yet in a position to comply fully with the standards as stipulated in the IMF and OECD recommendations.

In practice, the most important factors causing substantial discrepancies in international comparison are related to differing treatment of:

- *Basic data*: National data on international transactions reflect historically determined structures of institutions and capabilities. It makes a difference, for example, whether data are collected directly from the 'actor' or from an intermediary (securities dealer, firms' association) and, more importantly, whether flows or stocks are being recorded. As yet there are only a few countries in a position to provide genuine stock data as a meaningful input for structural analysis. These are based on periodically executed mandatory company surveys (US practice) and are thus far superior to simply cumulating past flows (even in Japan) as a rough approximation.

- *Reinvested earnings*: Since they are part of the capital engaged in the enterprise, reinvested earnings should be included in FDI. As this kind of venture capital does not cross borders, it is not reflected in balance of payments statistics. The older the direct investment stock, the greater the discrepancy between the figures of one country which records reinvested profits and those of another which omits them. Only half a dozen of the EU member countries are currently in a position to provide information on reinvested earnings. The US data comprise such earnings; they are not reported in the data from Japan. Practically none of the Asian NIEs is yet in a position to offer comprehensive information including reinvested profits. The differing treatment of reinvested profits is one of the major causes of distortion in international comparison of FDI data.

- *Loans*: Long-term loans are mostly dealt with as FDI. However, 'long-term' may have different meanings. In the majority of cases it is understood to cover periods of more than one year but it may also mean loans of over five years. Similarly, short-term loans and inter-company account balances are not uniformly recorded even within the EU. Insiders also consider this factor a major cause of asymmetry.

- *Reverse flows*: If capital is supplied by a subsidiary to its parent company it may be treated as disinvestment by the parent or an investment by the subsidiary. The problem is aggravated if subsidiaries in third countries are involved. Keeping the share of multinationals' activity in mind, this type of transfer may also contribute significantly to the built-in obstacles of international comparison.

- *Minimum requirement:* There is still a wide range in the minimum percentage of capital required before this amount will be considered as FDI. The percentage varies between 10 and 50 per cent of equity capital. Over the years this threshold between portfolio and FDI has gone down; the OECD recommendation is 10 per cent.[1] Fortunately, as most direct investment enterprises are majority-owned subsidiaries, this factor is of minor importance.

To sum up, an increasing supply of data on FDI obviously strongly encourages direct comparison. Empirical work with such data, however, stimulates second thoughts on how sensible this kind of exercise is. On the other hand, the sizeable discrepancies and obvious insufficiencies do not automatically preclude meaningful analysis. But the variations over time and the resulting regional and sectoral patterns should be interpreted with caution. For the future, a meaningful, that is, simultaneous, presentation of the geographical and sectoral distribution in the form of a matrix for a great number of countries would be a substantial improvement. The picture that can be painted at present should be interpreted as a pointer to likely trends rather than a precise reflection of the real world. The international organisations involved in the collection and dissemination of such data cannot solve the inherent problems. The reproduction of national data under their name may suggest comparability but, in fact, the underlying inconsistencies persist.

With this in mind, some figures are presented in the following section.

Global and Regional Trends

Irrespective of the data source employed (UN, OECD, or Eurostat), in the last 30 years world-wide FDI has grown about four times faster than GDP and three times faster than trade. The rapid increase in sales of foreign affiliates makes FDI one of the most important mechanisms of international economic integration. The spectacular rise in FDI has probably in most cases complemented and created trade rather than substituted for it (although there are good reasons also for a causal relationship in the opposite direction). Conservative OECD estimates show that at least 40 per cent of world trade is intra-firm trade, thus establishing a strong link between trade and investment. If compared with trade, FDI flows are only a fraction of international trade flows (around five per cent). This comparison is, however, misleading insofar as an investment typically involves a long-term commitment. Its world-wide effects on integration exceed the comparatively limited effects of trading relations.

The European Union[2] is by far the most attractive destination for foreign direct investors. Of the world's total FDI, which – in terms of *stocks* – amounted to US$1,650 billion in 1992, about 30 per cent is hosted by the EU (excluding intra-EU stock, estimated) [*European Commission, 1995*]. At the same time, the EU is one of the most important sources of FDI, also representing about 30 per cent of world-wide outward FDI (US$470 billion). The non-OECD countries play a minor role, but are becoming increasingly important. The EU, the US and most other OECD countries have a more or less balanced situation with regard to inward and outward FDI stocks. Japan is an important source of outgoing investment, by far exceeding incoming FDI. The same is true for Germany. The non-OECD countries are still mainly net recipients of FDI.

The OECD countries remain responsible for the bulk (95 per cent) of outward FDI in terms of *flows*, but recently their share of inward investment flows has declined markedly; it went down to half of its previous size within five years. The most notable feature of recent FDI development is the vigorous expansion of investment flows towards non-OECD countries.

At the same time, the more dynamic economies of South-East Asia and Latin America have themselves begun to invest abroad, predominantly but not exclusively in other countries of their region, with total FDI outflows of around US$9 billion in 1992 and US$14 billion in 1993. FDI from these countries is also directed toward the mature industrial economies of Europe and North America. After Japan had appeared as a major global investor, the Asian Newly Industrialising Economies of Hong Kong, Korea, Singapore, and Taiwan emerged as important regional investors after 1987, but have yet to become significant global investors.

As to the type of investment, FDI entry by mergers and acquisitions has become the dominant form, exceeding green field investment. There has been a clear increase in the numbers of mergers and acquisitions in the major industrial countries during the 1980s, including an increase in larger transactions. It is clearly related in part to the 'globalisation' process in the sense that a significant portion of the mergers and acquisitions are *international* transactions. Moreover, besides traditional green field investments or takeovers, modern operators resort to forms of business co-operation, for example, joint ventures, strategic alliances or the pooling of research and development resources. Particularly if there are explicit restrictions on foreign investment, companies tend to find alternative ways of gaining access to foreign markets. Alliances among enterprises of different nationalities turned out to be an effective way of entering the market, even without straight FDI.

East Asian Direct Investment Abroad

For Asia's dynamic economies – as was the case for the old industrial countries earlier – foreign direct investment is one of the ways to successful integration into the world economy. They became actors in this field as, first, consecutive export surpluses had fulfilled an important prerequisite for the export of their own capital and, secondly, pressure to keep costs down and to secure markets also forced more and more firms in the newly industrialising countries to establish foreign bases. Corresponding with the development of the current account and depending on the repayment of public debt – not considering special factors (for example, Taiwan's relations with mainland China) – phases of increasing liberalisation of capital transactions abroad could be observed.

As protection against actual, or simply against expected, protectionist measures, investors from East Asia increased FDI in the US and Western Europe in the second half of the 1980s. Towards the end of this period, the imminent completion of the European Single Market triggered a surge of additional investment flows.

For companies from newly industrialising countries there are different motives for making overseas investments. The main motive is to establish foreign branches in order to ensure continuous access to advanced technologies, production techniques and organisational structures. Investment does not necessarily have to replace exports, instead they may be mutually supportive. This occurs in two ways: first, investment supports the export of services; secondly, secure and growing markets ensure returns to scale which enable firms to remain competitive in their financial scope for acquiring advanced technological capability. In addition to this, there is design and quality improvement, where market proximity is advantageous.

In as far as East Asian firms have constructed their own production plants in Europe, the supplier system has already been partially 'exported'. On the one hand, small and medium-sized suppliers tend to follow large multinational firms – their main customers. In some cases the Japanese have effectively transplanted their *keiretsu* networks abroad. On the other hand, with the local production of components in the host country, the political demand for increased use of domestic intermediate goods and higher shares of value added can also be met. In fact, Japanese companies are the most advanced in this way of globalising production; however, competitors from Korea and of various Chinese origins (People's Republic, Hong Kong, Taiwan, Singapore) are moving in the same direction. Dominated by large associations, the organisational set-up of Japanese enterprises favours this trend. A similar structure can be observed in Korea ('chaebol') and in China ('guanxi') although they operate on a smaller scale as yet.

With respect to sectoral distribution, manufacturing is indeed the standard starting point for extensive investment in the industrialised countries, but a comparatively high proportion of Japanese and Korean firms have ventured into Europe in the service sector. Besides trade-related investment (banking, distribution), the EU's increased attractiveness – particularly with respect to (Japanese) financial services – is a result of the completion of the Single Market.

The large enterprises from East Asia which are permanently active abroad are trying to effect a long-term orientated strategy with the aim of continuously expanding investment abroad – largely independent of the economic situation in the country of origin and in the host country. In this context a hierarchy in geographical preference is noticeable. Asia remains the preferred region, with particular attention being paid to China. Recently, investment in the EU countries has not necessarily been given high priority, because some major projects have been completed and Europe's economic slow-down has begun to take its toll. Because of their long-term interest in the opportunities to participate in a growing market, most firms actively engaged in Europe are gearing themselves towards increasing sales and reducing distribution costs. The greatest changes are being witnessed in the manufacturing sector with the discontinuation of border controls and customs clearance and the establishment of general standards for safety, health and environmental protection.

In the end, the volume of direct investment from East Asia into the EU will also be dependent on how the foreign trade and payments regime looks in practice. The more restrictive the import procedures, the greater the attraction for foreign investors to enter the market from within the Single Market.

It can be expected that the future spectrum of foreign investment from the newly industrialising Asian countries will also be complex. Their outward direct investment has now developed a momentum of its own. Medium-sized firms, which are engaged in strong competition with each other, as well as firms with an oligopolistic position in their home market, create a 'pull-effect' on their way abroad: firms from the same branch follow in order not to lose ground to their rivals. The aim of developing global entrepreneurial ventures is clearly discernible in the strategy of firms from the NIEs. Korean firms, as well as firms from China and Taiwan, have focused on the dynamic growth area in East Asia and the Pacific region. At the same time, however, they do not refrain from participating, by means of direct investment, in the economic potential of other important regions.

III. THE EU'S INTERREGIONAL INVESTMENT RELATIONS

The EU has become increasingly important as a destination for foreign direct investors, and saw rapid growth between 1986 and 1989. However, the high level of investment attained in 1989 and 1990 was followed by a slump beginning in 1991. For 1993, a decrease of seven per cent was registered. Investment abroad has also been increasing since 1984, with a peak in 1989. Except for 1990 and 1992, the EU has always been a net exporter of FDI capital [*Eurostat, 1995*].

For comparison: the flows *within* the EU have been growing rapidly in recent years. From 1989, the intra-EUR12 outgoing flows remained higher than the extra-EUR12 flows. This also applies to receipts; member countries received larger flows from their EU partners than from EU-external enterprises. To give an example: in 1993, incoming extra-EUR12 FDI stood at 21 billion ECU in contrast to 27 billion of *intra*-EU flows, while direct investment going to the outside world was 22 billion ECU as compared with 34 billion going to the member states. The EU's overall contribution to world-wide direct investment amounted to slightly over 40 per cent of the total in 1993; as mentioned above, the lion's share is being distributed within the EU. The same order of magnitude applied to incoming FDI (Figure 8.1).

FIGURE 8.1
EU-12 DIRECT INVESTMENT, 1993 (ECUm.)

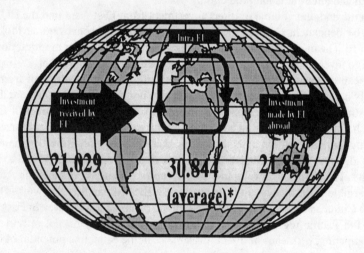

* To dampen the effect of asymmetry, reported investment accounts of both the investing and the receiving country have been added and divided by two.

Main Investors

The cumulative flows over the period 1984–93 show that the US and EFTA countries together accounted for slightly under two-thirds of the total investment made in the EU by outside investors.

The US was the single largest contributor with one-third of the EU inflows, just beating EFTA-sourced FDI. However, in recent years, the EFTA countries have been losing ground as a supplier of capital to the EU. This trend was accentuated by the virtual dissolution of EFTA with Austria, Finland and Sweden joining the EU. Japanese investment represented about 11 per cent of the total cumulated flows. Japanese investment in the 1990s fell, and has been stabilising at eight per cent since 1991. Japanese investors are more attracted by the US market. During 1985–95, the US hosted more than 50 per cent of Japanese investment abroad, in 1985 it was 40 per cent.

In 1993, US investment accounted for 43 per cent of the EU's FDI received from the outside world (1992: 51 per cent). The EFTA contribution totalled 17 per cent, leaving the EFTA countries as the second largest investor, with Switzerland as the dominant EFTA contributor. With Japan being the third largest investor in the EU, the combined share of these three investors together left about one third to other investors in the EU. 14 per cent of the total flow to the EU comes from APEC members, apart from the US and Japan. Among the rest, offshore centres were playing a major role, contributing 13 per cent of EU inflows in 1993.

Conversely, the US was by far the biggest recipient of EU direct investment capital, receiving around 70 per cent of total EU investment abroad. Even after the substantial slowdown in 1990, the US remained the main recipient of EU investment. The second largest recipient was the EFTA countries. In 1993, the US absorbed more than 47 per cent of the outgoing EU investment (1992: 37 per cent) – an increase compared with the period 1990–92, but still far from the level reached in the 1980s. EFTA members Sweden and Switzerland were, after the US, the main single recipients. With respect to Japan, EU investors were repatriating more capital than exporting in new flows to the country in 1993. This confirms the finding that, despite recent Japanese efforts to attract foreign investment, Japan remains a marginal target area for EU and US business in terms of direct investment. EU investment in other areas is gradually becoming more important. APEC countries (apart from the US and Japan) attracted seven per cent of the EU outgoing flows.

In particular, EU investment has been stepped up in the direction of its neighbours to the East, with the countries of Eastern Europe attracting 11 per cent of EU outflows in 1993. In fact, these countries were catching up to the level of investment received by the EFTA countries. For a variety of reasons, the successor states of the former Soviet Union apparently remained on the sidelines, and the investment efforts made by the EU, US and Japan towards this part of the world are either negligible or estimated at close to zero.

In the Asian region, the NIEs and China received only five per cent of total EU investment abroad in 1993. The US directed investment of the same order of magnitude to this area, while the figures for Japan (13 per cent in 1993) reflect that country's higher investment commitment to these countries. With regard to the rest, the offshore centres continue to play a role, giving a biased picture of the real destination of FDI flows: eight per cent of EU flows abroad were declared as directed towards offshore centres in 1993, 'and it is not possible to distinguish whether these flows are in transit towards other destinations, or if they remain as holdings' [*Eurostat, 1995*]. The imbalance in EU flows has been shrinking continuously, substituting the large surplus up to 1988 by a subsequently more balanced situation with regard to incoming and outgoing flows.

With particular reference to APEC-EU investment relations, in 1990 and 1993 these flows were (with the exception of EU outflows) generally dominated by the US and the UK.[3] Germany's and Japan's weight as source countries shrank drastically; both are negligible as destinations (see Figure 8.2).

FIGURE 8.2
APEC–EU MUTUAL DIRECT INVESTMENT RELATIONS

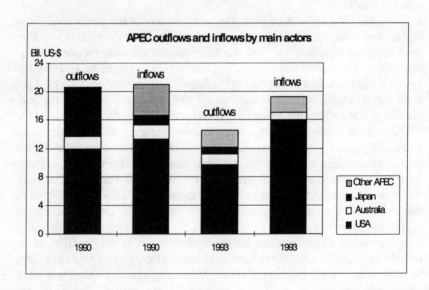

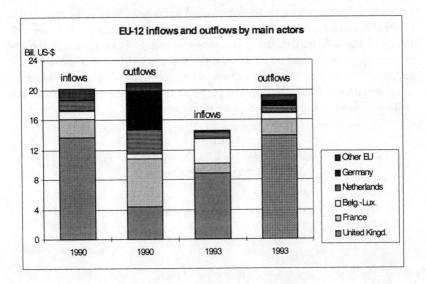

EU-12 inflows and outflows by main actors

Notes: Extra-EU flows only. In 1993, for Germany repatriation exceeded new flows: thus the net inflow wa negative. The same applies to Japan.

Source: OECD 1995b; DIW calculations.

In terms of investment volume, APEC's relations with the EU are more or less accounted for by four countries. Measured by incoming FDI, in 1993 90 per cent of the total was carried out by investors from the US, Japan, Australia and Canada (cf. Table 8.3).

Sectoral Distribution

Today the service sector has become both the largest and the fastest growing part of advanced economies. As services can be incorporated in goods or can 'travel' with persons providing them, most services must be produced at the location where they are consumed (as in professional consultancy) or used as intermediate inputs (for example, banking). This requires investment in local subsidiaries. But, to an increasing extent, international trade also requires investment facilitating sales across national frontiers.

The cumulative flows over the period 1984–93 indicate that more than 60 per cent of the flows made by foreign investors in the EU were hosted by the service sector, and about one-third were destined for industrial activities. Splitting the period in two parts (with the dividing line drawn at 1988/89) highlights some interesting features. The share of industrial activities declined from 40 to about 30 per cent, while in the service sector the corresponding figures were 37 per cent initially and more than 60 per cent more recently. In the majority of cases, FDI transactions in the service sector were linked to financial and banking activities. Deregulation and privatisation (beginning in the mid-1970s in the US, the early 1980s in the UK and in the mid-1980s elsewhere) have opened large and previously protected industries to international competition. For outflows, the pattern is similar. Total services accounted for more than 60 per cent of outgoing direct investment. The manufacturing sector abroad attracted only about a quarter of the EU flows going to other regions of the world.

TABLE 8.1

INVOLVEMENT OF APEC MEMBER COUNTRIES IN FDI RELATIONS WITH THE EU (ECUm.)

| APEC members[a] | Capital acquisition and other capital transactions[b] | | | | Cumulative percentage of the APEC share of EU-inward FDI | |
| | 1992 | | 1993 | | | |
	EU-inward	EU-outward	EU-inward	EU-outward	1992	1993
USA	11,619	6,523	9,044	10,167	76.9	65.4
Japan	1,816	432	1,662	-1,168	88.9	77.4
Australia	745	861	1,263	195	93.9	86.6
Canada	342	294	667	-78	96.1	91.4
Mexico	6	241	603	62	96.2	95.8
Hong Kong	310	-349	274	110	98.2	97.7
Korea (Rep.)	86	205	148	73	98.8	98.8
Singapore	104	217	134	-25	99.5	99.8
China	29	108	10	164	99.7	99.9
Thailand	15	235	9	152	99.8	99.9
Taiwan	11	-18	7	72	99.8	100.0
Indonesia	9	-74	3	136	99.9	100.0
Philippines	15	88	1	63	100.0	100.0
Malaysia	8	403	0	514	100.0	100.0
New Zealand[c]	-6	107		-35	100.0	100.0
Chile	-1	-61	-2	24	100.0	100.0
Total APEC	15,108	9,212	13,823	10,426	100.0	100.0
As % of extra-EU total	67.0	51.9	65.7	47.7	-	-

Notes: a) In descending order of investment amounts 1993. Brunei Darussalam and Papua New Guinea not listed due to lack of data; b) Reinvested earnings not included; c) Due to substantial negative entries in 1993 (repayments exceeding new flows), thus causing ratios above 100 per cent in the last column, these items have been deleted here.

Source: Eurostat, 1995, pp. 34/35 and 96/97.

IV. DIRECT INVESTMENT FROM THE INVESTOR'S PERSPECTIVE

Factors Determining Locational Choice Within the EU

The uneven regional distribution of Asian direct investment in Europe, as well as its concentration in few countries, gives rise to the following questions: What are the factors determining location? Why are the UK and the Netherlands the preferred destinations of foreign capital? Why is Spain relatively attractive to industrial investors? Why does Germany rank only in the middle of the foreign investment league table?[4]

With regard to firms in the service industry, particularly those in the *financial* sector, there is obviously a strong tendency to agglomerate. The large, well-known financial centres of Europe attract foreign finance companies like a magnet. The subsidiaries of Asian finance companies settle in Europe according to a similar pattern to that followed by the regional finance companies. The major concentration of such companies is in the Netherlands and the UK. There are only a few cases of overseas finance companies locating in Germany. *Trading* establishments tend to locate in those countries which offer large markets. This helps explain why up to now the trade sector dominates FDI activity in Germany and France.

What determines the choice of location for *industrial* investment, however, is less clear. Although basic patterns in the structure of the locational choice of countries and sites for direct investment abroad do exist, these decisions do not fully conform to formalised procedures [*Min, 1992*]. It is not merely a question of maximising profit, whilst taking labour costs, technology, intermediate supplies and market outlets into account. A series of socio-economic factors also play a part, such as labour force specifications, the ability of local management, national attitudes, language and social infrastructure. Government incentives for FDI may not be a decisive factor when selecting a location for investment among different regions of the world, but they do influence the decision taken when selecting production sites *within* a given region, like, for example, the EU.

Up to now, the most crucial determinants of investment in *Germany* have been the size of its market, its favourable position for distribution throughout Europe and the quality of its workforce. Furthermore, its infrastructure, particularly transport, is regarded as clearly superior to that of other European countries. Factors which fare less well in Germany than in comparable countries are, above all, the cost of labour, the general command of the English language and other 'soft' factors of location.

Unlike Germany, the *UK*'s attractiveness, as far as Japanese industrial firms are concerned, is due more to the language and other factors important for the establishment of production plants, than to factors related to the domestic market. Whilst the quality of the workforce is not different from that on the Continent, the UK with its low labour costs is considered far more favourable a location for investment than the Continental countries. That this advantage could be lost – since average labour productivity in the UK is clearly lower than in Germany – seems either to have gone unnoticed by overseas investors, or they assume that they will achieve above-average productivity in their plants. On the whole, the British infrastructure is also regarded as positive. In addition, low taxation in the UK and the numerous national, regional and local programmes for encouraging investment are regarded as attractive locational factors. Moreover, investment projects which promise to be of particular national benefit are supported by the Department of Trade and Industry. A lower rate of strikes and increased union flexibility have become known to a wider public and the old negative image of British industrial relations has been reversed.

Industrial productive capital is attracted to the *Netherlands*, above all, because of its central position in Europe, its highly acclaimed command of English and other workforce-related qualities. In addition, its components supplying industry and its transport network rank among the best.

As in Germany, *France* is chosen as a location for investment, above all, because it represents a large market and is a good location for distribution. However, the perceived limited knowledge of English makes a negative impact.

Spain stands out against other countries owing to its low labour costs (as does Portugal). In contrast, investors from the Far East class Spain's infrastructure as inferior to that of the Northern European countries.

Of course, these assessments leave some questions unanswered. Clearly the catalogue of criteria is inadequate, as 'other factors' often rank highest among the locational criteria in the whole of Europe and in individual countries. Thus, approximately one-third of the criteria seems to consist of subjective judgements, to a certain extent even influenced by emotional factors, and the remaining two-thirds, of hard factors [*Ernst and Hilpert, 1990*]. To a certain extent, personal experience played an important role in earlier contacts established with Europe, particularly when senior officials were involved influentially in the decision to invest. Among the criteria mentioned above were contacts made by executive personnel with people on the spot in connection with studies and periods of professional training in Europe. Another 'irrational' factor is the attitude shown towards foreigners. Not least, the racist incidents in Germany have had their effect on the choice of location for investment. Even though such factors have probably been absolutely decisive in only a very few cases, one can, nevertheless, conclude that such factors do have repercussions and their effects should not be underestimated.

Heading the list of the most significant decision-making criteria for objectively choosing a location for investment is the *policy employed to entice investors*. This applies to the basic attitude towards firms as well as the practical incentive measures employed for assisting firms to settle. For example, the popularity of the *UK* as a host country was established at the end of the 1980s to a significant extent on the basis of the energetic and confidence-building efforts of Thatcher and her government. Whilst Asian investors were certainly not always welcomed in the UK during the 1970s, the British government did systematically encourage the location of such industrial firms as a means of revitalising the country's industry. Subsequent policy has been geared towards job creation – particularly in structurally weak regions – and the establishment of technologically sophisticated production. Given the previous far-reaching decline of the British motor industry and in view of the subsequent FDI-driven establishment of motor production plants, this objective seems to be in the process of being realised. Such policy by the British government has been, and is, flanked by energetic recruitment and incentive measures at a regional and local level.

Policy in *France* is characterised by a rather more reserved or ambivalent attitude towards Asian investors. Public opinion in France differs widely on this topic. On the one hand, the contribution of Asian investment to the revival of British industry is widely recognised. On the other, there is a marked aversion to the influx of foreign, in particular Japanese, capital into France, as well as a fear of local industry being dominated. This anxiety is similar to the misgivings concerning American investment during the 1960s, which then gradually subsided. This is in stark contrast to the assiduous efforts of prefectures and communes with respect to Asian investment. In particular, Brittany and Alsace have been very active. The fact that France has a prominent place with regard to the number of production plants of Asian investors demonstrates that decentralised initiatives have more than compensated for the lack of enthusiasm shown by central government.

In the eyes of foreign management *Germany* has no explicit interest in a forced expansion in the presence of Asian investors. Indeed, despite the noticeable acquisition efforts of the *Bundesländer* and individual local authorities, the impression is given that a reserved position at the national level is intended to demonstrate that Germany, on the basis of its strong technological position and competitiveness, does not need actively to recruit foreign investors. Considerations regarding the market framework (*laissez-faire*) also play an important role here.

How do *incentives to settle* influence investors when deciding upon a location for their investment? Those countries which have made particular efforts in actively attracting investment by industrial firms, seem to have been able to entice these investors most frequently with what are, to a certain extent, massive locational subsidies (the UK and Ireland, for example). Naturally, firms have taken advantage of such financial assistance. This applies to investment aid awarded in the context of supporting structurally weak regions in specified development areas. Generally speaking, it is reported that in those local authorities where foreign firms wanted to settle more effort was made and higher levels of funding injected in order to improve the general economic setting for investors. This ranges from the establishment of special transport links to the provision of land which had been tailored to the demand of the respective investors.

The attitude of those foreign firms represented in Europe towards *direct* subsidies is not clear. Quite a few firms refuse to make use of these funds, either because they do not, in principle, want to be dependent on state assistance, or because they want to avoid possible public criticism in the host country. Such reservation seems less apparent with respect to *indirect* subsidies such as those which are offered by local authorities for the development of business parks. The effectiveness of subsidies as a means of attracting investment is unproven. There are indications that subsidies do not entice additional investment into Europe, but rather influence its distribution *within* Europe.

Incentives in the Target Area

The prime concern of investment promotion, not only when mobilising domestic saving but also when inviting FDI, should be the provision of conducive macro policies, as the overall economic environment is the prime factor in determining FDI flows. If potential investors are indifferent with regard to the attractiveness of competing locations, or if there are (actual or alleged) disadvantages which must be compensated for, extra government measures are important.

A number of measures are available to host authorities wishing to encourage the establishment of foreign manufacturing plants, including tax concessions, export subsidies, training schemes and preferential access to local credits, in addition to the various location grants which may be automatically available, discretionary, or a combination of both. Projects are increasingly sought by both local and regional authorities as well as national government agencies. In practice, the most important instruments in favour of projects in target regions and zones are tax privileges, accelerated depreciation, loan subsidies, and R&D support.

Despite continuous efforts in the past to curb the ongoing competition of public subsidisation, in the past, budget means have been employed to attract internationally mobile investment projects practically all over Western Europe. On the basis of an assessment made in a British study,[5] the activity of countries involved may be roughly classified as follows:

very active	fairly active	less active
Ireland	Austria	Italy
France	Belgium-Luxembourg	Spain
Netherlands	Germany	
United Kingdom	Portugal	
	Sweden	

Grants and financial incentives have been part of the regional policy tool-box for several decades in western Europe, with two main objectives usually being pursued: (i) to increase the growth (and improve the efficiency) of the indigenous sector of the economy, and (ii) to attract inward investment, either from neighbouring European countries, or – more likely – from international investors with their headquarters in the US and Japan.

Other objectives have also often existed, such as stimulating new technology or encouraging decentralisation. The latter used to be important in Britain, and is still very much the case in France. Inputs to the local economy and the creation of employment are not the only objectives sought by local or national authorities, given that foreign firms have a 'demonstration effect' for the region or country in which they establish themselves.

The attraction of inward investment has become the main purpose for offering incentives in most countries, and there is evidence that some internationally mobile firms are quite responsive if there are substantial amounts of grants and/or tax incentives available. Consequently, the provision of significant financial inducements as part of an incentive package to attract inward investment can indeed have an impact on locational trends for foreign manufacturers, although other factors, such as transport and telecommunications and the social environment, should not be ignored.

From a supranational point of view it is clear that competitive bidding with regard to investment incentives will be counterproductive. Incentives – a specific species of subsidy – in many countries are granted mostly by non-federal governmental bodies, for example, the individual states in the US and Australia, the provinces in Canada, and the *Länder* in Germany, and the federal governments in each of these countries have been reluctant to impose restrictions. But also, where issues of federalism are not as pronounced, subsidies are used actively as instruments of industrial policy by central governmental agencies, and governments have been reluctant to give up their power to use these subsidies.

Looking at the matter from an overall perspective – the OECD has been doing so and keeps trying to convince member countries – investment incentives represent an inefficient use of scarce public funds. The reason behind this assessment is that incentives have distortive effects similar to those of trade-impeding measures. Investment incentives tend to have little impact on the investment *total*; rather, they have an effect on the geographical *distribution* of the investment which is taking place anyway. In particular, they become most problematic when governments bid against each other to win a particular invest-ment project [*OECD, 1995a*]. However, as long as incentives are not eliminated altogether they will continue to be exploited by potential investors to gain as much external support for their projects as possible. In this way, investors tend to perceive incentives as a windfall but base their decisions on more fundamental considerations.

V. GOING REGIONAL OR MULTILATERAL – OR BOTH?

A crucial question to be addressed is whether regional integration is resulting in an increased regionalisation of the international economy, that is, a tendency for economic exchange to expand more quickly *within* a region than between that region and the rest of the world. Traditionally this assessment has been based on trade flows alone. Today the globalisation of production has led to a growth in trade and investment between related parties, so trade by itself is no longer an adequate guide. Foreign investment flows are also influencing the balance between regionalisation and globalisation. Investment flows suggest that, as for trade, faster growth in the share of intra-regional investment has gone hand in hand with faster growth in investment between regions. Intra-regional investment quadrupled within the EC over the period 1985–89, largely in response to the Single Market programme. But European investment in North America also quadrupled over the same period, and also grew dramatically in Asia, although from a lower base [*OECD, 1995c*].

Within East Asia there was also a rapid growth in intra-regional investment, with Japan and, to a lesser extent, the NIEs as the main sources. As with intra-regional trade, intra-regional investment in East Asia has grown much faster than in Europe. This has been both a cause and a result of rapid growth in the region.

Since the end of the cold war, regional integration arrangements have been part of a search for a stable international order and are, therefore, issues of high political priority. They ought always to be considered in terms of their strategic importance as well as of their impact on the multilateral world economic system.[6]

One of the outstanding features of the multilateral world economic system is the extensive coverage of the world economy by different forms of regional integration – from particularly deep formal integration in the EU, to informal, market-driven integration, as in East Asia. In recent years, the trend to formal regionalisation has accelerated noticeably, with the extension of the EU, the formation of NAFTA, CEFTA and MERCOSUR, major developments in APEC, and initiatives elsewhere.

Differences in the shape of agreements are closely related to objectives and policy choices. In fact, the approaches embodied in existing regional and multilateral arrangements are quite different. This helps to clarify how the various schemes compare with the traditional distinction made between (trade) liberalisation and integration. While liberalisation measures discipline the use of national policies without questioning their existence, integration involves changes in the domestic policies of the countries concerned [*OECD, 1995c: 37*]. The liberalisation matter corresponded to the multilateral approach of the GATT/WTO system, and integration to the regional approach (of the EU type). This distinction has, however, become less neatly cut in recent years. Indeed, some issues in GATT/WTO (like the stipulations for government procurement) touch upon national sovereignty in a way that only deep integration has done in the past. In contrast, important regional initiatives, such as NAFTA, are using the liberalisation approach, although going further in some aspects (for example, dispute settlement and partially affecting domestic policies). This is why it is important to be clear about the approaches used in both regional and multilateral arrangements.

The EU and APEC are outstanding examples of fundamentally different approaches in coverage and ultimate objectives to be achieved. The EU is aiming at far-reaching integration in a number of important policy areas (for example, the Common Foreign and Security Policy as outlined in the Maastricht Treaty). The coverage is comprehensive, with convergence of national policies an explicit target. The concept of competition among rules, made operational by mutual recognition of regulations in the country of origin, inserts an element of dynamism. The European approach is backed by institutionalised enforcement mechanisms at the supranational level and the jurisdiction of the European Court of Justice for EU rules.

On the other hand, APEC is not (yet) an entity constituted by a formal integration arrangement. As it is still in the process of identifying areas of joint activity as well as developing institutional structures, the governments of the member states are in full control of their various policies. There is no supranational element, and enforcement is strictly at a national level. As seen by the outside observer, there seems no intention to change this basic layout in the foreseeable future. The Committee on Trade and Investment takes care of policy dialogue on issues of member countries' interests. Because APEC investment principles are non-binding in nature, enforcement and dispute settlement procedures are generally irrelevant [*Brewer and Young, 1995*]. As APEC's ultimate objectives have not yet been fully spelled out, it seems that more weight will be given to some looser form of co-operation and to market-led integration rather than a formalised approach to integration. The basic idea is non-discrimination, with the notion being to strengthen economic relations among members, while also making the region more open to trade and investment with the rest of the world ('open regionalism').

In the interrelationship between the regional and the multilateral approach, the crucial question is whether regional agreements 'divert' political and economic efforts at the expense of multilateral negotiations, or is there a synergy between regional and multilateral negotiations? On the one hand, it has been argued that regional agreements divert from multilateral solutions. On the other, there were successful negotiations on the multilateral track running parallel to regional negotiations. The negotiations of the GATT Kennedy Round took place while the EEC was created, the Tokyo Round was concluded at the time the EEC was enlarged, and the Uruguay Round was accompanied by the completion of the EC Single Market and the founding of the US–Canadian arrangement and of NAFTA. The regional agreements comprise fewer countries than multilateral negotiations, with, in general, comparable levels of economic development; this facilitates mutual understanding. Regional agreements have sometimes also offered a more rapid route to liberalisation, whereas by contrast, multilateral negotiations, with the ultimate goal of achieving an agreement, are overladen by the wide range of interests of a large number of countries with quite divergent domestic policies and at different stages of development. Market-led initiatives of countries with a high level of economic interdependence may turn out to develop the proper driving force to push agreements ahead successfully.

With regard to the impact of regional negotiations on the multilateral process, there is in fact a high degree of interaction between regional and multilateral processes. Although this may have negative as well as positive effects, as yet the net effect has been positive more often than not. Case studies, carried out in an OECD research effort (see below), gave proof that experience in the process of regional integration is ultimately supportive of the acceptance of the need for international rules on the part of national governments and interest groups. Among the factors contributing in favour of more general solutions are the awareness of interdependence and the use of regional solutions as the testing ground for more comprehensive approaches.

Obviously there are examples of synergy or cross-fertilisation of ideas between regional and multilateral negotiations [*OECD, 1995c*]. Among others, investment provides an example of how regional agreements have helped to realise objectives set at the multilateral level. The OECD had provided the basic principles for investment in the shape of the OECD Codes. What was needed were concrete decisions to implement these principles. These were taken unilaterally by some countries (Australia, the UK). But decisions taken at the regional level have extended such approaches to many more countries. The EC decision to remove all capital controls in 1988 is a clear example of this. The liberalisation of capital controls within the EC also spread to neighbouring EFTA countries (Sweden and Austria) which had retained quite extensive controls on investment. In the North American integration scheme, the liberal US regime was extended to Canada; and NAFTA extended liberalisation to Mexico as a middle-income country.

Undoubtedly, occasionally multilateral solutions have occasionally been hampered or at least delayed by a lack of progress in regional arrangements. On balance, however, developments at a regional level seem to have tended to facilitate progress at the multilateral level. In addition, regional integration has prepared minds to accept multilateral liberalisation and wider competition, even in less liberal countries. Globalisation of competing companies also operates in the same direction, since there is a trade-off between companies' desire to keep a strong, possibly protected, national or regional market and their interest in being attached to the world-wide network of sourcing and selling.

VI. CONCLUDING REMARKS

As has been illustrated above, FDI relations between the EU and the countries constituting APEC are substantial. Since all the major players in the world economy are members of one or other of these two schemes, their mutual transactions come very close to the world total. The catalytic effect of the formation of APEC on such flows can hardly be proven for the past, its potential will have to be developed in the future.

There does not seem to be evidence of an overall trend towards regionalisation of investment. More often than not, regional arrangements have been 'laboratories' for new forms of co-operation which have not been to the detriment of the multilateral system. Rather, they were compatible and supportive of the world economic system organised on a multilateral basis. In this respect the market-driven, only moderately formalised approach in the APEC region may serve as an important impulse.

The 'open regionalism' approach during the period of uncertainty with respect to the Uruguay Round negotiations has been a good basis for the 'global option' that can be pursued now, after the conclusion of the Round. However, this does not preclude ongoing competition among schools of thought within APEC (fear of free-riding vs. unconditional liberalisation). Also, the interrelationship between APEC and the 'subregional' arrangements (AFTA, ANZCERTA, and NAFTA) might be subject to review aiming at increased consistency. Furthermore, differing notions on how to treat the agricultural sector within APEC ought to be reconciled at the outset. Here an important lesson can be learned from the EU's experience.

Admittedly, during the Osaka summit another important step has been taken to turn the 'APEC vision' into reality. It will be the member states' liberalisation programmes, to be tabled in 1996 in Manila, which will provide the prerequisite for the business community to step up investment in the region considerably (with repercussions for its presence elsewhere). In this context, the 'flexibility' formula – currently a euphemism covering up diverging philosophies about how to proceed with liberalisation in practice – has to be specified in detail. As yet, there is a wide spectrum of national points of view with regard to how closer economic co-operation is to be interpreted, ranging from Malaysia's clearly limited geographical concept to the approach of binding rules and targets preferred by the US in order to turn the common enterprise into a success story. Thus, the assessment that the 'Asian way' will prove more effective than western-style formal agreements still has to pass the litmus test.

In any event, APEC could play a crucial role in becoming a regional caucus within the wider multilateral negotiations. Furthermore, there is an opportunity to push ahead with substantive issues such as combining the subject of FDI with matters like trade policy or competition policy. In the multilateral negotiations APEC could make an important contribution to the extent that there is demand for integrating developing countries more completely into the multilateral negotiating process. Because APEC includes several emerging economies that are both host and home economies for FDI, it might turn into a platform for the better consideration of the positions of emerging economies.

NOTES

1. Until 1990 Germany used 25 per cent; currently it is 20 per cent.
2. For the statistical purposes of this chapter, the EU consists of twelve member states (EU-12).
3. After APEC was launched in 1989, the subsequent year was used as base period.
4. This section draws on the results of research by Ernst and Hilpert [*1990*].
5. Prepared for the Department of Trade and Industry.
6. Although GATT rules in general do not approve of regional groupings of a preferential nature (Art. I), departures from the obligation of most-favoured-nation treatment are possible, provided they meet (soft) conditions as specified in Art. XXIV, which were amended in the GATT-94 version (for example, inclusion of trade in agriculture).

REFERENCES

Akamatsu, Kaname (1962), 'A Historical Pattern of Economic Growth in Developing Countries', *The Developing Economies*, Preliminary Issue, No.1 (March–Aug.), pp.3–25.

Brewer, Thomas L. and Stephen Young (1995), 'FDI Policies in Regional and Multilateral Agreements', draft paper, 24 Aug.

Dunning, John H. (1981), 'Explaining the International Direct Investment Position of Countries. Towards a Dynamic or Developmental Approach', *Weltwirtschaftliches Archiv*, Vol.118, No.1, pp.31–64.

Dunning, John H. (1988), *Explaining International Production*, London:Unwin Hyman.

Dunning, John H. (1993), *Multinational Enterprises and the Global Economy*, Wokingham: Addison Wesley.

Ernst, Angelika and Hans-Günther Hilpert (1990), 'Japans Direktinvestitionen in Europa – Europas Direktinvestitionen in Japan. Bestandsaufnahme und wirtschaftspolitische Empfehlungen (Stock taking and policy recommendations)', *Ifo-Studien zur Japanforschung* 4, Munich.

European Commission (1995), 'A Level Playing Field for Direct Investment World-Wide', COM(95) 42 final, Brussels, 1 March.

Eurostat (1995), *European Union: Direct Investment 1984–1993*, Brussels/Luxembourg: European Commission.

Graham, Edward M. and Paul R. Krugman (1995), *Foreign Direct Investment in the United States*, Washington, DC: Institute for International Economics.

Krugman, Paul R. (1992), 'Does New Trade Theory Require a New Trade Policy?' *The World Economy*, Vol.15, No.4, pp.423–41.

Meyer, Klaus E. (1996), 'Theories of Direct Foreign Investment: A Review of the Literature', Chapter 3 of a Ph.D. thesis in progress, London Business School, University of London.

Min, Chung-Ki (1992), 'Korean Direct Investment in the European Community: Strategies for Korean Firms', in Chung-Ki Min, (ed.), *The Economic Cooperation Between EC and Korea: Problems and Prospects*, Seoul.

OECD (1992), 'Detailed Benchmark Definition of Foreign Direct Investment', 2nd Edition, GD(92)31, Paris: OECD.

OECD (1995a), 'Investment and the New Multilateral Trade Context' (by Edward M. Graham), Document TD/RD(95)5, Paris: OECD.

OECD (1995b), *International Direct Investment Statistics Yearbook 1995*, Paris: OECD.

OECD (1995c), *Regional Integration and the Multilateral Trading System: Synergy and Divergence*, Paris: OECD.

Tanaka, Takuo, Osada Hiroshi and Kinya Onoda (1983), 'Economic Development and the Structural Change of Trade in the Pacific Asian Region', *The Developing Economies*, 21, pp.340–56.

Wilhelm, Markus (1996), 'Motive deutscher und ausländischer direktinvestoren', *Ifo-Schnelldienst* 16, pp.9–18.

213

9

Regionalism and Trade Globalisation in Latin America: Options and Challenges

CLAUDE AUROI

I. INTRODUCTION: A DISCOURSE OF UNITY, A HISTORY OF QUARRELLING

It would be tedious to enumerate all the movements towards unity and those of disruption in Latin American history, although many of them are relevant for the topic of this paper. Recently the push and pull factors of regional economic integration in the sub-continent have become critical elements that need to be examined when considering trade globalisation in Latin America.

Nevertheless, it is necessary to have a general insight into the history of the last two centuries, in order to explain why integration is so slow and difficult, with constant ups and downs. Only a political approach based on regional relations between states can provide the background to present movements.

It will then be possible to understand that the rationale lying behind the present attempts of groupings like MERCOSUR, the Andean Group or the Central American Common Market is not a unique one, for example one driven solely by global considerations of the world economy. On the contrary, it responds to various types of sub-regional considerations. The central American conflict of the 1980s has little to do with the creation of MERCOSUR, or with Chile's strategy of liberalisation and opening. For that reason there is no such thing as a Latin American point of view on integration, as there is in Europe, despite all divergence within the European Union.

However, over the years speeches are delivered by Latin American politicians on the necessity of uniting the continent and giving it some kind of central institutions. In these speeches reference is normally made to Bolivar's dream of a great Motherland in Latin America,[1] although the endeavours he made then were defeated by the quarrels of local elites, caudillos of all kinds, nostalgic pro-Spanish elements, etc. Divergence prevailed because political and cultural diversity were the dominant traits of early nineteenth-century Latin America.

Have these fundamentals evolved? Are they now *outdated?* If this is so, then a bright future of convergent movements in the economy and at the political level can be foreseen. What we shall try to show is that, while the Bolivarian dream is no longer totally imaginary, reality changes only slowly towards various sub-regional forms of economic groupings, which have sometimes quite different views on their role in the world market.

The drive towards integration in Latin America can therefore be characterised in different ways. On the one side, there is a strong trend which argues that integration into the world market with better competitivity can be achieved through regional integration. This could be characterised as the Brazilian position. On the other hand, there are smaller countries like Colombia, Peru and Venezuela which have tried, and still do, to *protect* themselves from the world market through regional integration. A third line is the Chilean case of total openness to the world market with no fear of competitiveness. Political considerations concerning the relative weight of each country on the continent also play a major role, as the smaller countries always feel threatened by their bigger and more dynamic neighbours.

II. POLITICS AS A CURB TO ECONOMIC ALLIANCES

Latin American states have been described as *Neighbors in Turmoil* [*Cockcroft, 1989*], meaning that historically they have been riven by frequent internal upheavals, mainly military coups, but also by conflicts with the countries surrounding them. Territorial claims have been raised ever since the end of the liberation wars against Spain at the beginning of the nineteenth century, and have sometimes ended in serious armed conflicts, resulting in the loss of large portions of land by countries like Bolivia, Peru, Paraguay, Argentina, Ecuador, Colombia and Mexico.

Besides surrendering territory and resources, many Latin American states have developed a sustained and profound distrust of some of their former foes, and have preferred alliances directed against those unfriendly neighbours. Some main axes can thus be identified, which have become over time strong components of regional politics. To clarify the picture in a few lines we can distinguish:

Main axes of traditional friendship	*Main axes of traditional rivalry*
Peru – Argentina	Peru – Chile
Peru – Bolivia	Peru – Ecuador
Peru – Colombia	Argentina – Brazil
Argentina – Uruguay	Brazil – Uruguay
Uruguay – Paraguay	Brazil – Paraguay
Mexico – Cuba	Paraguay – Argentina
	Honduras – El Salvador
	Colombia – Panama

In some cases territorial disputes are not yet totally settled or have been settled only recently: namely, those between Bolivia and Chile, Ecuador and Peru, Argentina and Chile; and in one case at least there has been an open war no later than 1991 (between Peru and Ecuador). Under these circumstances it is quite understandable that the efforts towards the creation of free trade zones have been extremely slow and difficult between countries which fear the advantages others could draw and the disadvantages from which they could suffer themselves.

Two other elements must be taken as constants on the subcontinent: the relationship with the USA, and the special position of Brazil.

Role of the United States

The US has traditionally played a major role on the continent since the Monroe Doctrine. The construction of the Panama Canal further increased its commitment, especially in Central America where big interests were at stake. After the First World War the US became the dominant power in the area, both politically and economically, and all countries started trading primarily with it. Commercial links and flows therefore developed mainly North-South (the US with each individual country) and very little sub-regionally between neighbours. No significant regional market was created till very recently, intra-regional commerce remaining quite marginal compared with trade with the United States.

The Role of Brazil

The second main factor behind all attempts at regionalisation of exchanges has to do with the special position held and played by Brazil. This country represents almost one-half of the territorial space of the subcontinent and 40 per cent of its population. It also has a history which is politically and culturally different from that of the other countries, with a strong state, an important entrepreneurial class and a bourgeoisie aware of their importance and the importance of their country. It would be an exaggeration to speak of sub-imperialism in the Brazilian case, but one must not forget its permanent policy of territorial extension throughout the nineteenth century, at the expense of Peru, Bolivia, Argentina, Paraguay and Uruguay. As a consequence first of this and more recently of its unquestionable economic growth and power, Brazil's neighbours all fear to some extent entering into alliances with Brasilia, and until very recently (the 1990s) have not even dared to connect their road networks through the Amazonian jungle.

Nationalism has thus developed partly as a means of preserving internal unity, but even more in order to set up a barrier against attempts from other countries to interfere in internal affairs. Until the creation of the Organisation of American States (1948) no collective political system has existed on the sub-continent, and the OAS is not even a creation of the Latin states but far more a child of the United States.

At the economic level it was the creation of ECLAC (Economic Commission

216

for Latin America and the Caribbean of the UN) in 1948 which started the process of integration, and not the countries themselves. It would nevertheless be misleading not to recognise that the main stimulus for integration came from Latin American personalities like Raul Prebisch, the first general secretary of ECLAC, whose influence was immense. Overriding or bypassing narrow nationalism has therefore also been the endeavour of Latin America, at least of intellectuals with broader views than politicians.

But the road which finally led to the constitution of durable entities like the Andean Group, the Central American Common Market, CARICOM, and later on MERCOSUR and NAFTA, was a long one. There have been retreats, crises and above all a history of very slow progress towards forgetting or surpassing previous traditional animosity and resentment.

III. HISTORY AND TYPES OF ECONOMIC GROUPS

The general framework for economic integration in the area is constituted by *LAIA (Latin American Integration Association)* which replaced (in 1980) the defunct LAFTA (Latin American Free Trade Association). LAFTA had been created in 1960 but was never really effective, owing to the difference in the level of development of the countries in the area, their differentiated degree of trade openness and above all the ideology of *import substitution* prevailing at the time. LAIA took over without leading to generally higher trade exchanges in the area in the 1980s, but it did foster an intensification of bilateral economic relations. A whole set of agreements of a new type were signed in the late 1980s and early 1990s. The new bilateral agreements (24 agreements were signed between 1982 and 1993 [*CEPAL, 1994a: 43, Table II-5*], tend to open up trade. They concentrate more on a *positive list of products to be liberalised* and envisage total de-tariffication. They also include rules about the origin of products exported but they do not propose to introduce a common external tariff (CET) and do not contemplate measures for the protection of investments.

These agreements are certainly a step forward from the situation prevailing in the 1970s and are timid signals of an evolution towards increased intra-regional trade. *De facto* intra-regional trade has been booming since the late 1980s [*CEPAL, 1994c: 16, Tables 6 and 7*], major increases having occurred between neighbouring countries and between more advanced countries such as Brazil–Argentina, Argentina–Chile, Brazil–Chile [*CEPAL, 1994a: 50, Table II-8*].

At the same time, between 1980 and 1991, trade with the United States showed a tendency to increase in relative terms, the US share of Latin American exports rising from 30 per cent to 40 per cent. But the share of Latin American imports and exports has decreased in the US trade balance, as the Latin American countries' trade has increased more with other regions. Nevertheless the situation varies from one country to another, those closest to the US being economically more closely linked to it, in particular Mexico, with 64 per cent of its exports in 1991 [*CEPAL, 1994a: 25, Table I-1*]. Whether dependence on the North, and on industrialised economies in general, is diminishing, depends primarily on the trade strategies applied by the various countries of the region, and therefore also on the success or difficulties of the economic free trade zones that have been established.

The various groups that exist within the general framework of LAIA are the following:

(a) the *Central American Common Market* (CACM) is the oldest grouping, founded in 1960. It comprises the five Central American countries. In 1991 it changed its name to *Central American Integration System.*

(b) *CARICOM*, the Caribbean Community, joins four major countries, Barbados, Guyana, Jamaica, and Trinidad and Tobago, and eight smaller countries as well as various observers. CARICOM was created in 1965 as CARIFTA (Caribbean Free Trade Association) and converted into CARICOM in 1973. In 1981 seven former associated states decided to found the Organisation of East Caribbean States (OECS).

(c) The *Andean Group* resulted from the signature of the Treaty of Cartagena in 1969 and comprises at present the five Andean states. Chile was also a member at the beginning, but withdrew in 1976.

(d) The Market of the Southern Cone, called by its acronym *MERCOSUR*, was founded in 1991 in Asuncion by Brazil, Argentina, Uruguay and Paraguay. MERCOSUR is the largest economic group in South America, covering 58 per cent of the total area and 44 per cent of its population.

NAFTA, the North American Free Trade Area, must also be mentioned as undoubtedly the strongest group in economic terms, led by the United States. But it is not an association belonging to LAIA, although Mexico is a member. Nevertheless, it constitutes a focal point for many Latin American countries, and will have a decisive influence on the evolution of the other groups, either pushing them towards more cohesion, or on the contrary disrupting them by its own power of attraction exercised on some of their members.

Finally, one country, *Chile*, remains apart from the integration process and has chosen to follow a line of total *openness to the world,* although it tries to conclude special agreements with existing groups.

In this rather complex situation the existing groups have evolved in a context of institutional fragility where borderlines between groups have not yet been firmly drawn, and where new initiatives like the Initiative for the Americas by President Bush (1990), the Group of Three,[2] or other initiatives taken, for instance, by the Group of Rio,[3] could still reshuffle the whole setting.

This having been said, there are still some elements that must be stressed, which lie in the direction of strengthening the existing associations. The potential of the groups needs to be assessed, as well as their degree of openness to the new world trade regulations of the WTO.

IV. THE EXPANSION OF INTRA-REGIONAL TRADE

As already mentioned, intra-regional expansion of trade is a new phenomenon in Latin America, where traditionally there were very limited relations with neighbours and, as protectionism was the rule, no willingness to open markets. The poorest countries were also those which had fewest contacts among themselves, and instead looked for trade expansion with the richer nations. This was especially the case in the 1960s and 1970s with the Andean countries like Bolivia or Ecuador, the overall exports within the Andean group in 1970 being only 1.8 per cent of the total exports of the six countries [*CEPAL 1994b: 10, Table 1*]. For CARICOM the proportion of intra-regional trade was 6.4 per cent [*ibid.: Table 3*] in 1980, whereas for the more advanced countries, like those of MERCOSUR, in 1980 their exchanges already amounted to 11.6 per cent.

Since the 1960s LAIA intra-trade has almost tripled and for the Andean countries it increased ten times. The worst performing groups have been the Central American Common Market and CARICOM, because of serious internal political difficulties like the Nicaraguan conflict.

New Industrial Exports

There are, however, more fundamental factors that explain the greater expansion of trade in some groups and not in others. Since the 1960s a number of countries have gone through a process of economic structural change, consisting of a relative increase in industrial output and a decrease of agricultural production with a fluctuation of commerce along an upward trend. The countries that have experienced these changes are also those which were already more industrialised, which means, in terms of comparative development, that the poorer countries have not yet entered a phase of catching up with their richer neighbours. Furthermore, confirming the strategic association between industrial exports and development, in the period 1985–92 the six countries with the highest GDP growth revealed more rapid rates of expansion of exports of manufactures (Chile, Venezuela and Colombia) or of semi-manufactures (Costa Rica, Uruguay, Paraguay) [*ECLAC, 1994: 76*].

The expansion of manufactured goods is also clearly linked to the introduction of new technology in 'new' industrial sectors like *chemical products, transport equipment and non-electrical machinery.* Diversification has been stimulated by the relatively large amounts of foreign capital that were invested in the area from 1985 onwards. Regional markets and free trade zones are attractive for this type of capital, because the prices of these products are more stable and positive in the long run; but the regional markets are not exclusive for these products, rather they are complementary to extra-regional exports [*ECLAC, 1994: 81*]. A basic study of investments in Latin America [*Di Filippo, 1994*] has shown, however, that two types of industrial exports have to be differentiated. The first is the *maquiladora* type in Mexico and Central America and the Caribbean, which is basically linked to re-exports to the United States, and is therefore only weakly geared towards other countries of the area. The other more effective type in terms of intra-regional trade is the process of the installation of subsidiaries of transnational enterprises which in the 1980s have reoriented their exports towards the regional markets, because of the liberalisation of trade relations [*ibid.: 35*].

The new intra-regional export trend is also likely to have an influence on external dependency. The region has a high dependency as regards extra-regional imports in the same sectors, and therefore intra-regional trade in them benefits from having access to inputs and equipment which may be imported from third countries [*ECLAC, 1994: 81*]. In reality imports of intermediate goods may either be further stimulated if final production still increases, or could be reduced if a substitution process takes place within the area.

The Liberalisation Process

The liberalisation process has taken two different forms within LAIA: one the series of bilateral trade agreements mentioned above and the other the revitalisation of existing agreements, and the creation of new economic groups like MERCOSUR.

The bilateral agreements have had a minor influence on the growth of trade in the region, but they confirm that there has been a political will to enter into the liberalisation process, the reduction of trade and non-trade barriers, and so forth. At least one of them, the Argentina–Brazil Integration Act of July 1986, has led to more substantial opening and to the creation of a free trade zone and finally a common market among four countries (1995).

At the same time the Andean Group has also been dynamised, and integration was pushed forward at the beginning of the 1990s, leading to the Common External Tariff and almost total internal liberalisation of tariffs. But since 1992 this quasi-customs union has also been facing the reluctant attitude of Peru with respect to further integration and finally the announcement of its withdrawal from the Cartagena Agreement in April 1997. This setback could lead to a complete disintegration of the Andean Pact, each member looking then for its own solution, which will most probably imply closer links with MERCOSUR, as negotiated by Chile, but without full membership. Political second thoughts as well as trade arrangements with the global economy will hamper the creation of an overall free trade zone covering the whole of South America for quite a few years.

Following the Nicaragua crisis, at the end of the 1980s, trade has also increased slowly in the CACM and recovered its former levels. Progressively all the sub-regional groups are adopting the rules of the WTO Agreement and removing barriers to their exchanges and to extra-regional exchanges. Integration is at present clearly a synonym for liberalisation, as tariffs have been more or less equalised at around 20 per cent, with some lower rates of ten per cent for Chile and Bolivia. But this should not preclude analysing whether the existing groups will be consolidated, and thus become forcibly in some sense *exclusive groups,* or whether the present phase is just an *intermediate state* leading to a continental free trade zone. To answer this question it is necessary to analyse the fundamental problems of the various groups, looking again at the political aspects of those clusters, which historically are *contre-nature,* but may evolve towards reducing the emotional load of nationalism and gradually integrating apparently irreconcilable nations, as was the case with France and Germany.

V. PROBLEMS OF ECONOMIC GROUPS

For Latin America, a continent in between Africa and Asia (at least the South-East), the challenge is to speed up growth, as present rates of GDP increase are too low in most of the countries (four per cent, whereas the dynamic Asian countries were all above six per cent, and some of them around eight to ten per cent). The rate of investment is also too modest, at around 15–20 per cent, whereas a more than six per cent increase in GDP can only occur with a 25–30 per cent investment rate.

Given these basic facts, and the importance of assessing the relationship between increase of trade and increase of GDP, what still remains to be investigated in this chapter is the way Latin American countries can foster development through liberalisation in the context of regionalisation and sub-regionalisation. Along the road to the expansion of economic groups from simple free trade zones to customs unions and common markets, there are a series of sensitive items or steps that have to be tackled and mastered, because they are conflictual. The internal liberalisation of trade in goods and the fixing of a common external tariff are the first hurdles for integration. After these objectives are achieved in the context of global universal liberalism, the next step is more tricky because it touches national feelings. It is to liberalise the movement of production factors. Both capital and labour movements are sensitive issues in all countries. And Latin America is no exception.

The Cartagena Agreement contains a set of rules concerning Andean transnational companies. It also envisages the resolution of cases of double taxation, whereas the MERCOSUR agreement does not contemplate any of these measures. Nevertheless, the agreement between Argentina and Brazil explicitly foresees the creation of bi-national enterprises, and in the new types of economic agreement within the framework of LAIA there is generally a clause conceding MFN and national status to foreign investment. Out of ten agreements six have provisions on foreign investment, which shows that progress has been made since the 1970–80s, but also that there is still considerable resistance within the various countries concerning foreign capital. In many countries the sale of enterprises even to neighbouring countries is considered as selling off the country itself, its dignity and its security. This attitude prevails notably in Argentina with respect to Chile, which is a country which is beginning to export capital, that is, it has bought assets in Argentina, especially in the energy sector. Total Chilean investments in Argentina between 1990 and 1994 amounted to at least $1.5 billion [*Di Filippo, 1994: 41*]. Again, the countries which contribute most to intra-regional investment are Chile, Argentina and Brazil. Politics still intervenes heavily in the circulation of capital, and it will take time for public opinion to admit that liberalisation also includes investments.

As for labour mobility, it is usually assumed that these displacements are allowed, but in reality all kinds of obstacles are raised against Latin Americans wanting to relocate to another country. For instance, although the Treaty of Asuncion included advanced consideration about social justice and although MERCOSUR has a technical sub-group on labour standards, employment and social security (no. 11), social issues are decisively resisted by employers, and even by the government of a country like Brazil. Of course, this lack of social rules does not necessarily preclude labour mobility, but it does not facilitate it either, and it creates a climate of instability. The economic logic of regional integration does not necessarily lead to an extension of labour and social rights.

Institutional Loopholes

Apart from specific problems of the kind discussed so far, the regional sub-groups also have more general functional problems, because of a serious lack of directing bodies. In most groups the leading body is the council of ministers, which meets on specific problems. In the case of MERCOSUR, the most developed of the groups, the Council of Ministers is made up of the four Ministers of Foreign Affairs and of the Economy, with other ministers participating on a case-by-case basis. Decisions are taken by consensus. There is, as in other groups, an executive body (called the 'Group' in MERCOSUR, the Junta in the Andean group, the Permanent Secretariat in the CACM), but with limited powers. The Group of MERCOSUR is an intergovernmental body, which reduces its representativeness. In the case of the Andean Group the Junta has a supranational character, but decisions must be taken by consensus of all governments. In fact, the institutional state of development of the groups corresponds to their level of integration, which is somewhere between a customs union and a common market, free movement of factors not being totally implemented in any of them. But most of the groups are planning to evolve rapidly towards fully-fledged integrated markets, with some first elements of common economic policies, which will be the next step towards integration.

The policies of the individual governments remain influential for the future of the economic groups. These policies are sometimes dictated by the evolution of main indicators like the exchange rate and the rate of inflation, which play a considerable role in the stabilisation of the economy. Setbacks leading to the use of safeguard clauses because of high distortions in prices and exchange rates cannot therefore be avoided and have been used, as in the case of Brazil, where inflation has been on average much higher than in Argentina. In the case of the Andean Group, Peru temporarily suspended its participation in the liberalisation process at the beginning of the 1990s, to concentrate on internal price stabilisation. Competition is also currently resisted in practice by industrialists and labour unions, even if there is a theoretical adhesion to the principle. And governments, for electoral reasons, have a tendency to follow the advice of important interest groups in the economy.

Another important problem is the difference in the level of development of the various countries within the blocs. In the case of MERCOSUR, industrial synergy will certainly have a push effect on their economies, with an enhanced drive towards more sophisticated industries and in general a bigger stake in GDP. But most countries of the area, including Chile, are still heavily dependent on agricultural commodities for their exports. The industrial process is very slow and is hampered by the much greater productivity in other countries of the region and from other regions, mainly South-East Asia. These countries are therefore trying to diversify their production and exports towards non-traditional agricultural commodities and seafood, but this does not modify the differences between their economies substantially, and thus does not foster complementarity. It will only be when the countries within a bloc find some kind of specialisation that exchanges can increase drastically and accelerate the integration process. The challenge for these countries is to improve their competitiveness without competing too aggressively with their associates in the same sector and in the same markets. Otherwise political opposition will reappear and put the whole integration process in jeopardy. One solution would, of course, be to look for different external markets, some of the countries being more aggressive in their trade policy with regards to Asian markets, for instance.

Diversification of trade partners therefore becomes more and more important. Chile has proved that such a policy is feasible, with a net relative decrease in its exports to the US and a growing share going to Japan and Europe. In matters of products and of partners, Chile has reached a fairly satisfactory balance of its exports, which makes it less vulnerable to outside political and economic pressures and retaliation. The question to be asked is whether other countries of the area can follow this example. It must not be forgotten that Chile reached a high level of openness and a better diversification of trade because, *before* the other countries and the end of the GATT agreements (1994), it applied far-reaching liberalisation measures which have attracted a huge amount of foreign capital. One problem might precisely be that trade groups like MERCOSUR are more internal- than external-looking, and will favour, *volens nolens*, internal relations more than outside markets.

VI. THE END OF DISPUTES?

Regionalism in Latin America might lead to a renewal of protectionist policies within greater spatial groupings against the world market, but not necessarily in opposition to the WTO rules. These rules leave a significant margin of action to developing countries and do not prohibit the setting up of regional trade groups. If quantitative and non-tariff barriers are now condemned, it is still possible to use safeguard clauses for a number of reasons and even to manipulate tariffs within the consolidated tariff limit. Powerful groups of countries can therefore become less open than the average level of world trade regulations stipulates.

In Latin America this hypothesis is further strengthened by the creation of NAFTA, which has clearly shown that even the United States has chosen *first* to build up a larger market capable of competing with the European Union, and only *then* to favour global liberalisation. The countries of the South have been hesitating since 1994 on what path to follow, and some of them like Chile and Argentina have tried to enter or to get closer to the newly born northern Association. The December 1994 Mexican peso crisis with its resulting *Tequila effect* has curbed much of the enthusiasm, and the refusal of Congress to consider Chile's application to NAFTA has started a phenomenon of retreat towards the existing groupings, and fostered their internal integration process. The temptation of the *NAFTA syndrome* has momentarily faded, although it is premature to think that it will not return. All will finally depend on the US trade and economic policy with respect to the continent, and the capacity of some big countries of the area to avoid disruptions to the trade groups.

The dilemma remains as to whether Latin America can achieve integration on the present pattern of sub-groupings; the other option of a global free trade zone seems to be too remote. The problem of the borders of such trade groups is not yet totally solved, at least in the Southern cone. There is, of course, the Chilean free-rider, which could finally also be linked to one of the groups, either MERCOSUR or the Andean Group. But there are other countries like Bolivia which have strong links with Argentina and Brazil, and are therefore attracted by the Common Market of the Southern Cone. All things considered, MERCOSUR shows a greater potential for cohesion than the Andean Group, which stretches along a very long line where the extremes are not tightly anchored to the centre. Venezuela illustrates this case, with its initiatives in Central America and the constitution of the Group of Three with Mexico and Colombia.

Contribution of Trade Groups to Regional Security

The new pattern of economic zones in Latin America has disrupted to some extent the old friends-rivals scheme. The main breakthrough has been the constitution of an audacious Buenos-Aires–São-Paulo axis, the most powerful link in South America. The two former rivals have become collaborators in the field of industrial development and science and technology. They have grouped around their union two small states which in the nineteenth century were often at war with their bigger neighbours. If all these four states can benefit from their union, then a centre of tensions will be suppressed and regional security will be greatly enhanced.

But other sources of insecurity will remain, especially between Peru and Ecuador, which have been in dispute over eighty km of their frontier since 1942. Will the Andean Group be able to act as a mediator and find a mechanism to settle the dispute? Will other groups play that role in the future? The CACM was not able to intervene during the Nicaragua crisis, but its weakness comes from the modest size and lack of power of its members.

Collective security is not an objective as such of trade zones and even common markets. But they can indirectly play that role by developing trade and therefore functional links between countries which are still poorly connected, even by a road network. The extension of terrestrial relations like the Amazonian highway, and hence the connection of Brazil to the Pacific Ocean, is still felt by many countries like Peru or Bolivia as a threat more than an opportunity for them to find new markets themselves. The old ghosts of discord are still in the air and affect the opening up of Latin American societies, although liberalisation and the continuation of integration processes have contributed greatly to unlocking some of the key bolts of Latin American nations and people.

NOTES

1. Bolivar tried to build up a Confederation of Latin American States as early as 1826.
2. Colombia, Mexico, Venezuela.
3. The Group of Rio is made up of the twelve most important Latin American countries and has political objectives concerning the settlement of disputes, economic development, diplomatic relations with other regions, etc. It meets once a year at the level of heads of state since 1986.

REFERENCES

Auroi, Claude (1995), 'Chili II', *Effets de Uruguay Round sur les Pays en Développement*, Vol. 3, pp. 171–95 (Rapports par pays), Genève: IUED.

CEPAL (1994a), *El regionalismo abierto en America Latina y el Caribe. La integracion economica al servicio de la transformacion productiva con equidad,* Santiago de Chile: ECLAC.

CEPAL (1994b), *Desarrollo reciente de los procesos de integracion en America latina y el Caribe,* Document LC/R, 1381, Santiago de Chile: CEPAL.

CEPAL (1994c), *El dinamismo reciente del comercio intrarregional de la Asociacion latinoamericana de integracion (ALADI),* Document LC/R, 1436. Santiago de Chile: CEPAL.

Cockcroft, James D. (1989), *Neighbors in Turmoil: Latin America,* New York: Harper & Row.

Dembinski Paul, Forster, Jacques and Jaime de Melo (eds.) (1995), *Effets de l'Uruguay Round sur les Pays en Développement,* Comprend quatre volumes outre la Synthèse générale, 27p, Vol.1: Evaluation et perspectives; Vol.2: Synthèse des études par pays; Vol.3: Rapports par pays (Burkina Faso, Mali, Bolivie, Bangladesh, Maroc, Chili et Inde); Vol.4: Les mesures suisses de politique commerciale et de coopération au développement; Genève: Institut universitaire d'études du développement. IUED.

Di Filippo, Armando (1994), *Regionalismo abierto e inversion extranjera en America Latina,* Documento de trabajo, no.34, Santiago de Chile: ECLAC.

ECLAC (1994), *Policies to Improve Linkages with the Global Economy,* Santiago de Chile: ECLAC.

Page, Sheila (1996), 'The Integration of Regional Groups into Multi-Country Organisations', in Van Dijk and Sideri [*1996*].

Schultz, Siegfried (1996), 'Regionalisation of World Trade: Dead End or Way Out?', in Van Dijk and Sideri [*1996*].

Stallings, Barbara (ed.) (1995), *Global Change, Regional Response: The New International Context of Development,* Cambridge: Cambridge University Press.

Van Dijk, Meine Pieter and Sandro Sideri (1996), *Multilateralism versus Regionalism: Trade Issues after the Uruguay Round* (EADI Books Series 19), London: Frank Cass.

Varas, Augusto (1995), 'Latin America: Toward a New Reliance on the Market', in Stallings [*1995*].

10

CEFTA: Training for Integration

KATARZYNA ŻUKROWSKA

I. INTRODUCTION

Establishment of the Central European free trade area, CEFTA, was achieved painfully and with controversies about the model of functioning as an exclusive club of three members. In the beginning it was treated as a temporary solution. Five years of existence have shown that the initiative is important and will last longer than was originally foreseen by its founders. The organisation has gone through two processes: enlargement (increase in number of members) and widening (expansion of activities covered by liberalisation).

This chapter argues that CEFTA is a unique form of regional trade liberalisation arrangement among the post-communist states. It demonstrates that liberalisation is not harmful for the national economy, but on the contrary brings profit and helps to improve the negative balance of payments which occurs in most transition economies.

II. WHY WAS CEFTA ESTABLISHED?

The East Central European (ECE) countries were reluctant to form a regional trade-liberalising organisation. After 1989, all the ECE countries were oriented to Western markets and considered that liberalisation of trade with their former CMEA/COMECON neighbours was an irrelevant step in their economic policy [*Skodlarski, 1997*]. During the six months between April and October 1990 there were no signs of an agreement on economic co-operation in the region. In the autumn of 1990 a proposal of the Polish Parliament was sent to Prague and Budapest for consultation. In October representatives of the Foreign Affairs Ministries held talks. Gradually the countries came to realise that co-operation in the region would help to upgrade their position in Europe and the world. Moreover, establishing an organisation was considered to be a means to stabilising regional tensions in Europe, by accelerating integration with the European Community. The breakthrough in the negative attitude towards the creation of CEFTA was stimulated by two factors: on the one hand was the pressure of Western institutions; on the other, Poland, the most advanced in transformation, was close to association with the EC.

Five years of CEFTA have demonstrated that the negative attitude towards the establishment of this organisation was mistaken. The success of the organisation means that today all the original members try to take credit for the initiative to form a free trade zone.

Zbigniew Brzezinski suggested the establishment of CEFTA and Poland brought this initiative to life since it closely followed the Polish pre-war ideas of regional integration [*Marszalek, 1997: 373-87*]. The reservations of Hungary and Czechoslovakia about the initiative can be explained by the differences in size of the countries concerned and by the destabilisation of their economies at the start of the reforms. The main controversies among the members concerned two issues: (i) the depth of integration: should it go beyond trade liberalisation to incorporate the introduction of a common currency and political coordination, (ii) the establishment of some type of institutions. In the end it was agreed that the initiative should be limited to the establishment of a free trade zone and that there would be no new bureaucratic institutions.

On 15 February 1991 in Visegrad, a symbolic place where the Czech, Hungarian and Polish kings used to hold their meetings, a declaration on co-operation was signed.[1] This was the first of a series of meetings during which the practical details were discussed. The list of problems discussed covered: economic co-operation, ecology, local government, culture, exchange of information, and minorities. It was agreed that priority should be given to the creation of a free trade zone. On 6 October 1991 a declaration on that issue was signed in Kraków. The declaration stressed that the three countries should give priority in their foreign economic policy to association with the EU. Nevertheless, for the first time the three countries declared their interest in accelerating the abolition of their own barriers to trade. Negotiations on this issue were initiated in Warsaw on 30 November 1991, where the basic principles were decided. It was accepted that liberalisation should be symmetrical and should bring equal advantages to all the partners. Negotiations on detailed conditions continued till December 1992.

CEFTA, an agreement to create a free trade zone between three ECE countries (the former Czechoslovakia, Hungary and Poland), was signed on 21 December 1992 in Kraków. It is worth mentioning that at almost the same time two other trade agreements were signed by this group of countries: namely: Europe Agreements with the EU and with EFTA. The CEFTA Agreement came into force on 1 March 1993. It was structured on the model of the Europe Agreements, which is reflected in the organisation. Three groups of goods were liberalised according to different schedules: (i) raw materials and semi-processed goods; (ii) processed goods; (iii) goods which required a longer period of liberalisation (so-called sensitive goods, that is, textiles, steel products, coal, food and agricultural products). The main difference between the CEFTA agreement and the Europe agreements was that the former was based on a symmetrical solution, while the latter were asymmetric. Members of CEFTA were at a more equal level of development than they were relative to the EU members.

Three explanations are offered for why CEFTA was set up. One is that it was created to diminish the pressure of the ECE countries on the EU to expand eastwards. A second is that the creation of CEFTA acted as a test or demonstration, to show how liberalisation can improve trade and economic growth, focusing on national problems. A third is that CEFTA was intended to liberalise trade among the member states to bring their economies closer together and at the same time improve their eligibility to join the EU. The last argument seems to be the most appropriate. It combines the internal and external conditions of integration which should not be separated in a world of growing interdependences.

Baldwin gives three reasons for regional integration [*Baldwin and Haaparanta Kiander, 1995*]. According to the first, regionalism is an alternative to multilateral liberalisation, which is often considered to be a politically complicated process. According to the second, regionalism is forced by the withdrawal of the US from the role of locomotive in global liberalisation. The third is based on a simple assumption that deepening integration decreases neighbouring countries' 'indifference' to regional integration and increases their interest in participating in an organisation which offers better access to the markets.

The experience of CEFTA seems to support the third. Countries outside the zone are treated less favourably than the members. The protection of national markets influences the level and structure of prices. Protection also limits competition, one of the main tools helping to restructure enterprises and reform the structure of the economy, as well as being the mechanism which forces innovations and fuels inflation.

III. THE EXPANSION OF CEFTA

Widening

The first version of the Agreement did not foresee the possibility of enlargement of the organisation.[2] But this was changed in 1995. Since 1993 the number of member countries has increased in two ways: (i) by the division of Czechoslovakia into two separate states; (ii) by expansion of the membership (Slovenia became the first new member on 1 January 1996, Romania on 1 July 1997). A list of countries have expressed their interest in accession to the zone: Bulgaria, Latvia, Lithuania, Estonia and Ukraine. Turkey and Israel have also expressed an interest.

CEFTA has also widened its activities; this was approved on 11 September 1995, in Brno. This added Article 39a, which included free transfer of services and capital. Unfortunately these new items on the co-operation agenda were not put into practice. At the same meeting the decision was made to open the organisation to new members, by the formulation of membership conditions:

* signature of an Association Agreement with the EU (or at least some other type of trade agreement with the EU);

* membership of GATT/WTO;

* approval of all the CEFTA members.

Implementation of CEFTA

March 1998 marks the fifth anniversary of CEFTA's establishment. The primary commitments, which foresaw the establishment of a free trade zone for industrial goods and, selectively, for agricultural products by 2001, were modified in subsequent years. The first crucial change was introduced by the Amending Protocol to the CEFTA Agreement, on 1 July 1994. This amendment accelerated the liberalisation of trade in industrial products and promoted trade liberalisation in agricultural products [*Kopec, 1995*]. The second package of changes was introduced on 25 November 1994 during the CEFTA summit held in Poznañ, Poland. These changes incorporated the accelerated abolition of barriers to trade in agricultural products and the completion of free trade in industrial products a year in advance of schedule, with a limited number of exclusions. The final liberalisation of trade in industrial goods was applied from 1 January 1996. Liberalisation of trade in industrial products within CEFTA consisted of: (i) the progressive reduction of tariffs, concluded on a bilateral basis, leading to their complete elimination; (ii) the elimination of other protective measures, that is, non-tariff barriers; (iii) the elimination of quotas or limits [*Kisiel-Lowczyc, 1996*].

Industrial goods trade was liberalised four years ahead of the schedule foreseen in the agreement. Trade in agricultural products and food is subject to far-reaching concessions, introduced since 1 January 1996. The scope of the concessions was radically widened. Generally, countries have ended tariff quotas. Concessions on industrial goods are divided into four groups. Similar arrangements were introduced in the case of agricultural products (Table 10.1).

The contents of lists A and B are negotiated by all CEFTA members, and all member states use the same level of tariffs for the same goods from the two lists. The contents of list C are negotiated bilaterally and the tariffs are lower than the generally applied level. In some cases the tariffs are '0'. For some goods on the list, preferential tariffs are applied, but this concerns only goods traded within limits.

New members reduce their duties according to schedules negotiated with individual countries. They are not required to meet the level of liberalisation already achieved.

TABLE 10.1
CONCESSIONS IN INDUSTRIAL GOODS AND AGRICULTURAL
PRODUCTS

Concessions in industrial goods	*Concessions in agricultural products*
Goods with low sensitivity for competition. '0' tariffs were applied. List A.	Goods with low sensitivity for competition. '0' tariffs were applied. List A.
Goods with medium sensitivity. '0' tariffs were applied from January 1997. List B.	Goods with medium sensitivity for competition. Duties are higher than '0' but lower than generally applied. List B.
Sensitive goods. Preferential tariffs are applied, which are lower than generally applied tariffs. Since 1 January 1997 goods falling into this category are traded freely. This was 4 years ahead of the schedule, 2001, and a year ahead of the date agreed in the First Amendment Protocol. List C.	Sensitive goods on which concessions are granted on a bilateral basis. List C.
Limited group of very sensitive goods which are not covered by preferential tariffs. The list of these goods is negotiated bilaterally by the member countries. Since 1 January 1998 trade is free within the primary CEFTA members.	

Source: CEFTA documents

Different concessions were applied in the case of Romania, as this country joined CEFTA in the middle of 1997. Romania's membership is regulated by an Amending Protocol, supplementing the Agreement on Free Trade in Central Europe, dated 11 September 1995. Article 2 provides that Romania accepts all the commitments deriving from the CEFTA Agreement and its supplements in the Agreement on Accession. The status of Romania is regulated differently on the following matters:[3]

• Romania had the right to apply specific limits and restrictions on trade till the end of 1997. It then put an end to border charges on exports or imports into trade with CEFTA;

- Romania signed a co-operation agreement with neighbouring CEFTA countries concerning customs administration;

- the customs duties forming the basis for reductions are those of 1 January 1993;

- liberalisation of markets will be reached in a shorter period than planned in the primary agenda (including public procurement).

In summary, the beginning of 1998 brought full liberalisation of trade in industrial and agricultural goods among the original CEFTA members.

TABLE 10.2

SCOPE OF REDUCTION OF TARIFFS ON INDUSTRIAL GOODS IN CEFTA COUNTRIES AFTER THE URUGUAY ROUND

Country	Weighted average		Reduction in %
	Before the Round	After the Round	
Czech Republic	4.9	3.8	22
Hungary	9.6	6.9	28
Poland	16.0	9.9	38
Slovak Republic	4.9	3.8	30
Average	8.6	6	30

Source: GATT Secretariat quoted in Kisiel-Lowczyc [*1996: 105*].

Alongside reduction of trade barriers within CEFTA, liberalisation was conducted within the following international frameworks:

- the GATT Uruguay Round, which resulted in establishment of the WTO. This covered further reduction of tariffs in fields not previously included (sensitive products; food and agricultural production, textiles, leather products, etc.); liberalisation in services, intellectual property and transfer of capital; 'tariffication' of non-tariff barriers and their reduction. Five ECE countries took part in the GATT Uruguay Round, including Poland (see Table 10.2).[4] The reduction in Poland was deeper than in the remaining ECE countries because the starting point was higher. (This did not imply intensive protection of the market, as non-tariff measures were not applied);

- liberalisation within free trade regional zones (the EU and associated countries, within EFTA, or within bilateral agreements);

- exchange-rate policy, which went from a fixed rate through a series of devaluations and was finally floated within a margin. In all these phases the exchange rate was always either overvalued or undervalued, which served as a tool either to protect the market and limit competition, or to open up the economy.[5]

The CEFTA summit in Jasna, held in September 1996, brought about two important decisions. First, it finally rejected the idea of creating a Permanent Secretariat in Bratislava, supported by an argument that there was no need for the 'institutionalisation' of mutual co-operation by the creation of organisational structures. Secondly, it produced a common declaration, in which the Prime Ministers of the CEFTA member states expressed their desire to widen the economic co-operation by including new fields. The declaration included the following matters:

- acceleration of negotiations on certification of industrial goods and agricultural products, including mutual acceptance of the results of scientific research and certificates;

- support for meetings in which information would be given about the possibilities of investment in CEFTA countries and other promotions of activities to be conducted abroad;

- continuation of work on the liberalisation of transfer of services;

- extension of co-operation within CEFTA, including administration, arbitration of disputes and interpretation of the CEFTA Agreement by the Common Committee [Kopec, 1997: 76–87].

IV. TRADE AMONG CEFTA COUNTRIES

Trade within CEFTA plays an increasing role in the member countries, although each has a different share of CEFTA trade. In 1997 the CEFTA share in imports reached an average of 12.8 per cent and in exports 16.6 per cent. This share is distorted by the relatively high share of CEFTA trade for the Czech and Slovak Republics, because of the close integration of the two economies. Excluding trade between the Czech and Slovak Republics lowers the share of CEFTA to 8.0 per cent in imports and 9.4 per cent in exports (Table 10.3).

TABLE 10.3
SHARE OF CEFTA TRADE IN TOTAL TRADE[6] (%)

	1997		1996		1995	
	Imports	*Exports*	*Imports*	*Exports*	*Imports*	*Exports*
Czech Republic	15	22.9	14.7	22.8	16.3	21.4
Hungary	6.7	8.1	7.8	8.7	6.4	5.9
Poland	6.2	6.3	5.8	6.1	5.6	5.4
Slovenia	6.9	5.7	6.5	5.4	6.7	4.8
Slovakia	29.3	39.9	29.8	41.4	33.1	44.3

TABLE 10.4
GEOGRAPHIC STRUCTURE OF TRADE WITHIN CEFTA IN 1997
(US$m. AND %)

Total value of CEFTA trade	*% CEFTA*	*Czech Rep*	*Hungary*	*Poland*	*Slovenia*	*Slovakia*
Poland						
Import						
2160.5	5.8	53.3	19.7	-	7.0	20.0
Export						
1480.8	6.1	57.2	21.0	-	-2.9	18.9
Czech Rep.						
Import						
4069	14.7	-	6.8	19.9	3.8	57.9
Export						
4069	22.9	-	7.8	24.1	4.6	63.1
Hungary						
Import						
1256.8	7.8	38.8	-	23.7	7.1	30.4
Export						
1148	8.7	25.2	-	33.8	19.2	21.9
Slovenia						
Import						
613.3	6.5	38.5	38.6	7.9	-	15.0
Export						
449.6	5.4	32.4	23.4	31.5	-	12.1
Slovakia						
Import						
3258	29.8	82.3	6.7	8.3	1.7	-
Export						
3658	41.4	74.9	11.3	11.7	2.4	-

Source: CESTAT, *Statistical Bulletin*, 1997/1, pp.60, 68, 73, 77.

It is clear that the share of mutual trade is higher among countries at similar levels of development. In spite of this, there is a large amount of trade between neighbouring countries, that is, the Czech Republic and Poland, Slovakia and Poland, and Hungary and Czech Republic. The high shares of Poland, Hungary and the Czech Republic in the trade of Slovenia indicate that this country is active in searching for markets, which are found in the more developed countries of the group.

TABLE 10.5

COMMODITY STRUCTURE OF CEFTA TRADE,

1992 AND 1996 (%)

Contents	Import		Export	
	1992	1996	1992	1996
Poland				
Food, beverages and tobacco	11.0	9.8	13.0	10.8
Crude materials except fuels	6.0	4.7	9.0	3.4
Mineral fuels, lubricants	17.0	9.2	11.0	6.9
Chemical goods	13.0	13.8	9.0	7.7
Machinery and transport equipment	30.0	33.0	19.0	23.4
Other manufactured articles	23.0	29.5	39.0	47.8
Total	100.0	100.0	100.0	100.0
Czech Republic				
Food, beverages and tobacco	22.0	6.9	5.0	5.3
Crude materials except fuels	7.0	3.8	4.0	4.9
Mineral fuels, lubricants	3.0	8.8	15.0	4.5
Chemical goods	11.0	12.9	13.0	9.0
Machinery and transport equipment	21.0	36.7	30.0	32.7
Other manufactured articles	36.0	30.9	33.0	43.6
Total	100.0	100.0	100.0	100.0
Slovakia				
Food, beverages and tobacco	8.0	7.3	5.0	4.6
Crude materials except fuels	6.0	4.9	8.0	4.5
Mineral fuels, lubricants	1.0	16.9	27.0	4.9
Chemical goods	11.0	11.5	10.0	12.4
Machinery and transport equipment	18.0	35.1	33.0	23.2
Other manufactured articles	56.0	24.3	17.0	50.4
Total	100.0	100.0	100.0	100.0

TABLE 10.5 (cont.)

Slovenia

Food, beverages and tobacco	6.0	7.8	9.0	4.1
Crude materials except fuels	2.0	5.1	8.0	1.6
Mineral fuels, lubricants	4.0	7.9	7.0	0.7
Chemical goods	9.0	11.9	12.0	10.4
Machinery and transport equipment	29.0	33.8	34.0	33.1
Other manufactured articles	50.0	33.5	30.0	50.1
Total	100.0	100.0	100.0	100.0

Hungary

Food, beverages and tobacco	5.0	5.3	22.0	19.2
Crude materials except fuels	4.0	3.7	7.0	4.5
Mineral fuels, lubricants	15.0	13.6	3.0	4.1
Chemical goods	13.0	13.9	11.0	11.1
Machinery and transport equipment	30.0	30.5	21.0	25.5
Other manufactured articles	33.0	33.0	36.0	35.5
Total	100.0	100.0	100.0	100.0

CEFTA-5

Food, beverages and tobacco	10.4	7.4	10.6	8.8
Crude materials except fuels	5.0	4.4	7.2	3.8
Mineral fuels, lubricants	8.0	11.3	7.9	4.2
Chemical goods	11.4	12.8	13.0	10.1
Machinery and transport equipment	25.6	33.8	30.3	27.6
Other manufactured articles	39.6	30.0	31.0	45.5
Total	100.0	100.0	100.0	100.0

Source: CESTAT, *Statistical Bulletin* 1997/1, pp.46–8 and own calculations.

The structure of trade within CEFTA is similar to that of their trade outside CEFTA [*Misala et al., 1997: 12*]. The main difference is the higher level of industrial goods, which is accompanied by lower shares of fuels, machines and equipment. Generally, industrial products dominate in both imports and exports. This is true in value terms, dynamics and changes in exports. After a deep fall in 1990–91 imports were growing in the following commodity groups: chemical products, industrial goods, machinery, and transport equipment. This indicates growing investment and consumption demand in the CEFTA countries. The balance of trade in machinery and transport equipment was negative in all CEFTA countries, but import/export proportions were better for the Czech Republic and Slovakia and slightly worse for Poland and Hungary.

Despite the fact that intra-trade specialisation in CEFTA trade is still not high, there are certain indications that this is changing. Foreign direct investments into

CEFTA markets are one factor that can have a positive impact on this indicator in a short time. In general, opening the economies of CEFTA countries to inflows of capital and trade within the region and within the Europe Agreements will change the economies of the region spectacularly [*Kaminski, 1997; Kaminski et al., 1995*]. Access to advanced technology, know-how and management will help to exploit the natural and hidden resources in the countries of the region. According to prognoses about future growth in the region, this will result in quick catching-up as the rate of growth in coming years will be two to three times higher than in the EU [*Welfe et al., 1997*].

In such circumstances negative balances of payments have to be considered necessary costs for the present and future CEFTA members.[7] They reflect, on the one hand, differences in levels of development, while, on the other hand, especially when the commodity structure is taken into account, they reflect the process of restructuring the economies. In other words, they reflect processes which are fuelled by systemic changes: increased competition, ownership changes and deregulation.

Despite the fact that in the immediate future most CEFTA countries will face a negative balance of trade, relations between the dynamics of imports and exports should improve. They are improving already. First signs of this were seen in Poland in 1997, with liberalisation of trade in the region and plans to expand the zone. But not everything can be explained by liberalisation. Additional factors include the following: improvement of rates of growth in the main country and commodity markets and acceleration of the liberalisation achieved by the Uruguay Round, OECD decisions, regional agreements and bilateral arrangements.

In conclusion, it should be said that CEFTA has proved to be a route to the EU for countries that have joined the path later and are delayed in their transformation. CEFTA is not able to do the job of opening the economies of the latecomers on its own; it is supported here by conditions of membership in GATT/WTO, OECD, and the Europe Agreements. Together they lead the 'late-comers' slowly, step by step, to the European Economic Area, which still seems to be a distant goal but which will become more realistic quite rapidly.

NOTES

1. The place where three countries of the region accepted the idea of the liberalisation of their mutual trade resulted in their often being referred to as Visegrad countries. This is a mistake. The role of Visegrad ended with calling CEFTA into life. Visegrad was a political initiative and the countries in the region are not co-operating in the field of politics. This will come after further integration with the Euro-atlantic structures. Moreover, there were only three countries at Visegrad. This group cannot be expanded, while CEFTA today embraces five members.
2. Article 36 point 1 of the CEFTA Agreement announced that it deals with trade liberalisation among the signatory countries. Point 2 provides the possibility of creating free trade zones and

custom unions, as well as agreements on cross-border trade on a scale which should not disturb the conditions of trade of the signatory countries. It also takes into account the issue of the certificates of origin of traded goods, listed in the Agreement. This condition has formed the background for the gradual creation of the free trade zone between the member states.

3. The Concessions of Romania and CEFTA are included in Protocols 14–17 (industrial goods) and 18–21 (agricultural products). Concessions between Poland and Romania are in protocol 16. Also Supplement to Protocol No.3 of 1995 contains some conditions on agricultural trade, including some exceptions from List A and List B till the end of 1998.

4. In the Uruguay Round Poland was committed to reducing import duties for industrial products by an average of 38 per cent, that is from 16 per cent to 9.9 per cent. At the end of 1997 the average level of duties was 7.2 per cent and was to be lowered by opening the market to industrial imports from the EU and CEFTA from the beginning of 1998.

5. It is worth stressing that the Polish market in certain periods was protected only by an undervalued exchange rate. Most of the tariffs, reduced on paper, were not applied in practice as they were temporarily suspended. This, together with the biggest reductions of tariffs within the GATT, resulted in the shortest recovery from the transition depression and the highest rate of growth in CEFTA.

6. Data for 1997 indicate the values of trade in January. These are the latest available data in comparable values.

7. This is contrary to the controversial article of Baldwin, Francois and Portes [*1997*].

REFERENCES

Baldwin, R. and P. Haaparanta Kiander (eds.) (1995), *Expanding Membership of the European Union*, Cambridge: Cambridge University Press.

Baldwin, R.E., Francois, J.F. and R. Portes (1997), 'The Costs and Benefits of Eastern Enlargement: The Impact on the EU and Central Europe', *Economic Policy*, No.24, April, pp.127–76.

Kaminski, B. (1997), *Poland's Transition from the Perspective of Performance in EU Markets*, Washington, DC: World Bank.

Kaminski, B., Wang, Z. Kun and L. Alan Winters (1995), *Foreign Trade in Transition: The International Environment and Domestic Policy,* Washington, DC: World Bank.

Kisiel-Lowczyc, A. B. (1996), *Srodkowo-Europejska strefa wolnego handlu* (*Central European Zone of Free Trade*), WUG.

Kopec, U. (1995), 'Polityka handlowa w stosunkach z krajami CEFTA', in *Polska polityka handlu zagranicznego 1994–1995, IKiC HZ*, Warsaw. ('Trade Policy with CEFTA', in *Polish Trade Policy* 1994–1995).

Kopec, U. (1997), 'Postępy procesu integracji Polski z krajami CEFTA (Progress in Polish integration with CEFTA)', in *Zagraniczna polityka gospodarcza Polski 1996–1997 (Polish Foreign Economic Policy in 1996–1997),* IKiC.

Marszalek, A. (1997), *Unia Europeiska*, Lodz: WUL.

Misala, J., Kisiel, A. and B. Baranowska (1997), *Rozwoj handlu zagranicznego Polski w okresie transformacji i zarys perspektyw na przyszłosc*, Warsaw: Rzadowe Centrum Studiow Strategicznych, Departament Strategii i Integracji Miedzynarodowej.

Skodlarski, J. (1997), 'Grupa Wyszehradzka i CEFTA' ('Visegrad Group and CEFTA'), in A. Marszalek (ed.) *Integracja Europejska (European Integration)*, WU, 1997, pp. 409–21.

Welfe, W., Welfe, A. and W. Florczak (1997), 'Dlugookresowe prognozy rozwoju gospodarki polskiej do 2010 roku' ('Long-period prognoses for the Polish Economy until 2010') in *Gospodarka Narodowa (National Economy)*.

PART III

GOING BEYOND REGIONS

11

The Global Involvement of Small Island Developing States

LINO BRIGUGLIO

I. INTRODUCTION

There is a growing interdependence among nations in various matters, including trade, protection of the environment and resource management. Small Island Developing States (SIDS) have been directly affected by this process of globalisation, and, as this chapter will show, they themselves have made a contribution to the process.

Although the total population of such states is under 40 million, accounting for a very small fraction the world's population, and the land area they occupy is also a very small proportion of the earth's surface, SIDS have been directly involved in matters of global concern. To mention just two examples. Malta has taken a leading role in the development of the Law of the Sea and of the concept of the 'Common Heritage of Mankind' [*Borg, 1996*], and the Maldives, with other AOSIS (Alliance of Small Island States) members, has to a large extent been responsible for putting the issue of climate change and sea-level rise on the national and international agendas.

In addition, SIDS are sometimes considered to be microcosms of larger territories, and as a result issues affecting islands are considered as having global implications. Within the United Nations such issues have recently taken centre stage during the 'UN Global Conference on the Sustainable Development of Small Islands Developing States' held in Barbados in April/May 1994, where the discussion was not confined to problems affecting SIDS only but was extended to others affecting humanity in general. The decision to convene this conference was taken at the General Assembly by means of Resolution 47/189, following the Rio Conference and Agenda 21, which deals with sustainable development in general and in Chapter 17G with the Sustainable Development of Small Island States in particular.

This chapter discusses the impact that the globalisation process is having on SIDS and the contribution that such states are making to, and expect from, the global community. It is organised as follows. The next section describes the special characteristics of SIDS, where the problems of small economic size and insularity are prominent features. The following section discusses the role of

SIDS in the global stage. The next section deals with the response that SIDS expect from the global community in the endeavour to promote sustainable development on their own territory and on a global level, followed by a concluding section.

II. THE SPECIAL PROBLEM OF SIDS

SIDS[1] face special disadvantages because of their small size, insularity, proneness to natural disasters and environmental fragility. These factors make their economies highly vulnerable to forces outside their control - a condition which sometimes threatens their very economic viability. Many times a high GNP per capita in these states conceals this reality. Following the Barbados Global Conference, these problems have become of global concern, as evidenced by the fact that the global community, at the end of the Conference, approved by consensus the Programme of Action for the Sustainable Development of SIDS.

Small Economic Size

The size of a country can be measured in terms of its population, its land area or its gross national product. Some studies prefer to use population as an index of size, while others take a composite index of the three variables. As their name implies, smallness is a characteristic of SIDS, but some of them are extremely small when measured by any of three indices just mentioned, and therefore face severe constraints in this regard. Small size is economically disadvantageous for a number of reasons, the most important of which relate to limited natural resource endowment and small size of the domestic market. A small land area, which is a feature of SIDS, leads to very limited natural resource endowments, leading to a high dependence on imported raw materials and industrial supplies [*Briguglio, 1993: Appendix 4*].

The import propensity of SIDS tends to be high for another reason, namely, the limited possibilities for import substitution owing to the small size of the domestic market [*Worrell, 1992: 9–10*]. In many SIDS where import-substitution policies were adopted, the end result tended to be a protected economic environment, with products of inferior quality, higher prices and a parallel market in non-domestically produced goods. A small domestic market and the need for a relatively large amount of foreign exchange to pay the large import bill give rise to a relatively high dependence on exports [*Briguglio, 1993: Appendix 5*] and therefore on economic conditions in the rest of the world. These factors explain why the economies of very small states have a large foreign sector (see Table 1).

TABLE 11.1
INDICES OF TRADE DEPENDENCE

Averages for different categories of countries[a]	Exports/ GDP	Imports/ GDP	Diversity[b]
All countries	36.73	40.97	0.758
Island Developing Countries	57.31	66.11	0.845
SIDS	60.41	70.90	0.872
Non-Island Developing Countries	29.15	32.86	0.767
Developing Countries	38.02	43.44	0.841
Developed Countries	31.34	31.02	0.424

Notes: (a) For a description of the classification of countries see Briguglio [1995]; (b)The diversity index measures export concentration by means of a formula explained in Handbook of International Trade and Development Statistics [UNCTAD, 1991]. It takes a value of between 0 and 1, where 1 is the maximum concentration of exports.

Source: IMF, International Financial Statistics Yearbook, 1991.

SIDS tend to depend on a narrow range of products to generate income and employment. In many cases, small size restricts the country's ability to diversify its exports, and this renders it dependent on a very narrow range of goods and services [Briguglio, 1993: Appendix 6]. This carries with it the disadvantage associated with having too many eggs in one basket, and intensifies the problems associated with dependence on international trade. Small economic size leads to severe limitations on the ability to exploit economies of scale, mostly due to indivisibilities and limited scope for specialisation. In turn, this gives rise to (inter alia) high per unit costs of production, high costs of infrastructural construction and utilisation per capita, high per unit costs of training specialised staff, and a high degree of dependence on imported technologies, since small size inhibits the development of endogenous technology.

Public administration in small states also faces problems associated with small scale, the most important of which relate to the small human resource base from which to draw experienced and efficient administrators. Very often specialists can only be trained overseas in larger countries, without a guarantee that their services will be needed on their return. For this reason, many specialists originating from SIDS decide to emigrate to larger countries where their services are better utilised and where remuneration for their services is better. One outcome of this is that SIDS have to rely on larger states, generally the ex-colonial metropole, for certain specialised aspects of public administration.

A related problem is that many government functions tend to be very expensive per capita when the population is small, owing to the fact that certain expenses are not divisible in proportion to the number of users. For example, overseas diplomatic missions of small island states are often understaffed, and many such states are represented by roving ambassadors.

Disadvantages of Insularity and Remoteness

Island states are by definition insular, but not all island states are situated in remote areas. Insularity and remoteness give rise to some similar problems associated with transport and communications, and these two factors are considered together here.

TABLE 11.2

TRANSPORT AND FREIGHT COST AS A PERCENTAGE OF EXPORTS

Average for country categories[a]	Ratio
All Countries	18.73
Island Developing Countries	35.99
SIDS	43.24
Non-Island Developing Countries	15.71
Developing Countries	23.75
Developed Countries	4.66

Notes: (a) For a description of the classification of countries see Briguglio [*1995*]. Transport and freight as a ratio of export proceeds are for the years 1987–89. They therefore represent a medium-term average. This was done to avoid attaching too much importance to a single year.

Source: UNCTAD, *Handbook of International Trade and Development Statistics*, 1991: Table 5.1.

Transport costs in the international trade of SIDS tend to be relatively higher per unit of export than in other countries. This is confirmed in the index of transport and freight costs, given in Table 11.2. The main reason for this is probably that separation by sea gives rise to communications difficulties. Islands are constrained to use only air and sea transport for their imports and exports. Land transport is, of course, out of the question, and this reduces the options available for the movement of goods and of people. Problems associated with transport faced by SIDS include:

• uncertainties of supply from abroad;

• large stocks due to infrequency of calls by cargo ships;

• fragmentation and therefore high per unit costs of cargoes.

Proneness to Natural Disasters

Many island states experience natural disasters caused by cyclones (hurricanes or typhoons), earthquakes, landslides and volcanic eruptions. Although natural disasters also occur in non-island countries, the impact of a natural disaster on an island economy tends to be relatively larger in terms of damage per unit of area and costs per capita, due to the small size of the country. This tendency is apparent in Table 11.3, which shows higher readings for disaster proneness in the islands.

In some instances natural disasters threaten the very survival of small islands. Some of the effects of natural disasters on small economies include the devastation of the agricultural sector, the wiping out of entire village settlements, the disruption of a high proportion of communication services and injury or death for a relatively high percentage of the inhabitants.

TABLE 11.3

INDEX OF DISASTER DAMAGE AS A PERCENTAGE OF GNP

(1970–89)*

Averages for country categories[a]	*Ratio*
All countries with disaster incidence	28.10
19 Island Developing Countries	51.72
13 SIDS	66.52
46 Non-Island Developing Countries	20.58
61 Developing Countries	30.35
4 Developed Countries	5.10

Notes: * Countries with zero incidence are excluded; (a) For a description of the classification of countries see Briguglio [*1995*].

Source: UNDRO, *Preliminary Study on the Identification of Disaster-Prone Countries Based on Economic Impact*, 1990.

Environmental Fragility

As is well known, national accounts statistics do not take into consideration environmental degradation, resource depletion, and dangers to flora and fauna [*Dahl, 1991*]. In other words, GNP statistics may give a picture of development, whereas in reality a country might be undergoing a process which is unsustainable in the long term. Environmental problems are likely to be particularly intense in SIDS, because:

- economic development tends to have a much higher impact than in countries with large land areas;

- resources tend to be depleted and degraded faster, owing to their limited availability;

- the ecosystem tends to be naturally fragile;

- many SIDS face the problem of rising sea level;

- SIDS have a relatively large coastline in relation to their land-mass, and this gives rise to a relatively high rate of land and soil erosion.

Dependence on Foreign Sources of Finance

Some island states have a very high degree of dependence on foreign sources of finance, including remittances from emigrants and development assistance from donor countries. This is especially true in the SIDS in the Pacific region [Bertram, 1993; Connell, 1988: 27–8]. These transfers from abroad have permitted many SIDS to attain high standards of living and to offset trade deficits. Figures on these variables are summarised in Table 11.4. On the other hand, the figures do not indicate that SIDS tend to have a relatively higher debt burden than other developing countries.

TABLE 11.4

INDEX OF DEBT AND REMITTANCES AS A

PERCENTAGE OF GNP (1989)

Averages for country categories[a]	Remittances[b]	Debt[c]
All Countries	6.17	66.70
Island Developing Countries	9.36	55.55
Small Island Developing Countries	10.98	49.89
Non-Island Developing Countries	5.12	70.57
Developing Countries	7.40	66.70

Notes: (a) For a description of the classification of countries see Briguglio [1995]; (b) As % of GNP. These cover private and government net transfers; (c) As % of GNP. Developed countries are excluded from the averages.

Source: UNCTAD, Handbook of International Trade and Development Statistics, 1991.

Demographic Factors

Demographic changes in small islands are sometimes very pronounced, owing to emigration from the country or, in the case of multi-island states, migration from one island to another caused by the attraction of urban centres in terms of jobs and education. These movements sometimes give rise to brain and skill drains and social upheavals. This happens even in islands which are economically successful, because of the limited opportunities for specialisation in such islands.

The Vulnerability Index

Many SIDS register a GNP per capita which is relatively high in comparison to developing countries in general (in the region of US$4000 to US$8000), giving the impression that they have a strong economy. In reality, SIDS, by their very nature, have a fragile economy, because their economic activity is to a very large extent exposed to and dependent on what happens in the rest of the world. In contrast, a country like India, where GNP per capita is very low by SIDS standards, can rely on its own markets and its own resources much more than a small island developing state like Malta, which has a much higher GNP per capita. Larger countries are therefore more resilient, even if they may be poorer in terms of GNP per capita.

The question that may arise here relates to whether or not the economic fragilities of SIDS are in fact the reason for their relatively high GNP per capita. The fact that many SIDS have done relatively well in terms of this index has prompted some observers to argue that being small and insular is not a disadvantage after all. This line of argument may, of course, contain an element of truth, in that smallness has its advantages, including a high degree of flexibility in the face of changing circumstances. However, the handicaps and fragilities associated with smallness and insularity, described above, are a reality in many SIDS, and the success stories of some of them were probably achieved *in spite of* and not *because of* their small size and insularity. Unlike larger states, small ones can never take their viability for granted, and they are perpetually in a sink-or-swim situation.

One reason why many SIDS register relatively high GNP per capita scores could be their strategic importance. Many SIDS are situated in the sphere of influence of relatively large powers: the UK and the US in the Caribbean region; the EU in the Mediterranean region; and Australia, New Zealand, Japan and France in the Pacific area. The interest of these powers in SIDS has given rise to what may be called 'artificial' props to the economy of the islands, in terms of, amongst other things, (a) relatively large amounts of transfers and free technical assistance and (b) preferential access to the markets of developed countries in industrial and agricultural products. Because of their intrinsic economic vulnerabilities, many SIDS might not have survived as independent

247

states in the absence of these 'artificial' props. Furthermore, it could be argued that it is the relatively large financial transfers to SIDS which have pushed up their GDP per capita to levels higher than what one would expect from countries continually facing the constraints associated with small size and limited resources.

It should also be noted that the relatively high growth rates which many SIDS experienced during the 1980s may give a misleading picture of the strength of the economies of these countries. In many instances, their growth pattern has been unstable and erratic, as was the case in many Caribbean islands, and dependent on preferential access to markets in developed countries.

The present author has attempted to compute a vulnerability index, composed of three sub-indices, namely exposure to what happens in the rest of the world (represented by dependence on international trade), insularity and remoteness (measured by relative transport costs), and proneness to natural disasters (measured by costs of disaster damage as a percentage of GDP). The method used in constructing this index is explained in Briguglio [*1995*]. The results of this exercise are summarised in Table 11.5, which shows that small islands tend to be more economically vulnerable than other categories of countries.

TABLE 11.5

VULNERABILITY INDEX, GDP PER CAPITA AND HUMAN
DEVELOPMENT INDEX FOR DIFFERENT GROUPS OF COUNTRIES

Averages for country categories[a]	*Vulner. Index*	*GDP PC US$*	*H.D.I Index*
All 113 Countries	0.447	4468	0.588
28 Island Developing Countries	0.598	3165	0.670
20 SIDS	0.635	3384	0.698
85 Non-Island Developing Countries	0.418	4890	0.565
91 Developing Countries	0.475	2191	0.535
22 Developed Countries	0.328	16740	0.962

Notes: (a) For a description of the classification of countries see Briguglio [*1995*]. In the Vulnerability Index and the Human Development Index, zero signifies the minimum and 1 the maximum.

Sources: Vulnerability Index, Briguglio 1995. GDP per capita taken from UNCTAD, *Handbook of International Trade and Development Statistics*, 1991: Table 6.1. Human Development Index taken from UNDP, *Human Development Report*, 1991.

The types of vulnerabilities represented in the Vulnerability Index presented in Table 11.5 are not related to economic performance, but to fragility and lack of resilience. This is confirmed in the same table which gives averages of GDP per capita and of the Human Development Index of different country groups and compares them with the vulnerability index. It can be seen that SIDS do not fare badly in terms of GDP per capita, and of the Human Development Index. As a matter of fact, their scores are much higher on average than those of developing countries in general. However, as stated, these countries are characterised by high vulnerability scores.

III. THE GLOBAL COMMITMENT OF SMALL ISLAND STATES

Most SIDS belong to the United Nations, and therefore have the right to voice their concerns and their interests, and to participate in other ways in this global organisation and its various agencies. In doing so SIDS have also subjected themselves to a number of global regulations.

Small Island States and the UN

By joining the United Nations, they have committed themselves to promote development and good governance in the political, economic and environmental fields, not only in their own country but globally. This was inevitable because small states are very much exposed to what happens in the rest of the world. They lack natural resources, cannot adequately protect their sovereignty against aggression from larger states, and in isolation they find it difficult to exist as a sovereign entities. By joining the global community, SIDS have, ironically, strengthened their independence. In the process many small states have managed to recover their national identity and dignity, which could have been seriously threatened had they not joined the United Nations. Through their participation in the UN system, SIDS have also shown that small states can exercise sovereignty in a meaningful way within a global framework, and that they can contribute to global well-being. The case of Malta's initiatives in the Law of the Sea Convention is a case in point.

AOSIS

Many small islands with a UN seat have joined together to form a pressure group within the system. This group, known as AOSIS – the Alliance of Small Island States – was the main driving force behind General Assembly Resolution 47/189, which called for the convening of the Barbados Global Conference on the Sustainable Development of Small Island Developing States.

AOSIS was formed during the negotiations on the Framework Convention for Climate Change. This alliance proved to be a very successful and influential negotiating group, and its establishment enabled SIDS to act with one voice, giving them much more strength as a collective unit. As a result of this development, SIDS were taken more seriously and their demands were heeded much more by the larger countries, developed and developing alike. During the Earth Summit in Rio de Janeiro in June 1992, AOSIS, against all odds, was instrumental in negotiating the introduction of a few paragraphs in Section 17 of AGENDA 21, which recognised the special problems of SIDS.

The Barbados Conference

It is widely held that the Barbados Conference was a test case for the global community, following the 1992 Rio Conference, since it was one of the first actions of Agenda 21 to be discussed at a global level and to be implemented. The object of the conference was to produce a Programme of Action [*UN, 1994*], with a set of programmes involving the participation of the international community and the small island states themselves.

The conference was a global one not only in name, but in reality, since all the formal groupings within the UN General Assembly were represented. The participating countries could by and large be divided into three major groups, namely (i) the advanced countries, (ii) the Group of 77 and China, and (iii) the Eastern developing countries in transition.

Different Interests

The different interests of major groups within the UN, and their various subdivisions, were clearly visible during the Barbados Conference. Among the advanced countries, the European Union and the United States tended to oppose additional funding by donor countries over and above that agreed at the Rio Conference, and were in favour of improving the efficiency and re-distributing the existing development funds. Another group of advanced countries, which sometimes acted with one voice, were the Cairns group, made up of Canada, Australia, and New Zealand. These tended to be more sympathetic to the call by SIDS for additional funding for their requirements. Japan and some non-EU European states often took positions in between these two groups.

The Group of 77 and China, representing the interests of the developing countries, contained in it the AOSIS sub-division, which is basically an informal group and which evolved into a pressure group representing some 40 SIDS. On some occasions during the preparations for the Global Conference and during the Conference itself, AOSIS did not see eye to eye with the rest of the Group of 77, since the interests of the islands differed in many ways from those of the larger non-island states. However, at the Conference, a consensus document (the Programme of Action) was produced, admittedly after difficult negotiations. This would not have been possible without the negotiating abilities of the representatives of small states within AOSIS, chaired at first by

Vanuatu and later by Trinidad and Tobago, indicating once again that small states can contribute in a meaningful way within the UN system.

The Programme of Action

The Programme of Action is in fact a document of global involvement in island affairs. It is a carefully negotiated document, and is divided into 15 sections, covering issues of special concern to SIDS, including climate change and sea-level rise, natural and environmental disasters, waste management, management of coastal, marine, freshwater and land resources, tourism, biodiversity resources, capacity building, technical cooperation, transport and communications, science and technology, and human resource development. The final section, entitled implementation, monitoring and review, deals with the financing of the Programme of Action, and was approved by consensus by all the UN members represented at the conference.

The CSD Follow-Up

The Programme of Action of the Barbados Conference was recently reviewed at the fourth meeting of the UN Commission for Sustainable Development [*UN, 1996*] held in New York in April 1996.

Parts of the Barbados Programme of Action have already been implemented, but the CSD noted with some concern that many items in the Programme have not been given their due importance by the international community. For this reason, AOSIS, through the Group of 77, tabled a motion to the CSD meeting in April 1997, recommending, among other things, that the General Assembly convene a special session at its 54th meeting for an in-depth assessment and appraisal of the implementation of the Programme of Action adopted in Barbados.

IV. SIDS AND THE GLOBAL COMMUNITY

The Barbados Conference, discussed above, was essentially an appeal to the international community (meaning donor states and multilateral agencies) to support in concrete terms the implementation of the Programme of Action, with the aim of mitigating the disadvantages faced by SIDS, summarised above.

The problems listed pertain first and foremost to the SIDS themselves, and therefore call for national solutions. The report of the UN Secretary General, relating to Island Developing Countries [*UN, 1992: 19–23*], lists a number of policy options available to SIDS in this regard. These include: (a) improved flexibility to enhance their ability to withstand external shocks; (b) improved ability to compete, through niche-filling export strategy, flexible specialisation, enhanced entrepreneurship and economic deregulation; (c) environmental education and environmental management; and (d) regional co-operation to reduce certain per unit costs which tend to be high in a small economy.

However, as stated many times in this chapter, problems and issues pertaining to SIDS also have a global dimension, and these states have now obtained a commitment, unfortunately lacking a proper timeframe, from the international community to help them mitigate their economic fragility and to 'cope effectively, creatively and sustainably with environmental change' [*UNCED, 1992: Chapter 17G*].

The question arises here as to what basis exists to justify this commitment by the global community. A number of explanations can be put forward in this regard. There is the moral argument, in that donor countries, most of whom were the colonial masters of SIDS, have an obligation to help them attain maturity, after having dominated and at times exploited them. However, there are also 'mutual interest' arguments. SIDS now constitute a relatively large presence in the UN General Assembly (around 25 per cent of the seats) and therefore winning them to one's side is an advantage.

An extension of this argument relates to the fact that many SIDS are located in strategic positions and their predicaments cannot therefore be isolated from the global system of collective security. The South Pacific SIDS, for example, have jurisdiction over an extremely large, and potentially lucrative, part of the ocean, considering their 200 mile Exclusive Economic Zones [*McCall, 1996*]. Similarly, the domain of the Caribbean islands is of extreme importance to the Americas and, by extension, to the security of the Western world. As a matter of fact, it is now widely acknowledged that many SIDS have an important role to play in the strengthening of the global system of collective security [*Commonwealth Secretariat, 1985*].

There is also what one might call 'the microcosm' argument. Small islands can serve as a model for assessing the impacts of certain sustainable policies. It would be difficult to trace the path and to understand the impact of such changes in larger countries.

Finally there is a 'diversity' argument. Many SIDS possess cultural identities and environmental characteristics which make an important contribution to the global heritage. One reason for promoting the sustainable development of SIDS could therefore be related to the fostering of cultural and bio-diversity.

V. CONCLUSION

The globalisation process may be defined as the growing interdependence among nations – a process which is being greatly enhanced by the rapid developments in information technology. SIDS tend to be very much exposed to this process, primarily because they typically have a very open economy, which ties them to the fluctuations experienced by larger territories, especially those possessing large commercial centres. Thus for example, the fortunes of most Caribbean SIDS is tied to the economic performance of the United States, those of most Pacific states to the economic performance of Australia and Japan, and those of the Mediterranean SIDS to the economic performance of the EU. The globalisation process affecting the advanced countries is therefore also hitting SIDS. In addition, the insularity of SIDS is being eroded by means of modern means of transport and communications, rendering them increasingly open to what happens in the rest of the world, even if they remain separated by sea from other countries.

SIDS have not reacted passively to such developments. This chapter has shown that they have used the global forum – the UN – not only to gain world attention for their special problems, but also to make a contribution to global well-being, as was the case of the leading role taken by AOSIS in matters related to the Convention on Climate Change. The future of SIDS is becoming increasingly tied up with the rest of the world, in a give-and-take fashion. The globalisation process is, admittedly, dominated by the larger developed states, but it is becoming more and more possible for the small states to play an important role in this regard.

NOTE

1. It is not easy to give a precise definition of SIDS. The Commonwealth Secretariat defines 'small states' as those with a population of around one million or less. The Alliance of Small Island States (AOSIS), however, has at least three members which cannot be classified as small using this yardstick: namely Cuba, with a population of about 11 million, Jamaica, with a population of 4.2 million and Singapore with a population of just under 3 million. Some members of AOSIS, ironically, are not islands. These include Guyana and Surinam. The small island states referred to in this paper are those with a population of about one million or less. Many of these are located in the South Pacific Ocean and the Caribbean, two are located in the Mediterranean (Malta and Cyprus), two in the West Atlantic Ocean (Cape Verde and São Tomé/Principe) and four in the Indian Ocean (Comoros, Maldives, Mauritius and the Seychelles).

REFERENCES

Bertram, G. (1993), 'Sustainability, Aid and Material Welfare in Small South Pacific Island Economies 1900–90', *World Development,* Vol.12, No.2, pp.247–58.

Borg, Saviour (1996), *Malta and the Law of the Sea,* Valetta: Ministry of Foreign Affairs.

Briguglio, L. (1993), 'The Economic Vulnerabilities of Small Island Developing States', study commissioned by CARICOM for the Regional Technical Meeting of the Global Conference on the Sustainable Development of Small Island Developing States, Port of Spain, Trinidad and Tobago.

Briguglio, L (1995), 'Small island developing states and their economic vulnerabilities', *World Development,* Vol.23, No.9, pp.1615–32.

Commonwealth Secretariat (1985), *Vulnerability: Small States in a Global Society,* London: Commonwealth Secretariat.

Connell, J. (1988), *Sovereignty and Survival: Island Microstates in the Third World,* Monograph No.3, Department of Geography, University of Sydney.

Dahl, A. (1991), *Island Directory,* Nairobi: UNEP.

McCall, G. (1996) 'Nissology – the Study of Islands on their own Terms', paper presented at the conference 'The Effects of Economic Globalisation and Regional Integration on Small Countries', Nicosia, Cyprus, 4–6 Sept.

United Nations (1992), *Specific Problems and Needs of Island Developing Countries* (Report of the Secretary General A/47/414), New York: UN.

United Nations (1994), *Programme of Action for the Sustainable Development of Small Island States,* document of the Barbados Conference, 26 April–6 May.

United Nations (1996), *Progress in the Implementation of the Programme of Action for the Sustainable Development of Small Island Developing States* (Doc: E/CN.17/1996/L.17). New York: UN Commission for Sustainable Development (Fourth Session).

UNCED (1992), *AGENDA 21,* reproduced in an abridged form in *The Earth Summit,* London: Regency Press.

Worrell, D. (1992), *Economic Policies in Small Open Economies: Prospects for the Caribbean,* Economic Paper No.23, London: Commonwealth Secretariat.

12

Trade Issues after the Uruguay Round

MEINE PIETER VAN DIJK

I. INTRODUCTION

An export drive could help poor nations' development [*UNCTAD, 1996*]. With this objective in mind, this chapter will briefly discuss some recent developments in world trade. What was achieved in the Uruguay Round? What happened to the tasks which resulted from the Marrakesh agreement: further negotiations on services, diminishing subsidies, more open public procurement of services and a further harmonisation of domestic regulations? The Uruguay Round added new tasks to the World Trade Organization (see below). Have these been accomplished?

A number of trade issues which are still outstanding after the Uruguay Round will be reviewed.[1] A distinction will be made between major issues concerning developing and developed countries. Some issues are important for both and will also be discussed, before drawing some conclusions.

II. ACHIEVEMENTS OF THE URUGUAY ROUND

The GATT Uruguay Round can be seen as the basis for emerging international institutions and work should continue in this spirit.

In April 1994 the seven-year-long Uruguay Round of trade talks was formally closed in Marrakesh. Since then the major trading nations have ratified the GATT Accord, which became effective in 1995. Tariffs were to be reduced substantially and a number of non-tariff barriers removed. The agreement was signed, together with the agreement to create the World Trade Organization (WTO). There is now a system for the settlement of trade disputes, which is generally considered a major step forward.

An advantage of the WTO is that all parties have similar rights and duties of a binding character, irrespective of their economic power. The WTO is based on rules and regulations. The opposite of rules would be a series of protective measures. The negative consequences of protectionism for developing countries has been estimated to be US$45 billion per year [*Van Rooy, 1994*].

Tariffs on manufactures were on average reduced by 40 per cent. This is to be achieved by the industrial countries over a period of five years.

Negotiations in the Uruguay Round went beyond the question of tariffs which had preoccupied previous Rounds. The achievements in market liberalisation, strengthening of rules and institutions and extension of discipline to new areas will be far-reaching, according to the International Monetary Fund [*IMF, 1994*]. The trade negotiations were extended to areas such as phasing out the Multi-Fibre Arrangement (MFA), government procurement, Trade-Related Intellectual Property rights (TRIPs), Trade-Related Investment Measures (TRIMs) and non-tariff barriers (such as standards, procurement procedures and state aid) [*van Dijk and Sideri, 1996: Ch. 1*]. Sectors other than manufacturing (for example, tropical and temperate agriculture and services) also received attention, if only because the United States pushed hard for the latter.

III. WORLD TRADE AND TRADE ISSUES AFTER THE URUGUAY ROUND

Merchandise exports rose by seven per cent in 1996, more than double the increase in world output.[2] The rapid expansion in developing countries of processing trade (the assembly of manufactured goods for re-export using components and materials imported under special tariff regimes) is one contributing factor to the fact that merchandise trade continued to outstrip output growth by a wide margin.[3]

Above-average increases in overall goods trade were posted by the Asian 'Tiger' economies, Latin America and Eastern Europe. The ten leading Asian developing economies have become the fourth focus of global commercial activity, after the United States, the European Union and Japan; they are also the fastest growing (*Financial Times*, 30 March 1996). Trade in that region is not just large, it is also dynamic: the volume of imports into Asia as a whole grew at an annual rate of ten per cent a year between 1990 and 1995, while the volume of exports grew at 7.5 per cent [*WTO, 1996*].

Van Dijck and Faber [*1996*] list the following challenges for the WTO:

(i) The tasks resulting from the Marrakesh agreement: services, subsidies and public procurement of services, and harmonisation of domestic regulations, plus new tasks with respect to the trade policy review mechanism (TPRM), the new dispute-settlement system, the negotiations on the membership of a number of countries in transition (including China), the monitoring and co-ordination of the implementation of the Uruguay Round agreements, and co-operation with the Bretton Woods institutions.

(ii) The WTO must deal adequately with inconsistencies between its own multilateral and truly global rule system and rules that regulate trade among partners of preferential trading areas.

(iii) The WTO will have to cover new ground in areas referred to as the new trade agenda: namely, trade and the environment, rules on international investment and competition policy, and trade and labour standards (including child labour).

Van Dijk and Sideri [*1996*} also drew up an agenda for the WTO, providing the following list of issues to be discussed in the framework of the WTO:

(i)   further market liberalisation;
(ii)   liberalisation of the agricultural sector;
(iii)   trade and the environment;
(iv)   the services sector;
(v)   national competition and investment policies;
(vi)   integration of new competitors; and
(vii)   labour and environmental standards.

The lists are not the same and a distinction could be made between issues that are most relevant for developing countries and issues that interest developed countries in particular. This chapter will discuss most of the above issues for both types of countries. For developed countries the priority issue seems to be further liberalisation of world trade. Further liberalisation of services and agriculture will be discussed as the second and third issues. Finally, the issue of integrating other countries in the WTO seems to interest the developed countries more than the developing countries.

Developing countries are concerned about the erosion of trade preferences given under the generalised system of preferences (GSP). Secondly, many feel uncertain, because larger countries can threaten to accuse them of dumping practices. Third, they are interested in setting a date for free trade and in the zero tariff for the least developed countries, suggested at the WTO meeting in Singapore in December 1996. A fourth issue is the liberalisation of the textile trade which was promised during the Uruguay Round and of which they would be the main beneficiaries. Finally, most of them want to ensure a role for UNCTAD, which is considered the secretariat of the developing countries for the negotiations taking place in the WTO.

Both developed and developing countries face inconsistencies between the WTO multilateral rule system and rules that regulate trade in regional agreements. Are the two conflicting? Both types of countries have also benefited from the improved system of dispute settlement. The issue here is to keep the system respected by all the countries concerned. Finally, both are struggling with the new trade agenda, in particular the issue of labour and environmental standards.

IV. ISSUES FOR DEVELOPED COUNTRIES

Further Liberalisation of World Trade

Not much has been achieved since the conclusions of the Uruguay Round with respect to further market liberalisation. This subject was high on the agenda of the first ministerial meeting of the WTO in December 1996 in Singapore. Further market liberalisation is, in particular, important in specific areas such as, for example, steel and the production of civil aircraft. Other issues to be discussed are further harmonisation (of government policies, taxes and technical standards), rules of origin and liberalisation in the framework of intra-regional trade. Further liberalisation of the services and agriculture sectors will be discussed below.

Further Liberalisation of the Services Sector

Negotiations on the services sector, and in particular on financial services, have not ended with the signature of the Uruguay Round. The agreements stipulated that negotiations in some service sectors would continue for an unspecified length of time.

The weak obligations in the Uruguay Round concerning the services sector were seen as an indication of limited commitments to trade liberalisation in services (*Financial Times*, 5 Oct. 1994). Western countries are striving for an agreement which would allow foreign financial institutions, including banks, securities firms and insurance companies, to establish and operate on terms no less favourable than those applied to domestic institutions (the so-called principle of equal competitive opportunity) (*Wall Street Journal of Europe*, 11 Oct. 1991).

The announced follow-up negotiations failed to produce significant results. The European Union contended that the financial services and telecom talks failed because Washington pulled the plug for political reasons (*Business Week*, 20 May 1996). Agreements on opening up markets may be difficult to accept for developing countries, which have not yet been able to develop their financial services sector. Another worrying development is the lack of progress in the discussions about liberalisation of shipping. It has been agreed that the next discussions will take place only after 2000.

However, an agreement was reached on telecommunications quite unexpectedly in early 1997. According to the *Financial Times* (March 1997, 'Review of the Telecommunications Industry'), the WTO deal offers a framework with clear, simple and stable rules It could mean a boost to the world economy in the coming years, but the newspaper also notes that 'there will be teething troubles and that the agreement could still turn sour'.

The Agreed Liberalisation of the Agricultural Sector

Countries protecting their farmers promised during the Uruguay Round to convert non-tariff barriers and other protective measures such as quotas into tariffs. These could still be prohibitive, but a certain specified maximum will have to be lowered in the years to come.

The liberalisation of the agricultural sector under the Uruguay Round is very limited. Protection of Western markets may go down from 99 to 95 per cent, according to Van Rooy [*1994*]. The World Bank also concluded that the advantages of the Uruguay Round for agriculture are very limited (quoted in *Volkskrant*, 8 April 1996). It expects that many tariffs will still be higher in 2000 than in the period 1986–88.[4]

The Food and Agriculture Organization of the United Nations [*FAO, 1996*] argued in its *Annual Report* at the beginning of 1996 that the Uruguay Round is disadvantageous for African countries. Their agricultural trade surplus may be turned into a deficit in a few years time, because of increased prices for agricultural imports and the elimination of the preferential treatment which they still get in certain export markets.

Much depends on what the future of agricultural protection in the European Union will be. There is a trend to reduce subsidies for the agricultural sector in the EU. At the same time the world grain market seems to be turning into a real market instead of a dumping place for surpluses. This would have positive effects for countries growing agricultural products, although it also means that importing countries may have to spend more money, given the resulting higher prices.

The agreed liberalisation of the agricultural sector needs a follow-up. Agricultural trade liberalisation has been one of the difficult subjects. The WTO will start farm talks in 1999.

National Competition and Investment Policies

National competition and investment policies influence trade. As traditional trade barriers are lowered, attention is shifting to the impact of these policies. They remain an important issue, in particular for developing countries. Calika and Ibrahim [*1994*] conclude that 'Competition policy issues need better definition and analysis before multilateral approaches can be formulated to tackle emerging trade frictions in this area. Openness and non-discriminatory treatment of foreign direct investment will be critical in maximising the global gains from an international specialisation.'

Subsidies are often an instrument of national competition and investment policies. Developing countries, however, often do not have the money to subsidise their exports and, hence, will certainly be in favour of eliminating such subsidies. In discussion in the United States it was stressed that there can be no fair competition if national competition policies are not fair.

No real consensus was reached on investment during the Uruguay Round. The OECD countries are working on an Investment Code, but within the framework of the WTO the agreed TRIPs and TRIMs did not go very far. In fact a number of developing countries including Malaysia have issued a joint statement asking the WTO to stop discussing investment issues (*Malaysian Star*, 11 Nov. 1996). They warned that, since there is no consensus on the issue, continued discussion could cause greater controversies with adverse spillover effects on other issues.

The United States has made clear that it will press for WTO work on anti-competitive practices, bribery and corruption in public procurement, and the link between trade and labour standards. Developing countries have said that they oppose the inclusion of labour standards (*Financial Times*, 19 March 1996).

Membership of New Countries

Negotiations for full membership continue with a number of countries. Integration of new competitors like China is a problem for the WTO. Taiwan would like to become a member at the same time as China, and Russia would also like to join the WTO. A number of problems of creating a level playing field with, for example, Russia and China can be mentioned. China itself considers the US responsible for its slow integration into the WTO. The director-general of the WTO called for more intense negotiations on China's entry to the trade body ('Call to Speed China WTO Entry Talks' *Financial Times*, 24 April 1997). According to the *Wall Street Journal of Europe*, 26 May 1997, China has moved a step closer to joining the WTO, but the timetable remains uncertain.

Russia will not be a member soon according to the *Nieuwe Rotterdamse Courant*, 16 April 1997. According to diplomats in Geneva the country does not satisfy the requirements. Issues that need to be settled are the system of custom tariffs in Russia, its way of issuing export permits and the modernisation of its trade laws. Finally, the role of the state sector, the treatment of foreign investors and the need for fiscal reforms have been mentioned as requiring action before it can become a member.

V. ISSUES FOR DEVELOPING COUNTRIES

Erosion of Tariffs Allowed Under the GSP

For developing countries the positive effects of lowering tariffs have gradually diminished, since tariffs had already been reduced in the different Rounds and many countries receive lower tariffs in the framework of regional trade associations or through the generalised system of preferences. The tariff cuts erode the value of these trade preferences for developing countries and the advantages of the GSP will gradually diminish [*OECD, 1995*].

The United Nations Conference on Trade and Development [*1991, 1994*] has made several proposals to maintain the value of the GSP to developing countries, including one to establish a GSP system for trade in services, and another to set up a Green GSP under which environmentally friendly export products would receive extra preferences (*Go Between* 46, June 1994).

Anti-dumping

The opposite of a rule-based system would be a system of arbitrary import restrictions, including anti-dumping policies and so-called Voluntary Export Restrictions (VERs). Multilateral trading rules were eroded in the 1980s when countries resorted to protectionist and anti-dumping actions, VERs and other discriminatory measures.

Merely threatening to take a country before the WTO can be enough to secure trade concessions in certain cases. Japan suffered, for example, with the Clinton Administration when the United States called for sanctions against Japan under a domestic law in a car dispute (*Indian Express*, 4 May 1996). The US had also threatened Japan with sanctions because of a lack of openness of its market for films. Finally it decided to submit the case to the WTO, to avoid a confrontation. In this case the complaint would have taken a year and hence the results would be available only after the American elections (*Nieuwe Rotterdamse Courant*, 15 June 1996). However, the European Union also uses threats. In 1997 it threatened the United States with a complaint to the WTO concerning chicken and other bird meat (*Financiële Dagblad*, 13 May 1997).

One solution to this problem is to include in bilateral trade agreements a clause stating that both parties, in the spirit of the agreement, will not threaten to take each other to the WTO, but will seek other solutions. The EU could include this in its menu approach for ACP countries under the new Lomé Convention [*NAR, 1996*].

Achieving Free Trade and the Suggestion of a Zero Tariff for Poor Countries

Immediately after the signing of the Uruguay Round Agreement at Marrakesh some urged the WTO to set a date for completely free trade. A group of 34 economists took the issue up again just before the December meeting of the WTO in Singapore in 1996 (*Financial Times*, 6 Dec. 1996).

One suggestion concerning further liberalisation has been the 'free trade target date' discussion. F. Bergsten, head of the Washington-based Institute for International Economics, and (independently) M. Wolf of the London *Financial Times* have suggested that the WTO should commit itself to achieving global free trade by 2010 (*Financial Times*, 25 April 1996). The director-general of the WTO has said that setting a target date would be premature, while Sir Leon Brittan, the EU Trade Commissioner, said that it risked raising expectations too high and distracted attention from essential trade policy priorities. However, Ruggiero has suggested organising a large WTO conference to provide a new impetus to the liberalisation of world trade (*Nieuwe Rotterdamse Courant*, 5 April 1996).

The suggestion of a target date was endorsed by the secretary general of the OECD, and by the then UK Trade Secretary, Ian Lang. In reaction (*Financial Times, 25 June 1996*) J. Bhagwati stressed that the December 1996 meeting in

Singapore was the opportunity for undertaking a significant initiative on trade. With a group of economists, he supported the idea of a target date and urged the members of the WTO to make the endorsement of such a target their first priority. The arguments mentioned are that there are now so many regional preferential trade arrangements that a virtual 'spaghetti bowl' of criss-crossing preferential trade barriers has arisen, with different duties applying, depending on which country the imported product is assigned to.

Ruggiero called on the industrialised nations and the advanced developing economies to commit themselves in 1997 to scrapping tariffs on all exports from the least developed countries (*Financial Times*, 1 July 1996). It was noted that one of the biggest challenges would be to reach agreement on the types of products on which tariffs should be removed. The 48 least developed countries account for less than one per cent of world exports, but many of these are in sensitive sectors, such as textiles. The principle was accepted in Singapore, but its implementation is still facing a number of bottlenecks.

The Future of Textile Quotas

Under the Uruguay Round agreement quotas on textiles and clothing will gradually be eliminated after 1995 and completely abandoned in 2005. The dismantling of barriers to textile imports by such major importers as the US and the EU over a ten-year period is considered one of the major achievements of the trade pact (*International Herald Tribune*, 8 Dec. 1994). The Multi-Fibre Arrangement had been beneficial for the developed countries, who officially argued that it would give them time to restructure their industries to the competition from the low-income countries.

The main issue regarding MFA reform was whether most of it would happen in the first year or whether it would be postponed to the last year. Portugal, supported by Spain, used as an argument against an early opening that non-EU countries are failing to open their markets to European products – an argument supported by the European textile manufacturers. According to the industry, 100,000 jobs were lost in the European textile industry in 1996 because of growing competition from developing countries.

The EU Foreign Ministers agreed at the end of April 1997 to adopt a more flexible approach to import quotas for textiles, despite protests from Portugal that textile jobs would be lost across Europe (*Financial Times*, 30 April 1997). The report mentions that low-cost producers such as China, Indonesia and Vietnam have breached import quotas in certain clothing categories in recent years, often with the tacit acceptance of EU members 'happy to buy their cheap products'. Some countries were allowed to transfer unused quotas in certain clothing categories to other categories, or to compensate for exceeding quotas in one year by reducing imports the following year.

It will be necessary to look closely at this sector, to prevent certain countries from introducing new protective devices to support their textile industries. Secondly, the risk exists that some developing countries are not competitive and will see their exports decrease under free trade. Countries like Nepal and even Mauritius fear they are too small and not sufficiently competitive to benefit from completely open markets.

Future of UNCTAD

A question remains of what the role of UNCTAD will be in the future. Its Trade and Development Board has suggested that the organisation could play a major role in providing technical assistance to the least developed countries to strengthen their institutional and human resource capacities and their information management. More concretely UNCTAD should continue to do background work and build consensus on trade and economic policy issues before they become negotiable in the WTO.

Third World countries have an interest in a continuing role for UNCTAD. Most of them want to ensure a role for it in trade negotiations. The organisation is often considered as the secretariat of the developing countries for negotiations taking place in the WTO. UNCTAD could also try to implement the conclusions of the UNCTAD IX conference in South Africa in 1996, to provide developing countries with technical assistance to do better in world trade and world trade negotiations.

VI. ISSUES FOR DEVELOPING AND DEVELOPED COUNTRIES

Multilateral versus Global Agreements

In Van Dijk and Sideri [*1996*] multilateralism (such as negotiations within the framework of the GATT) is contrasted with regionalism, the trend to reach more liberal trade agreements within a regional co-operation framework.[5] While the European Union and North American Free Trade Agreement (NAFTA) are examples of the latter, the conclusion of the Uruguay Round is an example of successful multilateralism.

The WTO faces the issue of how to deal with regionalism. The Uruguay Round had to counter a wave of bilateral and regional trade agreements. The NAFTA agreement in 1994, like the creation of the Single European Market (SEM) between 1988 and 1992, has encouraged other regional trade blocs to form. The fact that these processes took place simultaneously made the conclusion of the Uruguay Round more difficult.

Regionalism is a reasonable answer to the prevailing difficulties of multilateralism. Regionalism can play the function of a laboratory, in which experience is gained with competition in the world market [*Hormats, 1994*]. GATT has official criteria for the approval of custom unions. Article XXIV of GATT allowed bilateral agreements under conditions intended to ensure that they would be trade-creating instead of trade-diverting. In practice they were always accepted and no supervision has taken place to assess the real functioning of these regional efforts to integrate.

However, trade agreements go against the Most-Favoured Nation (MFN) clause of the GATT and the WTO namely, that what one does for one country should be done for every country. One can say that they introduce distortions. Since Ruggiero became the director general of the WTO, he has urged regional groupings to aim at the creation of a global free trade area by moving to abolish all their barriers to trade with non-members (*Financial Times*, 25 April 1996). The risk is, he has pointed out, that the world will be divided in a number of years into two or three intercontinental blocs, each with its own internal free trade but with external barriers against the rest of the world. More than 100 groups exist but the top nine are, in order of size: the European Union, the ASEAN Free Trade Area (AFTA), NAFTA, the Asia Pacific Economic Cooperation (APEC), the Mercado del Cono Sur (Mercosur), the Southern Africa Development Coordination Conference (SADCC), the South Asian Association for Regional Cooperation (SAARC), the Andean Pact and the West African Monetary Union (UEMOA).

One of the interesting developments since the Uruguay Round has been the emergence of agreements between different regional groups. NAFTA is considering linkages with MERCOSUR[6] and the EU also plans a free trade zone with MERCOSUR.[7] The number of bilateral Free Trade Agreements (FTA) has increased rapidly. The EU, for example, has been very active in Eastern Europe, with South Africa[8] and in Latin America. The United States and Japan are also active. It is sometimes said that the US wants to limit the power of the WTO by these means.

The increasing number of bi- and multilateral agreements makes it very difficult to find out how rules of origin work out, because these are defined differently in the different agreements. For these reasons the Netherlands argued against a proliferation of trade agreements in Singapore in December 1996 and in favour of clearer criteria (*Financiële Dagblad*, 23 April 1996). Some EU member states seem to be unhappy with the large number of bilateral trade agreements, which are partly the result of there being three separate EU Commissioners, each dealing with relations with different parts of the world. Too many concessions have been allowed on a bilateral basis, instead of pursuing the multilateral track (*Nieuwe Rotterdamse Courant*, 23 March 1996).

Empirically, a number of questions have not yet been answered. Does regionalism lead to less trade outside the bloc? And does regionalism really challenge the multilateral system?[9]

Settlement of Trade Disputes

One of the positive results of the Uruguay Round is the improved system for settling disputes between WTO members. The matter had been discussed at length during the Round. Now disputes can no longer languish for years. The WTO's rules specify time limits that effectively mean a dispute can take no longer than 18 months from the filing of a complaint to a final verdict after appeals, if any. The WTO requires consensus to block this procedure, whereas the GATT required consensus to move a dispute towards resolution. The enhanced predictability and discipline provided by the integrated settlement mechanism should stimulate export-oriented investment and expansion of world trade. The subjects of dispute can be as diverse as a US ban on shrimp imports or tariff reclassification of computer equipment by the EU (*Financial Times*, 26 Feb. 1996). A few concrete examples will be given.

(a) Bananas. The United States, Ecuador, Guatemala, Honduras and Mexico asked the WTO to set up a panel to adjudicate a dispute arising from the EU's banana import regime, following a failure of consultations to resolve the dispute. Two GATT panels had previously ruled against the EU's banana regime, but the EU was able to block implementation of these findings. Research has shown that the European consumers spend about 3 billion Dutch guilders too much every year because the EU gives import preferences to so-called EU bananas (*Telegraaf*, 13 Aug. 1996). Its preferential treatment to bananas from African Lomé Convention signatories discriminates against the growers of so-called dollar bananas. The ACP countries argue that their banana-dependent economies face disaster if the EU regime is dismantled. This has resulted in a higher price for bananas, which has also reduced demand for the product. In any case benefits tend to go to the trading companies and not to the farmers.

The final report of the WTO banana panel ruled against the EU banana import regime, in May 1997. The panel's interim report upheld the EU's right to grant preferential duty rates to ACP or EU bananas under the Lomé Convention. However, the panel found other faults, notably in the way the import quotas were allocated. The EU had 60 days to appeal or agree its adoption. It appealed and lost. It must now comply with the findings or face trade retaliation.

(b) Hormone-fed beef. Since 1989 the European Union has banned imports of US beef produced with synthetic growth hormones, citing health concerns as the main argument. US officials have always argued that the hormones are safe. Consultations between the US and the EU to resolve this long-standing trade dispute had up to 1996 come to naught (*Wall Street Journal of Europe*, 12 April 1996). Subsequently, the US asked the WTO to set up a panel to adjudicate the dispute. Finally, the WTO ruled that the EU was unfairly banning US meat shipments (*Financial Times*, 9 May 1997).

(c) Scallops. In an interim report a WTO panel has also ruled against the

European Union's – more specifically, France's – trade description of scallops, which Canada, Peru and Chile claim hurts their exports (*Wall Street Journal of Europe*, 12 April 1996).

(d) The Fuji-Kodak dispute. In the Fuji-Kodak dispute the US and Japanese governments have presented evidence to a WTO panel investigating US claims that the Japanese photofilm market is rigged against imports in contravention of WTO fair trade rules (*Financial Times,* 18 April 1997).

Has the WTO's capacity to settle trade disputes improved? There were 26 disputes filed from January to August 1996, compared with 196 cases handled by the GATT over nearly half a century from 1947 to 1995 (*Financial Times*, 8 Aug. 1996). The report considered this figure an important vote of confidence in the WTO's strengthened dispute procedures. At the beginning of 1996 the total number of panels was 13 with over 30 others in preparation. Fortunately the Cuba investment conflict between the EU and the US, in which the US refused to co-operate with the WTO, has been moved to negotiations between the two, since a refusal to accept the panel's conclusions threatened to undermine the WTO.

The New Trade Agenda

The WTO is concerned with areas referred to as the new trade agenda: trade and the environment, rules on international investment and competition policy, and trade and labour standards, including child labour. Two, namely trade and the environment and trade and labour standards, have not yet been discussed. Trade and the environment is an issue which is rapidly climbing up the international trade agenda. At the closure of the Uruguay Round a decision was taken, for example, to revive the Committee on Trade and the Environment within the WTO. UNCTAD also decided to establish an *ad hoc* Working group on Trade, the Environment and Development, with particular emphasis on the special circumstances of developing countries (*Go Between*, June 1994).

Some developed countries see Agenda 21, the agreement reached in Rio de Janeiro, as the point of departure for the WTO (*Handelskrant*, July 1996). The WTO itself considers free trade to be an overriding principle, however. Wiemann [*1996*] has argued that a pro-active environmental policy (stimulating industrialists to adopt environmental measures to help them export their products) seems to be appropriate for developing countries. Donor countries and organisations can help developing countries to opt for cleaner technology. There are a large number of initiatives in this field, some co-ordinated by UNCTAD, others by a bilateral donor.[10]

The OECD countries, in particular, argue in favour of internationally accepted standards concerning labour conditions and the environment. The question is: who needs these labour and environmental standards? A number of Third World countries do not like the idea of setting internationally accepted labour and environmental standards. They fear more protectionism under a different heading. Some consider low wages and low environmental standards part of their competitive advantage. A number of developed countries, however, insist on minimum standards, often pushed by their trade unions. The discussion started during the annual conference of the International Labour Organisation and was taken up at the WTO meeting in Singapore. The director-general of the ILO argued in favour of a global system of 'social labelling' to guarantee that internationally traded goods are produced under humane working conditions (*Financial Times,* 23 April 1997). Child labour is a special part of this issue, and there is an ILO initiative on it.

VII. CONCLUSIONS

Trade is very important for the development of the industrial sector in developing countries. Developing countries face a decline of benefits from the GSP. The Uruguay Round has certainly created new opportunities and some developing countries have already benefited from the new possibilities.

Third World countries have an interest in maximising future gains from the multilateral trade system. This requires that their interests are adequately represented in the new monitoring and enforcement bodies. In this chapter we have suggested that UNCTAD could provide them with the technical assistance to benefit to the maximum from these new opportunities.

In general, the Uruguay Round created new opportunities for trade, although it also poses challenges for certain developing countries. It presumes, for example, the existence of domestic institutions and resources, which may be lacking in many developing countries.

The new trade agreement does not necessarily benefit a number of very poor and some African countries directly. The share in world trade is actually declining for a number of African countries. To understand the reasons for this, we have to differentiate between developing countries and even within them. Even within the successful developing countries certain groups or regions may not benefit from the dynamic process triggered off by international trade and may need special attention.[11] The least developed countries are likely to face particular problems in adjusting to the results of the Uruguay Round. They face the usual difficulties because of the erosion of preferential margins.[12] Many of them can also be expected to incur higher costs for imported foodstuffs. The main beneficiaries will be the more advanced developing countries, which have more to gain from tariff cuts and the liberalisation of agricultural, textile and apparel trade [*IMF, 1994*].

Governments can try to stimulate certain sectors, and create an enabling environment for industrial development. In the end, however, the market determines which industries are internationally competitive.

NOTES

1. During the ministerial meeting of the WTO in December 1996 in Singapore most of these issues were discussed, but not all were solved.
2. This compares with trade growth of eight per cent in 1995 and 9.5 per cent in 1994, the highest rates for a decade (*Financial Times*, 28 March 1996).
3. Processing and assembly factories in China accounted for nearly half the country's exports of US$149 billion in 1995 and 45 per cent of its $132 billion imports according to WTO estimates (*Financial Times*, 28 March 1996).
4. The examples given are the tariff for grain in the EU and the tariff for meat in the US. Both provide more protection than import restrictions on these two products used to give.
5. In the literature different stages of integration are distinguished [*Nielsen et al., 1991*]:
   • free trade area: no restrictions on visible trade;
   • customs union: the same, plus a common external tariff;
   • internal commodity market: the same, but also no restrictions on trade in invisibles;
   • common market: the same, plus free movement of factors of production (capital and labour);
   • monetary union: the same plus a common currency;
   • economic union: the same plus a common economic policy.
6. Chile, while applying to NAFTA, signed a free trade agreement with MERCOSUR which would result in zero tariffs on most trade within an eight-year period (*Financial Times*, 25 June 1996).
7. An inter-regional framework agreement for economic and trade co-operation between the EU and MERCOSUR was signed on 15 December 1995. It is the first EU accord of its type signed with any part of Latin America.
8. The negotiations with South Africa have not been easy. Germany and France had submitted long lists of products that they wanted to be excluded from trade concessions, while the Netherlands wanted to favour South Africa, given its role in the region (*Nieuwe Rotterdamse Courant*, 23 March 1996).
9. Does the Lomé Convention, with its non-reciprocal trade agreements, conflict with the multilateral trade systems? (For a defence of this point of view, see Chapter 4 in Van Dijk and Sideri [*1996*].
10. For example, the UK's Technology Partnership Initiative focuses on providing environmental technology on a commercial basis.
11. The trend seems to be to leave the fate of these groups to non-governmental organisations, which try to provide safety nets and sometimes socio-economic development funds [*Van Dijk, 1992*].
12. Some countries in North Africa and the Caribbean, which rely overwhelmingly on preferences on industrial products, could be especially adversely affected by the Uruguay Round.

REFERENCES

Calika, N. and A. Ibrahim (1994), 'Uruguay Round Outcome Strengthens Framework for Trade Relations', *IMF Survey*, 14 Nov.
FAO (1996), *Annual Report*, Rome: FAO.
Hormats, R.D. (1994), 'Making Regionalism Safe', *Foreign Affairs*, Vol.73, No.2.
IMF (1994), *World Economic Outlook*, Washington, DC: IMF, Oct.
NAR (1996), *The European Union Development Policy and Lomé*, The Hague: National Advisory Council.

Nielsen, J.U., Heinrich, H. and J.D. Hansen (1991), *An Economic Analysis of the EC,* London: McGraw-Hill.

OECD (1992), *Employment Outlook,* Paris: OECD.

OECD (1995), *Trade Preferences for Developing Countries: How Much Are They Worth and For Whom?* Paris: OECD.

UNCTAD (1991), *Trade and Development Year Book,* Geneva: UNCTAD.

UNCTAD (1994), *The Outcome of the Uruguay Round: An Initial Assessment,* Geneva: UNCTAD.

UNCTAD (1996), *Trade and Development Report.* Geneva: UNCTAD.

Van Dijck, P.F.F.M. and G. Faber (eds.) (1996), *Challenges to the New World Trade Organisation,* The Hague: Kluwer Law International.

Van Dijk, M.P. (1992), 'Socio-Economic Development Funds to Mitigate the Social Cost of Adjustment: Experiences in Three Countries', *The European Journal of Development Research,* Vol.4, No.1, June, pp. 97–112.

Van Dijk, M.P. and S. Sideri (eds.) (1996), *Multilateralism versus Regionalism: Trade Issues after the Uruguay Round,* London: Frank Cass.

Van Rooy, Y.C.M.T. (1994), 'The Consequences of GATT for Developing Countries' (in Dutch), speech delivered at the Dutch Chapter of SID, Amsterdam, 9 Feb.

Wiemann, J. (1996), 'Green Protectionism: A Threat to Third World Exports?' in Van Dijk and Sideri [*1996*].

WTO (1996), *Year Book,* Geneva: WTO.

Index

EADI BOOK SERIES